MY WEST

By
Patricia Nell Warren

Wildcat Press
www.wildcatpress.com

Wildcat Press

Inquiries should be addressed to: Wildcat Press, 8306 Wilshire Blvd. Box 8306, Beverly Hills, CA 90211. Phone: 818/246-2766. Fax: 818/246-2767. Email address: wildcatpress@aol.com. Website: www.wildcatpress.com.

FIRST EDITION – First printing June 2011

Production credits:
Jacket and book design: Renne Rhae, Tyler St. Mark and Patricia Nell Warren
Jacket photo: John R. Selig
Typesetting: Linda B. Jones and James Stelzer
Printing: World Trade Printing Center, Garden Grove, CA

10 9 8 7 6 5 4 3 2 1

Library of Congress Control Number: 2010929595
ISBN-13: 978-1-889135-08-3 ISBN-10: 1-889135-08-9

To Conrad

"Time will last till all the stories are told."
-- EarthThunder

OTHER BOOKS BY PATRICIA NELL WARREN

Nonfiction:

The Lavender Locker Room (2006)

Fiction:

The Wild Man (2001)

Billy's Boy (1997)

Harlan's Race (1994)

One Is the Sun (1991)

The Beauty Queen (1978)

The Fancy Dancer (1976)

The Front Runner (1974)

The Last Centennial (1971)

Ukrainian poetry under the name Patricia Kilina:

Horse With the Green Vinyl Mane (1970)

Rose-Colored Cities (1969)

Legends and Dreams (1964)

A Tragedy of Bees (1960)

Table of Contents

FOREWORD

By Gregory Hinton

I have always known the name Patricia Nell Warren. Since I am an author myself, the success of her most famous book, *The Front Runner*, astounds me. I first saw Patricia at a Palm Springs book festival, where I was reading from my first novel *Cathedral City*. She was manning a booth for her own imprint Wildcat Press.

It was hot that day, a humid 105 degrees, and Patricia was seated on a stool, elbows on the counter, her white curly hair billowing up from her beautiful face like a rolling Montana thunderhead which has just cleared a distant limestone bluff. I was too intimidated to introduce myself but I can see her to this day.

At the time I had no idea that Patricia, like me, was also a Montana native. Had I known I would have certainly overcome my shyness and said hello. A shared profession as a common denominator doesn't carry the same clout as coming from the same place.

Seven years ago, I flew from Los Angeles to Billings, rented a car and drove northeast on I-94 toward Glendive. It was early October and the rolling Montana plains were dotted with golden cottonwoods. I was headed to Wolf Point where I was born, on the Fork Peck Reservation tucked away in the far northeastern corner of Montana. Lewis and Clark made camp on the banks of the Missouri River, a mile south from the center of town. On the same banks where my family picnicked, Sacagawea bathed in the shallow waters.

My father was a country editor, first at the Wolf Point *Herald News* and then the *Cody Enterprise*, originally founded by Buffalo Bill in the charming historic Western hamlet of Cody, Wyoming.

Although I had lost both my mom and dad much too young to lung cancer, many of their old friends still lived in Wolf Point, and I was greeted by them like a prodigal son. An old family friend offered me a ride in his private plane, which was hangared at the Wolf Point Municipal Airport a mile up the road from his house.

He flew me all over the reservation, dipping the wings low over Fort Peck Reservoir, where he and my dad used to go duck hunting. When we landed I remarked that I hadn't been a bit nervous. Through watery, twinkling, old-man eyes, he studied me for a moment and teased, "Why *would* you be nervous?"

We whistle at the past at our own risk. The more we learn about where we come from, the more we wonder why we ever left. It is also true that the more we learn about our ancestors, the more we understand who we are as people; our values, our sense of humor, our need for solitude and open space. I have since returned to Montana and Wyoming many times. When I send landscape photos to urban friends, I inevitably generate the same responses. What are you *doing* up there? It looks so *lonely*.

Not so, I write back in reply. *I can finally hear myself think.*

My West, Patricia Nell Warren's remarkable anthology of 47 previously published articles, essays, and blogs about the West, is a masterwork by one of our most gifted storytellers. Grouped in sections ranging from Agriculture to Zest, Patricia's always informative, often humorous, and deeply evocative individual stories will quickly transport even the most dug-in urban reader to the heartland that is the rural American West.

Take for example Patricia's "Gates," originally published in the Hot Springs Little Baldy Press. "A gate is not a façade," she dryly states the obvious. "Facades are not meant to be gone through."

A regular contributor to *Montana Magazine*, Patricia reminisces in "A Gift of Pheasants" about raising dazzling Ringneck pheasants for food and profit on her tiny co-op farm. From a cardboard box filled with a hundred mail-order peeping chicks, Patricia offers a detailed history of pheasants as a culinary delight; from Roman banquet tables all the way to the release of her remaining beloved and uneaten grown Ringnecks back into the wild from her rural Northern California barnyard.

My West is a tonic to an apocalyptic 2011 America, plagued with natural and manmade disasters, financial collapses, and schoolyard mass murders. I chose to read Patricia's collection of articles scattershot, rather than front to back. Like the last peanut in a bowl full of shells, each time I discover a story I haven't read, the grace and simplicity of her straightforward writing takes me to a simpler place.

When I read Patricia's prose I recall the smell of sweet peas climbing the rickety fence abutting the alley behind our house in Cody. I can taste fresh bib lettuce snipped from the garden and rinsed in a beat-up colander with a garden hose. I can see elderly Assiniboine women standing in line ahead of my mother in the Red Owl grocery store in Wolf Point.

I finally met Patricia Nell Warren when she attended a lecture I gave in the Western film gallery at the Autry National Center in Los Angeles. It was a remarkable event, hosted by Mrs. Gene Autry, commemorating the installation of the iconic intertwined shirts worn by Heath Ledger and Jake Gyllenhaal in the seminal movie *Brokeback Mountain*. In addition to both being novelists, and native Montanans, Patricia and I share another common characteristic. We are both country Western gay, in that order.

Patricia's advice and encouragement have been vital to the creation of Out West, an educational program series we have created to shine a light on the contribution of gays, lesbians, bisexuals and transgender people to the history and culture of the American West.

In her article "Girl Grassroots," Patricia recalls her personal odyssey from Deer Lodge to Manhattan, from chaps to Chanel, from the closet to Grand Marshall of the International Gay Rodeo.

I am proud to say that because of our mutual love for the American West, Patricia and I have become good friends. With *My West*, the circle has completed.

My West reminds me how exotic the virtues of simplicity have truly become.

The son of a country newspaper editor, Gregory Hinton is an author, filmmaker, and independent curator. Hinton was born on the Fort Peck Reservation in Wolf Point, Montana, and raised in Cody, Wyoming. After graduating from the University of Colorado at Boulder, Hinton moved to California to pursue a writing and film career.

Hinton has published many critically acclaimed novels, including *Cathedral City* (2001), *Desperate Hearts* (2002), *The Way Things*

Ought to Be (2003), and *Santa Monica Canyon* (2007). His films include: *Getting it Right* (1989), *It's My Party* (1996), and *Circuit* (2003).

For *Night Rodeo*, his novel about a small-town editor struggling to save his weekly newspaper, Gregory Hinton holds a 2009 residency at Ucross Foundation in Wyoming. In July of 2009, Hinton delivered his acclaimed lecture, *Waiting for a Chinook: Searching for My Father—A Wyoming Country Editor* at the Buffalo Bill Historical Center in Cody.

Gregory Hinton is the creator of *Out West at the Autry*, which he is currently producing at the Autry National Center in Los Angeles, sponsored by HBO. Out West is a historic program series designed to illuminate the contributions of the lesbian, gay, bisexual, and transgender (LGBT) community to the history and culture of the American West.

AUTHOR'S INTRODUCTION

When I was a kid, aged 10 years or so, I used to climb on my cowpony and wend my way to a pasture that the family called "the Eighty." It stretched across a big prairie on the east side of the state highway. On the white man's record books, the Eighty had started out as an 80-acre desert claim taken up by my greatgrandfather Conrad Kohrs.

Out of that gravelly prairie, six or seven low mounds rose like gentle waves from some geological deep. They were greened by native short-grasses and sage that made gentle whistling sounds whenever the wind blew strong across them. You couldn't miss the mounds – they looked like they didn't belong there.

Often I got off my horse and sat there on the biggest mound, chewing on a stem of grass and listening to the sound of wind in the sage. The world was still very quiet in those days right after World War II – as yet, no commercial jets were flying overhead, trailing their blue thunder. Nor did any huge 16-wheeler trucks roar by on the highway. From the distant town, I might hear a faint whistle from a steam engine in the Northern Pacific switching yard. Or perhaps – if it was noon – the siren on City Hall would crank up to tell everybody that it was time to go home for lunch.

Other than that, the prairie was quiet, quiet. Now and then, a long-billed curlew ran through the grasses, with its mournful cry of "Eeeee, eeee, eeeee.....pur-eeee! Pur-eee!" Nearby a colony of prairie dogs had built their own little mounds, and one or two of them might be standing guard there, keeping an eye on me and clucking warily.

I wondered and wondered about the mounds.

According to my father, this was a place where the tribes once stopped to pray when they traveled through the valley in the fall, on their way to hunt buffalo east of the mountains. He'd heard this from the old men of the family – his grandfather Kohrs and his greatuncle John Bielenberg. In his own childhood, he had felt drawn to the mounds too. Dad told me that he remembered poking around over them and finding hunks of decayed old buffalo skulls buried in the grass – splintered horns, weathered eyesockets, with vestiges of red and blue paint still on them. According to him, his old Uncle

Johnny had told him that the People always said thanks for a good hunt by leaving the painted skulls there.

So I wondered. Who built the mounds? How long had they been there? Hundreds of years, like some people said of the Medicine Wheels around the West? Or were they just natural heaps of gravel and dirt, left behind by glaciers, perhaps, that the tribes had adopted for their prayers?

Back at the house, nosing into books in the family library, I found archeologists and scholars who stated in authoritarian tones that "American Indian mound culture could only be found in the Mississippi Valley." But other books I found later would make mention of mounds in western North America – clear north into Canada. Clearly the experts didn't agree on the wheres and whyfores of mounds.

Why had Greatgrandfather taken up a desert claim right there, when he could have grabbed from anywhere near the ranch buildings? Was he protecting that spot somehow? He had been friends with the white and mixed-blood stockraisers who first settled in the Deer Lodge area in the early 1800s. All of them had Indian wives that he knew.

Why did this spot seem so familiar and dear to me – as much my heritage as clapboard churches in New England or Greek temples in Europe? Why did I feel like praying there myself?

Why did the wind sometimes sound like little voices talking to me – right there, buried in the grasses, yet too far away for the words to be heard?

So the wonderings took on an open-air blue-sky spiritual tinge. It was the beginning of hearing the faint far-off talkings of hidden history, of almost-lost human time and human doings, and stories that were as many as the stars I couldn't see in the daytime. It was the start of learning how words on a printed page can be made to lie – of learning how unprovably accurate an unwritten tradition can be.

Fast forward to 2009, when I became involved with Gregory Hinton's new "Out West" lecture program at The Autry National Center of the American West in Los Angeles. The association with the Autry prompted me to look back at all the material about the

West that I had generated over 54 years of writing and publishing – not just several novels with Western settings, but several short stories and dozens of nonfiction articles. I was stunned to see how much of my total "short-format" output was occupied by ponderings about that vast region of the U.S. where I had grown up.

The subjects had a wide range – from the popular history themes that one would expect, like free-grass ranching and old-time cattle, to contemporary controversies like racism, human rights, land use, wildlife conservation, censorship, marriage. Today's West is as much about styrofoam as sagebrush. It's as much about the 1994 L.A. Riots as it is about the 1876 Battle of the Little Bighorn. It's as much about the immigrant Muslims and Bantus and H'mong who settle here today as it was about the immigrant Irish and Chinese who built the railroads. My West is the Sons of the Pioneers singing "Cool Water," and it's also Stevie Ray Vaughan singing "Texas Flood."

In my West, the "frontier" is still out there. But the "frontiers" are different ones today. They are economic and political and social and environmental horizons that our country is crossing, with no possibility of ever going back to what it once was – life-and-death decisions that our society is being compelled to make.

Even when the subject of a piece wasn't entirely Western, I found myself harking back to some west-of-the-Missouri perspective in order to find a measure for something, or a good example of something, or a what-not-to-do.

Indeed, growing up on a ranch had given me a crassly practical view on many political issues. As my dad always said, "When your horse is caught in some barbed wire, you don't stand around making speeches. You grab the goddam wire-cutters and get to work." These days, it seems to me that the White House and Congress and state legislatures are way behind on wire-cutter time. Indeed, neither political party is very fast with the wire-cutters right now.

So my body of Western writing is rayed through by a changing perspective over half a century – as I evolved from young hopeful college scribbler to published best-selling author. As I left Christianity to become an ever-questioning pagan. As I came out to live the life of a gay woman.

These writings ranged from editorials, commentaries and essays, to history pieces, blogs, letters, speeches. Most were published by print media, including *Acres U.S.A., American West, Atlantic Monthly, Corporate Africa, Denver Post, Gay & Lesbian Review, Los Angeles Times, Modern Maturity, Montana Magazine, Persimmon Hill, San Francisco Chronicle, The Californians, The Reader's Digest.* Some appeared in anthologies. Others were posted online, in Web publications like *Whosoever* and *Outsports*, or at political sites like Politech, or blogs like Bilerico Project and Huffington Post. Some were distributed on an online newslist that I did for several years in the 1990s, called "News You Didn't See on TV." Still others appeared in a series of public-health columns that I've written for *A & U Magazine* since the 1990s.

Out of this mass of material, I've picked the 47 nonfiction pieces in this anthology. They include those that I could get permission to reprint at this time, as well as some for which I retained ownership of publishing rights. Most are in their original word-for-word version. In some cases where a piece was long, I've abridged it or excerpted a section that seemed pertinent. For some pieces that touched on newsy issues, an update was needed at the end.

Some choices are editorials that never got published (because news editors wouldn't touch them with a 10-foot pole).

I've dedicated this book to my brother, Conrad Warren, a gifted writer in his own right. Though he's spent his life in the type of creativity called for by being a pilot, engineer and inventor, I still hope he will do that book he plans to write about our native West – especially that ranch where we both grew up. His unique perspective on the Grant-Kohrs and the technology side of rural life, shared with me through constant phone calls and visits over the years, has contributed richly to my own understanding of that place and time that has shaped us both.

At publication date of this book, I will be 75 years old. I'm still asking questions. My views are my own, and they're still evolving. I do not belong to, or say that I represent, any established tradition or belief system. In a mysterious kind of way, I'm still a kid sitting on that grassy mound, trying to ponder everything out.

– Patricia Nell Warren

A WESTERN BIO

I was born in 1936 and grew up on that ranch. Today it's known as the Grant-Kohrs ranch at Deer Lodge, MT. My parents were Conrad Kohrs Warren and Nellie Flinn Warren. I have one brother, Conrad Warren II.

The ranch was one of the first to be established in the Pacific Northwest – by mixed-blood Canadian trader John Grant, who settled in the Deer Lodge Valley in 1860. He sold the ranch to my greatgrandfather Conrad Kohrs in 1866.

Kohrs and his half-brother John Bielenberg were German immigrants from Holstein, then part of Denmark. They launched a lifetime partnership, and were among the pioneers in crossing Spanish and English cattle in search of an ideal type for grass finishing and winter ruggedness in the Northwest. By 1900 they expanded their holding to 50,000 deeded acres and 2 million acres of leased grazing. For a time, in the early 1900s, the CK shipped more beef to the Chicago stockyards than any other American ranch.

After Kohrs and Bielenberg died, my father Conrad Warren took over the ranch in 1932. He was a pioneering rancher in his own right, who put to work the latest in everything from range conservation to veterinary medicine. Both my parents had a passion for Western history that rubbed off on me as I grew up. My mother's passion, in particular, would later serve to protect and preserve the ranch as a future historic site.

Ethnically and spiritually speaking, my family drew its red threads from all over the Western Hemisphere. On my dad's side, there were English Quakers, German Mennonites, French Huguenots, Irish Methodists, Sephardic Jews and Cherokees. My dad's father, Dr. Otey Yancey Warren, had left West Virginia, where his side of the family spent several generations, and migrated west to Montana, where he married into the Kohrses. On my mother's side, it was a shade less mixed – mostly Irish Freemasons and Norwegians whose bent in politics and religion somehow didn't get on the record. Her father, Roland Flinn, worked for the Milwaukee Railroad most of his life.

I started writing at age 10, and told everybody who would listen that I wanted to be a writer when I grew up. My first stories were done in the ranch office, hunting-and-pecking on the big Underwood typewriter with an extra-wide carriage for cattle and horse pedigrees. The carriage made an extra-satisfying *thunk*! when you hit the return lever. I always loved that sound.

Both my parents, especially my mother, encouraged my writing bent. Their liberality on this point was remarkable in a time when women were mainly encouraged to be housewives, secretaries, nurses or airline "stewardesses." My first efforts were short stories – mostly (and predictably) about wild horses and ranch life.

The interest in writing came up as naturally as the grass in the fields. My family's library was well-stocked with classics and current bestsellers, including that new-fangled postwar thing called nonfiction. In fact, the home library still included venerable morocco-bound German-language tomes that my greatgrandmother Augusta Kohrs had brought over from the old country. The family's oral tradition was strong, and resulted in endless storytelling at the dinner table.

So all that word magic conjured a lifetime fascination with following the many trails of Western history. They are as many-laced as the cow trails and game trails across a mountainside. The trails included recognition of the many Western families like mine with a blended heritage, and many ways to look at Life.

In addition to helping my dad on the ranch, I participated in high-school rodeo, including that new sport called women's barrel racing. On the print-media front, I jumped into publishing activities at Powell County High School – editor of the school paper and yearbook. Printers' ink was definitely my thing.

Already in high school, I knew somehow that I was "different," and had my first closet relationship with a girl in town. But it was not a time when Americans talked openly about other brands of sexuality, so I stayed firmly in the closet till 1973.

Like many Montana kids of my time, especially those from the older families, I got sent "back to the states" to college. In 1954, my first year at Stephens College in Missouri, I won the

Atlantic Monthly College Fiction contest with a short story about ranch life titled "Slave of the Sky." I also continued working on publications at Manhattanville College of the Sacred Heart in Purchase, NY, where I edited the campus literary magazine, *The Essay*. Graduation came in 1957.

Later in 1957, I married Yuriy Tarnawsky, a Ukrainian émigré writer that I had met through a Ukrainian student friend at Manhattanville. His family were World War II DPs (displaced persons) who settled in New Jersey. They had fled western Ukraine to avoid living under communism after the Soviets occupied it. This was the beginning of my involvement with émigré literary life for 16 years. Though I was never actually to visit Ukraine, the country fascinated me with its vast steppes – grasslands and wheat-fields and histories of galloping Cossacks – so reminiscent of my West.

Throughout the 1960s, I kept to short stories and poetry. U.S. poetry magazines were not very interested in my work. Having learned Ukrainian, I published three books and most of a fourth in that language with a New York-based Ukrainian poetry co-op, the New York Group. Later on, my work became known in Europe, and appeared in translations of émigré Ukrainian writing – in German, Czech, Polish, Portuguese. After the Soviet Union dissolved in 1989 and Ukraine became independent, a few of my Ukrainian works were published there in anthologies.

Meanwhile, in 1959 I got a copy-editor job at the *Reader's Digest*, working at the magazine's corporate headquarters near Mt. Kisco, New York. Like many Montanans of my generation, I definitively left my home state to make a career elsewhere.

At that time, RD was still at the peak of its power and prestige. Professionally speaking, it was a great place to work, though ideologically I evolved into one of the staff liberals who were forever writing memos in favor of more diversity in magazine content. In 1964, I was promoted to book editor, working on both nonfiction for the magazine, and fiction for the Condensed Book Club. I continued in that capacity for the next 17 years, occasionally writing an article for the RD magazine on the side.

In the mid-60s, my husband and I took a sabbatical from our jobs and lived in Spain for two years. We fell so in love with

Spain that we bought property there and returned to spend a month of vacation every year. There I worked with the Digest's Spanish edition, *Selecciones*, assisting the staff in developing various original book and article projects of interest to their own readers. As a Westerner who grew up in ranching, I found many points of connection in Spain, especially with the horse and cattle industry.

By 1971, my personal creativity had expanded to full-length fiction, and I published my first novel – *The Last Centennial* – with Dial Press. My agent in those days was John Hawkins at Paul Reynolds, Inc. My editor was Bill Decker, who really knew the West. The book was my way of reconnecting with those little voices that I'd first heard singing in the grass. It consisted of three novellas about three different people in Cottonwood, a small Montana town. Their different stories were linked by a common time and place, namely the town's 100th-anniversary celebration.

Last Centennial got excellent reviews, but didn't go much of anywhere.

By 1973, with the gay-rights movement happening, I had decided to come out and divorced Yuriy. The following year, with John Hawkins' help, I published my first gay-themed novel, *The Front Runner*, with William Morrow. My editor at Morrow was Jim Landis. It became the first such novel to get on the *New York Times* and *Time Magazine* bestseller lists. Though set in the world of Olympic sports, TFR managed to have a Western thread, which would continue – whether thicker or thinner – through most everything gay-themed that I wrote.

Publishing *The Front Runner* meant coming out personally. This I did in an interview with the *New York Post* sometime in mid-1974. I had wondered if my conservative employers would have issues with this. To my surprise, the Digest seemed pleased that one of their editors had a book on the bestseller list, and they ran an article about me in the company magazine.

In 1976, I returned to the fictional Cottonwood locale with another national bestseller, *The Fancy Dancer*, also published with Morrow. TFD was about a small Montana town and its struggling Catholic parish. The young priest there was struggling with his closet attractions to men, and his changing relationship with cow-country parishioners as he became more self-honest.

Meanwhile, my family's ranch had been following its own course. Since my brother Conrad and I had gone into other professions (he to the Air Force and later to engineering and inventing), my parents pondered what to do. My mother's suggestion: get the attention of the National Park Service, which was beginning to add small parks of historical interest to its system. My dad agreed that this was a good idea. In the early 1970s, the National Park Foundation acquired a quarter section that comprised the original Grant-Kohrs area of the ranch, complete with 19th-century documents, structures and artifacts, making it a time-capsule of ranch history.

In 1977 the Grant-Kohrs Ranch National Historic Site had its grand opening for the public, with my dad cutting the ribbon.

Later on, after my mother died in 1979, the Park Service acquired another 2000 acres of the home ranch that adjoined the town of Deer Lodge. My dad retained a lifetime estate in the house and adjacent horse barns, and lived there till he passed on in 1993.

In 1980 I left the Digest and moved to California to become a full-time writer. I had just signed a contract from Random House/Ballantine to write *One Is the Sun*, a historical novel set in Montana Territory of the mid-1800s. It was to be based on the story of a mixed-blood woman who was a powerful Medicine Chief. My agent on this book was Morton Janklow.

Meanwhile, I did freelancing on the side, with a focus on historical and contemporary Western material. Articles on this subject were published in *The Reader's Digest, Persimmon Hill, American West, The Californians, Montana Magazine, Denver Post, Modern Maturity, Los Angeles Times, San Francisco Chronicle, Métis Courier* and others

For the Digest, I did a piece about the ranch, titled "Saga of an American Ranch," that won the 1982 Western Heritage Award for magazine writing given by the National Cowboy Hall of Fame that year. This was the same year that my father was inducted into the Hall of Fame (greatgrandfather Kohrs was already a Hall of Famer.)

In 1991 *One Is the Sun* was published by Ballantine as a paperback original. The publisher didn't promote it, so the book didn't go much of anywhere at first. Only later, by word of mouth, did OITS find its readership.

By then I was unhappy with trade publishing over various contract issues, notably creative control and accountability on royalty bookkeeping.

Starting in 1994, I got most of my book rights reverted, then licensed any that I couldn't retrieve, and went into business as a small independent publisher, Wildcat Press, with a business partner, Los Angeles media specialist Tyler St. Mark. Fittingly, Tyler is from an old Arizona ranch family himself – namely the Mannings, who once owned the Canoa, one of the biggest cattle outfits in the Southwest. We capitalized our new company partly with funds from my mother's trust. This was fitting, since Mom had always supported my writing career so strongly.

Wildcat Press published two gay-bestselling sequels to *The Front Runner*, namely *Harlan's Race* and *Billy's Boy*. We got almost all my previous titles back in print. These were followed by a new gay-themed novel in 2001, *The Wild Man*. This story was set mostly in a 1960s Spain awakening to change, but had its thread of Western interest.

Next came my first nonfiction book, *The Lavender Locker Room*, with profiles of LGBT greats in sports. It won an Independent Publishers Gold Medal, and was a finalist in the Benjamin Franklin awards. As always, the Western thread continued with a piece on gay cowboys that was widely reprinted. This article reflected my connection with gay rodeo, where I had been grand marshal or special guest at several IGRA rodeos up and down California.

Now in its 16th year, Wildcat Press has gotten some recognition, including an ACLU award as a "champion of free speech." This was for our involvement as a plaintiff in the 1996 lawsuit against the Justice Department over the Communications Decency Act, which resulted in a U.S. Supreme Court decision striking down the CDA.

Several of my titles have been translated into foreign languages – notably *The Front Runner*, which has appeared in a total of 12, including Complex Chinese and Ukrainian.

Today I live in the San Fernando Valley, and continue my work with diverse types of writing – including political blogging and new books in the works.

My Montana ties are still strong. Though my parents have crossed the Great Divide, I still have cousins and friends around the state. I enjoy a warm relationship with the Park Service staff at the GKRO, and serve on the board of directors of the ranch's Grand-Kohrs Ranch Foundation, a nonprofit that does fundraising for the park. I've been grand marshal of Montana Pride, and lectured around the state on various subjects – books, literature, free speech, LGBT people, mixed-blood people and human rights. Organizations and institutions that invited me have included the Montana ACLU, Montana Authors Coalition, Montana Human Rights Network, Montana State College in Butte, Montana State University in Missoula, and the Myrna Loy Cultural Center in Helena. I've done events at public libraries, including the William Kohrs Memorial Library in my home town.

Today I'm moving into film development, hopefully to produce some feature films and documentaries that focus on lifetime interests of mine – including documentaries about my West.

I'm also active in the biomedical sector of the West – working with BioClonetics Immunotherapeutics, Inc., a Texas-based biotechnology company. BioClonetics is engaged in the development of new technologies for use in both vaccines and treatments for HIV/AIDS and other infectious diseases caused by retroviruses. The BioClonetics approach also has potential applications in veterinary medicine. My dad would be pleased to know about it.

Last but not least, I'm working on my autobiography, to be titled *Girl Grassroots*.

MY WEST

Personal Writings on the American West – Past, Present and Future

AGRICULTURE

GATES

Originally published in *Hot Springs Little Baldy Press*, March 10, 2010

Westerners are into – and out of – gates. Especially ranch gates.

Our gates say a lot about us. They say who lives here.

For many people, the generic gate will do – the kind that is crafted from lodgepole pine or 2 x 4s. It comes in two colors: "utterly unpainted" or "bare-bones barn red."

Yet many of our gates reflect some human fantasy. The sentimental gate of old wagon-wheels. The monumental gate of massive pine, with a state-of-the-art cattle guard. The heraldic gate, burning its brand into the sky. The junkyard gate, with an old Model T tractor parked on top.

Oh yes ... and that murderously effective barbed-wire thing, that is variously known as a Dutch gate and a South Dakota gate. Everybody blames this gate on somebody else. If New Yorkers had invented it, they'd call it a Midwest gate. If Montanans had created it, they'd insist it was a California gate.

But a gate is not a facade. Facades are not meant to be gone through.

The gate is a gift from our most ancient geniuses. After humans monkey-puzzled through what mathematics is, they used numbers to build the first wheel, the first ship, the first house... and the first fence, complete with a gate and rawhide hinges. How else could the ancients keep their ponies in and the thunder-lizards out?

A gate must be skillfully engineered – or it falls over like a bad joke. It is a creation of technical genius – a marvel of weight and counter-weight. It must have hinges that swing at the touch of a child's hand – yet stand solidly in place when a herd of 5000 buffalo hits it at full gallop.

Any well-built gate can outlast a marriage, a bank loan, a belief, even an era. On the ranch where I grew up, a few gates are older than me.

In addition, a gate should be designed so a cowgirl or cowboy can open it from horseback. What impatient rider can wait forever to get down and un-snap the chain?

The best gates are also wide enough between the poles for a kid to slither through.

As it swings open, a gate invites us into a new place, a new time, a new view, a change of venue. It takes a bunch of cows in, to new grass. Or it can take them out, to the packing-plant that changes them to tasty steaks. The gate brings a 4-H Club to visit, friends to dinner, the veterinarian to heal, the auctioneer to disperse a herd. The gate takes children away to school, the soldier away to the Middle East, the RV away to discovery, the grandparent to the cemetery – and brings the new baby and mother back from the hospital.

How we westerners love our gates. Some of our grandest, most historic places of passage are gates opening to new peoples and great Time. Hellgate Canyon. Gates of the Mountains. The Golden Gate. The four gates to Yellowstone.

Gates also have their partners in symbol. For the First Nation peoples, there are the leather gates – lodge-doors opening to a magic world of firelight within, to the magic world of sunlight without. The leafy cottonwood gates of the Sun Dance Lodge. The limestone temple gates of Uxmal.

For the European arrivals, there are the Iron Gates of the Danube, the Great Gate of Kiev, the Brandenburg Gate, the Lion Gate of Mycenae.

Even our planet is a gate of Life and Death, ever opening and closing as billions of lives speed through Her like electrons every day. The word “gate” sounds like Gaea – the name of goddess Earth.

Like minds, gates aren’t useful, or diplomatic, if they always stay shut. When a gate is flung open, both sides of the argument can mingle.

Magical things happen with gates. They keep saddle horses in, but let the butterflies and jackrabbits circulate freely. Unlike doors and windows, they have the power to let in the smell of rain even when they’re shut.

In short... a gate by any other name would still have squeaky hinges.

Yes, we humans have designed gates that are not things of beauty. Prison gates with peeling paint. Castle gates with rusted iron hinges that scream of ancient cruelty. The Gate of Hell. And that Gate of Hollywood grillwork thing, operated by electronic sensors, that only stays open long enough to let a stretch limousine hum through to a Beverly Hills palace.

But I’ll take the gate of lodgepole pine, wintered to a silver hue. The kind that opens into an alfalfa field. The kind that has a pair of pickup tracks curving away to the horizon.

The grass may be greener on the other side of the fence – but only a gate can get us there.

HAYING AT THE CK: FROM HORSE TEAMS TO BALING MACHINES

Excerpted from unpublished information provided to the Grant-Kohrs Ranch National Historic Site

One of the intriguing things about history is how quickly we forget the little wrinkles of past technology that preceded our personal lifetimes. Few people remember the whys and wherefores of pre-transistor radios, or pre-digital printing, or pre-antibiotics medicine, or pre-freezing food preservation. Where Western ranching is concerned, that sad fact is also true of humble technology called haying, upon which the lives of rural Americans depended.

Everybody had to put up their own hay. If you were forced to buy hay to get through a hard winter, the extra expense could put you out of business.

But how exactly did people handle that messy, cumbersome stuff called hay? It's an intriguing tale of home-built engineering.

Lately the media spotlight has been turned on old-time haying at the Grant-Kohrs ranch. Rural Heritage has sponsored the RFD-TV airing of a documentary, "Horse Drawn Loose Haying," that was filmed during GKRO's re-enactment of haying on the ranch during the

Kohrs and Warren eras. It shows haying being done with a small beaverslide stacker and an entire crew of horse-drawn equipment, with support from the Academy of Living History. The film is available at www.ruralheritage.com.

Since the haying project is evidently going to continue, with Kohrs-Warren haying history being portrayed to visitors as well as young park personnel who are learning, I would like to describe in detail how a century of our haying was done – and how that process in the hayfields transitioned from horse-power to machine-power.

The prime source on haying information was my father. With Dad passed away, my brother Conrad and I are the last living witnesses of the ranch's haying operations during World War II and the post-war period. We have our oral-tradition resources – recollections of personal conversations with Dad about haying – as well as our own personal memories about same.

Conrad's information is especially important. He actually worked on the hay crew from when he was old enough to steer a tractor straight. When he was older, he helped build and maintain the machinery. He also worked as a stacker. To this day Conrad can tell you the exact models of the different tractors we used, and the name of which man drove what machine for some years.

I wasn't involved with the machinery and engineering to the extent my brother was, but I certainly remember how it was done during my childhood, since I was born in 1936. As soon as I was old enough to sit on a horse, it was my job to ride out to the haying site with messages from my mom, or a jug of lemonade and a sack of cookies for the crew. So I spent a lot of time hanging out at the haying site.

Conrad and I have spent some time reviewing and comparing our memories about haying. Up until 1947 or 1948, we personally participated in haying that was still done with an old-style swing stacker. But even this antiquated technology was not what the ranch used when Dad was a little kid.

Starting Out With Pole Stackers

When Greatgrandfather Kohrs and Uncle Johnny Bielenberg were still alive, our dad spent time with them at the ranch as a small boy and saw how the old men had their hay put up. According to

Conrad, our dad explained to him in dctail how the CK used a type of pole stacker. "The CK" was how the ranch was often referred to then, after the cattle brand.

Before 1900, a great variety of pole stackers, derrick stackers and cable stackers were used around the U.S. According to period books on farming equipment that I've been able to consult online, most of these stacking apparatuses were home-built – so varied in design that they almost form a category of folk art. Most were likely inspired by models that were brought to the U.S. by European immigrants.

During my European travels between the mid-1950s and 1970, some of which occurred in rural areas where people used farming methods that were still antiquated, I saw how some European farmers still used a simple pole derrick to build a small stack, or to raise loads of hay into their hay loft. Generally, given the small acreages that typically prevail in Europe, and the fact that it rains so much in non-Mediterranean areas, most hay storage was done in barns. Pole derricks were (and still are) used in parts of England.

Since Kohrs and Bielenberg were both natives of Holstein, in north Germany, they may have adopted haying models from their home country.

But in the United States, as the West was settled, haying technology got a new urgency. Given the vaster-than-Europe acreage of many farms and ranches here, as well as the larger numbers of livestock being run, it became imperative to process larger amounts of hay than could be stuffed into a hay loft. The drier climate in most areas of the American West made it practical to stack a great mass of hay for storage outdoors. But hay had to cure properly, and stacks had to be made waterproof, so hay didn't mildew or combust. So there was the right way and the wrong way to do it.

U.S. patents for stackers were on file as early as 1858. Drawings of various pole stackers can be found on pp. 318-19 of *Farm Buildings*, edited by Sanders Publishing Co. The drawing of a single-pole stacker on page 318 probably comes closest to the model that our dad saw during the last years of the Kohrs-Bielenberg era – except that it used a fishing-boat type of net instead of a fork, to swing the load up over the stack.

According to Conrad, our dad described the one that he saw at the CK. It worked like any construction crane or dock crane of today, with its upright tower and a boom sticking out at a right angle, that can swing around to drop a load wherever needed.

First the hay was evidently cut by hand, using scythes with cradles that left the cut grass laying on the ground in a row of bunches. After the hay quickly cured in the sun, the bunches were shocked like grain. From there the shocks were pitchforked into a cargo net on a wagon. According to Conrad, our dad said that Uncle Johnny described these wagons as "boats" – maybe because the net operated like a fishing-boat's net.

When the net was full, the "boat" was hauled over to the stack site. There the net was hooked to the end of the boom. A cable and series of blocks and tackles ran down to ground level, where the cable was hitched to a team of horses. When the team hauled the cable, the net was lifted and the boom swung out over the top of the stack. The bottom of the net was tripped open, and the shocks dropped onto the stack like a load of fish.

There, the stackers arranged the shocks carefully on a slope, with the head-end of the stems pointing towards the outside of the stack and a little downhill, so they would shed rain downwards to the perimeter of the stack, just like a European thatched roof does. They were careful to cap the stack with a final "roofing" of well-placed shocks.

The process was very labor-intensive, and probably didn't result in a whole lot of hay.

My brother and I conclude, from this, that Kohrs and Bielenberg didn't keep a lot of livestock there at the home ranch. Probably only the Thoroughbreds were there, along with the little band of native-bred brood mares that produced the "big circle" cowponies for use down on the range – plus a few saddle horses, work horses and buggy horses, and a few milk cows to service the cookhouse. The big herds of range cattle were all located elsewhere, and had to rustle feed right on the range in order to get through a winter.

So the home ranch's winter hay needs were probably quite limited.

Transitions, Big and Small

Haying technology on the CK evolved gradually, according to Conrad. When Kohrs and Bielenberg finally died, and our dad took over the operation, there were seldom any radical and abrupt changes.

At some point, Dad replaced the old scythe and cradle by a horse-drawn mower, with its bar containing two rows of sharp teeth that worked against each other like scissors. Conrad isn't sure what year this happened. The horse-drawn mowing machine had actually been invented during the Civil War, according to Robert L. Ardrey in *American Agricultural Implements*. But evidently its use was slow to penetrate Montana… or at least to penetrate the CK.

Our dad used the horse-drawn mower through the 1930s and into the early 40s. We remember a photo that was around the house in the historic photo collection when we were kids, of Dad sitting on a horse-drawn mower. Conrad remembers that Dad had several models of mowers around. When we were kids, a few of them were still stored in the sheds where the older machinery got junkpiled. In the 1970s, when Dad was downsizing the outfit and dispersed some of the old machinery, he evidently sold some of the antiquated horse mowers. But the GKRO may have found one or two of these old mowers still kicking around in the machinery storage sheds.

About that same time, Dad also adopted the horse-drawn side-delivery rake, the horse-drawn bunch rake or dump rake, and the horse-drawn buck rake, sometimes called a bull rake. They too had been around since the 1800s, and made it possible to address a logistical problem that emerged when the hand scythe went away. The problem was this: each bunch left on the ground by a sweep of the hand scythe had made a thick layer, that let the hay cure better before it was shocked. But the mowing machine with its long bar left the grass in a thin layer on the ground, that bleached and lost vital nutrients if you left it in the sun too long.

So the side-delivery rake was designed to fold the hay into neat wind-rows, where it could cure better in a thicker layer. Then the dump rake/bunch rake would move along the wind-row, pulling the hay up into big individual bunches with its long curved tines.

Next came the horse-drawn buck rake, and scooped up bunches till it had a full load. The one that we used looked pretty much like the one in the Rural Heritage film. The big fork with the long teeth on it was actually "pushed," not pulled, by two horses who worked independently, not as a team, driven by the guy sitting on the back. It pushed the load over to the stacker and onto the fork.

Onwards to the Swing Stacker

As the crowning improvement on the new "assembly line" of haying machinery, Dad started using a swing stacker.

We don't know if its construction was his own homebuilt idea, or if he got the design from someone else – though this general type of stacker was evidently used in various places around the West. We also don't know what year Dad started using it. Conrad and I remember seeing pictures of the swing stacker in the family photo collection, and trust that these are now among the photos now in the archives. If so, GKRO can know what the swing stacker looked like.

The swing stacker was actually a bigger, more sophisticated evolution of the pole/boom stacker, and was also operated by a long cable pulled by a horse team. When the team moved forward, the cable levered the fork end of the swing-arm off the ground, with its load of hay, and swung it on a curve up and then over the stack. When a lever was tripped, the fork dropped its load on the stack.

Then, while the stackers went to work, the horse team backed up slowly to lower the fork down to the ground again. This stacker was better suited than the pole stacker to process the big loose piles of hay that were delivered to it by the buck rake.

I remember the swing-stacker vividly – it was painted barn red, and the teeth in the fork were made from sharpened lengths of wood, possibly lodgepole. The swing-arm was mounted on a wooden derrick with a strong square base. You couldn't build a very big stack with it – maybe 10-12 feet tall. If I remember correctly, it had heavy iron wheels, so it was easy to move to a new stack site with a horse team. It was also small enough that Dad could get it across the bridge over the river, between the hayfields on the West Side and the hayfields adjoining the ranch buildings.

After the swing stacker was retired from use, Dad parked it on the West Side, over by the flume near the county road and the gate into the Williams & Pauly property to the west of our ranch.

A Brief Note About Horse Teams

Five teams were required for the swing-stacker operation. During the 1930s and into the World War II era, Dad used some of our Belgians. A last few purebred Belgians were still bred at the ranch when I was little, though Dad had given up showing them during the World War II period, with gas being rationed and the market for these big horses dwindling. But there were still a few brood mares and foals in the pastures north of the barnyard when I was a little kid.

Dad greatly valued the Belgians' gentle temperament for work around the ranch. Even in their workday harness, with mud all over their feathers, a team of Belgians looked very sharp. The new haying machinery was dangerous enough that teams had to be very quiet and dependable. Runaways had to be avoided at all costs. Especially with the dump rake – a runaway incident could hurl the driver off his seat and down onto the lethal curved tines beneath. He could be dragged and mutilated for quite a distance before the runaways were stopped.

During the winter, a horse team hauled a loaded hay wagon around the meadows, so hay could be dumped out for the cattle wintering there. If snow was deep, Dad used the wagon with sleigh runners on it.

Eventually the older Belgian stallions, including Bloc II (the ranch's big star during the big showing years), died or were sold. By 1946, just one stallion remained on the place – a young horse, maybe 5 years old, that we called Prince. Dad didn't have time to work with him, so he was pretty unruly and not broke to harness. Since Dad didn't need Prince for breeding, he sadly sold the horse to the only buyer around...which happened to be the state prison farm. At that time, the prison farm was located just down the valley, north of the Hansen dairy and west of the state highway. There Prince was finally broke to drive, and ended his days working for the trustee convicts who raised vegetables for the prison.

A few favorite old Belgian mares were pensioned, and spent their days in that big pasture west of the railroad tracks and north of the chutes-and-sheds complex. This pasture was the ranch's winter home for saddle horses not being used at that time of year, as well as the "retirement home" for old horses. Dad's favorites were Gonval (he pronounced her name "gone-volley") and Ariste. This latter mare was the namesake for the sailboat *Ariste* that he owned after retirement from ranching. Gonval lived on for many years in that pasture, into the 1950s.

As the aging Belgians were phased out, Dad acquired one younger team that I remember. They weren't a matched pair, but they worked together well, and we had them for many years. I'm not sure of their names – Babe and Tiny are what come to mind. One was a Clydesdale, and the other was a big sorrel horse, possibly a Belgian crossbred.

Some Beaverslide History

The beaverslide first came to the ranch in around 1947 or 1948, when I was 11 or 12 and Conrad was 8 or 9.

The Rural Heritage film goes into a little historical background on how the beaverslide stacker was invented in the early 1900s, and how it was used in the Big Hole and other big Montana haying districts from a fairly early date. The beaverslide was a giant step forward in haying technology – it could process vaster amounts of hay than the older methods. Our cousin Gary Tavenner told me last year that he is working on a book about the history of beaverslides in Montana. A member of his family held a patent for the beaverslide.

So it's a fact that the beaverslide was adopted by other Montana ranches at a far earlier date than ours. Why didn't our ranch jump on this trend in the early 1900s, when we had always been such trendsetters? That is a good question.

In his *Autobiography*, my greatgrandfather wrote that between 1910 and 1915, the CK operation was downsized sharply, with only "remnants" of livestock left after 1915. These remnants would have been located there at the home ranch, since outlying properties, like the range headquarters at Prairie Elk, were being dispersed. It's possible that Kohrs and Bielenberg kept on using the old pole-stacker method because their hay needs at the home ranch were minimal. They saw no advantage in the effort of introducing the new-fangled beaverslide when they were essentially retiring from the business. The old method would be adequate for the ranch's sunset needs.

When my dad took over the ranch in the 1930s, he elected to bring in the swing stacker instead of the beaverslide. We don't know why he made this choice. But it's possible that, during the Depression era, the swing stacker was adequate for the needs of Dad's relatively small cow herd and the Belgian purebreds – through the 1930s and into the World War II era.

It's also possible that Dad delayed shifting to a beaverslide because of some logistical problems relating to its use that I'll mention later.

More Hay Needed

But the haying imperatives started getting urgent when Dad began expanding the ranch's carrying capacity, as well as its grass-growing power.

His expansion had started with re-seeding and improving the played-out hayfields on the West Side, along with installing pumps and making other improvements in the ditch system that watered them. He re-planted the hayfields with a mix of meadow grasses that were good for hay – brome, redtop, bluegrass, Junegrass, timothy, etc. Into the mix went a certain percentage of alfalfa, red clover and Dutch white clover. He also started a program of fertilizing the hayfields, by mining the rich layer of old manure out of the feedlots along the river.

To further expand the ranch's hay capacity, Dad purchased two old homestead properties on the West Side that were reachable by his irrigation ditches. If I remember right, the original owners went bankrupt during the West's most recent long drought, and their homesteads went into foreclosure. Dad obtained them by paying the tax liens on them. One was the Keating place, located opposite the cemetery. The ruins of the Keating home can still be seen on a little rise north of the hayfield – the house foundations and several crabapple trees that the Keatings planted. The other was the D'Alton place, which was directly west of the spot where our bridge crosses the Deer Lodge River. When I was a kid, there were still vestiges of old farm buildings on the D'Alton place, notably a weathered old shed that was leaning over in the direction of the prevailing winds.

Dad also acquired an old working hay ranch that we called the Upper Ranch, because it was located up the valley from Deer Lodge.

This was where Harold and Florence Fisk lived during Harold's tenure as our ranch foreman. The Upper Ranch had a weathered late-1800s frame house on it, along with a few log barns and sheds, and maybe a few hundred acres of good hay meadows along the river bottoms.

I was very little when I visited the Upper Ranch during World War II. Now and then Mom got me out of her hair for a couple of days by sending me up there for Florence to tend. So I remember some general details about the ranch's operations. The Upper Ranch had its own haying equipment. All the equipment was old-model – in fact, the ranch itself was not even electrified, so the house was lit with kerosene lamps, cooking was done with a wood stove, and Coleman lamps had to be carried to the barns for any errand after dark. At that time, there were still areas in the valley where the federal government's Rural Electrification project hadn't reached yet. How things have changed!

Rather than hauling Upper Ranch hay down to the home ranch, we usually wintered some cattle there – yearlings, I think.

But after World War II, Dad faced the fact that he needed to expand the number of cattle still further, if he was going to be able to support the family and make money. By then the swing stacker couldn't handle that need for increased hay production. Having two swing-stackers operating, with two crews, was ridiculous from the economic point of view.

Mechanization With the Beaverslide

So Dad evidently decided to head into the logistical problems and the beaverslide stacker made a belated debut at our ranch.

Its arrival coincided with the arrival of our uncle and aunt, John and Charlotte Potter, who came to the ranch after World War II to live for several years. Uncle John had been a fighter pilot instructor during the war, but now he was out of the Marines and wanted to do something else with his life.

So Uncle John helped Dad build the beaverslide. He and Dad went down to the Big Hole and consulted with a big hay ranch there. Dad studied their operation and took measurements on their beaverslide. The man who built that Big Hole beaverslide came up to Deer Lodge and helped Dad and Uncle build the one at the ranch.

It was a complicated piece of engineering, and according to Conrad, they had to tinker with it quite a bit before they finally got it working right. The two huge beams that framed the ramp had to be purchased from the Montana Power Company – they were actually power poles. Since today's super-fancy power tools were not yet invented, the beaverslide was built using mostly hand adzes and hand saws and other manual carpenter tools available then. I.e. a lot of sweat equity went into it.

Since the beaverslide could process bigger loads than a swing stacker, and build bigger stacks, and get more hay put up in the two-month window of summer weather available, it was imperative that the machinery used by the hay crew had to process more hay too, so it could keep up with the beaverslide.

Conrad always talked about keeping the beaverslide "fed."

So the assembly line now was motorized.

The horse teams disappeared – except for the bunch rake, which continued to be powered by a horse team. This part of the operation still worked better that way – the driver sat right on top of the rake, driving the horses and tripping a lever with his foot, that lifted the tines of the rake when it had gathered a big enough bunch of hay. Since the bunch rake moved at plodding horse speed, Dad operated two of them in order to stay ahead of the motorized buck rake.

During this period, just a couple of work teams were still active on the ranch. One was a Belgian team. The other was the unmatched pair I remember. Dad had gotten them somewhere, to replace old Belgians that he'd pensioned. These were the horses that I remember pulling the bunch rakes.

For raising the basket on the beaverslide, a small tractor was used to pull the cable.

So technologically speaking, beaverslides and motorized equipment had to go hand in hand.

While some of the new haying machinery was purchased ready-made, a few items were custom-built there at the ranch. Conrad remembers that Dad hand-built mowing bars onto two different tractors. The side-delivery rake was a shiny new industry model.

As for the new buck rake, it was a unique Con Warren creation. My brother remembers it vividly. With that genius for thrift that Dad always had, he took an old truck chassis and turned it into something like an open-wheel hot-rod. It had to be driven in reverse in order to position the hot engine in the rear, away from the dry hay. Conrad says that Smitty, the welder in Deer Lodge, built the buck onto the chassis.

Uncle John loved driving the buck rake – it was noisy and fast and brought out the fighter pilot in him.

Building a Beaver-Size Stack

Constructing the bigger stacks (20-25 feet tall or so) was also a technical challenge. The Rural Heritage film shows the GKRO crew using a four-sided frame covered with wire mesh, building the stack inside the frame. I've also seen the stacking frame used in some present-day beaverslide haying operations in southwest Montana.

However, our ranch was purist when it came to stacking. We never used a frame, as far as Conrad and I remember. Generally the expert old-time beaverslide crews avoided using a frame, because it resulted in a weak stack that might fall over.

These bigger stacks, even more than the smaller ones of old that were constructed with shocks, had to be built like a brick house. The stackers were professionals, well paid and regarded as the elite of the crew. They knew how to build a free-standing stack in a perfect rectangle with firm straight sides.

The stack's only support, as it was going up, was the back wall of the beaverslide. As each load of hay fell onto the stack, the stackers had to find any natural bunches in it, and move these around like they were shocks. As they finished off the stack, the stackers layered the last swathes of hay to form that thatched-roof kind of cap, so that rain would follow the stems towards the edge of the stack, and the stack would shed water like a duck. Only the top few inches would get wet, while the inside of the stack would stay dry and cool. Otherwise any wetted hay deep in the stack would mildew. Indeed, there was an art to stacking, that is probably remembered by just a few living elderly people today. Conrad is one who remembers how to do it.

The absence of a frame made stacking a dangerous job. There was a high rate of injury, even death, to stackers who slipped and fell off those high stacks.

Before winter came, Dad would have the men go back and throw up a fence around each stack – simple panels made of lodgepole pine. This was done in the hope of keeping out the elk that often moved down from the hills to winter along the river. Deer and pronghorns, of course, had no trouble getting through (or over) the stack fences.

The arrival of the beaverslide spelled the gradual end of our need for the Upper Ranch as a hay ranch. At some point, after Harold Fisk died and his two boys grew up and left home, the Upper Ranch disappeared off our radar screen. (Not too many years ago, on a drive around the valley, I went up that road and found that the old Upper Place was still there, very rundown, but still relatively intact and recognizable.)

Problems With the Beaverslide

We used the beaverslide stacker for perhaps five years. While it handily increased our hay production, it did give Dad some headaches.

To drag the beaverslide around, we had to have a big tractor. The structure was too heavy for wheels, so it had to be skidded on its bottom timbers. When it was moving slowly, grandly, ponderously along, it looked like some giant medieval war machine. To get to the West Side, it had to be laboriously dragged across the river, since it wouldn't fit across the bridge. There was a particular shallow ford that Dad always used for this purpose.

Also, the beaverslide had to be gotten under the power line on the West Side, so it could be hauled over into the D'Alton Place and the Keating Place. This required Montana Power to come out and lift the lines for us.

In addition, our dad wanted to develop irrigated hay pasture in the "80" east of the state highway. It would have been difficult to drag the beaverslide over the highway and under yet another powerline to that side of the ranch.

By the time I graduated from high school in 1953, the beaverslide era was over, and Dad had switched to a hay baler.

Retired in its turn, the beaverslide was hauled over to the West Side and left sitting in a spot just east of the power line.

As a side note: some big hay ranches in the Big Hole went on using the beaverslide for many years. They snubbed the baling machine, which rapidly got much more expensive to buy and operate. The vast open level hayfields in the Big Hole made it practical to stick with the beaverslides, since the ranch owners had little problems moving them around.

In 1991, when I was book-touring around Montana, I drove through the Big Hole and was surprised to see how many beaverslides were still in use.

Baling the Hay

The ranch books noted the date of the first baling machine's purchase. Conrad remembers it as a New Holland model that did round bales. But Dad didn't like the round bales because they were so cumbersome to handle.

Next he tried a New Holland model that did square bales. It tied the bales with twine, and the knotter didn't work well, so the bales often fell apart.

Finally Dad settled on an International Harvester 340 model that used wire instead of twine; he was happy with it. The baler was easy to move anywhere on the ranch – not only back and forth across the river, but across the highway into the 80, where he was harvesting quite a few bales.

Now was when the support machinery was reduced. The buck rake went away. Only the mower and side-delivery rake were needed. On occasion, Dad did get a man out with the dump rake and team to do some cleanup along the edges of a particular field.

My dad and my brother did the baling operation together. By now Conrad was old enough to drive ranch equipment. First, Dad would go out and mow like crazy. He never let anybody else drive the mower, because he worried about safety around those razor-sharp metal teeth. He also grieved about small wild animals in the grass, like baby birds, that got caught in the teeth and killed when the mowing bar came along.

When the hay was cured, my brother came wheeling along with the side rake and made the wind-rows.

For the third phase of the operation, Dad drove the baler and Conrad worked on the wagon hitched to the back of the baler. Dad's favorite International model had a conveyer on one side, that picked up each wind-row and fed it into the ram. As the finished bales came off the back end, Conrad hooked them onto the wagon. When the wagon was full, two other men hauled it over to the stack site and threw the bales onto the stack.

Baling hay had its dangers too. Herewith a hair-raising tale:

One summer day around 1952 or '53, Dad and Conrad were busy baling when a thunderstorm came racing across the valley. Dad decided to delay quitting for just a few more minutes, because the hay was nice and dry, and a rain squall might wet it. Just then the baling machine was hit by lightning. Both Dad and Conrad were knocked colder than a mackerel for a few minutes. When they came to, Conrad found that he was laying on the bales in the wagon. Dad found that he was laying right on the wind-row, in front of the baling-machine's conveyor belt. When he had toppled unconscious from the baler, his body had somehow shifted the transmission into neutral, so the machine stopped in its tracks. But the engine was still running, and the conveyer was still operating ominously, just a few feet from him. If the machine hadn't stopped, Dad would have been carried up the conveyer into the ram, and mangled to death.

In winter, a big stack of rectangular bales wouldn't shed water, but a huge canvas tarp over the top solved that problem. Stacks were located at convenient places around the ranch, where they'd be handy for winter feeding.

Dad had now reached the limit of his ability to maximize hay capacity on the land he owned, within the time frame of weather and season that Montana gave him. Essentially this "window of opportunity" was from the start of mowing in the last week of June, until the first of September, or whenever he had to drop haying in order to start grain harvest – which was that fleeting moment when the grain fields were ready.

An End to Haying

Dad used that basic baling operation till he finally stopped operating and started leasing the ranch. He never did get comfortable with the big round bales that everybody else fell in love with. And he was glad to get out from under haying, because of what had become the enormous expense of operating and repairing a baling machine.

"Goddam baling needles," he complained bitterly. "They used to cost five bucks. Now they cost a hundred bucks. Inflation is going to ruin this country."

Hopefully today, at the GKRO and Rural Heritage, there may be interest in building a reconstruction of that cantankerous old swing stacker. The Grant-Kohrs Ranch could have *two* haying demonstrations, both of them going on simultaneously for the visitors to see. The swing-arm model with the all-horse crew, and the later-model beaverslide with its largely motorized crew... to show how radically the technology changed in just a few years.

Few Americans were paying attention to what happened to haying, of course – even though they continued to eat beef and drink milk that comes from animals who eat hay. People were more awestruck by the rapid shift to color TV, space-age plastics, spandex clothing and pre-fab houses. Not to mention that humble invention that makes it possible for me to write this piece at my desk – the personal computer.

Further reading:

American Agricultural Implements: A Review Of Invention And Development In The Agricultural Implement Industry Of The United States, by Robert L. Ardrey (published by the author, Chicago, 1894).

Farm Buildings (Sanders Publishing Co., Chicago, 1909).

FARM SUBSIDIES: ONE AMERICAN'S VIEW ON AFRICA

Originally published in *Corporate Africa* (Summer 2006)

One of several commentaries that I was invited to write for this publication owned by the Times-Mirror Corporation of London. My concerns about Africa date from conversations with my father in his later years, when he used to worry about the global effects of climate change, and of agricultural policies that don't make sense.

Today's challenges around global agriculture marketing are not new, but they are more urgent than ever. As I write this article, WTO negotiators missed a vital April 30 deadline. They were supposed agree on details by which 147 member nations could end export subsidies by 2013 and improve market access. The agreement had been pushed by fierce litigation by developing countries with WTO – the aim was to have U.S. cotton dumping and EU sugar dumping declared illegal. But resistance by rich nations continues, especially by the United States. *South African News Features* commented on this latest disappointing development: "The future of a new international deal on agriculture hangs by a thread as agreement remains elusive on key targets."

What will happen to dozens of vulnerable African economies and populations who must wait seven years for any significant market relief?

A look at the U.S. past might help illuminate the African present. In my opinion, a grim line can be drawn back to 1933 from African anxiety about subsidies. This was the year that modern subsidies were first put in place in the U.S. during the Great Depression. African leaders – especially the 37 nations who qualify for U.S. help under the African Growth and Opportunity Act (AGOA) – would do well to study the U.S.'s own history on how its agriculture subsidies have affected its own citizens. Perhaps they could learn from the U.S.'s mistakes, and profit by them.

I first heard the word "subsidy" as a child living on a cattle ranch in southwest Montana before World War II. Growing up during that time of tumultuous agricultural change in the U.S., I learned a great deal from my rancher father, Conrad Warren – from his lifelong struggle with subsidies and other critical trade issues that were linked to them.

Before 1933, under the administration of President Herbert Hoover, the U.S. federal government had done little to alleviate the rampant joblessness, despair, natural disasters and hunger, which created social unrest and occasional violence across the United States. The traditional views – that government should take a passive role, that farmers should solve their own problems through their own sheer will and thrift – had prevailed. Yet U.S. agriculture was being decimated – not only by the global economic collapse that had occurred after 1929, but also by drought and dust storms that had blighted much of the American Midwest and West since the mid-1920s.

Taking Care of the Grass

My family's ranch was the oldest in the Deer Lodge Valley, a historic ranch dating back to 1860, to my greatgrandfather's generation. With the old man's death in 1922 and no son to carry on, the ranch had gone into hiatus. Most of its land and livestock were sold off, just a few old Hereford cattle and draft horses left, its small bills paid by the estate. In 1932, my father – then a young man – dropped out of medical school and took over the ranch's management.

The scene was enough to discourage any young person. All across the valley, smaller ranchers and homesteaders were going bankrupt. They signed their land over to their creditors and emigrated to bread lines in the city. With export and domestic markets sagging, commodities were selling dirt cheap. A cow with calf at side was worth just $10. Winter and spring wheat dried up as it sprouted, and the bared soil blew away on the hot winds, along with a bumper crop of dried tumbleweeds – that botanical marker of American rural disaster – that rolled along to pile up against fences. The ranch's rangeland was grazed down to the dirt by hungry cattle, and invaded by undesirable plants like Russian thistle.

Since the ranch had dwindled to a size that wouldn't support a family, my dad persuaded the estate to buy several adjoining parcels that had gone into foreclosure. Fortunately the land was as cheap as commodities. The expanded property now totaled 5700 acres of pasture and 500 acres of hayfields. If only grass could be persuaded to grow, the summer pasture would support 600 cows @ 10 acres per cow-calf unit, and the hayfields would produce enough hay to get the herd through the long Montana winters.

Finally, with President Roosevelt's election in 1933, the new administration was willing to take action. As part of the historic "Hundred Days" of emergency legislation, the government started providing financial aid to farmers, urging them to adopt conservation-oriented farming practices, and paying them for cutting production of core commodities – cotton, wheat, rice, tobacco, beef, hogs, milk. Subsidies were viewed by many as a wonderful new idea. The intentions were good – to cushion American farmers and ranchers from the jolts of extreme climate and market fluctuations. If agriculture produced less (the reasoning went), the market price of its products would go up.

My dad was an inventive, energetic and forward-looking man who helped pioneer new techniques in ranching – like artificial insemination and scientifically mixed cattle feeds. With his medical background, he put himself on the cutting-edge of animal-health practice. There were few veterinarians in Montana at that time, so he did most of his own veterinary work. I grew up helping him at the chute as he vaccinated cattle and tested for disease.

His basic operating principle was: "Does it work? If it doesn't, how do I make it work?"

So his efforts focused on making his property "work" again. embracing the new principles of land conservation – contour ditches as the most water-efficient way to irrigate hayfields, planting shelterbelts, etc. Most important, he patiently reseeded thousands of acres of our rangeland with native grasses, using a team of horses and a drill. The hayfields got worked over too, with a mix of clovers, alfalfa and grasses. Neighboring ranchers scoffed at him, saying the seed would never grow.

But in 1938 the rains did start returning, and the seed did grow.

Soon our summer range was a vista of waving green grass, belly deep to a horse. Other ranchers and agricultural officials came to see it. The deed would eventually cause my dad to be recognized as one of the pioneers of rangeland conservation in the U.S. Meanwhile, as we could afford it, he had put together a herd of top-quality registered Herefords, breeding new heifers a few at a time.

The experience taught Conrad Warren that economic survival is linked to being a good steward of the land. For instance, he noticed that the renewed growth of native grasses on his range stopped the invasion of sage, Russian thistle, tumbleweed, spotted knapweed and other plants that cattle won't eat. Later on, when agribusiness came up with toxic chemical sprays for these invaders, my dad refused to use them, saying they weren't necessary.

"If we take care of the land," he liked to say, "the land will take care of us."

Signs of Trouble

World War II made the U.S. government a huge beef and produce buyer, and agriculture was suddenly booming. Peacetime brought a decade of heady prosperity – but suddenly the subsidy thing was getting more complicated. Huge surpluses were again bursting thc grain elevators everywhere, and the U.S. government went deeper into paying farmers not to grow. The Department of Agriculture imposed an annual allotment on certain crops. My dad grew our own cattle feed, so every spring the government man came to tell us how many acres of wheat and oats we could plant. In 1947 came the Soil Bank Program, where government paid farmers and ranchers to put surplus arable land into water impounding, wildlife habitat, etc.

In 1946, when my dad was appointed Montana livestock commissioner and elected president of the Montana Stockgrowers Assn., he made himself more widely known as a progressive thinker and problem-solver. His positioning was not always popular.

By the 1950s, as I entered high school and was active in cattle-breeding myself through 4-H, U.S. subsidies were proliferating everywhere – from alfalfa seed to sugar, even subsidies to sheep-raisers for lambs killed by coyotes. Some ranchers, included my dad – operating off their old tradition of crusty independence and mistrust of bureaucracy – grumbled that subsidies were becoming a form of welfare. Many big ranchers took the subsidies gladly, and became used to them.

As I finished high school in 1953, it was clear to many that subsidies were not the solution that everyone hoped. Instead, they complicated an agriculture scene that had stayed complicated even after the Dust Bowl ended. Inflation meant not only rising retail prices of food, but rising costs for the food producers – whether parts for machinery, costs of fuel and feed, or wages for farm and ranch employees. So the very strategy that was supposed to cushion agriculture from risk was actually operating to shrink agriculture's profit margin. With "trade, not aid" the new philosophy in Washington's dealings with other countries, imports increased and American cattlemen complained bitterly when cheap Australian and Brazilian beef started undercutting their domestic sales.

But there was no shortage of "bright new ideas" coming out of Washington – ideas like deficit financing. Traditionally, farmers and ranchers had taken a loan only as a desperate measure. Farm credit had started in the 1920s, when a farmer might buy his first mechanized farm equipment. Now that farmer went for the annual loan every spring. With his own shrinking profit margin, and his own need to stay modernized, even my dad was compelled to visit the banker in spring, hat in hand. In fall, if everything went well – if his wheat crop wasn't shredded by a hailstorm or the cattle market didn't fall, he paid off the loan. After taxes, there might be a 2 percent net profit at the end of the year – hardly enough to get us through winter, let alone to start operations next spring.

About that time, my brother and I decided – not surprisingly – that we would not follow our parents into this stressful occupation called ranching. So we joined the flow of young people "exiting" American agriculture. My brother went off to be a pilot and engineer, while I wound up in New York working for the media.

By 1980, because of spiraling costs and interest rates and other factors, smaller family farms and ranches were starting to crash and burn again, as they had done in the late 1920s and early 30s. Most of them operated so close to the edge that it didn't take much of a loss – a few sick animals, an untimely rainstorm during harvest – to default on that farm loan.

In the 1980s, a wave of horrible bankruptcies swept through the Midwest and West, with some desperate and angry ranchers turning to suicide or gun violence as a reaction. So many families fell victim to this latest wave of foreclosures that it emptied large areas of the West of active farming. In eastern Montana, entire towns were empty and boarded up. Foreclosed farmlands were often resold to large emerging agricultural corporations – the media now referred to them as 'agribusiness." Or land was taken out of cultivation entirely, and sold to real-estate developers. The steep "death tax" on inheritance of farms and ranches was yet another factor – so rural properties were sold and the children moved into urban life.

All in all, the long-term effects of billions of dollars spent on subsidies was that they had subsidized the destruction of small farming in the U.S.

By then my mother had died and my dad ran the ranch alone. Genetic problems had come up in purebred cattle, so he had switched to commercial cattle. Still inventive and thrifty, he bought young steers in spring, getting him fat on his good grass, then selling them to feedlots for finishing in the fall. Since he didn't need hay to feed cattle through the winter, he could sell his hay crop. Meanwhile, he continued pioneering – increasing the ranch's water storage by having the state wildlife agency plant beaver on every creek, so they would build dams and impound water. Out of the beaver ponds, he did sprinkler irrigation of some pasture.

Though my father had always loved science as a way to improve agriculture, he didn't like the brave new world of agribusiness and factory farming and biotech that was emerging – use of toxic chemicals, farming practices that contributed to soil loss, inhumane treatment of animals. Most of all, he hated the vanishing of the independent self-sufficient family farm or ranch, which he felt was the backbone of any national community. My dad's attitude was that any agricultural practice – and that included subsidies – that resulted in human misery and environmental damage should be stopped.

"They're putting money first," he said. "Nothing wrong with money – I spent a bunch of years chasing money. But if you don't put the soil and the grass and the people first, the money won't last."

In 1982 at age 75, my father was honored nationally for his lifetime of forward-looking and socially conscious agricultural practice, by being named to the National Cowboy Hall of Fame.

Often I wished that he had the vigor to travel the world and become politically active. His views and experience – a perspective of nearly 80 years of American agricultural history, his keen sense of what worked and didn't work, could be invaluable. He enjoyed being recognized, but he was getting to be a "broken-down old cowboy," as he put it, tired and worn from the years of struggle. He had retired from active ranching and leased the grazing to another rancher.

In those final years, his thoughts turned to Africa. In his office, he kept a big pile of world-news and agriculture publications, and read obsessively about emerging disaster in the Sahel – desertification, famine, starving people and animals.

"They're having a helluva time there," he'd say, "a lot worse than we did here."

But he was also deeply concerned about his own country, and pointed out that the hard 1930s lessons about conservation had suddenly been forgotten by a new generation. He tried to point this out, but found that new people in agriculture often didn't want to listen. He often predicted to me that the accelerating abuse of land in the western U.S. – everything from clear-cutting timber to large-scale plowing of wheatlands with no use of windbreaks, to overgrazing of public lands – was contributing to climate change – drier, more open winters with less snow pack, more drought, more erosion. He foresaw a time when the western U.S. might experience a Sahel-like human and environmental disaster of its own.

In the early 1980s, I moved to California and returned to agriculture for several years, as an small-time organic farmer. There, too, I saw the trends he talked about. For instance, many cotton growers in the San Joaquin Valley had taken land out of cultivation because water prices had shot up. They had simply left hundreds of thousands of acres unplanted by any protective cover crop, so the soil was bleeding away onto the winter santa ana winds like in a 1930s Dust Bowl. One November when I was driving the 5 freeway, I ran into a huge dust storm in this area that was blowing across the road. I narrowly escaped being caught in a huge traffic pileup involving over 100 cars.

Whenever I went home to visit Dad, he was fading physically, but his stack of books and magazines about Africa was bigger than ever. Often he woke up in the middle of the night and sat on the edge of his bed, smoking a hand-rolled cigarette and brooding on the fate of agriculture across the world.

In 1993 my dad finally gave up the fight and crossed the Great Divide to the spirit world.

What "Works" Today

Today I do still have a "ranch" of my own. It's a corner residential lot in West Los Angeles, where my intensive garden produces some fruit and vegetables year-round.

As I finish writing this commentary, I ponder thc ongoing stupidity of many U.S. politicians who seemingly don't get it about food security in the U.S., let alone parts of Africa that they probably couldn't find on a map. The end is near for L.A.'s famed South Central Farm, largest community garden in the U.S. Fifteen years ago the Farm was developed in the poorest part of the city, on a 150-acre property that the city wasn't using. Thanks to the initiative of a group of black and Latino families, who won an arrangement with the city, this property became an oasis of organic green in a zone of industrial blight. Bursting with fruit trees and vegetable plots, the Farm fed hundreds of poor families for years. Recently the city reneged on an agreement to keep the property available to these urban farmers. Now the L.A. County sheriff is evicting them so the Farm can be bulldozed and yet another warehouse built.

Not a single prominent politician or corporation stepped forward to save the South Central Farm, though they could have set an inspiring example by doing so. If my dad were alive, he would be outraged.

The South Central Farm's destruction is a telling symbol of the shockingly strange things that the American establishment has done, and still does with agriculture, at that critical juncture where greed intersects with human need. In recent years, the U.S. has been exporting to the world, and to Africa, a number of agricultural programs and practices that may fill the pockets of politicians and corporate executives but that haven't exactly been ideal or enriching for the rest of us here at home. There's no doubt that subsidies are among them. Currently U.S. subsidies stand at 108 million payments totaling $118 billion a year – yet for the most part subsidies appear to have outlived any real usefulness they may have once had in the 1930s, and are hated by many.

What remains to be done? How can AGOA be encouraged to work more effectively?

As I already pointed out, seven years remain before those subsidies might be lifted through WTO action in 2013. This surely seems like a lifetime to African livestock and plant growers who are anxious for things to happen with their businesses.

One thing that might bridge this 7-year gap is for U.S. firms and NGOs – as well as firms and NGOs of other developed countries – to increase their investments in AGOA countries. But it's best, I think, if they invest at a level that would start with greater food security for people in the more at-risk Sub-Saharan areas. Food security for a nation's entire population – especially its poorest people – should come first, because without food security, there is no political stability for a country – and without political stability, both African and non-African firms will hesitate to invest. With food security in place, there may be a better chance for export market farming to succeed.

Food security, especially for the subsistence farmers, is best achieved by sustainable methods – for the simple reason that most subsistence farmers can't afford the high-tech corporate types of farming. They can't afford the patented seed, the pesticides, chemical fertilizers, etc. Reclamation of damaged land, improved soil fertility and water supply, emphasis on sustainable agriculture methods rather than corporate biotech, and concentration on basic food crops rather than non-edible cash crops – these are all important. In good years, subsistence farmers can market their surplus, but in the bad years, hopefully they will be able to scratch by and always have enough to eat.

A notable example of failing food security, and the tragic consequences for a non-AGOA nation, is Zimbabwe. As I wrote this article, eight years of economic and political meltdown have resulted in widespread hunger. The Zimbabwean government is sending their army to confiscate farms and launch an emergency program of growing maize, the basic food staple. Crops already on the ground, like tomatoes, are being plowed under to plant maize.

Recently I got an email from a Zimbabwean friend of mine, a young medical technician with a wife and child and a large family, who had this to say about the current situation:

"All the way until the late 1990s, Zimbabwe was literally a land of milk and honey. All the money in the world couldn't pursuade most of us to live abroad. Images of starving Africans from other parts of the continent used to shock us just as much as it does Europeans or Americans. Zimbabweans have been master farmers for hundreds of years. Even the poorest villages would have herds of fat,healthy cattle and fields of corn and vegetables. The commercial beef ranches produced world class steaks that countries all across Europe would clamor for. No one was ever hungry, certainly no one ever died of hunger. Even those that were dirt poor. So to see the devastation one man's greed has caused to an entire nation makes me feel shame."

Two years ago, this young man and his wife gave up trying to cope, and fled Zimbabwe. They now live in the U.S., where he works long extra hours for money that will help get other members of his family out of the country.

Going by what I've studied, and what I learned on our Montana ranch, I would hope for a greater emphasis on organic farming in Africa.

According to Brian Halwell of the Worldwatch Institute, "Two recent studies reveal that a global shift to organic farming would yield more food, not less, for the world's hungry. Organic farming tends to raise yields in poorer nations, precisely those areas where people are hungry and can't afford chemical-intensive farming. Where there is a yield gap between conventional and organic crops, it tends to be widest in wealthy nations, where farmers use copious amounts of synthetic fertilizers and pesticides in a perennial attempt to maximize yields. In poorer nations, organic farming techniques like composting and green manuring and biological pest control may be farmers' best hope for boosting production and reducing hunger."

Organic methods can usually offer good logistical solutions for specific problems – like East Africa's battle with witchweed, a parasitic plant that thrives in poor soil and saps corn growth. East Africans do have the option to go the biotech route, and put themselves under the control of giant corporations who will provide yet another toxic chemical and charge them a lot of money for it. But some East African farmers have discovered that keeping up soil fertility by planting nitrogen-fixing trees will keep out witchweed.

My dad would would applaud their choice. Natural control was the method he used to eliminate undesirable plants from our rangelands.

"Take care of the grass," he'd say, "and the grass will take care of the weeds."

Final Thought

If I could bring my father back, and restore his health, and set him to traveling, he would be a good "agricultural ambassador." He would have a great time sitting down with African farmers and ranchers in different countries all the way across the African continent. As farmers and ranchers have always done, he and they would swap stories and vital information – about what worked and didn't work in American agriculture, about what works and doesn't work in Africa today. Indeed, it looks to me like more of this real farmer-to-farmer talk is needed, not only across the borders but also at the big global meetings.

Maybe if African farmers talk directly to U.S. farmers, they will have a better idea how to lobby their representatives and make AGOA work for them. Unlike most bureaucrats and many members of our U.S. Congress, who (in my opinion) live in a bubble, people who are really engaged in agriculture are aware of the life-and-death nature of the issues before AGOA. They are sensitive to the real losses when yet another growing season goes by and little is done, when millions of people in a region continue to be faced with little market outlet for their produce, perhaps even little food security. Farmers have a permanent built-in urgency about getting things done, that seems to be somewhat lacking in AGOA.

One thing of which I feel sure, based on my own experience with growing up in agriculture, is this:

When you are deciding what and where and how to plant, and why, you can never lose your grip on common sense. As my dad put it, "Does it work? If it doesn't, how do I make it work?" "What works" involves global principles that all farmers have learned the hard way, no matter what their culture or spirituality is, no matter what color their skin is, or what language they speak. The sun and the rain, the good years and the bad, the bumper crops and the famines, come to all parts of the Earth.

Our power to deal with natural disasters, to direct these natural forces so we can have the basics of human life – food, shelter, tools and clothing – can never be dictated wholly by politics, or by bureaucratic rules or human laws. When we remember this, peoples and nations can prosper.

ESPERSETH: A LITTLE-KNOWN FORAGE PLANT

Originally published in *Acres U.S.A.*, March 1992

Today, near the small Montana town of Deer Lodge, a non-native cultivated forage plant has made itself at home in the wild. This perennial plant – an almost forgotten immigrant from Europe – holds promise for helping to revitalize abused fields and range lands. In my family, this plant was known as esperseth. The name possibly translates as "sharp seed" – a vivid description of its one-eighth-inch burr-like protective seed pod. The pods contain the actual seed.

Esperseth is a legume – possibly a relative of alfalfa – that was imported to Montana from the alpine pastures of Switzerland. Distinguished by small pink-and-blue blossoms and vetch-like pinnate leaves, this plant matures over years into massive and deep-rooted clumps. Each clump measures as much as three feet wide at the base, and grows over 20 inches high when in full bloom.

For centuries Swiss farmers cultivated esperseth. They used it for livestock forage and soil enrichment, as well as erosion control on their steep and sometimes unstable mountain slopes.

The Montana locality mentioned earlier is the only spot in the U.S. (as far as I know) where esperseth is naturalized on a long-time basis today. It has survived there untended and unhampered for almost a century, through winters where the wind-chill factor can drop temperatures to 80 below zero. The plant has toughed its way through "normal" years of rainfall (Montana is classified as semi-desert" and averages 12-13 inches of rain a year). It has also gritted through the dry cycles – including that landmark drought of 1930-1938 that denuded the grasslands. This was when the local county agent told my father, Conrad Warren, and other ranchers, "Boys, the grass is gone forever."

In the spring of 1940, the drought ended locally, says my father, "when three feet of snow fell on the first of May." When the snow melted off, the grass was already springing a foot high – and with it the esperseth. This record shows that at least that one strain of esperseth is extraordinarily hardy and drought-resistant.

In the mid-to-late-1800s, my German greatgrandparents (Augusta and Conrad Kohrs) and my great-granduncle (John Bielenberg) pioneered in southwestern Montana. There they established a cattle ranch whose old historic headquarters is now a national park, and is on the maps today as the Grant-Kohrs Ranch National Historic Site.

In the late 1800s, with rampant over-grazing of Western grasslands and the great cattle die-up during the winter of 1886-87, my forebears started pulling back from grazing huge herds of grade steers on the public lands. Instead, they began experimenting with purebred cattle, and looking for ways to manage and re-plant ranges, so they could graze smaller areas more intensively.

The headquarters at Deer Lodge, Montana, was the focus of their breeding and planting experiments. Now and then, Conrad and Augusta returned to Europe to visit relatives. According to my father, it was on the last of these trips in 1898, as they were traveling through Switzerland and Conrad got to talking with stockgrowers there, that he became aware of esperseth. He obtained some seed, and took it back to Montana – along with a crate of fine Swiss woodcarvings and brass cowbells that he and Augusta had purchased as souvenirs.

Back home, Kohrs and Bielenberg sowed esperseth in an experimental pasture somewhere on the west side of the Deer Lodge River. The import may have been interspersed with alfalfa and mixed pasture grasses – the kind of mix that is still today a standard Montana favorite for grazing and grass hay.

The family men hoped that esperseth would prove superior to alfalfa as a Montana hay-pasture plant. Reason: alfalfa is dependent upon enormous amounts of irrigation water. It is also not reliably hardy or long-lived in Montana. Esperseth was evidently iron-clad hardy. While the European alpine climate is far moister than Montana's, esperseth had survived unaided in the Swiss pastures, so it did not require surface irrigation and intensive human effort to survive.

But the immediate result of Kohrs' experiment was not heartening. In the drier Montana summers, esperseth performed differently than in moister Switzerland. As the grazeable stalks matured in summer, they lost their juicy lushness and turned woody. The CK cattle didn't like to eat esperseth, especially after it set its thorny seeds.

So the experiment was abandoned.

Between 1920 and 1922, both Kohrs and Bielenberg died. When my father, Conrad Warren, took over the ranch in the 1930s, he worked most of the West Side into standard irrigated hayfields. The esperseth planting survived only in a narrow unfarmed strip north of the county road that runs towards Rock Creek Lake. There my dad continued to keep an eye on it, and pointed it out to me in the late 1940s and early 1950s, when I was a kid helping him on the ranch.

There on the West Side, the esperseth thrived on its own terms. It leaped south across the county road and spread on several neighboring properties, including unused portions of Hillcrest Cemetery and the boundaries of the county airport. It also leapfrogged west along the county road and up the slope of the bench there – where I found it when I went looking for it again in the early 1990s.

It was clear that the old Kohrs import was flourishing in a variety of situations, from gravelly benches to creek bottoms. Its most impressive performance was on some steep road banks. There it does the highway department a favor by helping hold up the shoulder. The banks are hot and dry – and nothing else grows there but sagebrush, spotted knapweed, snakeweed and thistles. The esperseth was duking it out with these gnarly competitors, and giving them no quarter.

The most distant plants I found from the historic center were approximately 1 mile. As far as I know, this is the plant's radius of spread in nearly a century. In short, esperseth is not a rampant grower, even though each mature plant drops thousands of seed-cases in August. So it cannot be classed with noxious invaders like spotted knapweed.

I watched this colony of esperseth for many years now, starting in the late 1940s as a teenager in 4-H Club range management, into the 1990s, when I was a small organic poultry-grower in northern California and experimented with growing it there. The plant's nitrogen-fixing power seems to improve the soil, because grass is always thicker in the vicinity of the esperseth clumps. I noticed that even "outsider" plants like feral perennial baby's-breath (for which the Deer Lodge area is famed in the local florist trade – florists come to pick baby's-breath in the pastures around the Hillcrest Cemetery) appear to like growing near esperseth.

Here are a dozen unanswered questions about esperseth:

(1) In parts of the United States where there is greater summer or year-round rainfall than in Montana, would esperseth have a more tender growth, and be as palatable to stock as it was in Switzerland?

(2) In these rainier areas, can esperseth begin to replace commercially grown alfalfa – both as hay for dairy cattle, and as fresh forage in dairy pasture? If it can, it would be a gift to farmers in water-critical areas like the central valley of California, where alfalfa farming is now under fire because it demands so much water.

(3) Would the rugged deep-rooted plants be more resistant to close grazing and trampling by livestock than are the more fragile grasses?

(4) Do sheep like esperseth? Goats? Horses? Llamas? Sheep and goats feast on many plants – like leafy spurge and spotted knap – that cattle shun.

(5) In drier parts of the U.S., would esperseth provide good drought-resistant grazing for sheep and goats, who don't mind woody stems?

(6) What about ranging poultry? Can esperseth stand up better than standard pasture to the incessant scratching and digging by ranged chickens and turkeys? Ranged poultry is an attractive

alternative to "factory chicken," but it can be destructive to land in the same way as intensive grazing by hoofed animals.

(7) What are the possible dangers to horses, of grazing on green esperseth? Every horse-owner knows the risk of bloat from fresh alfalfa.

(8) What is esperseth's long-term value (since it is a slow grower, but long-lived) in revitalizing farmland and rangeland that is eroded and leached of nutrients?

(9) Does esperseth have survival value for wild grazers like elk and deer? Some private land-owners are learning that their strategy for environmentally saner ranching and farming can also help support local hard-pressed wildlife. I have seen whitetail deer feasting happily on the Montana patch. Esperseth is still deep green in August, at a time when most Western grasses are already cured on the stem.

(10) What can esperseth add to our array of plants used for reclaiming strip mines and other such damaged areas?

(11) Does esperseth have any value as a single-season green manure?

(12) Does esperseth – like alfalfa – have any medicinal value for humans?

These and other questions about this intriguing plant deserve to be answered.

Today, with the urgent need to learn about little-known plants, and to care for our gene pools of every kind of cultivated seed, I have made the decision to write about this plant, so that more agriculturists might work with it.

Update in 2010

The foregoing article was written with my father's encouragement, and he reviewed it for factual accuracy. When it appeared in 1992, it sparked some lively discussion that eventually found its way onto the Web, where links can still be found today that mention my article.

While Dad always spelled the plant's name as "esperseth," I found that the plant is known in Germany and Switzerland as *esparsette*. Other European languages use similar-sounding names. It apparently occurs as a large number of species, that can be distinguished from one another by the shape of the seed pod. It belongs to a distinctive family of legumes known as the sainfoins, and has been cultivated in Asia, the Middle East and Europe for many centuries.

Today, according to sources I find on the Web, there is growing revival of interest in the whole sainfoin family.

Further reading:

INTERNATIONAL LEGUME DATABASE & INFORMATION SERVICE (ILDIS) (2005): Genus Onobrychis. Version 10.01, November 2005.

BOBCATS AS PEST CONTROLLERS

Originally published in *Acres U.S.A.*, November 1992

Many farmers who switch to biological agriculture are discovering how wildlife can be of benefit. For centuries, "dominion over the Earth" has been translated as "war on wild animals that get in the way." But balance is possible, and both farm income and valuable wild resources can be enhanced. This balance is crucial, I think, to revitalization of those farmlands and ranchlands that are now America's "empty quarter."

A few decades ago, the idea of getting beneficial insects to kill pests was considered outlandish. Today, with the beneficial insect industry a reality, perhaps we can talk about help from another outlandish creature. This creature is the small wildcat.

Small wildcats are part of the Earth's life support system for human beings. By keeping small plant eaters in check, they protect our croplands, grasslands and forests. The magnetic arc of life's circle passes directly through the cats' stomachs. Today, four small wildcats still live in the continental United States. These are the lynx, ocelot, jaguarundi and bobcat.

But only the bobcat still ranges in enough states, and enough numbers, to offer a positive boon to farmers.

Our culture's attitude that predators are "bad" has made it difficult for agriculture to seek a sensible coexistence with some wild animals. Large predators such as mountain lions, eagles and wolves are an explosive political issue. While controversies rage, the beneficial *small* predators – raptors, snakes, mammals – have drifted into a perilous backwater of public inattention.

This article will not take sides on any legislation or Earth Summit post-mortems. *Acres USA* readers will doubtless agree with me that learning, not legislation, is the only real way to change.

My subject is one seldom discussed: bobcat logistics on the ranch and farm. I'll also share a few personal observations.

Why Balance Matters

This underestimated but useful little animal is not presently on the CITES or U.S. endangered species list, therefore, the bobcat presents an intriguing challenge to the intelligence and initiative of the American farmer and rancher.

Across the world, recent decades have seen huge swings in natural imbalances. As we already know, pesticides destroy birds and insects that feed on undesirable plants and insects. When these natural allies die, the number of undesirables explodes. Human beings then step in,and their manner of predation has often skewed the imbalances even more wildly.

The classic example is Australia. a continent with no native wildcats. There, farmers tried to eradicate the wild dingo dog, and introduced rabbits. The rabbit numbers exploded, uncontrolled. into the vast interiors. The result was breath-taking forage destruction and soil erosion. Australia had to undertake a costly rabbit eradication program.

On the landscapes of rural America, many smaller predators have now vanished, or are scarce. Mice, rats, grasshoppers, rabbits, gophers and other animals multiply unchecked. Ranchers and farmers spend millions annually on traps and poisons.

Some plant-eaters can also delay forest re-growth when their populations soar. Deer graze heavily on seedling trees, including conifers.

Supreme Hunters

The small wildcats number 28 species, out of a total of 37 species of felines found worldwide. In a recent issue of *Zoonooz* featuring small cats, the San Diego Zoo said of the cats: “As a group they are, perhaps, the most efficient and highly developed hunters in the animal kingdom. No other carnivore surpasses them in this ability.”

Indeed, many of us have valued the superb varmint hunters among domestic cats – the mother tabby who relentlessly, year after year, sweeps the garden and nearby meadows. Mice and rats that are killed in these hinterlands do not invade barns and granaries.

But if the domestic cat is good, the small wildcat is better. It ranges more widely. It has an explosive energy that can handle bigger, more agile prey.

Thousands of years ago, the first smart farmers got wildcats to help them, and this is how cats were “domesticated.” Ancient farmers recognized the importance of wildcat patrol around their fields and storage. A few of these felines had a mellower nature, and wound up on Granny’s lap in the house. Others were more feisty, undomesticable – yet they were amenable to living on the fringes of human habitations. Wildcats make lousy pets. I advocate only hands-off cooperation with free-living cats.

Our ancestors also knew that farm pest control is linked to disease. For instance, the Chinese knew that rodents are linked to bubonic plague.

Today, prey of small cats carry serious diseases that can be spread to domestic animals and humans. Rabbits harbor tularemia. Farm rodents contribute heavily to the salmonella problem in the poultry industry. Deer and certain rodents carry Lyme disease, which is transmitted through ticks. I personally had Lyme disease – a bobcat could have shielded me from this affliction.

Mice and rats alone share 32 different diseases with humans. Today, with exploding human populations spilling into undeveloped areas, we need to remember that many wild burrowing rodents on Western lands are a natural reservoir for the bubonic-plague bacillus, especially as the bobcat is steadily eradicated.

The wildcat’s only serious threat to humans is as a possible carrier of rabies; however, with the humane new bait-administered rabies vaccines that can be scattered about for wild animals (see May 1992 *Scientific American*), this threat will surely wane.

Last, but not least, wildcat pest-control is non-toxic, low-tech – and free.

The World Picture

Endangered big cats – cheetahs, tigers, etc. – have commanded world attention because they were the first felines to slide toward extinction. And because they are big, they are dramatically visible. But many of the little cats weigh less than 20 pounds, a few as little as three pounds. Many of them live shy, nocturnal, hidden lives. Little is known about many.

Beyond size, what distinguishes a small cat from a big cat? One of the most striking differences is voice. Most little cats purr, and yowl. Most big cats roar, but cannot purr. These distinctions depend on the anatomy of the larynx.

In other countries, many small wildcats have names that Americans consider unpronounceable and, therefore, forgettable: tigrina, kodkod, caracal, manul, chaus, serval, colocolo. Few Americans get excited over the jaguarundi, which looks like an otter/weasel hybrid. Or the fishing cat, with its partially webbed feet. Or the flatheaded cat, whose name needs no further explanation. Yet, historically, many of these odd little creatures have lived close by humans, and hunted for them, without becoming domesticated.

In ancient Egypt. the chaus and the North African wildcat were so useful and beloved that whole cemeteries of little wildcat mummies have been found. In southeast Asia, the tiny leopard cat is still cherished in some commercial palm plantations, where it controls palm rats. The same with parts of rural India, and the caracal with its long-tufted ears. In Central and South America, some farmers still keep jaguarundis around.

Rccently I interviewed Patricia Quillen, who is one of the world's ranking experts on little cats. Her Society of Scientific (*S.O.S.*) Care, Inc. is a non-profit conservation foundation dedicated to preserving the world's small cats. She was working within IUCN as a member of the Species Survival Commission,

Cat Specialist Group. In 1989, Quillen was nominated for the Chevron International Conservation Award.

Quillen's work had a common-sense message: small cats have bigger economic value alive than dead. Because of this, a growing number of foreign governments seek her advice on small wildcat husbandry and conservation.

In the past, pelt hunting was harder on the little cats than was agriculture. CITES fur-trade figures show that, from the 1950s into the 1980s, countless millions of small-cat pelts were marketed. Complicating the issue is a profound human reality – in many countries, wildcat pelts have been a cash crop for poor rural families. But suddenly, in the early 1980s in many countries, pelt "catches" plummeted – many cats were being fished out.

Today, both abroad and in the U.S., it is chemical agribusiness, population growth and the more shortsighted kinds of logging that hurt our wild helpers most. With hungry people proliferating, with forests razed for everything from firewood to pulp, with steady bleeding of rural lands to development, with intensive marketing of petrochemical products into developing countries, the little wildcats quietly die, with survivors making last stands in tiny pockets.

Statistics are scarce, because wildcat apparent naturals usually go unreported. Causes of death can range from timber clear-cutting, to poisoning by pesticides and heavy metals, to shotguns.

Close-up on the Bobcat

Bobcats are highly adaptable, and thrive in almost any temperate-zone North American habitat. In north Los Angeles, where I live today, suburban neighborhoods run right to the foot of the Angeles National Forest. There, I have seen the occasional bobcat disappearing through hedges in search of suburban rodents. I have also seen them in the Malibu canyons and chaparral ridges, just a 45-minute drive from the Los Angeles Airport.

Bobcats eat a long menu, from rattlesnakes to grasshoppers. Film footage in slow motion shows the incredible dexterity with which they run down their meals. Occasionally a good-size cat will even tackle a weak deer floundering in snow. Bobcats are known to travel long distances, to seek out new territory where there is food.

Three centuries ago, bobcats numbered dozens of subspecies and millions of individuals, in every continental U.S. state. In colonial times, it was stamped as a chicken-killer, with most states offering bounties on its head.

Starting in the 1930s, the bobcat became a major target of the federal predator control program. Some conservationists commented that attractive subsidies, and little documentation of bobcat predation required, created the motive and the loopholes for some stockgrowers to cheat. By 1970, with introduction of high-tech poisoning devices, some Americans felt that the bobcat was in trouble.

The fur business also takes bobcats off farmers' hands. In 1971, suffering a slump in high-end fur sales, the industry invented the low-price mass marketed "fun fur." Since the bobcat was not protected, it was fished like cod on the Grand Banks – by 1977, 100,000 pelts a year were exported abroad, where the bobcat is considered exotic.

Nose counts of bobcats are difficult, owing to the animal's elusive nature. But the cat's decline was visible enough that CITES listed it as threatened when the treaty went into effect in 1973. However, the U.S. Endangered Species Act kept the bobcat in the "safe" category, thanks to pressures from fur, hunting and agribusiness lobbies.

Today, Gail Foreman, an American wild feline observer, tells me that the bobcat is virtually wiped out in the heartland of American farming – the Midwest. In Ohio, the cat is listed as "endangered" on the state level. In Nebraska, it has "protected" status, yet is hunted. Sizeable populations still rove the Southeast and West. But solid population studies are lacking.

In less intensively farmed areas, and in ranch country where enough cover remains, bobcats can still handily breed.

It is here that agriculture operations – especially those involving vegetable crops and grain – actually create hotspots where rodents bloom like plankton in the springtime seas. These blooms create a problem for the farmer. They also attract the cats.

In Foreman's opinion, the bobcat's biggest attrition comes from continuous shooting and trapping by individual farmers and ranchers.

Sheep growers, and the increasing numbers of poultry farms that grow birds on range, have a legitimate concern about small-wildcat predation. Sheep growers claim that 3% of their annual losses are due to bobcats; however, there are those eco-agriculturists who can reasonably tolerate a bobcat family for neighbors, if they wish. Bobcats pose little threat to large stock, and zero threat to any and all plant crops.

If bobcat acceptance is starting anywhere, it is among these people.

My Own Observations

My education about small wildcats started in the 1940s on my family's 6,000- acre Montana ranch. There, until around 1977, we ran Herefords. For a time, during World War II and after, we also farmed wheat, oats and potatoes.

The ranch terrain varied from riverine hay meadows to high mountain pastures, and bobcats could be found almost anywhere. A few lived within a half-mile radius of the main buildings. Now and then we glimpsed a distant swirl in the ripening wheat, as a mother bobcat nailed a mouse. Or we noticed a blurred short-tailed shape that was just leaving the potato field with a gopher in its mouth.

I remember a spring day, in the late 40s, when my father, Con Warren, showed me bobcat tracks in the muddy road 50 feet from our house. He pointed out that the cats were important to his rodent-control program.

"I've got them working for me," he said. "Like the beaver."

The beaver were one of the ranch's best "conservation" stories. They had been planted at his request by Montana Fish and Game, so the pond storage they created could be his irrigation-water backup. And the project had worked, supplying him with enough extra water to sprinkler-irrigate an additional 80 acres. Now and then, my dad shot a coyote, or grumbled about elk that invaded his haystacks. But today, when I think that he headed the Montana Livestock Commission and Stockgrowers' Association during an era when poisons were in almost universal use, I realize that his personal forbearance about bobcats was unusual.

My next close look came during 1975-81, in New York State. Here, I worked as a volunteer associate with Reg Riedel's captive breeding program for endangered small exotic cats under a New York State Fish and Wildlife permit. Such programs, both private and zoo-run, can create a hedge against extinction, and restock wild habitats.

During these years, I got to observe several species of small wildcat – tigrina, chaus, Geoffroy's cat. Because the animals lived in large tree-shaded outdoor runs, we had an effective varmint patrol on the place. Any wood rat, snake or mouse that blundered through the chain-link fence into the runs, was fast food. I was amazed at the sheer quantity of beetles, hornworms, moths and grasshoppers that those wildcats scarfed.

Several years later, I moved to northern California. There, I had an illuminating experience.

Some Métis relatives and I settled on a 300-acre farm in the coastal range of Mendocino County. We decided on organic produce, with hopes for a modest market operation. The land, formerly grazing for a large ranch, had never been chemically farmed. From the start, however, our little operation was overrun by ground squirrels and pocket gophers. Potato plants, even full-grown corn plants, disappeared overnight. Dug-in wire did no good. Neither did traps, or those nontoxic "environmental" widgets that supposedly scare gophers away.

The plant destroyers were already out of hand when we came. Why? For years, the land had been unposted. Poachers and hunters roamed through freely, blasting at anything that moved. The grazing had been leased, and ranchers eliminated varmints. By the time we arrived, that property was echoingly empty of wildlife. No coyotes, fox, bobcats, raptors. Just a few gun-shy deer. In the absence of predators, the plant nibblers had exploded, Australian style.

I didn't want to escalate to poison. This was my chance to test if the natural balance could return.

Our first step was to discourage trespassers with guns. After two years of posting, patrolling, and a court case that we won, and with the dedicated support of our game warden, word got out that we meant business, and the illegal hunting stopped.

Just as I was about to ask our game warden if we could legally release bobcats there, the first one – a female – showed up. She stayed aloof, on a slope a quarter-mile away from our planting area, but we heard her springtime yowls, found her tracks along the stream and occasionally glimpsed her trotting off towards cover. After that, we saw a few other bobcats, so perhaps she denned and raised kittens.

In one year after her arrival, we were seeing fewer ground squirrels and gophers. Eventually, other predators moved in – fox, badger, a pair of golden eagles. The numbers of produce-nibblers kept ebbing. Grey squirrels, chipmunks, wild turkeys, and more deer came.

The bottom line:

• After two years of bobcat help, wildlife on our farm was more varied.

• We now raised vegetables with minimal losses to nibblers.

• Balance was restored without chemical warfare. The main human input was patience.

• The cats appeared to be the first to come. Their propensity for roaming evidently means that they are among the first predators to spot new food.

Some Final Thoughts

Protecting our beneficial predators is going to be a touchstone of our courage and dedication to Reality.

Unfortunately, for a few small-cat species, appreciation comes too late. In South America, the Andean mountain cat is evidently gone. In Southeast Asia, the bay cat and several others are down to a few dozen individuals. Other small species are imperiled as long as the anti-predator rage lasts. Each species that disappears will leave a gaping tear in the dynamics of rural life – a wound that the petrochemical doctors will insist they can Band-Aid with their products.

Fortunately, the picture is not all gloomy. Pat Quillen's expanding advisory work, and that of others, gives a profile of awakening world consciousness. Currently, through AAZPA, with Purina funding, Quillen is cooperating with Brazil, which is creating a major program.

These efforts will succeed if rural Americans, and rural people everywhere, come to see the small wildcat as a valuable living resource. The only thing that will help the animals is if enough of these ordinary citizens want them around.

The poisoning and blasting of wildlife will affect us profoundly – and in ways that we do not foresee right now. Contrary to current propaganda, wild animals do not stand in the way of filling human needs. The only thing standing in the way is the unwillingness to look for creative solutions, and the stubbornness of vested interests that profit by the status quo.

Agriculturists can have a decent living because of intelligent wild-animal conservation, and not in spite of them.

Thousands of years ago, farmers and cats started the long, long road together. If today's eco-farmers have been inventive enough to discover beneficial insects, ELF waves, brix readings, rock dust, and carbon, then surely we are inventive enough to rediscover the helpful little hunters that still make their distant waves in the wheatfields.

Update in 2010

Sad to say, since I wrote this piece, the global effort to save a wide range of small wildcat species has largely failed. Too much of their habitat was being destroyed, leaving nowhere for them to live. It cost too much money, and fundraising was getting increasingly difficult to get as the global recession worsened. In recent years, many big cats and small cats are now seriously threatened or endangered – even African lions, which used to be thought of as "common."

In the U.S., bobcats are still fairly common, and listed as CITES Appendix II species, which can be traded commercially only if it does not harm their survival.

I haven't changed my opinions about bobcat value for farmers, however – especially after living in Malibu for five years, 1991-96 and personally witnessing one more example of bobcat cleanup on pest species. I rented part of a house halfway up Latigo Canyon, in an area well-surrounded with typical brush and no houses nearby. The property owners had a fear of rattlesnakes, and industriously killed every snake they saw. With the snakes gone, they found their property being overrun with pocket gophers, mice, rats and rabbits.

Just when things were completely out of hand and my landlord was about to call a pest-control company, Mother Earth said, "Cue the bobcats."

The one that showed up was a female. She seemed quite unafraid of us, and would appear in early morning at first light, sauntering along the sidewalk beside the house, till she reached the railroad-tie terraces overlooking the canyon slope. There she would sit at the top of the steps for hours, patiently watching. If anything moved down there, she'd be off in a flash to stalk it. It took a year, but she pared my landlords' overpopulation of rodents back to normal size.

GRASSES:
THOSE GRACEFUL DANCERS

Originally published in *Montana Magazine*, August 1993

No doubt about it – I was on a quest. One as fraught with challenge as galloping my charger in search of a wise witch who keeps a magic sword. In this case, the "charger" was my silver Toyota pickup. And the object of the quest was a patch of sweetgrass somewhere... anywhere.

This lovely grass, used as incense by native tribes and early settlers, perfumes every breeze of Montana history and spirit. A county, a range of mountains and several streams are named after several species of this distinctive plant, known as *Hierochloe* or sweetgrass. Though it was once found across all of Canada and much of the U.S., I had heard tell that in recent years, sweetgrass was becoming scarce in Montana. Long decades of grazing and haying have eradicated it from many of the river bottoms where it grows.

I started by asking ranchers. They'd all heard of sweetgrass, but – "I haven't seen it in years," admitted one. Since this grass is not of major economic importance to ranching, most had no idea what it looked like. But I persisted, calling ecological organizations and Forest Service botanists. Some people are understandably protective about top-secret locations of their favorite grass. But finally, like every good quester, I managed to get a map, with somebody's X marking the spot.

Armed with the map and a botanical drawing, I sallied forth in search of Chloe.

Grass Roots

Being a writer, I like to quest into the meaning of the key word in a story. Whole eras of forgotten human history can be found hidden in every word, if only we look. Peoples, wars, trade, migrations, hate, beauty, goddesses, gods – all are there in the *American Heritage Dictionary's* glossary of root words. "Grass," and a related word, "grace," go back to the ancient Mediterranean. Graecia is Greece. The word could be translated as "the goddess Grass." Perhaps "grace" also came to mean "lithe and beautiful movement" because of the way that grasses dance in the wind.

Grasses are flowering plants that sway on hollow, jointed stems, with their supple sword-like leaves whispering on the lightest breeze. Their tiny flowers burst from the lofty heads, or "spike1ets," whose swaying throws pollen into the wind, and onto the fur of passing animals. In size, they range from the short grasses of the northern plains, to the giant bamboos of the Far East.

Thousands of grasses are known in the United States. They grow in two ways–either in individual clumps, like the bunch grasses so loved by Montanans, or in masses that spread by means of underground rhizomes.

My map sent me west of Augusta, toward the Benchmark Wilderness. As I jounced along a dirt road, thundershowers were sweeping the grasslands, as they had for days. The hills were unusually green at a time of year when grasses are usually sun-fried on the stem. Climbing the grade into Willow Creek Canyon, I passed the sleekest range cattle I'd seen in years. They were Charolais, technically white, but with a golden tint on their hides that comes from carotene in the grass.

The Graces are the most important plant food for humans and land animals – perhaps that is how their name came to mean prayers of thanks at meals. Corn, rice, wheat, oats, barley, rye, millet, sorghum, sugarcane, triticale – all are grasses. Every meat animal is fattened on "grass" in some way, whether sheep on an Argentine range, or chickens picking at grass seeds near a Chinese village, or hogs stuffed with corn in a Midwest piggery.

New grass was a reason why Europeans emigrated to America. In overpopulated Europe, most of the grazing land was controlled by aristocracy and church. This left the swelling population of "common people" hungry for meat, and without land to produce meat. In Montana, our highly nutritious northern grasses have been – and still are – the source of our lives, our food, our history, our feeling for beauty.

Ancient native peoples in this area dined on big grass-fed mammals, as well as on the bounty of small animals nourished by the prairie. Vast herds of bison, elk, deer, and pronghorn antelope grazed these northern grasslands. By the 1700s, northwest Native Americans took up horse-raising in the grassy mountain basins of western Montana, as well as on the plains of eastern Oregon and southern Idaho. In the early 1800s, some enterprising mixed-blood traders moved from the declining fur industry and started bringing cattle and horses onto Montana grass. After the Civil War, those early ranchers were politically eclipsed by white immigrant cattle-traders.

Today, other Montana industries – mining, oil, logging, tourism – may come and go. But agriculture has always been – and still is – the biggest industry. Range grass still feeds several million Montana cattle a year, and the Montana grain harvest nourishes millions of lives in the U.S. and abroad.

The Little Grass Shack

Through the centuries, grasses also have given us shelter, tools, weapons and clothing.

Rope, paper, shoes, straw hats, baskets, mats, saddle-pads – all have been fashioned from grass. Grasses have gone to war as bamboo armor, lances, arrows. As "Montana feathers," they filled many a pioneer mattress and pillow. Layered into shingles, they create a thatched roof. Cut into squares, grass-sod made prairie homes that were warm in winter, cool in summer. In earthquake-shaken Japan, many residents prefer a flexible bamboo house to the more "modern" concrete and steel structures.

The Graces also feed our need for beauty. Some, such as lemon grass, yield aromatic oil for perfume. Florists use them for delicate accents in dried arrangements. And what country child has not shaped a switch of green grass into a doll?

Some grasses can heal, steeped in boiling water to make herbal tea. Several are listed in the *United States Pharmacoepia*, including rye-grass. These, like all native plants that contain healing substances, were made known to immigrant doctors by Native American doctors.

In sweetgrass, we have an incense as wondrous as sandalwood. *Hierochloe odorata* is the most fragrant of four sweetgrass species. Together, the four blanket northern Europe, Canada and much of the U.S. The common name "sweetgrass" and the scientific name both describe the plant well: Chloe was a goddess in ancient Greece, and the word "chloe" means "to clean" as well as "young green shoots." *Odorata* means "fragrant." People have burned *Hierochloe* to clean the air during ceremony. They have also stored it with clothing, like a sachet. Old-timers in Montana tell about riding along the river bottoms on a hot August day, their horses' hoofs stirring up clouds of powerful scent from the acres of ripe sweetgrass.

Today, in the West, some people still harvest sweetgrass, by braiding it green from the ground up, then cutting the braid and drying it. The braids retail for as much as $5 each, leading me to suspect that the grass's growing scarcity is due to this trade.

The economic importance of grass dances far beyond our personal survival and comforts. Example: Our highway system. It would be a moonscape of erosion if shoulders and interchanges were not held in place with grasses. Highway engineers like go-get-'em grasses that are quick-growing, drought-resistant and tough-rooted. Roadside stands of grass are often so magnificent that they show us what a pristine rangeland could look like. Ranchers even lease some roadsides to cut for hay.

Like the Dutch boy in the story, Grace also keeps her finger on the hole in the dike. Across the U.S., grasses hold down many earthen dams as well as river levees near towns and cities. Grassy levees also guard some of our finest farmlands – along the Mississippi River, and the Sacramento River in California.

Grass is a vital partner to many kinds of land healing – such as timber clear-cuts and old strip-mine sites.

Grass to the Rescue

My quest also took me to Sweetgrass County. While zigzagging around the state, I saw that some of Montana's grasslands are badly overgrazed.

In agriculture, disregard for the delicate nature of grasses has created a world crisis. As borders change, and money and politics go global, we Americans need to look at our own grass crisis with world eyes. Today, a significant percentage of our Western rangeland – both public and private – is seriously overgrazed. Much of the topsoil is gone. Many areas are overgrown with inedible brush and gullied by erosion and flash floods.

In addition, erosion is increasing on our farmlands. Many farmers have cut corners on soil care in order to wring more bushels and more profit out of every acre.

In the early 1900s, America was shaken by a collision between unwise agricultural practices and a long drought. The result was the 1930s Dust Bowl. Our nation experienced massive human suffering and massive loss of precious topsoil as fierce dust-storms darkened the skies and swept thousands of families from their ruined lands.

Afterwards, shocked into the need to care for what soil was left, our agriculturists did employ wiser methods for a time. But in recent decades, it seems that too many have forgotten the horrible lessons, as agribusiness chases ever harder after profits and exports. Once again, as in the early 1900s, we stare directly into a possibility of dust bowl – meaning the loss of more precious topsoil.

In some areas, the future is already here. In the grain lands of eastern Oregon, road signs warn of severe dust storms. In California's drought-stricken San Joaquin Valley, dirt blowing from unplanted cotton fields now threatens traffic on Interstate 5. On Thanksgiving 1991, a sudden dust storm covered a section of

I-5 and caused a 125-vehicle pile-up that killed 16 people. I was driving on the 5 at that time, and missed encountering that lethal pile-up by 60 minutes. In eastern Montana, concerned ranchers have tried to use legal action to block massive plowing of grasslands.

Hair-Raising History

As our very lives blow away on the wind, it is important to consider why our grasslands are so fragile and need such care.

Unlike woody trees, grass plants do not live for hundreds of years. Some clumps of bunchgrass can live for decades. But ultimately the individual plant dies and must be replaced by new plants if the great robe of grass enclosing a region is to be kept whole.

Our ecosystems function well when only a certain percentage of grass seed feeds the grass-eaters. When populations of wild herds are in balance with the available grass, the uneaten percentage of seeds falls to the earth, there to sprout into new plants. But when herds grow too big, and/or when drought limits grass growth, the grass-eaters destroy the grass – then starve in masses. Their die-off gives the grass time to recover, while the herds re-build their numbers slowly to the delicate balance-point again.

When humans enter this design with fences that limit grazing space, and the tendency of some to value profit over common sense, a herd of 1,000 animals can be thrown onto a rangeland that only has grass for 500. These animals not only chew the plants right down to the crowns, but also gobble all the seeds. They can even destroy the crowns with their desperate pawing and trampling.

Western history books show us some spooky examples of how fast a "limitless" grass country can be decimated. In the early 1860's, the mountain basins of southwestern Montana were described by my amazed Greatgrandfather Kohrs as "a sea of waving bunch-grass." My dad always remembered him using that phrase. When gold was struck in 1864, beef herds poured in to feed the Army forts and growing towns. In just five years, those local "seas" of grass were gone. By the late 1860s, stock-raisers were moving north into the lush Sun and Judith river basins. By 1870, the bison were being decimated to free up grass for cattle. No sooner were the Plains tribes conquered in the late 1870s than the ever-growing beef herds were gushing east onto the high plains of eastern Montana. There, in an area measuring approximately 90,000 square miles, the waving grasses lasted only till the "big die-up" of the 1886-87 winter.

That "die-up" has been blamed on a major blizzard. Actually, the eastern ranges were overpopulated and overgrazed after a dry summer. Many of the 10 million cattle were weak. A number of big herds belonged to absentee speculators who cared only about money. So when the blizzard hit, several million cattle died. It was a rebalancing jolt to a cycle that ranchers had thrown out of balance.

In short, land can be overgrazed in just a few years. With reseeding repeatedly thwarted, bare spots appear. These wounds are rapidly occupied by new plants that livestock don't want to eat – like sagebrush, snakeweed, spotted knapweed, ground lichens.

Today's money crunch speeds up the destruction. With ranchers often in chronic debt, an outfit can often be tempted to squeeze several hundred more head onto the range.

Desertification

When humans abuse the land enough, the result is "desertification" – making a region barren and desert-like. One horrible example is the Sahel – that swath of new desert that sweeps from the Atlantic coast of Africa to the Nile valley. Until 1968, it was farming and grazing country. Now it is littered with cattle bones, its seared villages disappearing under sand dunes. The new Sahel desert has already engulfed the future of eight entire African nations, and the lives of millions of starved refugees.

But the Sahel is only one example. *The Arid Lands*, a Time-Life book on deserts and desertification, reports that "nearly 70 countries in the world ... are afflicted by desertification. Each year 15 millions of acres of useful land are lost." This figure should make a Montanan's hair stand on end. Fifteen million acres translates into 23,437.5 square miles – the equivalent of 16 percent of Montana lost every year. In the final years of his life, my dad kept that book on his kitchen table and often leafed through it, deeply worried.

Certainly, with five years of Western drought, and weather patterns changing over our continent, the threat of new deserts is one that should jolt awake even our most soporific citizens. How ironic that our great big nation might have to import most of our meat and produce. Our vulnerability to the Middle Eastern oil squeeze, and the war we just fought in the Gulf, would be the whine of a single mosquito compared to the big sting of a food squeeze.

The Need for Appreciation

Today, most Americans experience grass only as lawns, that must be sheared like sheep. The idea of manicured lawns originated in England, where it rains a lot. So vast is our cultural insistence on a lush greensward that irrigating lawns is a major factor in the nasty interstate wars over water rights – especially in the Southwest and California. Homeowners, estates, campuses, city parks, industrial landscapers and golf courses spend millions annually on lawn chemicals and high-tech irrigation equipment.

Most lawn-lovers never let themselves enjoy the delicate beauty of the grass-flowers, or hear the sound of the wind playing the harps of a million grass-stems. Instead, the moment a single spikelet appears, these folks race out and mercilessly raze their grass down to doormat level. Indeed, for many people, the lawn is not a living being, but an extension of their living room carpet.

Ironically, homeowners and golfers have learned what some range managers have not – that they have to reseed now and then. Weekly machine-mowing thwarts the natural process of reseeding, just like overgrazing does.

Fortunately, more and more Americans realize that we are fighting for our lives. Publications like *Beef Today* and *Acres U.S.A.*, and organizations like the National Cattlemen's Association, are actively campaigning for grass conservation and management. The crisis has created sophisticated new commercial sources of grass seed. For instance, Granite Seed is located in Lehi, Utah. Not only does Granite offer dozens of varieties of native and exotic seed, but they assist with soil testing and provide custom mixes.

Like the redwood trees and the whales, the graceful grasses also inspire new friends. In Salina, Kansas, the Land Institute has been working for many years to breed high-protein perennial grains from native grasses. In Montana, members of the Native Plant Society cooperate with the federal government in listing plants – grasses among them – that are threatened or endangered.

Sweetgrass is not yet on the list. But its possible growing scarcity, and its value in the restoration of damaged riparian areas, has prompted one major Western seed company to tell me they are thinking of growing it commercially.

After days of driving, my silver "charger" finally carried me to the object of my quest – a patch of sweetgrass. As I sat down in that meadow with Chloe, sniffed her wondrous fragrance, and watched her graceful purple stems do their sword-dance in the wind, I thought of the Sahel. If a Nigerian cattle-herding mother could see this, she would probably throw herself down in the grass, and kiss it, and weep with joy.

It's no wonder that the history of words offers us this pungent phrase, "grass roots" – meaning *people*.

Update in 2010

Today the USDA Plant Database lists sweetgrass as endangered in three states – Maryland, North Carolina, and Pennsylvania. Expert observers continue to comment that sweetgrass is in trouble, and getting hard to find, owing to development and over-harvesting of wild stands.

ANIMALS

THE GENTLE BEING

Originally published in *Cat Fanciers' Almanac,* September 1992

When I was doing the research for my novel, *One Is the Sun*, I got this story from a Montana Métis (mixed blood). He in turn heard it from Cree relatives of his, who live in northern Canada, lynx country, up near the Arctic Circle.

It's the kind of story that comes out of that country. And it's the kind of country where, today, you fly in for hours in an elderly decrepit plane, a Cessna 170, that is based in some tiny bush airport. The Métis told me how the plane bores into a brilliant vista of hundreds of miles of northern skyline, well north of the 50th parallel – sun flashing off the wild rivers and lakes below, sun glaring off endless stretches of boggy meadows and timber and muskeg, where technical incursions are finally grinding their deadly tracks across those of moose and wolf.

Finally the blue glare of Great Slave Lake is below. The engine of the 170 changes its pitch as it descends onto the tiny landing strip at Yellowknife. Relatives are there with smiles rearranging the wrinkles on their weathered faces, with warm handshakes and their different tongue. Mail, dogs and sundries are dumped off the plane, and other sundries thrown aboard. The plane is already lifting off as you jounce away with your relatives in the old Ford pickup. A .3030 rifle rides on its rack in the pickup cab – till not long ago, the weapon of choice was still an antique muzzle-loader. This was thought to be a more practical weapon because you could be independent of the trading post for a whole year – dig your lead out of wherever it went and re-load your own ammo.

It is a different world, the Métis told me, where stories are still legal tender. Stories are still traded, as they once were on those lake shores, when husky young northern children were traded for rare southern plant drugs and parrot feathers, to the southern traders who would walk those slaves far, far, many moons of walking, back to jaguar country – Mexico. Those slaves would grow up on the journey, and when they got to Mexico, they would grow corn and build pyramids.

It is a different kind of story, told with different rhythms, and the different viewpoint of that world.

One of the Métis' relatives had traded for this story of the Gentle Being. He got it from some Inuit who lived up near Point Barrow. In spite of the incursions of the Alaska Pipeline, and television, and liquor, and all the sadness and anger that go with being poor and indigenous in a wealthy white's world, many of the things of the white man are still strange in this north country. Some of them were held at arm's length with a fury – and others were accepted because, however strange they may be, they were seen as wondrous gifts that came from Life, not from the wealthy whites.

The People had that kind of thinking for a long time about the Gifts. Such a gift was the Gentle Being.

Many years ago, said those Inuit, in the times when their grandfathers were young, a white man's Big Canoe, a whaling ship, got caught in the ice just off Point Barrow. The ship was squeezed tighter and tighter, with the great slabs and shelves of ice piling higher and higher around her, giving off flashes of rainbow light in the freezing sunshine. After awhile, with a great cracking groan, her timbers gave way, and she sank swiftly.

Watching from the shore, the Inuit ventured towards the wreck as far as they dared, across the deadly heaving groaning ice. They wanted to see if they could rescue anyone, or find anything good to use or trade. But they found no white men alive. Nothing remained of the ship but some shattered wood sticking out of the jumbled ice, right where it had closed over the ship. Nothing was alive there –

except a little Animal Being that the Inuit found wandering on the ice.

It was the strangest Being that any of them had ever seen. This little Being was possibly a relative of the lynxes, yet it did not look like a lynx at all. It actually walked right up to them, trembling with fright and cold. They scrutinized it a little nervously, weapons ready to kill it, if necessary. But it did not try to hurt them, and it was also not afraid of them. Instead, it rubbed its side on the legs of their mukluks, with a questioning cry in its high little voice.

The Inuit knew well the great silent lynx of those lands. They knew that the lynx did not ever do such a thing as rub on a person's mukluk.

This Being was much smaller than the lynx, with little round paws that were not suited to walk easily over the snow. It did not have the thick coat or the ear-tufts of the lynx. Nor did it have the same color. Its pelt was painted with white and red and black, in the same way that the northern Crees painted their faces sometimes.

The people were so amazed at the gentleness of this Being that finally some woman courageously bent and picked it up. The Being nestled into the front of the woman's parka, and made the sound of warm coals glowing that the lynx always makes when she is happy with her kittens. This was a very good sign.

So they took the Being back to their village.

They wondered if it was good to eat. But it was so small, and there was only one of it. It had no fat on it at all. The whole village would have been able to give each person only one bite of that Being. Besides, they were curious about it, so they let it live.

They had no word for this animal in their Inuit tongue, and so they called it the Gentle Being.

Quickly the Gentle Being learned that it was welcome everywhere in the village.

When the sled dogs barked at it furiously from their hide tethers, it puffed up its hairs like a summer porcupine and spat back at them. If a dog gave chase, the Gentle Being was very smart and raced like the wind into the nearest igloo, where the dogs knew they were not allowed.

Inside, in the warmth of fur rugs and the golden light of the seal-oil lamps, the Gentle Being went from lap to lap. The people had already noticed that the Being was a female, and they never tired of touching her, and studying her, and sharing stories about her curious doings.

They showed her off to visitors, because she made the village richer in her way. In fact, they even bragged about her a lot.

The Gentle Being loved to be touched. She would arch her back and make that soft, comforting fire-sound in her throat. The children loved to put their ears against her sides, so that they could listen to this sound. When everyone curled up to sleep, the Gentle Being always picked someone to sleep next to. She curled up with her paws tucked under her chest in the most amazing way, to keep them warm, and she comforted that person with her Fire Song.

How wonderful her eyes were! Bright and clear yellow they were – but not like the wolf's eyes. No, no! Her eyes were like the Sun! The pupils opened and closed in a magical way when the light shone into them.

And her fur! How soft it was! With time, it grew thicker from living there. The People were very glad of this, because they had always been afraid that she would freeze to death. During the coldest winter days, she did not go outside much, or she might have frozen the delicate skin-pads on the bottoms of her feet.

Now and then, when the weather warmed, she would sit at the outer entrance of the igloo, out of the wind, catching the feeble sunlight that came her way. But that was only before, or after, the long arctic night.

When the People returned from the hunts, she always ventured out then. She sat with great dignity near the butchering work, and they gave her little gifts of tasty bits, fat and flesh. She liked that, and carried these little gifts off to eat them with great care. What a dainty eater she was!

Afterwards she washed herself and washed herself, till they wondered if she would wear her fur out with her tongue.

When summer came, the People left their igloos to melt away behind them, and found trails across the summer tundra to hunt summer meat and gather herbs, and enjoy the Sun and the smells of vegetation. The Gentle Being went with them.

She was an excellent little traveler, staying clear of the dogs, and trotting right along the trail, following this family and that, with her tail straight up in the air. The tip of her tail always quivered gently with the good eager feeling in her. The People always liked seeing her tail standing straight up like that.

Now and then, the Gentle Being angled off into the tundra, and they had the chance to learn what an excellent hunter she was. Their march stirred up mice and birds, and she pounced on a mouse more swiftly than any wolf, stopping to eat it daintily with her delicate white fangs, and then racing to catch up with them again. Sometimes she caught songbirds, and ate those as well.

Now and then she brought a mouse as a Gift, to this or that family. She did this as a mother lynx bringing food to her kittens. This touched the People deeply.

"She cares for us," they told one another.

All during the summer, as the People lived in their hide shelters and watched the Sun do Her summer dance along the horizon, the Gentle Being went from shelter to shelter.

When the Sun once again sought Her own winter shelter in Her great igloo below the horizon, the People built their shelters of snow once again, and the Gentle Being went indoors with them, and flooded their lives with her warmth.

She was a Sun Being of warm light, shaped into fur and fangs. They wondered how long she would stay, and how long she would live.

Every spring, and summer, she called loudly for a mate, as the mother lynx does.

"What a pity that there is not another of these Gentle Beings with us, a male one," said the chiefs. "If there were, we could have them breeding, like our dogs. In this way, we would always have these Gentle Beings with us."

The chiefs talked about this often. But no other Gentle Beings were coming their way.

And they were afraid to ask the occasional white trader if there might be a second Gentle Being to trade for, because the whites might want this valuable first one back. And, in the manner of the whites, they would simply steal this Gentle Being, and not even trade for her. This was the way the whites always did things.

With time, the People learned a very interesting and intriguing thing about the Gentle Being. They learned that she knew about healing.

When anyone was sick, a child or an adult, the Gentle Being went to that person right away, and sat close by and comforted that person with her Big Sound.

When the Medicine Woman or Medicine Man came to do the doctoring, and sang, and drummed, and worked with feathers and summer herbs, the Gentle Being sat right there, with her big yellow eyes fixed on the sick person. Her eyes brought the Sun's healing into their winter, the People said.

"She knows just what to do," the healing women said. "She goes right to the part of the body that needs the work, and there she sits. Sometimes it is at the head. Other times the feet. And she stays till the work is done."

As the years passed, the fame of the Gentle Being spread through that north country. Stories about her were traded through many bands of the Inuit – and to the Crees, even. Many were the Cree and Inuit traders who offered fine and valuable things in order to have this Gentle Being go with them to their own people, and do this healing work.

But the Point Barrow Inuit did not want to part with her, not even for valuable things of the white men, not even guns.

"She is Good Medicine," they said. "She is healing. Her value cannot be measured in guns. It would be Bad Medicine to trade her away. She has come here to be with us, and here she can stay."

So it came to pass that, in summer, when people could travel, that other Inuit, even the Crees, made long journeys with their sick people across the tundra, and came to find these Point Barrow people in their hide shelters. They asked to have healing ceremonies with the Gentle Being present, doing her doctoring work. This meant that the Inuit doctors were very busy in summer.

And since the sick people always made give-aways of appreciation, the Inuit were becoming wealthy with the give-away guns and pelts and blankets and metal needles and other wonderful things.

The stories of those healings were yet more stories to tell and be traded – stories added to the growing Story-Belt of the Gentle Being.

Once some white traders even heard about the Gentle Being, and came far to see her. However, the People were afraid that the white men of the Big Canoes had heard that she was there, and sent these others to take her away. So they hid the Gentle Being. They told the white men that she was visiting another people to do her healing work. The whites were very disappointed, and they left.

Yes, it could be said that the Gentle Being changed their lives. It could be said.

She lived with those People for perhaps ten winters, warming their lives with the Sun-glow of her eyes and the comfort of her Gentle Sound. She grew old, and slow, but never less gentle.

One summer, she could not keep up with the People along the tundra trails. So one of the women put her in the thrown-back hood of her parka. The Gentle Being rode happily along in the hood, behind the woman's dark head, peering out over the furred edge of the hood. Her golden eyes still opened wide and dark at the sight of the songbirds, but she no longer hunted much, so the people trapped mice and brought them to her.

That winter, she got sick. The Medicine Women and the Medicine Men all drummed over her, and sang their most powerful songs, and worked on her with their best feathers and other Medicines. But it was her time to journey. So the glow of the Sun faded from her golden eyes. In the morning, they found her small body cold and stiff among the furs.

The People knew that her spirit was speeding into a new life. Perhaps she would be born out there on the tundra somewhere, as a Being of that great land – a lynx kitten, or a white wolf cub, or a polar bear. Or perhaps a musk ox, or one of those little songbirds that hatch in summer, and fly south by autumn. Or even a seal.

"Perhaps she begins to move into the Human Circle," said one of the old men wisely.

This thought comforted them all. At the same time, they missed her gentle presence, and they all cried.

Then the women discussed what to do. They wanted to keep the warmth of that Gentle Being in their circle for always, and call her spirit to touch their sick ones.

So gently, respectfully, the women tanned that wonderful soft many-painted pelt with the greatest care. From it, they sewed a Medicine Bag, in which to keep all of their most precious healing things – teas, crystals, feathers, whatever was needed. The most powerful of the Medicine Women became the Keeper of the Gentle Being Bag. This position became an influential one among the People. Only the most honorable and powerful woman could have it.

In this way, the Gentle Being would be with them for always.

The Inuit man who told the story to the Crees had seen that Medicine Bag himself, because his grandmother had been the Keeper of it. By then, the bag had been handled and used for two generations, and the fur was wearing off, just as the Inuit had always feared when she licked herself. But the Healing Bag was no less loved for being worn, and would surely keep going till it fell apart.

The Montana Métis who told me this story confided that his northern Cree cousin had to trade away four of his best stories, in order to get the story of the Gentle Being.

The Métis himself presented me the story as a Gift. He gave it to me with all the care of a mother lynx bringing a mouse to her kittens.

THE SPOTTIE: APPALOOSAS, AND WHY PEOPLE WANTED THEM

While historians have said much about the old-time cattle industry, the horse industry was just as important. Cow business of yore simply could not happen without the right kind of horses. For many years, my family's ranch, the CK, was a major breeder and supplier of good cow-horses to the Northwest. Our old-time horses can be seen in the photographs that frontier photographer L.A. Huffman took of CK range operations in the late 1800s and early 1900s. Here and there is a roany-looking horse – one or two with "blankets" on their rumps. One Appaloosa breeder who studied these photographs told me: "It looks like some of these horses had a strong Appie background."

I became intrigued with the question of why the spotted strain was so strong in the CK horses. Our horse-breeding program never did anything without a good reason. Yet our forward-looking outfit had decided *not* to concentrate on breeding Appaloosas per se. Why? The questions started me down a long trail of thinking about why anybody would want to ride a spotted horse.

Montana Indians and Métis (mixed-bloods) whose great-grandparents knew my family in the frontier days have talked with me about Appaloosas.

"We had many names for them," one Métis told me. "My relatives were traders in those days. We traded a lot of those horses, for sure. In the kind of Crow I speak, we call them 'cat horses' and 'star horses.' And 'hail-paint horses' also."

In those times, the Indians, the Métis and even the earliest white arrivals agreed that the native horses were usually superior to any "American horses" brought in from the states. Bred on green pasture and grain, the "American horse" did not have the endurance of the native horse, who could go almost forever when he was tired, on a few bites of dry grass. Supreme among native horse-breeders were the Northwest peoples who became known to the whites as Nez Perce, Umatilla, Palouse or Cayuse.

With time, white Westerners called all native horses by the name of "Cayuse."

In talking with my father, Con Warren, I also discovered that a spotted horse appeared at a key moment in the ranch's history.

In the early 1860s, when my German great-grandfather Conrad Kohrs and my great granduncle John Bielenberg migrated to Montana Territory, they found a big healthy horse-trade already being operated by the tribes and the Métis free traders. Early-day writings mention that horse herds were constantly coming and going over the mountains. The two Germans settled in the Deer Lodge Valley. Through this valley, every fall, the Nez Perce traveled every year to hunt buffalo. They were led by young Joseph and his mentor, Mirror. At that time, the tribe had thousands of horses. The mass of "hail-paints," passing through the valley under a great billow of dust, must have been a magnificent sight.

The Nez Perce always paused to trade with the prominent horse-traders who lived in the valley: men like Louis Maillet and Thomas LaVatta. All these men became friends of Kohrs and Bielenberg. But the most influential horse-trader in the valley was John Grant, a Canadian Métis. He was said to own thousands of cattle and horses, and staked my great-grandfather in his first ventures as a cattle-trader.

Kohrs had decided to start a butcher business in the mining camps, and he needed good road-horses to get around and buy cattle. Grant could afford to have the best in Cayuses. So from him, and possibly from others like Maillet, my great-grandfather Kohrs put together a string of the best Cayuse road-horses in the territory.

These super-horses carried Kohrs all over western Montana. Kohrs had his mounts staged at different ranches, and delighted in beating the stagecoaches between towns.

According to my father, one of these road horses was the Spot Horse, or Spottie. He had no idea where and by whom Spottie was bred.

"A horse could be traded many times," an old Métis told me, "and wind up many months' walking away from where his dam dropped him. And no one would know where he was bred. A good star horse, like that one you tell me about, would trade for many hanks of blue beads."

The old man was talking about the high value placed on sky-blue trade beads by the Northwest tribes. Usually, he said, it was the other way around – with a hank of blue beads costing several common horses.

For a few years, during the 1862-1870 period when Kohrs was parlaying the butcher shops into a range-cattle business, and veering towards married life, his half brother John Bielenberg roamed off to live with the tribes. "Onkel Johnny" was an independent and unconventional spirit, and he liked the Indians and the Métis. Decades later, after World War I, he would still make pemmican every summer, and spoke a little mangled Indian around the ranch – my father still remembered a couple of the phrases he used.

Why "Cat" Horses?

Kohrs and Bielenberg were probably intrigued by the American spotted horses because of an old European love for spotted horses. Both men had grown up in Holstein, a German-speaking duchy that belonged to Denmark when they still lived there. Holstein was the home of the Knabstrupper, a big bold coaching-type leopard-spotted horse that was popular with army officers. Some of the Kohrs and Bielenberg men had fought in the Schleswig-Holstein wars between Prussia and Denmark, so they may have known these horses.

Why had Europeans – and almost every other horseback civilization all over the world – singled out the "cat horse" for such appreciation?

And why did some indigenous American peoples favor the spotted horse?

One reason may be cultural. All over the world, spotted horses were prized by the wealthy and military elite. Art history shows us that English kings, Mogul emperors, Chinese warriors have sat tall on spotted horses. Spots make one think of the big spotted cats. All these same civilizations honored the big cats as symbols of courage in war and – most importantly – as clan symbols of powerful families. To this day, in English, an athletic and brave horse is described as "cat-like." So I think that spotted horses were favored as an allusion to the feline status-symbol.

With the spread of horses to the Americas, the indigenous peoples were quick to see the resemblance between the coat of the spotted horse, and the coat of their own big spotted cats. Trade and travel kept Northwest Indians in contact with the more southerly peoples who cherished the jaguar. In those days, the jaguar could be found as far north as today's Arizona and Texas. The Aztecs and other Mexican peoples ruled, fought and prayed in jaguar skins. The Cheyennes, who loved to wear spotted cat-skins and filled their ledger-art of the 1800s with spotted war-ponies, are known to have traded all the way to Mexico and jaguar country. This fact, I think, explains my old Métis friend's comments about "cat horses."

The term "star horse" is understandable when we remember that the jaguar was also a native symbol of astronomy – its coat marked by stars. Medicine People have told me that one of the native names for the Big Dipper constellation, with its obvious long tail, is the "Big Jaguar." Theirs was a world where people saw everything, even features in the natural world, as symbols of something sacred and amazing.

The Art of Camouflage

But there were also practical reasons for valuing spotted horses.

The American indigenous peoples led a hard and disciplined life, and they were ruthlessly practical people. In those hard lands of ours, Western tribal life demanded a high level of survival skills. The Indian horse had to be a "survival tool" – fast and tough on the battlefield, and in the hunt. Indeed, I think that the Peoples liked the Appaloosa for its natural camouflage.

My old Métis informant agreed with me.

"You see, we had to hide," he explained. "After the fight with Custer at the Little Horn, many of us survived because we hid – not because we won battles. A lot of our military tactics were based on hiding – shooting from cover, and so forth. You had to hide your horse, too. It's hard to hide a pinto, or a white horse."

Amidst the historical glamorizing of male Indians, the horse's importance in family survival is often overlooked. During long treks to escape the U.S Cavalry, Indian horses might drag the heavy lodge poles, or pull a travois loaded with the buffalo-hide lodge-cover – even a travois-load of sick children or old people. The horses did this heavy work over long distances, with little rest or food. Many women and children had to know how to fight (a reality that many historians overlook in their haste to laud the deeds of warrior males). So a travois horse might be hastily unhitched from his load to stand duty as a war pony. A woman and kids had an extra edge if their war pony was spotted.

My Métis informant told me:

"When I was little, one of my grannies told me about standing hidden in the brush while the pony soldiers rode by. She was just a kid, and she was scared to death ... shaking in her tall grass-boots. She had her fingers over the nostrils of her spotted travois horse, so he wouldn't whinny. She had her sick baby loaded on the travois. She'd gotten lost from the rest of the family. The pony soldiers were just yards away. But they didn't see her, or the horse. They just rode on by."

War always demands the art of camouflage.

To learn more of "camo," I talked with war veterans, especially special-warfare men who had excelled at jungle fighting in Vietnam. In a word, they knew how to hide. The idea is to disguise an object by covering it with a repeat design in several colors. This way, the object – tank, artillery, the human body – literally disappears into the terrain that the designs and colors mimic. Blue-grey paint fades a warplane into the sky, while pure white camo is for a platoon of arctic troops.

The speckled roany hides of spotted horses – in all their variants, from the starred-all-over "leopard" to the classic "blanket" on the rump – are painted by Mother Earth with a natural camo pattern that had to be irresistible to the indigenous military minds of America's yesteryear. Basically, the Spottie was the only horse who could magically turn into leaf-shadows and brush – perfect for hiding amid the chokecherry brakes and cottonwood stands of the Northwest. A small mounted Indian war-party waiting in ambush could stay as well-hidden as the Navy SEAL in Vietnam, with his tiger-stripe head-rag and tiger-stripes painted on his assault rifle. Or his Viet Cong opponent, with black uniform disguised by foliage tied on.

Today, as the art of war gets ever more sophisticated, there are many camo patterns on the uniforms of the world – from the steel-grey-and-tan ASAT pattern favored by many SWAT teams in urban "war," to the Rhodesian army's unique pattern designed for grasslands warfare. Our own U.S. troops wear distinctive patchy beige-and-tan desert camo in Iraq and Afghanistan.

The camo design that is probably closest to Appaloosa spotting is called "woodland camouflage." Today, this design is cherished not only by the military, but also by ranchers, deer-hunters, hikers and campers. It is sold in practically every Army-Navy and sporting-goods store in the U.S.

Since the native peoples were such superior tactical fighters, the tactical advantages – or disadvantages – of a horse color would not have been overlooked by them. In certain situations – buffalo hunting, for instance – it was a good idea to pick a horse that could be seen for miles. In the paintings of Charles M. Russell, the old-time buffalo hunters are often depicted on white or light-colored horses. Russell had spent time with the Canadian Crees, who were great buffalo hunters, so he knew his stuff. If you ran buffalo on a light-colored horse, your buddies could keep track of you amidst the mass of plunging dark-colored bison and churning dust. If your horse went down, they could spot you easier, and hopefully rescue you before you got trampled into pulp.

My great-grandfather Kohrs's close friendship with the Métis traders may have awakened him to the advantages of a camouflaged horse. For him, "war" included the dangers of his long cattle-buying rides. He was always carrying a saddlebag full of gold-dust to trade for cattle. After the Montana gold rush exploded in 1862, the territory rapidly became infested with "road agents," a wry frontier term for highwaymen. Kohrs became a prime target for the local road agents.

In his *Autobiography*, Kohrs tells about the time in 1863 when he was almost overtaken and killed by road agents. He had just sold steers in Bannack, the boom camp, and started home to Deer Lodge 60 miles away with $5000 in gold dust in his saddlebag. His mount was another of his road horses – a dappled grey named Billie. A grey horse is visible from a distance, so the two road agents, Dutch John and George Ives, had no trouble keeping Greatgrandfather in sight – and catching up to him slowly but surely.

To lighten his horse's load, Kohrs hid in some brush for a few minutes to shed saddle, guns and blankets. Then he galloped on, riding Grey Billie with just a surcingle, and clutching the saddlebag of gold dust with all his might. The two fugitives covered 60 miles over the mountains in 6 hours, and got to safety at Deer Lodge 15 minutes ahead of the outlaws. Unfortunately Grey Billie was ruined by the hard ride. But Kohrs lived to tell the tale.

Kohrs' native friends might have ribbed him about picking a grey to carry his wealth on. A typical choice for a Skunk Person (their humorous term for many whites). Perhaps it was after this close call that Kohrs decided to get himself a couple of horse colors that were easier to hide. The following year he paid John Grant $300 (a small fortune) for a brown road horse named Woodtick.

And eventually he got that Spottie that Dad always talked about.

"Financially," I told Dad, "it was the frontier equivalent of buying a $30 million Harrier jet with a good paint job."

My dad agreed with this supposition.

"I'll bet," he said, "that Spottie cost granddad a whole bagful of gold."

A Mystery About Mares

So where did those spotty coats in the CK horses come from? Was the Spottie a stallion? Probably not. Stallions could be noisy and obstreperous – not a good strategy for road riding if you needed to keep a low profile.

In 1877, after a series of fierce battles across the Northwest, Chief Joseph's people failed in their attempt to escape to Canada. They surrendered to the U.S. Army in south-central Montana. Over a thousand of their best war horses and breeding stock were captured. Many of these were spotted.

A rich plunder, these fine animals were not herded in front of a Gatling gun and shot to shreds, as were many captured herds of common cayuses. Instead, according to historian Francis Haines in his classic study *Appaloosa:The Spotted Horse in Art and History*, the horses were trailed to Fort Keogh, near present-day Miles City, MT, and sold at auction to private buyers. Later, a similar thing happened to most of the Nez Perce horses still roaming on the tribe's home ranges in Washington. These were confiscated and sold to Western cattlemen.

In 1870, Bielenberg had returned to the CK with an Indian blanket in his bedroll and a beaded buckskin sheath on his Sharps rifle. From what I know, he had little to say about his experiences. The people with whom he'd been roaming, the free brown people he loved so passionately, were now prisoners of war being herded onto reservations. Things had gotten too hot for a blue-eyed German to stay among them.

In 1878 – at the very time when captured Nez Perce horses were becoming "available" – Bielenberg and Kohrs decided to breed some good cow-ponies. To handle the big crossbred steers appearing on the northern ranges, they wanted a big vigorous crossbred horse. Their choice was to blend the Cayuse, for bottom and intelligence, with the Thoroughbred, for size and speed. So they put together a herd of over 100 of the best Cayuse mares that they could find.

Yet, despite the CK's German penchant for meticulous record keeping, little in the way of records have survived that document the origin of these unregistered brood-mares. No pedigrees were kept on their crossbred offspring. When Western historical records are silent on a subject relating to native peoples, it is usually for a reason.

Were some of those mares from the Miles City auction?

It is logical to speculate that some were. Kohrs and Bielenberg sold beef to the military, and were well acquainted with Montana army officers. After the army's fight with the Nez Perce at the Big

Hole, the CK had helped the Army to transport wounded soldiers. So the ranch had a good "in" to learn about the auction. Maybe they even got a pre-sale crack at these horses – this would explain the absence of bills of sale. The CK valued horses that could "deliver," and the Nez Perce horses – especially the ones that had campaigned hard across Montana – had certainly delivered. The CK wouldn't have passed up such a golden opportunity.

John Bielenberg took charge of the CK horse-breeding. He mated these Cayuse mares to registered Thoroughbred stallions. With time, every year saw half a hundred well-broke five-year-old crossbred cow-horses coming out of his breeding program. The CK kept some of these horses to use, and sold the rest for top dollar to other outfits. They became known as "big circle horses" because, during roundup, they could lope non-stop for 20 miles or so while making a big circle to gather cattle out of a given area.

Paradoxically, Bielenberg and Kohrs evidently declined to get into spotted horses in a big way. Several reasons possibly influenced the ranch in this decision:

Reason #1: personal sadness. Times had changed. In 1866, fed up with increasing violence and anti-Indian feeling in the territory, John Grant had sold his ranch to Kohrs and moved to Canada. Many other Montana Métis left the state with Grant. Both Kohrs and Bielenberg may have been profoundly saddened that the old friends who gave them their start in business, and first acquainted them with the Cayuse, were vanishing from the country.

Reason #2: more practicality. With Indian wars over, and road agents hung, the need for the "camo horse" had passed. On the range, cowboys needed to stay visible like the buffalo hunters, not hidden like soldiers.

Reason #3: no time or energy for breeding to get Spotties. Kohrs and Bielenberg liked vigorous cross-breds, and they were aware that the strongest hybrid is always the F-1 cross. "Hybrid vigor only lasts for one generation," my great-grandfather was fond of saying. Therefore the ongoing CK interest in F-1 crossbreds might have kept Bielenberg from doing the intense selective breeding that is needed to get a spotted horse.

Reason #4, the most likely: racial prejudice. In the new state of Montana, now heavily populated by whites, the old fur-trade tolerance among Indians, Métis and whites had vanished. Many pioneers who had married Indians or Métis now nervously covered up their old associations if they could. They put away their native wives, married white women, and did any social bobbing and weaving that they thought would erase the past. As white history began to be written, many family biographies stopped mentioning their Indian mothers or grandmothers.

So the word "Cayuse," once high praise for a horse, now became a put-down. The spotted horse was so identified with the brown-skinned enemy, that many whites now felt a strong bias against this horse color. On the Nez Perce reservation, missionaries actually preached sermons about the spotted horse being evil ... a symbol of the "devil's ways."

Reacting to these prejudices and wanting to avoid questions about whose side they were on, most cow outfits avoided mounting their cowboys on the pintos and spotties so favored by the tribes. If you look at the paintings of Remington and Russell, and the photos of L.A. Huffman, you see the white men riding mostly solid-color horses.

Kohrs and Bielenberg did not bob and weave. In company with some other white Montana pioneers, they remained publicly labeled as "Indians" because of their early-day associations. The native "taint" didn't keep these two "Indians" from being elected to political office when Montana became a state in 1889. Ever the one to thumb his nose at convention, Bielenberg named one of his Thoroughbred racehorses after Tendoy, the well-known Shoshoni chief who was the brother of John Grant's wife Quarra. Yet even Bielenberg may have decided not to flaunt the past too hard by breeding this most notorious of Cayuses as a working ranch horse.

Reason #5: money. With all the prejudice in the air, who would buy Spotties? The CK would go broke breeding Spotties.

Changing Times

From the late 1800s into the early 1900s, many of the scanty surviving Appaloosas did find a ready market elsewhere – in circuses and Wild West shows. Yet even the high prices that these horses commanded in show biz did not lure the CK into breeding them.

Shortly after 1900, with the decline of open-range ranching, CK cowhorse-breeding closed down.

After Kohrs died in 1920, and Bielenberg in 1922, a few American horse lovers were finally banding together to locate the last of the good spotted horses, and build them back to the outstanding breed that they'd been.

Today the triumph of the Appaloosa, and the related Pony of the Americas, is almost complete. The cat-horse who carried emperors in triumph, and feathered warriors in battle, now carries riders in endurance races, and jockeys in horse races, and winning kids in show rings, and cowboys in rodeos.

Those spots even turn up on miniature horses. During a trip to England in 1992, a friend took me to visit the noted Falabella breeders, Lord and Lady Fisher, at their farm in Sussex. They had imported one of Julio Falabella's original spotted Argentine stallions, Menelek, and launched the breed in the UK. The morning we got there, Lady Fisher walked out of the mares' paddock to meet us, proudly toting a tiny leopard foal in her arms like a puppy.

All that's missing today is the military victory. With horses made obsolete by Patriot missiles and drones, no one needs a mount with natural-born war paint.

At the CK, what remains is the old Huffman photos – speckled horses with blankets on their rumps, half-hidden and almost lost in the big drifting herds. And the stirring tale of the spotted road-horse, to whose camo coat my great-granddad probably owed his life.

Further Reading:

Appaloosa:The Spotted Horse in Art and History, by Francis Haines (University of Texas, 1963).

WHY DO TEXAS LONGHORNS HAVE LONG HORNS?

Excerpted from unpublished commentary provided to the Grant-Kohrs Ranch National Historic Site, relating to my family's oral history on the nature of "Spanish cattle" in the West

Like many history-minded ranch kids of my generation, I grew up reading J. Frank Dobie's *The Longhorns* and was captured by the mystique of these beautiful, rugged and wily animals. My personal answer to the big question about the big horns began to be answered in the 1960s, when my husband and I took a sabbatical from my Reader's Digest job and spent several years living in Spain. There, as we traveled around the country's rural areas, I found much with which to connect in Spain's ranching and cattle-raising traditions and how they influenced the Americas.

There was a magic moment, in the fall of 1965, on our first trip to the province of Galicia, when I looked at a pair of yoked oxen standing in a field and said to my husband, "*!Vaya!* Look at those horns!"

Defining the "Longhorn"

What did the term "longhorn" mean in the mid-1800s, vis a vis what it means today? "Texas cattle" were often mentioned – we have to ask what that term meant as well. After Anglo settlers started moving into Texas in the early 1800s, not all cattle raised in Texas were "Longhorns" in the sense that we understand today, since hybridizing with Anglo breeds was already being done.

Some Texas Longhorn breeders like to say that "Texas Longhorns were brought to the U.S. by the Spanish." Is that true?

Western historical sources of Greatgrandfather's era talked about "horned Spanish cattle," and it's clear they weren't necessarily talking about the Longhorn of today that fanciers are re-establishing with a breed standard. The fact is, many strains of cattle existed in Spain. More than one of these were exported to the New World. Spanish colonials needed cattle for meat, milking and draft work. So they shipped a variety of breeds for those purposes. Indeed, the 19th century term "horned cattle" was a generic phrase that distinguished bovines from sheep, which were called "woolen cattle."

Some Longhorn historians, like Alan M. Hoyt, insist that all Spanish cattle brought to the New World originated in southern Spain. But the New World was Hispanified from both northern and southern Spain. Spanish colonial records that list families and points of origin reveal that the run of settlers, whether wealthy *hidalgos* or foot soldiers and farmers, came from many regions. For convenience, colonists tended to sail out of the nearest major port, and to bring their local cattle with them – breeds which their families had dealt with for centuries. So many shiploads of settlers sailed out of northern Spanish ports like Santander and La Coruña. As a result, some Spanish cattle imports to the New World would reflect northern Spanish strains.

Some Spanish strains had horns that were characteristically longer than others. But on the average, all of them carried more horn than the English breeds favored by east-coast American colonists. The Spanish have an iconic reverence for horns that dates back to before Christianity and is celebrated in ancient Iberian art. Both in the North, where ancient Celtic tribes settled the coastal provinces, and in the South, where the indigenous people had old ties with Rome and North Africa, there was a reverence for cattle with striking horns. Some Bronze Age bull-heads found in Mallorca have horn spreads that rival anything in Dobie's book.

Whereas the English were happy to get rid of horns, if they could. It was Englishmen who created the Shorthorns, and dairy breeds with crumpled horns, as well as polled varieties of several beef breeds.

So I think that these 19th century historical commentators got to using the term "longhorn" partly as a generic alternative for "horned Spanish cattle." They also may have used it as the Anglo equivalent of the Spanish term *corniancho* (wide horned), of which more later – especially since many Spanish terms were adopted into Anglo ranching lingo.

Corriente Cattle

Probably the most numerous Spanish import was the ancestor of cattle that Americans know today as Corrientes. The Spanish colonials didn't call them Corrientes, of course. That name is a modern U.S. usage, while in Mexico they're referred to as Criollo or Chinampo cattle.

Originally, ancestors of the Corrientes belonged to a stock of grade (i.e. non-purebred or "common") cattle that was widely distributed across Iberia. Several different subtypes thrived in different regions throughout Andalusia, Extramadura, Castile, Navarre, the Basque region, Galicia and Portugal. But all are thought to descend from *Bos taurus ibericus*, a distinctive type of auroch that was indigenous to the Iberian peninsula since ancient times and domesticated at a fairly early date. In post-medieval Spain, these regional subtypes were known by local names, such as the Retintas of the south, and the Moruchas in the Castilian uplands.

These cattle weren't maintained as a *raza* or pure breed with standards – they were used mostly for work animals, and only secondarily for beef, because the Spanish were also fond of pork, chicken and goat meat.

But they did have (and still have) some signature characteristics. Typical of Mediterranean and hot-country breeds, they had a flat, slick coat. They tended to be lean, light-framed and narrow-bodied, with a high-set tail. Horn spreads were mostly not humongous – probably never exceeding 3 feet or so, even in older animals. The animals didn't carry as much meat as an English breed. But they were tough, and easy calvers. Best of all, they kept themselves fat on next to nothing, especially the sparse grazing typical of hot, dry Mediterranean regions, where cattle must graze like deer on a variety of plants and woody shrubs. Plus they had a gentle nature and were easy to handle.

Coat colors were predominantly (and still are) *negro* (black) and *retinta* (red), which are the baseline bovine colors, along with the occasional dilutes. The red coats were dominant enough that these cattle became collectively known as Retintas or Rubias.

But actually the full range of colors and markings of Iberian cattle is dizzyingly varied. As I traveled around the country, I noticed that Spanish stockraisers of a certain region tended to prefer a certain color. In Andalusia, for instance, they liked the blacks and *cardenos* (blue roans). In other areas, I might see *berrendos* (white with large pinto-like markings). In Cantabria, the mountainous northern province of Spain where my husband and I owned a residence from 1965 till 1972, the farm people favored a dun-colored strain with a distinctive mascara-like marking around the eye that they called *ojo de perdiz* ("partridge eye").

These Spanish beef/work cattle evidently share a common ancestry with the Iberian fighting cattle – *toros de lidia*. These distinctive cattle are thought to have their own origins in the aforementioned *Bos taurus ibericus*. Sometime in the late middle ages, individual animals began to be selected for their peppery temperament and bred by noble families as a *raza* for the purpose of *lidia* (fighting bulls on horseback, and later on foot). First to export *toros de lidia* to the New World were the Gutierrez family from Navarre. The Navarrese fighting cattle were a distinctive strain – small but feisty and athletic. In 1552 a number of these bulls and cows were shipped by galleon to New Spain.

Today the native Spanish beef/work breeds and the *lidia* breed still share some similarities of DNA and phenotype, though their temperaments are as different as night and day.

What a Spanish Expert Had to Say

When I lived in Spain, the towering Spanish authority on Iberian bovine history was (and still is) José María de Cossío. Since he lived in Cantabria, I had the pleasure of meeting him – visiting him at his family home in a mountain village above Santander, sharing a snort of the fiery local hooch called *orujo* and talking cow with him.

The full title of his great encyclopediac work is *Los Toros, tratado téchnico e histórico*, first published in 1943. But the Spanish refer to this opus affectionately as just *El Cossío*. The author took part of a volume to lay out the rich glossary of Spanish cattle terminology. In just a few words, you can give a precise description of an animal, right down to its horn size and curvature.

First comes Cossío's long list of coat colors and patterns. Since the fighting cattle stayed wild till well into the 2nd millennium, they were not subject to color selection by humans. So their coats expressed an astounding array of roans, brindles, dilutes, distinctive marking patterns like *bragao* (white belly) and *ensabanao* (white wrapped mostly around the animal like a sheet), as well as diverse spotting patterns and several different shades of black. All these color genes may have been floating around as recessives in the Corriente's genetic background as well.

When it comes to the horns, bullfight people use the wry word *trapío*, meaning "equipment." Variations in "equipment" size and curvature also have their glossary, which Cossío detailed. They range from *brocho* (curving down and inward, towards the jaw) to *bizco* (crooked) – from *astifino* (fine and sharp) to *astigordo* (thick and blunt). Most ominous are *corniancho* or *cornalon* (wide) and *veleto* (curving sharply upwards). For centuries, Spanish breeders have often selected against super-*ancho* in both the beef/work cattle and the fighting cattle, in order to make the animals safer to handle.

Neither toreros nor farmers want to deal with a four- or five-foot horn spread.

Coloration of the horn can't be overlooked either. Different breeds of European bovines have their typical horn colors – on English Herefords, for example, the horn is a rich ivory or cream color that is solid from tip to base. Whereas the Spanish cattle most typically wear horns with a distinctive black point, shading to a lighter hue at the base. The work/beef cattle share this characteristic with fighting cattle, whose horn-point is called the *piton*, sometimes the *diamante* (diamond) in torero slang. Below the black point, the horn shades to cream, or a streaky grey, even a slate-green hue. Sometimes the entire horn will go almost black, or a light caramel shade.

When I was living in Spain, these indigenous strains of cattle still provided most of the beef eaten by the country, as well as agriculture's muscle power in many rural areas. Even fighting bulls were sold for beef after being killed in the ring. Tractors and machinery were still uncommon in the mountainous regions.

So the teams of oxen, with their hardwood yokes richly chiseled in folk designs, could be seen plowing the steep alpine cornfields of Cantabria, or hauling wagons loaded high with fresh-cut grass or produce. Though northern Spain's dairy industry had modernized with "foreign" Holsteins, the native beef stock had stayed popular enough to bar English beef breeds from getting a foothold. This was especially true in the hot dry southern and central regions, where the indigenous cattle were better suited to Iberian climate and grazing conditions than the English breeds.

It was ancestors of these cattle that Spanish conquerors and colonials introduced to the New World – all the way from Florida across Texas and the Southwest to California, as well as Mexico and points south.

In the U.S. West and Mexico, the descendants known as Corrientes or Criollos or Chinampos are still populous. Though they too became heavily hybridized, they are being revived as a pure breed, and a number of ranches have websites that advertise their straight-bred Corrientes. The *puro Corriente* is even being touted as environmentally friendly with its thrifty grazing habits. They are also familiar to rodeo fans and contestants as the critter of choice for bulldogging and steer roping, because they're athletic, small enough for easy handling, and not too feisty, plus they have good solid horns for the needs of the sport.

Double-Wide Horns

Now for the $64 question – where did the Texas Longhorn get the genes for those horns? Some have a distinctive corkscrew shape that came to be called the "Texas twist."

Some historians posit that the big horns just somehow "happened" out of the blue when Texas cattle were running wild before the Civil War. Certainly the dynamics of population genetics – especially the long-term results when an existing breed is transported to a new geographic setting somewhere else on our planet – can explain much about the emergence of those horns.

Some DNA studies have been done on Texas Longhorns. According to the American Livestock Breed Conservancy, their profile is consistent with DNA profiles of Mexican (i.e. Criollo or Chinampo) cattle of Iberian origin. Another important study comes from K. K. Kidd, W. H. Stone, C. Crimella, C. Carenzi, M. Casati and G. Rognoni, titled, "Immunogenetic and population genetic analyses of Iberian cattle." In it they compared DNA of Longhorns with that of four strains of Iberian cattle, including *de lidia* stock. Conclusion: "Analyses … show a closely related group of the 4 Iberian breeds and American Longhorn, confirming the close relationships among the Iberian breeds and the Iberian, probably Portuguese, origin of American Longhorn cattle."

In my opinion, the classic "long horns" – the ones with a spread of 7 or 8 feet – are not the result of a spontaneous mutant. Rather, they are the expression of a particular regional Spanish ancestry. The genes were already in the gene pool of stock imported from Spain, and re-emerged here in the Americas because of some unique historical circumstances.

When I traveled around Spain in the 1960s, I noticed that extra-large horns were visible on a few regional strains – for example, in the rolling plains around Salamanca in Old Castile, which has long been an important cattle country. There I was seeing "equipment" of around 4 feet on the Morucha beef/work cattle, which usually had black or blue-roan coats. Significantly, the Salamanca area exported many colonists to the New World, along with its indigenous ranching traditions. Even the traditional vaquero dress of the *charro*, which the world now thinks of as "Mexican," was actually imported from Salamanca. So I don't doubt that some big Morucha horns voyaged to the New World along with those *charro* jackets.

But the biggest horns, by a country mile, were those that I saw on the Rubia Gallegas of Galicia.

Cattle Market in Santiago

In the 1960s, Galicia was the poorest, least modernized region of Spain. The indigenous language spoken there, Gallego, is closer to Portuguese than Spanish. Customs of *gallego* land ownership and agricultural practice had been undisturbed for centuries. Likewise the Rubia Gallega breed had been used for both beef and draft work for centuries.

So, on that fall day in 1965, as our VW chugged into Galicia along the narrow highway towards the pilgrim city of Santiago de Compostela, with the smell of woodsmoke in the cold rainy air, my husband and I first saw these magnificent cattle in action in the fields, plowing in yoked pairs.

As the day passed, we kept seeing more of these cattle teams. They were hauling big wagonloads of newly harvested potatoes, cabbages and chestnuts into the market at Santiago. The next day, we visited the livestock area of the market, and I got to inspect a few of these animals at close hand. I actually got my eager hands on their slick red hides, while they stood patiently waiting to be sold. It was an enthralling experience to touch their horns – one that I've never forgotten – because I was 100 percent positive that I had stumbled on the historic roots of the Texas Longhorn.

The farmers were intrigued to meet somebody from that Wild West that they'd all heard about on their TVs. Galicia might have been dirt poor, but every village already had its first TV antenna or two.

These Rubia Gallegas were the only Spanish cattle I saw with those classic double-wide Texas Longhorn-type spreads. Many had a dramatic corkscrew twist to them.

Indeed, the *gallego* farmers had developed a unique strategy for dealing with this impressive "equipment." Otherwise the spreads on older animals might have reached 7-8 feet, making it impossible for them to work in pairs.

So the farmers explained to me how they trained the horns to grow into a tight coil. Cattle horns are alive and continually growing, like tree branches. So if you start when an animal is young, the horns can be bent in any direction you wish, by attaching weights, pulleys or other contraptions, in the same way that a live tree can be sculptured into a bonsai. This way, two oxen could comfortably walk along side by side without their horns tangling.

The *gallegos* also used a type of yoke that fitted around the base of the horns, instead of around the two necks. This yoke braced the two heads firmly apart, in order to keep the animals from poking each other's eyes out.

Typically the Rubia Gallegas I saw were as big as Longhorns too. They were tall, deep and heavy-muscled, perfect for both working and beef. Indeed, their beef is prized by Spanish gourmets. The coat color was typically solid red and red dilute, so they ranged from chestnut-brown to pimento-red and cream.

When I first saw these breath-taking cattle, I immediately suspected that northern Spanish colonists must have exported some of them to the New World – making it possible for a dose of *gallego* horn genes to wend its way to Texas.

Today, sad to say, the Rubia Gallega is heavily hybridized, and that distinctive strain has almost disappeared. According to the Spanish breed sources I find online, Spain has hybridized almost all her native cattle stock, or switched to imported breeds.

From Mexico Into Texas

When I got back to the United States and dug into Spanish colonial cattle history, I learned that Galician immigrants did indeed play a major part in colonizing the New World.

The long-festering poverty of that northern region motivated many single men, and some families, to migrate to the New World in hopes of better things. When the Spanish crown finally crushed the First Nation cultures of central Mexico and established an administrative region they called *Nueva España* (New Spain), they began looking to colonize northwards into North America. In the early 1500s, the crown established a new region called *Nueva Galicia* (New Galicia) in what is northern Mexico today. The region's very name testifies that many of its first settlers were from Galicia. I don't doubt that settlers brought some of their native cattle.

New Galicia's first governor was Francisco de Coronado himself. In 1540, he organized a historic exploration northwards into what would be New Mexico and northwest Texas – and he took a big herd of cattle with him. From the late 1500s till around 1800, thousands of colonial settlers moved north to start settling in California, Arizona, New Mexico and Texas. Official records of these settlement expeditions show that a significant number of settlers came from Galicia.

So I posit a slow-but-sure flow of Gallego cattle genes – from post-medieval northern Spain through northern Mexico and New Mexico, straight into the Texas heartland.

The Texas Longhorn Emerges

When the Longhorn was first noticed by what we call "American history" today, it was the early 1800s. By the 1840s, Anglo settlers were moving into Texas with their English beef breeds, only to realize that Texas already had well-established Hispanic ranching operations and a large population of cattle.

By then, thousands of Spanish cattle were running wild in the brush country, as described so compellingly by J. Frank Dobie. Feral *Tejano* cattle had existed since the 1700s. Their numbers had built up dramatically from animals that strayed or were deliberately driven away from *ranchos* or missions by Indians during the periods of fierce warfare between the freedom-loving native tribes and the Hispanic invaders.

These feral cattle had thrived in the wild with no care because the *Tejano* climate and grazing were not all that different from the latitudes of Spain where their ancestors had ranged. Texas sits just north of the 30th parallel, as does Spain. So vast herds of these wild cattle were there for the picking, ready to be gathered up by Anglos with entrepreneurial instincts, who exported them to a beef-hungry America.

By then, California had been densely colonized by Hispanic emigrants as well. Herds had become immense there too, by the time California was annexed by the U.S. and gold was discovered in 1849. There was already a huge trade in dried meat and hides, which *Californios* tended to export rather than live cattle, owing to the difficulties of trailing large herds overland across the vast interior deserts to the east. But California never had the feral cattle population that Texas did. The California Indians were decimated at an earlier date than the Texas Indians; they were either herded into virtual slavery at the California missions or wiped out altogether. So the California herds got more supervised tending, and presumably experienced more genetic interference by human selection – meaning that they stayed more genetically similar to their *Retinta* ancestors.

But evidently the Texas cattle – especially the feral ones – got some powerful nudges from natural selection, as a result of Texas climate and geography. Their descendants held onto the Spanish hot-country flat coat and the ability to get fat on sparse grazing. They even chowed down on prickly pear, spines and all – a feat that tender-mouthed English breeds couldn't match. When it came to coat colors, the wild Texas Longhorn blossomed out in the full rainbow of primordial Iberian genes – possibly because of indiscriminate matings in the wild among different imported subtypes of cattle. These random matings released any and all coat-color recessives that might have been hidden for centuries in the genetic background – not only the traditional *retinta* and black solids, but also the full range of colors that Cossío describes in the fighting cattle – the brindles, roans, dilutes, etc.

I do concede that some of the red and red-roan coats seen on late 19th-century Longhorns might trace back to Shorthorn mixes, because solid red and red-roan are standard Shorthorn colors.

Most important, something in the Texas conditions favored the survival of genes for wider, more spectacular horns. Possibly it was the absence of human interference, which was not there for a dozen generations to cull the feral herds in favor of smaller, less dangerous horns. Possibly, too, a specific infusion of genes from those Galician cattle with their corkscrew twist were somewhere in the original Texas mix. At any rate, the horn spreads of Texas cattle established a range of impressive width.

Based on what I've read, the iconic Texas Longhorn spread would typically start at four feet for a mature adult, and ranged up to 7 and 8 feet on older animals.

Crowded Cattle Cars

As the livestock business modernized, those iconic horns started getting in the way.

At the beginning in 1867, when Texas ranchers did their first big drives to markets or northern ranges, the herds were trailed overland. As the animals moseyed along on their daily stages of travel, they could spread out comfortably so their horns weren't knocking together. But in the late 1870s, when ranches started shipping by rail, cowmen made an unpleasant discovery. Loading Longhorns into cattle-cars through the narrow stockyard chutes could be a nightmare. As my Dad used to point out, a steer with a modest four-foot spread might get through the chute okay if he tilted his head sideways. But bigger "equipment" wouldn't fit easily through the chute. There was danger of a hang-up, a panic by the animal, and a broken neck. A cattle-car packed full of Longhorns was guaranteed to deliver an extra measure of crippled and dead cattle to Chicago....thus cutting into your profits.

Problems with the horns, along with the Longhorn's unique genetic link with tick fever and its vulnerability to non-Mediterranean weather on the northern plains, combined to convince many cattlemen that it was time to move on to other types of cattle. They wanted an animal with less horn, more meat and more resilience to northern weather. By early in the 1900s, the Texas Longhorn was so hybridized that it almost vanished as an identifiable strain of cattle – except on a number of die-hard ranches, including the Elkhorn Ranch belonging to Theodore Roosevelt. These outfits hung onto a few aging specimens because they loved the horns and the stamp of these magnificent animals. Today's purebred Longhorn has been rebuilt from a small gene pool of cattle surviving on those ranches.

In recognition of Roosevelt's fondness for the Longhorn, the north unit of Theodore Roosevelt National Park has maintained a few of these cattle. Thanks to these efforts, and others, the iconic horns of ancient Iberia will go on being worn with magnificence by living cattle in North America.

Further reading:

The Longhorns, by J. Frank Dobie (Nicholson & Watson, New York, 1943)

Conrad Kohrs: An Autobiography (privately published by Conrad Warren, Platen Press first edition, 1977)

*A Son of the Fur Trade: The Memoir of Johnny Gran*t, ed. Gerhard J. Ens (University of Alberta, 2009).

Bancroft Works, Volume 31, History Of Washington, Idaho, and Montana, 1845-1889, by Hubert H. Bancroft (The History Company, Publishers, San Francisco, 1890)

Shorthorn Cattle, by Alvin Howard Sanders and Bryant O. Cowan (Chicago, Sanders Publishing, 1918)

Genus Bos: Cattle Breeds of the World, 1985, MSO-AGVET, Merck & Co., Inc., Rahway, N.J.)

"Immunogenetic and population genetic analyses of Iberian cattle,: by K. K. Kidd, W. H. Stone, C. Crimella, C. Carenzi, M. Casati and G. Rognoni, *Anim. Blood Grps biochem. Genet. 11 (1980) 21-38.*

Tipologia del toro bravo, Portal Taurino (http://portaltaurino.com/ganaderias/tipologia/tipologia.htm)

Los Toros, tratado téchnico e histórico, 4 volumes, by José María de Cossío (Espasa-Calpe, Madrid, 1951)

A GIFT OF PHEASANTS

Originally published in *Montana Magazine*, August 1989

As the postmaster carried the cardboard box out of the back room, she wore a broad smile on her face. Out of the box's vent holes came a soft cheeping, incredibly musical, and a warm poultry smell.

"Rhode Island Reds?" grinned the postmaster.

"Ringneck pheasants," I explained, taking the box. "We're going to eat some, and release some to be wild."

The postmaster frowned. "I always wanted to eat pheasant under glass, in a fancy restaurant. Never could afford it, though."

"Well," I smiled, "we think we can raise them cheap."

With food prices rocketing and drought devastating crops all over the West, another woman and I had started a tiny co-op farm on our adjoining five-acre parcels. We were lucky to have good wells from which to irrigate. My friend, May, who had a lot of garden experience, took charge of our big vegetable operation. With my Montana ranch experience, I provided the poultry. We were sharing the work, fun, expenses and good eats. Best of all, May's children, who were city-raised, were excited at learning more about life.

Scanning a poultry magazine, I had noticed that ringneck chicks, available from game farms, were not much more expensive than chicken chicks. A hundred day-old chicks, shipped priority mail, ranged from $50 to $75 total. The ads inspired me to remember the big Montana State Game Farm, gone today, which stood upriver from our family ranch at Deer Lodge where I grew up. As a child, I had always been intrigued by the thousands of pheasants in the mazes of pens, and I learned to love these dazzling birds.

Many Westerners think of the ringneck as a native bird. Wily, volatile, it represents the ultimate challenge for many American game-bird hunters. Portraits of pheasant roosters in flight reign among our "sporting art."

But, like many human Americans, this noble and intelligent avian is an immigrant! Although it's related to the American turkey, the ringneck is Asian, as are all other members of the pheasant family. The smaller Chinese ringnecks shimmer with every color of the rainbow. The Mongolian ringneck is bigger, equally iridescent, but more red-bronze in hue. These days, many Asian pheasants are endangered species bred in captivity by specialists, under special permits. They are all exquisite, though not necessarily meaty.

Some fanciers of rare exotics loft their noses at the "common" ringneck, as I learned when trying to buy chicks. "Oh, we don't have *those*," one lady informed me haughtily. If the ringneck were a "rare bird," more people would appreciate its rainbow grace, I think.

In ancient times, silk-trade ships imported these birds for Roman banquet tables. "For many centuries now," a learned Danish friend of mine said, "European nobility have bred pheasants and loosed them into our highly managed forests." He had been a gamekeeper in his native land, and understood how the pheasant came to be an aristocratic dish.

European colonists brought the taste for pheasant to America. Here, the bird went democratic and forged west in the wake of the pioneers. By 1890, pheasants reached the Northwest, and probably began filtering into Montana around 1900.

American Indians, who had long appreciated the taste of their native game birds, recognized the delicious new opportunity. I know a number of Montana Indian and mixed-blood families who added pheasants to the poultry flocks on their ranches. They also relished the challenge of hunting them with .22 rifles, instead of the fancy over-under shotguns favored by white hunters. Getting your speeding bullet to intersect with the head of a speeding ringneck calls for some real sharpshooting.

"Never got any that way," grinned one Métis friend of mine.

Few people today realize how great was the destruction of our native game by the West's massive influx of settlers between 1800 and 1900. Montana created its Fish and Game Department because of an echoing absence of wildlife that suddenly embarrassed Montanans. Pheasants, though not native, were introduced because these adaptable birds, which have re-settled in almost every clime save the tropics, can shift easily between "domesticity" and "the wild."

Today, across the U.S., hundreds of licensed game farms hatch literally millions of pheasant chicks a year. A few tamer, heavier strains – "jumbos" or "table birds"– dress out at close to five pounds for specialty meat markets. Other strains remain "wilder," more wary and lightweight; these are valued by gun clubs, who raise and release them.

Our plan was to start eating them at 16 weeks, when they'd weigh around two pounds – the hunter's equivalent of young chicken broilers. They would feed us until the turkeys were big enough. We'd release about half of the remainder, and keep the rest to breed more birds next year.

When I got back to the farm with the chicks, May's three children met me with wild excitement. Elise, 10, Shawna, 8, and Gage, 7, volunteered to be my helpers.

Carefully opening the box, we placed the gold-and-brown barred chicks gently in their round wire enclosure, under the warm brooder lights. I had designed the rain-proof brooder right on the ground outside, so the chicks could pick and scratch nutrients from the rich earth. The children cradled each chick in their hands before putting it down. They were learning how fragile those feathered sparks of life are.

The tiny chicks had been traveling for 24 hours. So they eagerly gobbled high-protein turkey starter and sipped water. Then they ran around at breakneck speed and fought comically with each other, leaping up and down. Now and then, suddenly tired, they crouched down and nodded off for a few minutes. As they dreamed their pheasant dreams, their large eyes twitched under their eyelids. Then they'd wake up suddenly and race off, to begin the cycle again. Their energy was incredible.

"Look at them!" Elise kept saying. "They just never stop!"

That chilly night, we noticed that they piled on top of each other – jostling, nuzzling, pushing, peeping loudly, searching for the warm breast-feathers of Mother Hen that their tiny brains told them must be there.

Watching them "pile" like that, and seeing some die, was how the children and I learned that pheasant chicks must be kept very warm (but not too warm) during the first couple of weeks. Chicks that are already "down" and half-dead from cold can revive with amazing speed if they are warmed up. I added another light and learned to watch the brooder temperature closely, letting their contentment be the measure.

The 84 survivors grew fast. At two days, they sprouted tiny curved wing-pinions. At three days, they could whir like hummingbirds across their little enclosure. Any moth that flew under the bright lights was doomed – the chicks hunted it down with greedy gusto.

The children, who were getting very wise already, said: "They're *hunters*! They need to eat meat!"

In just several days, some individual chicks already stood out. In the wild moth-races, there was one consistent winner – a tiny lightning spark of a hen chick, darkly barred. We named her Warp Speed, thinking of *Star Trek*.

The pheasants grew swiftly. We scrambled to stay ahead of them, for they needed space – ever more space.

The biggest single cost of raising pheasants, we discovered, is the run. Its walls can use one-inch chicken wire. But it also needs a wire roof – else the pheasants will fly out into the universe. We wanted to give our birds plenty of room, and added bay after bay onto their run, until finally they had a wondrous 20-by-120-foot stretch of sunny slope above our creek. It enclosed some small trees and brush, where they roosted at night.

Next, we had to rent a ditch-digger and bury the wire walls into the ground 18 inches deep. Predators, like foxes and raccoons, can dig into a pheasant run. And the pheasants, now plowing the earth with their saber bills in search of worms and bugs, could dig their way out – as we learned the hard way. Total cost, including scrounged wire, posts, machinery rentals, etc.: $800.00. Fortunately, this expense was a one-timer.

Pheasants raised in captivity have one real problem: they can be cannibalistic. Because they are wild animals that don't tolerate crowding, they peck each other when they molt. The new pin-feathers bleed if pecked, and blood keeps the pecking going. The first sign of trouble is drooping, broken trail-feathers. Some professional pheasant-breeders clap little plastic anti-pecking goggles on their birds.

But I learned a simpler tactic: a long-handled fishing net and dog nail-clippers. Netting each pheasant, we nipped the tip of the saber beak. After four rounds of beak-trimming, they were fully armored with their new feathers, and the pecking stopped.

Pheasants also peck each other if they don't get enough meat protein in their diet. Ours delighted in meat scraps and bone meal or blood meal. As Warp Speed ran down a scuttling beetle or sow-bug, we could imagine a little winged pterodactyl swooping to seize its prey in its teeth.

The birds love to hone their beaks on the earth like fighting knives – and they use them to eat just about anything. Ours ate baled alfalfa, fresh lawn cuttings, any kind of grain, all table scraps except citrus, and boxes full of free cleanings from the supermarket produce department in town.

Growing pheasants turn themselves into wondrous feathered dragons, brilliantly shimmering as their adult colors flood their plumage. The roosters develop a warrior look, owing to their emerald helmet and massive scarlet wattles: a fitting look, for nature has made them the noisy fighters that lure enemies away from the hens.

For the female, nature has chosen camouflage–subtle hues of buff, plum, umber and lavender. These colors, delicately barred, help them blend into the shimmering light and shade of grasses when they sit on their nests.

At the slightest sign of danger, the roosters trumpet their raucous red alerts: “Kuk-kuk! Kuk-kuk!”

Only one thing could hush them. One morning, hearing the noisy “kuk-kuks” suddenly stop, May looked out the window.

“Look!” she called. “Hurry!”

We all rushed to the window, to see a golden eagle sitting on top of the pheasant-run gate. The pheasants were all hunkered to the ground, motionless, pretending they were large rocks. Calmly the eagle inspected the situation: run covered with wire everywhere. How would she get her meal? She looked over her shoulder at us, and I swear that she frowned.

All these events reminded us powerfully of the life cycles of which we are all part. Through the magic of eating, wheat and cucumber peelings and oyster-shell and bugs became shining feathers and proud bodies and swift roadrunner legs.

Our feathered dragons killed to live. In turn, as August came, we would kill them to live also.

One late summer morning, we killed our first four pheasants. The children had matured enormously. As they helped me to net the first rooster, they could accept the pheasants’ gift of life without a lot of emotional upset.

“When the head is cut off,” I explained to them, “they die right away. But they flutter around for a few minutes. This doesn’t mean that they are suffering. It’s their nerves reacting. They can’t feel pain because their brain isn’t connected to their body anymore.”

When the green helmet fell loose, the headless rooster flushed into the air one last powerful time, soaring, soaring into spirit. Then he arced to the ground like a spent skyrocket. There, he fluttered himself in thunderous circles. Finally he beat his way north along the run, and stopped, still vibrating, under a bush.

“Wow!” Shawna shouted triumphantly. The little girl ran and picked up the dead bird with great care and awe. “Did you see how he FLEW?” she asked. “When I eat him, will I be able to fly?”

In the big garden, May was plundering the heavily-laden tomato plants of a bowl-full of their fruit. Up out of the earth, amid the tines of the spade fork, came new potatoes, red as living rubies. Cornstalks cracked juicily as she tore off ripe ears. All these plants, too, would die to give us life.

It had been 30 years since I had plucked and drawn a ranch chicken, but I remembered how. Everyone pitched in, learning to dress the birds, seeing the amazing innards come out. In the crops were the plants and seeds that the birds had eaten that morning. In the gizzards, earlier meals were now crushed and digested.

"This is better than biology class," insisted Elise.

"I'll betcha," added Shawna excitedly, "this is how people first learned about 'natomy, and stuff."

Shortly, those birds were in the oven, sprinkled with flour, salt and pepper, and herbs from our garden, and a stuffing made with their giblets and lots of chopped onion – a Métis recipe that I'd learned from a mixed-blood family. As the smell of roasting pheasant drifted out the kitchen windows, and over the run, the remaining 80 birds calmly excavated for worms.

In the dappled shade of a cottonwood tree, we spread our feast on the picnic table outdoors. There we talked, laughed, told stories and ate. The pheasant meat was incredibly tasty, and so rich that small servings were enough. Finally we all leaned back in our chairs, stuffed to the gills.

"Counting what we spent on the run, it figures out to be about $11 a bird," commented May with a burp. "Not cheap meat."

"Next year, we won't spend near that," I reminded her. "And look at it this way. We raised the meat, not somebody else."

Then it was time to keep our promise about releasing birds. The children and I went to the pheasant-run gate. Elise opened it wide, while Shawna and Gage gently shooed three dozen pheasants into freedom.

True to their nature, the roosters exploded into thunderous steep-angle flights, like jet fighters taking off. And the hens – led by Warp Speed – sped silently, ducking and weaving, into the nearest brush.

Within a few days, however, they were back, picking at grain around the run. No doubt about it – those birds were *ours*.

Ringnecks are hardy birds. With adequate feed and winter cover, they can endure cold winters. Most of our loose pheasants made it to spring, and we began the adventure of breeding our own birds.

In April, our 30 captive hens began laying an abundance of eggs – one a day each. The eggs are colored with every shading imaginable, sometimes richly speckled with starlike spots. Watching, we learned that each hen always laid the same color egg. So we named some hens after their personal egg-color. There was Pink, Galaxy, Ivory and Morning Blue.

Because pheasant eggs are very tasty, many went into custards and egg sandwiches. The balance went into a used incubator, the kind that automatically turns the egg-trays, that we lucked into for $150. We learned that a ratio of one rooster to two or three hens gives the highest egg fertility, and we hatched more than 200 chicks.

With our growing experience, we lost few chicks. By the next autumn, we had 80 birds in the freezer and 90 to release.

Meanwhile, our wild birds were doing their own chick-breeding. As that year passed, our wild hens built hidden nests in the sunny brush, throughout the meadows and along the creek. In due course, they all came to visit us and feed, with clouds of yellow chicks around their feet. The children were wildly excited to see them. Some hens calmly tolerated close inspection of their broods, although Warp Speed warily kept her seven babes at a distance.

Watching the wild pheasants, we learned all over again how critically the chicks need to be kept warm. For 10 or 15 minutes, they would swarm after the mother, feeding. Then, suddenly, they would start to peep loudly with cold. She would immediately call to them and crouch down. They would run to her and burrow into her warm feathers. When they were warm, she'd stand up, and off they'd go again.

Sadly, many of our wild chicks were killed by visiting cats and dogs. Marauding pets, we decided, are big enemies of wild pheasants – as much as wild predators or human destruction of pheasant habitat. Most adult wild pheasants can evade attack – but not the brooding hens, who can be killed on their nests. And the chicks, despite their incredible ability to run and fly, are the most vulnerable of all.

One afternoon, we happened to be around when Warp Speed was attacked by a neighbor cat that was stalking her three remaining chicks. The cat, a tom, was used to easy kills on tiny fluttering victims called songbirds. So he was taken by surprise when Warp Speed launched a counterattack. Screaming with rage, her neck outstretched like a small dinosaur, Warp Speed fired herself at him. She chased the terrified feline for nearly 100 feet. Then she came back to her little family and led it off into the brush.

Beautiful, bountiful, bright – even brave – the ringneck pheasant deserves its honored place in the human world.

And releasing pheasants is a beautiful way to give something living and magical back to the land.

ARTS

AN ORIENTAL LOVE AFFAIR

Excerpt from an article originally published January 12, 1969 in the Denver Post *Contemporary*

Thanks to our Victorian grandparents' craze for Oriental rugs, which brought clipper ships loaded with them into U.S. ports, many American families might have at least one heirloom Oriental. "American homes today are the world's major source of fine old Oriental rugs," I was told at Oskar Harootunian & Sons, a leading U.S. antique rug dealer. Yet. ironically, most Americans remain unaware of the artistic value of Oriental rugs. A friend told me of an old Chinese rug that ended up literally in his doghouse, slept on by the family dog. Filthy, frayed, riddled with moth-holes, these minor works of art are finally carted away by the junkman. Yet with a little appreciation and care, they might have given pleasure to their owners for a century more.

I was lucky enough to inherit a whole batch of old Orientals. Studying my rugs opened a new world of passionate interest to me – not just in their beauty, but in the people and history that wove them.

What exactly is an Oriental rug?

The term is exotic, but vague. Many Americans think all Orientals come from Persia (today's Iran). Actually, from the

16th century – the golden age of carpet-weaving – until World War I, the lands that wove them spanned half the globe: from Spain across the Middle East and Asia to China. Today, thanks to steady Western demand that transformed this demanding art into a profitable industry, Iran and India still export significant numbers of Orientals, along with Pakistan, India, China, Spain, North Africa, Turkey. While many new rugs aren't as fine as those predating commercialization and use of modern chemical dyes, some are still of high quality.

Wherever they come from, Orientals have a few basics in common. They are all handmade. Nearly all have a soft pile of thousands of wool (sometimes silk) knots – as many as 500 to the square inch. Finally, all display rich designs charged with centuries of tradition.

In old (and many new) rugs. the wool yarn is first hand-dyed with natural colors obtained from plants, minerals, insects. Then skilled weavers tie the yarn into knots, row by row, onto foundation threads strung the length of the loom. They may spend a year or more weaving a large rug. Time means little – even today Persian weavers get only 25 or 30 cents an hour.

Ever since Biblical times, when Moses hung the Hebrew tabernacle with Oriental weaves, these rugs have played dramatic roles in history. Cleopatra had herself carried in to Julius Caesar wrapped up in one. Political assassins smothered victims' cries with them. Caliphs and nomad chieftains counted their wealth in rugs. When Tamerlane ravaged Asia and Persia in the 14th century, he slaughtered whole cities – but spared the carpet weavers. The great European carpet industries (Axminster, Savonnerie, Aubusson) were inspired by Oriental rugs. During World War II, Hitler ordered many fine ones looted from occupied countries for his personal art collection.

The Oriental played its part in American history, too. It may have come over on the *Mayflower*. Just 27 years after the Pilgrims landed, a Salem, Mass., estate inventory listed "one old Turkey carpitt." The Spanish conquistadors taught sheep-raising to the Navajo Indians, who used the wool for rugs. New England wives borrowed Oriental designs for their hooked rugs. Wealthy Virginia planters imported Orientals along with the fashionable European furniture they wanted for gracious living. George Washington had one of his best-known portraits painted while standing on a "Turkey rugg."

My own Orientals played their part by pioneering around the turn of the century. They went west on the railroads, or came through the port of San Francisco – and landed in Helena, Montana, formerly known as the wild and wooly gold-rush camp called Last Chance Gulch.

By then, Helena had grown swiftly into an elegant state capital. Helena's wealthy cattlemen, mine owners and politicians wanted Oriental rugs to complete the atmosphere of Victorian opulence in their big turn-of-the-century homes. So to meet this demand, a prominent New York textile-importing firm named Khoury opened a branch store there. It was in Khoury's that my rugs caught the eye of my great-grandmother, Oma.

Oma was, as family legend puts it, "Khoury's best customer in Helena." Like most Victorians, she knew less about rugs then we know today – real research on rug history didn't begin until well into the 20th century. But she collected them with the same enthusiasm – although not on the same grand scale – with which J. P. Morgan was collecting them back in New York.

Whenever Khoury's acquired a choice rug, they always took it to Oma first, practically sure of a sale. One by one, some 50 Orientals from the four corners of the earth flocked into her big brick house on Dearborn Avenue. There they cheerfully jostled with Tiffany lamps, needlepoint chairs, and the usual bric-a-brac. One rug draped a library table where Greatgrandfather, a pioneer cattleman, discussed rustlers and cow prices with cronies in the evening gaslight.

Once Khoury's showed Oma a positively ancient but admirable prayer-rug. Naturally Oma bought it. Then, excitement of purchase over, she noticed that it was worn very thin. (Myth falsely has it that a thin Oriental is ready for the garbage can.) She sat around in a temper for days, eyes flashing, wondering if she'd been taken. But she hadn't – that tough little rug outlived her. Oma died in 1945, at the ripe age of 96. And the prayer-rug is alive today at the young age (for a rug) of some 200 years.

When I married, in 1957, my parents were using some of Oma's rugs. But many lay mothballed in several trunks in our ranch house basement.

"Why don't you take some?" my mother suggested. "And while you're at it, study up on them and find out where they were made."

She gave me 12 rugs, plus a copy of Walter A. Hawley's *Oriental Rugs Antique and Modern.*

So the rugs backtracked across America again to New York's Westchester County. Shortly our 3½ room apartment looked like the Istanbul rug bazaar. I had studied art, but rugs I knew absolutely nothing about. So I started from scratch.

Armed with Hawley, I spent evenings lying on my stomach on a rug, studying the various colors, patterns, weaves. Finally I succeeded in identifying nearly all. And I discovered that even the most ordinary ones could, like King Solomon's carpet, fly me back into the lives of their makers.

For instance, the wool of our Hamadan rug was probably clipped by some tribesman somewhere on the Mt. Alvand slopes in central Persia. He must have sold it to a woman in one of some mud-walled villages on the Hamadan plain. She spun it into yarn, took it to the local dyer. He had tramped the foothills collecting madder-root for pink, pounded indigo dust-fine for blue. Now he brewed his vats from age-old recipes, boiled the yarn in them.

Finally the woman worked several months to knot the rug, selecting its medallions and rosettes and S-shapes from among the many motifs she had known since childhood. She sold the rug in the town bazaar. From there, baled with other rugs, it found its way into importer Khoury's hands.

A single design could be a key to history. Our blue Feraghan rug from Persia had rows of star-like henna flowers merely because Mohammed happened to remark, back in the 7th century, that the henna was his favorite flower, "the chief of this world and the next." In fact, Mohammed so concentrated on other-worldly things that he died in 632 without naming a successor to rule the Islamic empire. Thus burst open the longest goriest feud in history, as two rival groups grappled for control. The defeated Omayyads fled off to conquer Spain, and the schism divides Islam to this day – all mirrored in the little henna flower.

I learned to relish my rugs' human imperfections. Muslim weavers, believing that only Allah is perfect, would deliberately add an extra flower to spoil the symmetry, or plonk a tribal mark into a bare space. All my nomad rugs had streaky breaks in color. Called *abrash*, these are graphic proof that the dyer colored his wool in small non-matching batches.

Most fascinating was the large rug that Oma bought in 1898 for her dining room. The family always called it "the gold rug" because of its blaze of golden-yellow background, against which reds and blues trace out stiff cypress trees, lilies, iris, brooks flashing with fish. I discovered that its garden design has an ancestry going back some 1,300 years, to the most famous rug ever woven.

In 637 A.D., the Arabs galloped over the Persian Empire. When they clattered into the emperor's abandoned palace in Ctesiphon, they found an amazing carpet glittering on the floor. It was 100 feet long, woven in gold and silk, studded with pearls and precious stones. Its design was a walled Persian garden in spring, with brooks and blossoming trees. The emperor's entire surplus treasure – more than $200 million worth – had been put into it. Visiting diplomats were dazzled by it, historians have been tongue-tied trying to describe it.

The hard-boiled Arabs decided, after discussion, to follow their usual custom and divide all spoils equally. So they coolly cut the carpet into some 60,000 pieces, which the soldiers pawned in Baghdad for spending money. Not one fragment of this fabulous work of art survived to our day. But its legend lingered on. Through the 19th century, a small number of plain wool "garden carpets" were woven in Persia and Turkey, with that same design of brooks and flowerbeds. Oma's rug, I was sure, was one of these last glimmers of the legend.

But not wanting to be guilty of overvaluing, I checked my conclusions with a New York rug authority.

"You're very lucky," he said. "It's a rare old Turkish weave, maybe an Oushak. All that crazy yellow...I've never seen another quite like it." He smiled. "Add it to your house insurance."

An old Oriental rug needs certain good care. Weekly light vacuuming, yearly cleaning (moths, dirt and damp are Orientals' mortal enemies). Slippers preferable to high heels. Gently swat the cat if he tries to sharpen claws in it. Otherwise just enjoy it. We sat on ours to read, laid on it to listen to music. We'd found out what the Persians knew 1,300 years ago on their sunbaked Plateau: a rug can be a year-round, portable, indoor garden.

Learning more about Orientals is easy: read, look and ask. Besides Hawley, two books that authorities recommend are *Oriental Rugs and Carpets (revised)* by Arthur Urbane Dilley, and *The Persian Carpet* by A. Cecil Edwards. I visited exhibitions and museums to study the great velvety centuries-old court carpets. I have stared at Orientals in store windows, movies, Renaissance paintings, waiting rooms, photographs, friends' houses, business offices.

Visiting New York rug stores to ask questions, I found that many of the best Oriental dealers like to share their enthusiasm and knowledge with beginners. "You can't stay sane in this business unless you are really crazy about old rugs," one of the Harootunian brothers explained. "You have to be in it for more than money. It has a slow-paced Middle Eastern economy. It's an accountant's nightmare. And, as an investment, it's idiotic – you pay thousands for a fine rug, are stuck with it for years, maybe, before it sells."

"Once in a while," he added thoughtfully, "you find you've bought a rug you can't bear to sell. "

I found that American collectors today ranged from people like New York executive Joseph V. McMullan, whose 200 rugs were perhaps the world's finest private collection just then, down to a young editor I know who has one rug and is living on hamburger to buy her second. "Many of our customers are kids," the Harootunian brothers told me. "In fact, the main reason for this Oriental revival is that young Americans are better educated today, more widely traveled, more aware of art in general."

European dealers hop jets to the U.S. to buy rugs too. Some American dealers are worried about this rug drain. Says one, "Quietly but effectively, we are being raided. The clipper ships brought them, the jets are taking them away."

When a collector sees a rug that, as dealers say, "speaks to you," it's an instant rapport between a person and a piece of weaving that he or she can't explain.

It doesn't make sense to love an old Oriental because it's worth $10,000 or because George Washington once stood on it. It should be valued chiefly for its beauty. Only if its colors are lovely, its designs well-drawn and balanced, its workmanship good – only if it "speaks to you" – can it beautify your home and your heart for years.

THE JEWELRY OF HEYOEHKAH MERRIFIELD

A longer version of this piece was published in the *Cat Fanciers Assn. Yearbook, 1983*

The best way to talk about Heyoehkah Merrifield is to tell how I met him, and how he made a magical cat-necklace for me.

In 1982, I quit the cat fancy, left my job as a magazine editor and moved to California. As a Montana-born Métis (mixed-breed) who was finally ready to act on a lifelong connection with native American spirituality, I got to know some Medicine men and Medicine women who live on the West Coast. In due course, during the summer of 1982, I happened to meet Heyoehkah at a Medicine man's home.

The popular image of an internationally famous jeweler is: someone in a striped business suit, surrounded by the hushed chic of high-paid accountants, design assistants and marketing consultants. Couriers bring him briefcases of diamonds from Amsterdam. His creations are seen in the bullet-proof display windows of famed jewelry stores in New York, Paris and Rome.

Heyoehkah dances free of this image. He wears faded jeans, cowboy shirts and a well-worn brown leather vest. His black hat is the wide·brimmed kind that is still worn by some reservation Indians. He works out of a small studio in eastern Washington State, on the Colville Reservation. He built his house himself, and drives a dusty Dodge van.

Heyoehkah is half Cherokee. His long black hair, usually worn loose, frames a thin pensive face. He is a slender, wiry man of 43, standing about five foot eight in his old cowboy boots. Around his sinewy neck, he wears one of his own necklaces – an Indian-style choker of rock-crystal pipes with a turquoise jaguar pendant on it. I noticed that he is very feline in his movements. His hazel eyes fix swiftly on anything that moves. He walks along a forest path with the soft swaying saunter of a felid. His nose, about which he is affectionately kidded by his friends, is the large, long and solemn nose of a big cat.

When I first met Heyoehkah, I looked at that choker of his and felt an instant connection with his works, which he calls "Shields" or "Mirrors." With time I met a number of people who owned Shields of his. I attended a couple of his one-man jewelry shows at California galleries.

Inevitably, I decided to ask for a Shield of my own.

Being self-employed, living in a camper and not very rich, I didn't have a pile of cash to spend. But I learned that many of Heyoehkah's clients are people of modest means, and work it out with him on a barter basis. If a person has some heirloom gems and metals, Heyoehkah is willing to craft some of these materials into a Shield, and keep the balance as his payment.

I had some small antique rose-cut diamonds, and some other odds and ends of family jewelry, three gold-dollar medallions that my mother had given me, several fine old Navajo and Zuni silver bracelets, and a solitaire ring of my mother's with a Montana sapphire in it.

So, the next time Heyoehkah was in southern California, he came to see me.

An Opening of Memory

My camper was parked in the shade of some pepper trees, in back of a friend's house in Ojai. We sat cramped at the little camper table, drank many cups of herb tea, and talked. Heyoehkah had me flip through his portfolio, which was filled with color photographs of Shields. They dated back to the early years of his meteoric rise to jewelry stardom, and showed the many styles and symbols that had inspired him: Greek, Egyptian, alchemy, art nouveau, Mayan Indian.

"Do any of these pictures give you an idea of what you would like?" he asked.

My eyes were riveted to a Shield with a Mayan-style jaguar on it. Its name was "Jaguar Pyramid."

"I've always felt a strong connection with the Mayans," I said.

Heyoehkah's face lit up.

"I'd like doing something along those lines," he said. "The Mayan symbols are a newer thing for me, and I'm still exploring them."

We drank more tea. He talked about how the jaguar was sacred to the pyramid schools of the Americas, as a keeper of memory. Contrary to what many historians today believe, he said, the pyramids were originally *educational* institutes – the equivalent of universities. All knowledge was taught there, and all knowledge was considered sacred, from mathematics to philosophy. The jaguar helped the priesthoods and educated people to remember masses of information. Through the jaguar's Medicine power, they were able to draw on the knowledge that is in the collective consciousness of all humans, not just the surviving written records, as we do today.

Where did ancient Americans get their association of jaguars with memory?

I shared with Heyoehkah something that I had learned when I was a *Reader's Digest* editor and worked with South American wildlife expert Stanley Brock on his autobiography *Jungle Cowboy*. Brock talked a great deal about a unique habit of the jaguar. This great cat is the only feline that doesn't kill by biting into the spine or windpipe at the neck of its prey. Instead, its powerful jaws and fangs bite through the top of the skull, into the brain.

Heyoehkah nodded excitedly and explained further. Ancient American art has many depictions of humans wearing jaguar headdresses with the cat's jaws and teeth fitting down over the top of the human's head. Sometimes the jaguar simply embraces the human protectively, with its chin resting on top of the person's head. Ancient peoples knew that the brain is the seat of memory. So jaguar power is about the "opening of memory."

As I sat with Heyoehkah that day, the jaguar symbol was speaking to me strongly because I had already realized how much writers lean on memory. It seems to me that writers draw on personal karmic memory and on collective memory to write convincingly about things that he or she may not experience directly in this life. For instance, authors of detective novels don't have to go out and kill people in order to write about murder. Writers also use symbols to get their point across.

I realized that the jaguar could tell me much more about my chosen art.

"Please put a jaguar on my Shield," I told Heyoehkah.

We poked through the valuables that I had assembled. Heyoehkah inspected the stones expertly.

"The diamonds are nice," he said. "I love the old rose-cut diamonds. They have so much more depth and fire than the shallow-cut modern stones. The silver bracelets – well, I always hate to melt down things like that. But I'll take them."

He studied my mother's ring dubiously.

"I don't know about this sapphire," he said. "It's really bad. It's murky, grey, a lot of sadness and pain in it."

I told him a little about my mother's final years – illness, convalescent home, slow death.

He nodded. He talked softly about the incredible power that gems have, to collect and direct energy of all kinds. He said, "The spirits in gemstones are very old, possess great strength, and must be given the proper respect. So they are the most powerful of crystals, and have always been used for healing."

From my Métis relatives I had heard about an old Medicine man, living somewhere in North America until recently, who used ten phenomenal Brazilian emeralds in his healing ceremonies. They had been passed down in his family for many generations. But gems can kill too. Famed gems like the Hope Diamond roll through the centuries, soaking up all the powerful energies of hate, greed, intrigue, and power that surround them. They become glittering time-bombs of lethal energy that affect the lives and fortunes of all who dare to own them. Hence the reputation of "bad luck" that such gems have.

"Before a gem can be used for healing," Heyoehkah explained, "it needs work. It has to be cleaned with ceremony, and awakened. Even the Hope Diamond could be cleaned. Of course, that would take a *lot* of work."

Before we parted that day, I gave Heyoehkah a gift of pipe tobacco – the traditional honoring gift that is presented to a Medicine person.

Heyoehkah put all my odds and ends into his briefcase, and drove off with them. Since Medicine people are trusting folks, I didn't ask him for a receipt.

The Question of Magic

Jewelry has always expressed the ways in which we see the magic and the sacredness of the human being. We see it in the diamond-encrusted crown of a king. We see it in the cheap locket around a young girl's neck. We see it in the cat pin with rhinestone eyes that a middle-aged exhibitor wears to a cat show. Since ancient times, jewelry is worn not just to adorn – but to protect, heal and empower the person wearing it.

But what is magic? After a thousand years of relentless anti-magic propaganda by Christianity, magic is a misunderstood thing. Ironically, as Daniel Lawrence O'Keefe points out in his bestselling book *Stolen Lightning*, Christian ritual is full of hidden magical function – starting with the mystique around the cross.

The word "magic" goes back to the Indo-European roots: *magh*, meaning "to be able", and *mag*, meaning "to make". Magic involves the use of *images*, and the *imagination*. We can't make anything, whether it's baking a cake or building a bridge, without seeing a picture of it in our imagination first. Then we bring that thing from spirit into substance. If a person finds that a dream or a nightmare has come true in real life, it is because he or she has "made" it – created certain realities from images in the mind. If World War III finally happens, or if California falls into the ocean during an earthquake, it will be because the collective subconscious of humanity has brooded too long on these terrible images.

Most people's everyday magic is messy, because they have been taught that imagination is "not real," so they let their images slop into reality everywhere. But a magician is a creative and disciplined person who knows exactly what he or she is doing with images.

At a certain point, some images become powerful symbols. Symbols are designs or figures that are born from the collective conscious mind, into our culture, and we all agree that each has a particular meaning. Jung calls them "archetypes." Through our cultural creativity – the "making" of poetry, painting, novels, sculpture, movies, journalism, photography, even advertising and politics – we bring symbols into being. Mickey Mouse, Marilyn Monroe, the Marlboro cowboy, are all symbols – along with the sphinx, and the swastika, and the Statue of Liberty.

When we see a symbol, it reflects powerfully back into our subconscious. When the king's subjects see his jeweled crown, their subconscious notes this glittering and indestructible circle of protection around his head. When a young man sees the heart shape of the girl's locket, his subconscious sees the unfolding of her young mind, her teen philosophies and instincts. When we see the middle-aged lady with her cat pin, we know that here is a person who takes her cat magic with her everywhere.

So symbols have enormous power. They can be used to teach, protect, heal. Unfortunately, they can also be used to kill. Symbols can be manipulated by governments, religious cults, big corporations, and used to enslave people.

Heyoehkah pointed out that many people say that they don't believe in magic. Yet, if we look at the collective subconscious of Americans today, we see people still using the old pagan charts of birthstones and their powers. We see them reading millions of fantasy novels where people wear magic rings. We see them attending church services where faith healings are done.

Merrifield told me: "People laugh at magic until they need it."

A Sapphire Transformed

For six months, Heyoehkah and I didn't meet. I was traveling all over the West, researching *One Is the Sun*. He was home at his studio in Washington State, working on my Shield and other projects.

We did talk on the phone a couple of times, and I learned that he'd decided to keep the small diamonds as the trade. He didn't have the heart to melt down the silver bracelets so he had given them to family members and friends. The gold medallions and other odds and ends had gone to the refiner.

In December, I returned to California, and settled down in the Sierra foothills. Heyoehkah came to visit, and he had my finished Shield with him.

Such a piece of jewelry is not just handed over. Medicine has to happen.

We went to a teepee and Heyoehkah burned some dry sage in an abalone shell, and incensed both of us with it. The teepee filled with the powerful astringent smell of the sage. Heyoehkah took out his Pipe, and smoked it in the sacred way. Then, with his Pipe still laid out, he opened up his briefcase, took out the Shield and gently laid it down on the blanket before me.

There they were – the family odds and ends, freed of the burden of being possessions. I looked at the Shield in stunned silence for several minutes.

Then I said, "Where did you find that beautiful little sapphire?"

Heyoehkah grinned. "Don't you recognize it? That's the one from your mom's ring."

I was amazed. Finally I muttered, "It looks like a different stone. Before, it was so cloudy and grey. Now it's so clear, so blue ..."

Heyoehkah chuckled, pleased with himself.

He talked to me about the use and care of the necklace.

"I've already done the ceremony to awaken it," he said, "so it's all ready to work. The jaguar side is the strongest side. You'll probably want to wear that side out for ceremony only. But that's up to you – there may be times when you'll want to show it. Whatever you do, keep the Shield real clean. I use sage to clean mine. Some other way might be better for you."

That very day, I started wearing my Shield, which I named "Smoking Mirror."

The Shield quickly soaked up a lot of stuff. I was going through a time of powerful learning and changing, and the "Smoking Mirror" quickly reflected any imbalance and battlings within me. I was learning to trust the changes I saw in things, and noticed that it shaded visibly and dramatically after I'd worn it for a day or so. The gold and silver looked duller, and the gems suddenly looked opaque again. Polishing it with a cloth and jeweler's rouge didn't help.

First, I cleansed it with sage smoke. This method did not work too well.

Next, I tried running water. Near my house, there was a beautiful mountain stream edged by giant ferns. Now and then I put the Shield in a shallow pool. There it would lie on the pebbles, with the clear Sierra water rippling over it. Water has great power to cleanse away collected energies. When I fished the necklace out, it was nice and bright again.

Finally, I tried hanging the Shield in a tree, right among the fresh leaves. That worked best – I am strongly connected with plants. They infused the Shield with a distinctive radiant energy that was noticed by others.

Biography of the Artist

How did this Cherokee mixed-blood come to choose the Path of the Magical Shields?

Heyoehkah was born Edward Merrifield in Santa Barbara, California, in 1940. His father was a white Baptist minister. His mother, a hairdresser, had Cherokee blood on both sides.

"I don't think there was ever a time when I wasn't creating things with my hands," says Heyoehkah. "As a five-year-old kid, I was already interested in gemstones. I had a treasure box full of stones from old jewelry, and I used to imagine myself as someone from the Arabian

Nights. I also had an instinctive understanding of my Cat Medicine at that age – I fantasized that I was a black panther!"

His aunt, a Sunday painter, encouraged his artistic gifts.

When he went to San Diego University, he took jewelry courses, and became a jewelry-teaching assistant. Finally he studied with the well-known jeweler Arlene Fish. She had learned from Danish silversmiths, and her technique was what jewelers call "fabricating" – cutting, soldering and overlaying with thin sheet and wires of precious metal – instead of "casting" in solid forms.

"Interestingly enough, much of the beautiful ancient American Indian metal jewelry is fabricated, not cast," says Heyoehkah.

At that time, Heyoehkah preferred sleek contemporary designs. He showed his works at jewelry shows all over the Los Angeles area, and supported himself by selling jewelry. He also started to do sculpture – very architectural modern stuff, made of welded steel and plastics.

Suddenly, however, his mind and his memory began to awake to the magic and power of the old symbols. An art-history course exposed him to the power of archetypes as used in ancient Greek and Egyptian art as well as in modern art-nouveau.

"The Egyptian jewelry really blew me away," he says. "I began to realize that I was remembering – that I had made some of those things – and that I also wore some of them. Art nouveau impressed me too. It was full of symbols taken straight from nature. Those artists love the tendril. It's really the spiral, one of the most powerful archetypes there is."

So, abruptly, he stopped making modern-style things. Gods and goddesses made their appearance in his jewelry – sphinxes, heroes, Tritons, Furies, winged horses, all laced together with elegant tendrils and flowers. His new style, especially the Egyptian things, met with instant enthusiasm from clients.

When the Tutankhamen Exhibition toured the United States, Heyoehkah was invited by CBS to do the narration for their TV special. So Heyoehkah attended the show, eager to see the famed jewelry that had come from the tomb of the Boy King. But he approached the display cases with an instinctive caution.

"Those things," he says, "have been steeped in death and decay for a long time, and they're full of that kind of energy."

By now, around 1965, Heyoehkah was the epitome of the

successful West Coast artist. There was the dizzy round of galleries and shows and cocktail parties, where he had to butter up rich people who were possible clients.

All of a sudden, that summer while staying in a cabin in the mountains near Santa Barbara, he woke up to the ego trip that he was on.

"It all started to seem ridiculous to me," he says. "So I quit. I sold all my works, or gave them away. Then I moved to a remote spot near Mt. Palomar."

There, living in the wilderness, he began to look into himself, seriously and methodically. He read books about different spiritual disciplines, and found himself drawn powerfully to Medicine Ways of the First Nation peoples. After a year, he started making jewelry again – low-priced brass stuff that he could sell quickly at street fairs. He moved to his present home on the Colville Reservation. It was miles to the nearest neighbor. Twice a year, he drove down to California to sell his jewelry.

Then Heyoehkah made the next big step. He became a Pipe Carrier. With the sacred Pipe, he started doing ceremony for himself. This was how he learned of the power that ceremony could put into his new jewelry creations. Native Americans speak of "waking up" masks, pipes and other Medicine things. Heyoehkah learned what was meant by this, and how to do it.

"So now," he told me, "I was also waking up my pieces before I sold them. People started reporting back to me about how the jewelry was healing, helping and protecting them – changing their lives. The symbols in my jewelry had always been speaking to people's unconscious. But now the symbols were working in a more powerful way, because they were awake – because of the ceremonies."

This was a second period of dizzy success. Heyoehkah traveled widely to do special commissions. His pieces were hungrily bought out of top galleries. In 1975, he moved back to the L.A. mainstream, and lived there for five years.

"I had a big house on the beach at Malibu. I drove a Bentley. The whole banana," he says, smiling.

Most of his clients were creative people – artists, writers, musicians, actors. They included Joan Baez, Cher, Genevieve Bujold, Carol Burnett, Glen Campbell, Neil Diamond, Fleetwood Mac, George Harrison, Joni Mitchell, Cheryl Tiegs, Bob Dylan.

Why (I asked him) so many Shields for people in the art and entertainment fields?

"Hollywood is a difficult place to live in," says Heyoehkah. "Actors are constantly bombarded by the energies of people who want to approach them – energies that are often hostile, demanding, weird, bizarre. Publicity agents and the public create huge myths about actors – make them into archetypes when they are just ordinary people. In Hollywood, any connection with the spirit is hard to come by. When a person does find this connection, it helps him or her to survive."

Sacred Clowns

Heyoehkah also found his way to a few teachers whose ancestors had come north from Mexico, and who still teach about the Sacred Twins, the mathematics of the Mayans, and the efforts of Quetzalcoatl to stop human sacrifice long ago. These teachers (he said) have a lot to say about the jaguar symbol, because they still work with it. According to Heyoehkah, they told him that the Medicine of all cats is to be keepers of the balances in the universe. And the Medicine of the jaguar is to be the keeper of memory within balance. They teach of the cosmic balance existing in the universe between the Sacred Twins, who are also the Creatress and the Creator.

As he heard these things, Heyoehkah said, his hair stood on end with delight. He realized how deeply his creativity was rooted in his Medicine – and how unerringly he had been led by memory along the path of self-discovery.

Heyoehkah also gained more insight into why other artists – people like me – need Shields.

"I learned about the ancient American concept of the *heyoehkah*," he says, "and I took it for my Medicine name. *Heyoehkah* is an old word that means 'contrary' in English. For thousands of years, many native American peoples governed themselves by a democracy based on the council circle. No law could pass the circle unless it was debated and unanimously accepted by all the men and women who sat on the circle. The persons who formally introduced any proposed new law into the circle were the *heyoehkahs*. They were always the most brilliant minds in the tribe – often artists. They helped the council to look at all the effects that the new law would have. They did this by acting out the law in hilarious ways – dressing up in it, turning it upside down and inside out. They were sacred clowns.

"Artists are the *heyoehkahs* of today, in American society. With our government and our institutions becoming more and more deaf to the needs of the people, it is usually the writers, and the song-lyricists, and the actors, who hurl the call for a new law into the circle. Or they dress up in the old law and clown around to show us how bad it is. They need all the protection they can get."

He adds, "My creations hinder those who seek to do harm to the wearer. The subconscious recognizes the full power of the shield. A warning is sounded deep within the one who desires to do harm, warning that a Great Reflective Mirror is at hand. Terror or harm is reflected back to its source."

Today, Heyoehkah lives a full life. He is often on the road in his van – visiting Medicine people, doing ceremonies, taking new pieces to galleries and jewelry shows. He has returned to sculpture, and is doing a series of small bronzes. He has two apprentices now.

To be interviewed for this article, Heyoehkah visited me at my own little studio in the Sierra foothills. I still had a couple of cats. They loved Heyoehkah and climbed all over him.

He was delighted when he learned that the article would be read by cat-lovers. I agree that it is fitting, for this man who is a jaguar.

Update in 2010

In more recent years, Merrifield travels more widely in countries south of the U.S., and is an activist on behalf of the rights of indigenous peoples of the Americas. Today he lives in Montana.

He has authored several books of spiritual sharings in his White Buffalo Woman series – *Eyes of Wisdom, Painted Earth Temple* and *Lying Down Mountain.*

In 1986 his jewelry and sculpture work was celebrated in a book titled, *Heyoehkah Merrifield: Magical Art* (Rain Bird Press).

ART TREASURES OF AN OLD RANCH HOUSE

The Needlework of Augusta Kohrs

Visitors can walk into the old ranch house today and see the rooms almost exactly as they were in 1890. The rooms are unusually luxurious and artistic for a frontier home designed in such a rough country. This is because the woman who beautified it, my Oma (German for greatgrandmother) was an unusual woman, and an artist.

That ranch house is the glowing centerpiece of the Grant-Kohrs Ranch National Historic Site at Deer Lodge, MT. The whole site intrigues because it is not a restoration. It is still a working ranch, whose historic barns and corrals, historic blacksmith shop and bunkhouse and hayfields – are intact, and in use by Park Service personnel. Most of the original historic artifacts – including Oma's handiwork – are still there.

My greatgrandmother's spirit must enjoy the idea of 40,000 people a year traipsing through her house. Though she was a very private person, she loved to entertain. And she loved being a culture-carrier. Witness her efforts to bring opera to Helena, and build the William Kohrs Memorial Library in Deer Lodge.

In 1849, Oma was born Augusta Kruse in the duchy of Holstein, then a possession of Denmark. With its twin-sister duchy,

Schleswig, it was a hotspot over which Germans and Danes had been tug-of-warring for more than a thousand years.

Though the Kruses were not wealthy, they were educated gentry. Her mother, Anna Katherine nee Schnoor, was a midwife who revered learning. Though a tight-lipped Lutheran, Anna was also progressive politically – it was unusual for a German woman of those times to be that much of a "blue stocking," or trained in medical arts. A favorite book of Anna's, bought in 1835 when she was 15, was "*SELECTION OF READINGS BY GERMANS FOR TEACHERS TO CULTIVATE A SENSE OF BEAUTY AND CULTURE*."

In 1845 Anna had married Johann Christian Kruse, who started out as a civil servant but parlayed his musical talents into a position at the Danish court as musician, composer, and tutor to royal children. In later years, Oma would mention childhood memories of visiting the court with her father.

Then in 1854, Johann Kruse died – at just 50 years of age.

Frau Kruse found herself in straits both financial and political. Augusta was five, and her older sister Christine was 8. With her husband's earnings vanished, she now worked grindingly hard as a midwife. My father's sister, Anna Bache, who visited the family in Germany, described the Kruses' lifestyle in the great port city of Altona: "They lived in a narrow city house with a basement kitchen. Both girls attended private school where they sat on benches and learned English. Augusta and her sister did much of the heavy work, including carrying water."

Meanwhile, Prussia and Denmark were fighting their latest round over Schleswig-Holstein. Frau Kruse may not have been eager to live under Prussian occupation. Prussia looked less kindly on women's ambitions than did Denmark, which was shuddering its way towards an English-style constitutional monarchy and democracy. During the war, Frau Kruse had renewed her acquaintance with another Holstein family – the Kohrses from Wewelsfleth. In 1848, young Henry Kohrs had been wounded in the battle of Frederickstadt, and Mrs. Kruse was called in to nurse him. Henry's younger brother Conrad, who had served in the army as a teamster, was also briefly on the scene in Altona. A restless spirit, Conrad had already been roving the U.S. as far west as the California gold fields.

Despite what the Victorian era termed her "reduced circumstances," Augusta was getting her own unusual degree of education. She read poetry, history and philosophy. She studied piano and collected sheet music. The widow Kruse also taught both girls to do exquisite needlework. Though a stern *mater familias*, Anna Kruse beautified their stark home with needlework – at one point, beaded velvet lambrequins would grace the windows. Still on display was the exquisite pipe-rest that she had made for Johann when they were first engaged.

In 1866, Frau Kruse lightened the load on herself by putting 17-year-old Augusta on the passenger ship *Allemania*. Chaperoned by a Kruse relative and Henry Kohrs, and accompanied by a trunkful of books, music and embroidery tools, Augusta went to America. There, in the German immigrant community of Davenport, Iowa, she found work as a governess.

Just one year later, in 1867, Prussia had annexed Holstein and Altona.

The stereotype of a German woman insists that she is stern, blonde, cold, methodical, with a potato dumpling inside her head instead of a brain. The teenage Augusta Kruse certainly shattered this stereotype like a Wagnerian thunderbolt. She was a dark-haired blue-eyed beauty with a quick mind. She had a ready laugh, paired with a ready glare that could melt a cast-iron stove. Her regal bearing was doubtless inspired by those distant court memories.

"That woman thinks she's a queen," one discomfited cowman would later remark.

In 1868, Conrad Kohrs, then 38, caught up with her. He remembered seeing her as a little girl, and had heard glowing reports about her. The tall husky Conrad had already experienced years of frontier life, and established himself on a growing ranch in Montana Territory. He took the measure of the young Prussian lady, and decided she would survive on the other side of the Missouri.

So Augusta packed her trunk again, and rode the steamboat *Octavia* upriver to Fort Benton.

In the rough little community of Deer Lodge, Augusta must have been dismayed at the clutter of log cabins and raw new brick business buildings. On the ranch, the two-story clapboard house was a former trading post built by John Grant; purchased by Kohrs in 1866, it was now a cowboy bachelor digs. The "queen" was not amused. After the first scowling inspection, she tied on an apron and fired the male cook. She scoured the wood floors herself, and made war on the bedbugs with kerosene.

As her husband became known as Montana's "cattle king," Augusta transformed their home into the frontier version of a palace – with paintings, etchings, bisque figurines. Out of the newly curtained windows, sweetly heard amidst the bawling of cattle, there wafted the notes of a Schubert air played on Augusta's new rosewood piano. Cowboys and visiting cattle-traders learned quickly that they did not spit tobacco on the floors – they meekly used the new brass spittoons that she ordered from "back east." She had a greenhouse built on the south side of the house, and downhill from it, an outdoor garden rich in blooms to cut for the house.

But the most striking additions were her own. For she had found herself as an artist –- a painter with needle and thread.

The needlework art proliferated through the house. For the parlor, she did her own designs of Montana wildflowers and embroidered them on broad strips of trim for the velvet slipper-chairs. Sofa cushions had French designs in petitpoint and needlepoint. A fanciful tasseled cover draped the top of the rosewood piano. Though she was never a horsewoman, Augusta crafted an elaborate saddle-cloth for the ranch's Thoroughbred racehorses. It's even possible that she did the red-velvet mount on a pair of longhorns that hung over the dining-room door.

But her most ambitious work was a large petitpoint scene beloved to her from German music and culture: the Lorelei maiden, standing on cliffs above the Rhine, hair and gossamer garments billowing in the wind as she strums her bardic harp. The stitches were so tiny that the colors flowed like oil paints.

Another creation – a footstool with cow-horn legs – won her a first prize at the territorial fair in Helena. The seat was covered with a petitpoint scene of a naked Greek warrior lancing a lion from a rearing horse. She copied it from a bisque pair of figurines in the parlor – the mate was a naked Amazon on another rearing horse. Since the lion is a symbol of royalty, Augusta might have been making her own progressive sympathies clear.

With time, the Kohrses had two daughters, Katherine and Anna, and a son, William. Yet amidst the cares of motherhood, her busy needle and crochet hook kept brightening the house. There were dresser scarves, monogrammed napkins, crocheted edgings on pillowcases, tea-towels, antimacassars, with every kind of knot and stitch.

After Frau Kruse died in 1883, Oma's still-unmarried sister Steenie visited Montana. The two of them really went to town making things – Steenie had her own gifts with needle and embroidery hoop. Photographs of the period reveal how both women adored dresses that were tailored with every excess of Victorian needlework and passamanterie. Augusta hoped that her sister would stay. But Steenie didn't like Montana – still a rough place – so she went back to Altona.

As the century drew to a close, the Kohrses were tireless travelers. To California, to visit Conrad's sister. To Chicago, to shop and do business at the stockyards. To New York, where they heard opera.

"My wife overdid while shopping," my greatgrandfather's autobiography reported drily.

For many years, they spent the winter holidays in Germany, where they visited the relatives in Altona. They sniffed out every tourist hot spot and spa in Germany – including Bayreuth, where they took in the Wagnerian festival. In Egypt they boated on the Nile and visited the Pyramids, guided by a Syrian dragoman named Francis Moffa, who became a friend of the family.

Whenever they went, they hauled home more of other people's treasures. A collection of magnificent Black Forest wood carvings. More Dresden bisque figurines, Persian and Turkish rugs, damask tablecloths. And her sharp eye never missed foreign needlework to buy. It was perhaps in San Francisco's Chinatown that she bought some Chinese embroideries on silk, featuring Peking knots. In fact, she and Conrad happened to be staying at the Brown Palace Hotel in 1906 when the historic earthquake hit.

"Dear, could you get me a fresh collar?" her husband asked her as the building swayed and they were dressing hastily.

"Get it yourself," said the Queen as she hurried off down the hall in her wrapper.

My grandfather Warren married her youngest daughter, Katherine, and my dad was born in 1907.

Meanwhile, her own needle was never still. To the new damask linen napkins she often added her own and husband's monograms. Beds throughout the house featured the colossal pillow-shams starched stiff as a board, with rich borders crocheted or embroidered in white on white. Often Augusta had help from her daughters, and all their needles flew in unison, like the spinning scene in *The Flying Dutchman*.

In a time when most Victorian interiors were dark and overstuffed, Augusta kept her rooms bright and spacious. Windows were uncluttered by drapes, so the sunshine poured in. Colors were chosen carefully – brilliant blues and crimsons balanced with her favorite yellows, saffrons and swipes of gilding. Perhaps her inspiration flowed from those sunlit Montana hills where her favorite wildflowers grew. Though Augusta had never been an outdoor girl, the home was a reflection of outdoor beauty – a landscape painting to live in – a silk and velvet garden.

During the presidential campaign of Theodore Roosevelt, her home also became a Montana center of political activity. Prior to running for President, Roosevelt had run cattle in eastern Montana, so he knew the Kohrses. Augusta's parlor, with its naked Amazon killing a lion serving as an appropriate symbol, also saw meetings of ladies who supported the vote for women. It was 1914 and her husband was now serving in the state legislature.

On the morning of the historic vote at the Montana Capitol, Oma evidently felt a shadow of doubt on which way he might go.

"If you don't vote for suffrage," she told Conrad, "don't come home tonight."

Montana became one of the first states to enfranchise women.

After my greatgrandfather died in 1920, Oma did not fade into a fashionably yellowed widowhood. By then she was spending her winters in her Queen Ann-style townhouse in Helena, but she always returned to the ranch in summer. She used her fortune to build the library in Deer Lodge, a hospital wing in Helena. Frequently she took hard-luck children under her wing and gave them an education.

Steenie's death in 1932 ended Oma's visits to Germany.

In the early 1940s, when I knew Oma as a little girl, she was already past 90. Till she was 94, she still left Montana for a few weeks every winter to travel grandly by train to New York, where she stayed at the Biltmore Hotel and spent every moment possible in her box at the Metropolitan Opera.

Her summer visit usually began on Memorial Day, when the whole family assembled in the Deer Lodge cemetery to decorate Conrad's and other family graves. Everybody could hardly wait for her to come.

I remember her as fragile but straight-stemmed as the sweet-peas that grew in her garden. Regal in the black ankle-length crepe dresses that women of her generation still wore in the Forties, she always had her white hair perfectly coifed. That mind of hers was still sharp as a needle. She ran the family like a Teutonic chieftainess from her favorite oak chair beside the north window in the sitting room. But we greatgrandchildren knew her soft spot – her willingness to chuckle with us over a silly story, her tales of Napoleonic Europe that seemed so fantastic to us. Later in life, I would ponder having been able to talk to someone who could remember the arrival of steamships and railroads, who had seen a real queen at the Danish court.

By then, her hands were too gnarled for fine needlework, so she was knitting – afghans, mittens for greatgrandchildren. The sewing cabinet beside her chair was crammed with projects.

Augusta had a special affection for my mother, whose hard-labor Depression childhood and love of education echoed her own. So it was inevitable that Augusta's passion for needle art rubbed off on my mother – even a little bit on me. While Mom never mastered the more arcane crafts that Augusta had spent a lifetime doing, she did fill our own house with needlepoint. It was everywhere – on sofa cushions, covers for footstools, and those pairs of oval pictures with old-fashioned roses floating in space that everybody had on their walls during that time.

My cowgirl fingers labored their own way through a lumpy needlepoint seat-cover for the piano bench where I was supposed to sit for an hour and practice. I was also drafted to help Mom embroider vegetables in the corners of dishtowels, which Mom was still making from old flour-sacks. This was the artistic ethos of the day – that even dishtowels must be beautified.

Whatever linens Mom didn't have time to beautify, she bought. Every year a Syrian lady merchant made the rounds of her best customers in Montana. Sada La Touf was sent to Mom by Oma, and probably was a connection to old Francis Moffa's family. She always drove into the ranch with a big car loaded with fine Irish, Italian and French linens. Mom was always good for a sizeable purchase – everything from little tablecloths for bridge-club luncheons to dainty lace-edged hankies. Gradually Mom's collection of fine needlework overflowed her own linen closet in the same way that Oma's works already overflowed the oak cupboards down the road at the Old House.

I haven't mentioned the ironing yet. Miles of artful linens meant a full clothesline on washday, and hours of drudgery at the ironing board. It was one thing to be well-to-do and have a housekeeper do all that ironing for you – quite another to do it yourself. I ironed enough of those dainty hankies to pave a road to that Moon that Americans talked about visiting someday. Mom insisted that even the dishtowels be ironed.

Inevitably, through 1945, the clicking of Oma's knitting needles fell silent for good as her health failed. When she read in the Helena *Independent-Record* that a terrible new weapon called the atom bomb had destroyed two entire cities in Japan, she probably decided that she had seen enough. Death came to her in October 1945.

When I got married in 1953, my Mom inundated me with some of Augusta's hand-embroidered linens – and some of her own too.

In 1975, when the National Park Service purchased the ranch for a historic site, they found themselves cataloging piles of Oma's needlework along with the guns, saddles and ledgers full of cow business. Family members, including myself, gave back some of her finest items. Even a few random works by Augusta's mother and sister found their way into the collection – a black velvet beaded lambrequin, Johann Kruse's pipe-rest, a doily or two. And these were but the survivors of a century and a half of hard use.

One day, needing to do repairs, the GKRO staff lifted the grill of the heating register in the floor by her old chair at the sitting room's north window. Underneath they found an archeological trove of needles, buttons, colored thread, even a yellowed page of embroidery patterns.

For the moment, many "liberated" Americans were seeing women's needlework as an inconsequential and ephemeral art – not in the same class with "fine art." But that attitude is changing today, as more and more museum collections and exhibitions acknowledge the powerful creativity that women have long channeled into the domestic arts – whether a carpet embroidered by 16th-century Spanish nuns that I saw at the Metropolitan Museum of Art while researching an article for *Antiques Magazine*, or a patchwork quilt pieced in Appalachia, or the finger-woven sashes made by tribal women that I would study while writing *One Is the Sun*.

Today, at the Grant-Kohrs ranch, Oma's rooms can be seen almost exactly as they were. The embroidered slipper chairs stand in the parlor. The door of her greenhouse is open, releasing the scent of geraniums and herbs. The sheet music is still on the rosewood piano with its tasseled topper. Those heavy German books are still lined up on the shelf. On the parlor wall, in that gilded baroque frame, the Lorelei plays her petitpoint harp. If the notes could be heard, they would surely be an emigrant air from Wagner.

Today I don't even own an iron, and everything comes out of the wash tumble-dried. I'm doing good to sew on a button.

But I remain in awe of my greatgrandmother's body of work – as impressive in its way as if she had written a shelf full of books. It deserves to be seen as a treasure trove of pioneer art.

"MY MOTHER IS OF THE PEOPLE" – THE MÉTIS SASH IN CHARLES M. RUSSELL'S ART

While doing the research for my novel *One Is the Sun*, I took a fresh look at a body of art that I had grown up with. In the Montana of my childhood, you couldn't avoid running into Charles M. Russell. Reproductions of his paintings were on every ranch office wall, and many calendars in many stores. Russell was everywhere, like dandelions and tumbleweeds.

The second look gave me a lot to think about.

Russell intended his work to mirror the rich diversity of the frontier world where he spent his youth, and he sweated to capture every detail. As a result, his art gives us a loving close-up on a group of Westerners whose importance is not always acknowledged by Americans today – and the sash is a clue to their identity. They are known today (mainly in Canada) by the name Métis, which is French for mixed-blood.

In fact, Russell shows us how frontier society was divided along visible lines into three big camps – Indians, whites and mixed-bloods.

Today the English term "half breed" is generally shunned as offensive, though I know Métis who use it among themselves the way some black people use the "n" word among themselves. Russell used the word matter-of-factly, though some whites of his time might have spit the term with contempt. The French word Métis reached the

Northwest through the fur-trading networks – many Canadian traders and trappers had a mixed French Canadian/tribal ancestry. With time, its application narrowed to the sizeable mixed-blood population of Canada, who proudly identify themselves as Métis to this day and are legally recognized as such. In the U.S., sad to say, no such official identifier has ever been established for those non-tribal Americans who have some significant degree of Indian ancestry.

But the French weren't the only ones who blended their DNA into the tribes. In Russell's time, some Montana mixed-bloods might have been English, Scottish, Irish, German, Portuguese, Mexican and Spanish on one side of their parentage, and Cree, Crow, Blackfeet, Bannack, Shoshoni, Cheyenne, Arapahoe, etc. on the other side. Indeed, many of Russell's closest friends had these ethnic roots.

What's interesting is that Russell painted a number of self-portraits in which he wore the Métis sash himself.

"The sash sent a message," a Métis friend of mine who is passionate about Montana history told me. "It said, 'My mother is of the People.' So we call it the Mother Belt."

Living in the Twilight Zone

Today, it is now illegal to discriminate against anyone because of their ethnic ancestry. But in Russell's time, racial biases were still legal and blatant. There were no courtrooms where an Indian or a tribally affiliated mixed-blood could find justice under the law. Western tribes were confined in prisoner-of-war camps called reservations. Their status was little better than that of Muslim combatants held at Guantánamo Bay today. Since they weren't U.S. citizens, the U.S. Constitution and Bill of Rights did not protect them.

But there were many mixed-bloods who didn't wind up on the "rez." These people lived in a Victorian twilight zone between Indian and white. They were despised by any whites who felt the anti-racial passions of the day. Indeed, they were also despised by some Indians – a natural consequence of the U.S. government's use of "half breeds" as scouts and spies during military campaigns against the tribes. Yet, during that frontier period that ended in

Russell's time, the mixed-bloods were an economic force to be reckoned with on the frontier – men like Canadian Métis cattleman John Grant, who was known as the "wealthiest man in Montana" at one point. The Métis excelled in certain occupations precisely because of their experience and knowledge of both the white and Indian worlds.

In Russell's art, the three-way split in frontier society is visible in the clothing, weapons, tools, horse gear, hair styles – even the type of horse being ridden. Wardrobe reflected not only the differing occupations – but even a differing vision of good looks and style. We see Russell's mixed-bloods in blue-collar occupations – trapping, trading, scouting, guiding, boating on the big rivers, wild-horse hunting, horse handling, freighting, and of course cowboying. Often, in a painting, we'll see the Métis guy with his red sash, longer hair, Indian hat-band on his hat, colored shirt, and moccasins and gaiters – involved in some explosive action alongside a white guy with close-cut hair, plain hat, white shirt, cobbled boots and a regular leather belt instead of a sash.

So the mixed-bloods occupy a central place in Russell's art. The red sash may be discreetly half-hidden under a cartridge belt, but it is often there. According to my Métis cousins, it is sending that message that the wearer's ancestry is "of the People."

Historians wonder what message Charlie Russell was sending by wearing the sash. So do I.

Roots of the Northwest Métis

Russell's mixed-bloods have their genetic roots in colonial times, in Canada and Mexico as well as the U.S.

Many of these intermarriages were intended to ensure good business between tribes and the newcomers. My Métis cousins call them "trading marriages." Both sides had things that the other wanted. The tribes wanted guns, wool blankets, cloth, brass kettles, glass beads, whisky. The whites wanted horses, buffalo robes, furs and more furs, not to mention information about geography and routes. Often white traders were careful to marry into powerful and prestigious Indian families, in order to protect and enhance their business. But some white men married Indian women simply because of the scarcity of white women, or because they fell in love. Still others married into the tribes because they were powerfully attracted to what George Bent called the "wild life."

Russell's artistic adventures with the Métis sash were limited to men. Traditionally, the sash was worn by men. Because they were blue-collar men, they went on wearing it at work long after the fur trade ended.

The sash itself has an intriguing history. Some might imagine that the Métis borrowed the idea from Europeans, who often wore sashes with regional folk costumes and military dress uniforms. Today the European sash's descendant is that cummerbund worn with a tuxedo. Unlike the Métis sash, it was usually sewn of plain cloth, often silk or satin. But there would be no logic to taking an Old World sash and turning it into a symbol for New World ancestry.

So the Métis sash has no ancestry roots in Europe. It is finger-woven, not sewn from cloth. It is usually worn wrapped twice around the waist, with the fringed ends dangling dramatically, so it could be 8 feet (or more) in length. To weave it, a "finger loom" is used. Long threads of different colors are simply knotted along a short stick, which is then hung from a peg in the wall, or a teepee pole. The weaver starts at the stick and works downwards from there, to the desired length. All the threads function as both warps and wefts, depending on which way the pattern needs a particular color to go, so the weaver has to keep track of everything in that tangled mass of threads.

Some years ago, when noted Canadian sashweaver Carol James got a commission to copy a magnificent historic sash in a Manitoba museum, she needed 496 threads of different colors. It took her 420 hours to complete the 12-foot sash in a classic "arrowhead" or chevron pattern.

For thousands of years, finger-woven sashes were created by different peoples up and down the Americas. The oldest bit of finger-weaving known to North American archeologists was dated to 6000 years ago. North American finger-weavers used a variety of fibers – from buffalo and moose hair to hemp, cotton – even soft bark. When Europeans arrived, the weavers added wool and silk to their threads of choice. The sash could be very wide and fine, with a high thread count, or it could be narrow and coarse and workaday, like the ones we see wrapped around a cowboy's waist in a Russell work.

Red was a favorite color – for obvious reasons, since it symbolized blood and life itself. I once owned a vintage 8-foot sash made in Canada in the early 1900s, signed by the woman who made it. It was about six inches wide, finger-woven of red wool and heavy white cotton thread, with intricate diamond designs along it.

A skillful weaver could manipulate colors to create a wide variety of patterns and symbols. Often they were intended to send silent messages about one's clan connections. Indian women often wore belts with their family genealogies on them.

According to MetisNation.com, "The sash was also valued for its practicality and versatility. It was used by voyageurs, many being Métis, to carry belongings during transportation duties as a practical item of clothing. It could also have been used to replace a rope or tumpline if none were available. Not only decorative, the sash was warm and could be used as a scarf. The sash itself served as many other things: a key holder, first aid kit, washcloth, towel, and as an emergency bridle and saddle blanket. Its fringed ends, also useful, could become a sewing kit when the Métis were on a buffalo hunt."

Sashes in Different Russell Works

In Russell's paintings, men who are visually identifiable as Métis are too numerous to list all of them here. Some notable examples:

"*The Scout*." The man has shoulder-length loose hair and is wearing an Indian-style fur hat, coat made from a Hudson's Bay blanket, Indian-style gaiters, and moccasins. He is carrying a long-barrelled muzzleloader of the type so liberally traded during the fur days. The saddle looks Indian-made. The sash is visibly tied around his waist.

"*When Horseflesh Comes High*." The rider dismounting hastily on left is a Métis. His hat is the round-crowned model favored by Indians, with a beaded hat band. His loose hair is shoulder-length.

The colored shirt, gaiters and moccasins complement the sash so visible under his gunbelt. The rider at center, the one who is shooting, is dressed white man style – no sash, cobbled boots, short-barbered hair, white shirt. The painting's social message: a mixed-blood guy teamed up with a white guy to heist some horses.

"*Carson's Men*." Kit Carson was associated with the Bent family of traders. The red belt is visible on a rider to the right. Carson is wearing some Indian-made clothes, but not the red sash – after all, he was a white man. More about the Bents later.

"*Wild Horse Hunters*." The rider on the far left wears the red sash.

"*Caught With the Goods*." The outlaw on the left has a red sash, along with Indian style hat, gaiters, moccasins. And his face looks very Indian His partner is dressed in white man style – no gaiters, no sash.

Drawing of a Red River Métis. This man is magnificently turned out in the full-dress outfit – hat with round crown, and long hair, and the archetypal sash with visible chevron design and fringed ends hanging down the left leg. What looks like the Indian-style "possible bag" (for odds and ends of personal effects, including a pipe) is hanging from the sash. He wears moccasins and a buckskin shirt with flower designs typical of Métis beadwork, and carries that little clay pipe so favored by the Métis.

Among the Russell self-portraits, there are:

Drawing showing him wearing an "American" tailored jacket and tie, hat with the round crown often favored by Indians, no suspenders and the Métis sash.

Drawing showing the artist on his horse Red Bird– he's wearing an American jacket, with tie flapping in the breeze – and the sash.

1899 drawing – Russell wears a wide fringed sash with what looks like the classic chevron pattern in it.

"*Charlie Russell and His Friends*." In this work, the artist's red sash is barely visible above his cartridge belt.

Russell's Big Hint

Why was the sash so important to Russell? Many of the artist's historians, collectors and admirers have believed that

Russell simply adopted that red sash as a way of expressing his sympathies for the native peoples, and his nostalgia for their wild, free life – a nostalgia that some historians have called "romantic."

Yet the red sash may go deeper than nostalgia. Among the Métis that Russell knew, that sash was charged with meaning and reverence. It was never displayed casually. Even today, when the Canadian Métis have political meetings, they drape a sash across the table where presiding officers sit, in the same way that Americans post a flag at public meetings.

Russell's published writings don't reveal whether he ran into any racist reactions to his sash, but he must have walked a fine line on this issue. In his later years, when he was finally accepted as a leading artist, many older Montanans still knew what the red sash stood for. By then the term "half breed" had become a fighting word for many – "breeds" were still viewed with loathing and contempt by racist Americans.

By 1880, when Russell first arrived in Montana, most of the Canadian-born Métis families who settled there during the fur-trade days had fled back to Canada. New laws had made it impossible for Canadian citizens to claim land in Montana. Racial hostilities had exploded across the state after the Civil War, when many defeated and disgruntled Southerners migrated into the state.

Yet the Montana population still abounded in mixed-bloods – especially at the low-income end of the rural work force. Many of Russell's closest friends were mixed-bloods – like Bobby Stuart, half-Shoshoni son of rancher Granville Stuart. One good friend, Joe Cosley, a mixed-blood who was the first ranger hired at Glacier Park, made himself famous for wearing a Métis sash.

As Russell became famous himself, he wore the red sash around Great Falls, his city of residence, and across Montana, probably without making any public comments about what it stood for. Only the old-timers knew what it really meant. He also wore it to artist appearances in New York City and London – even on occasions when his wife, who was a stickler for protocol, made him wear black tie and tails. The high-society folks with whom he hobhobbed must have viewed the artist's sash as an eccentric and colorful leftover bit of frontier wardrobe.

So what statement *was* Russell making about his family, if any?

The Bent Cousins

Russell's father's mother, Lucy Bent, came from a trading dynasty that was well-known for its tender ties with the tribes. All four of Lucy's brothers – William, George, Charles and Robert, who were Charlie's great-uncles – worked in the Indian trade. In 1826, with their French business partner Ceran St. Vrain, William and Charles Bent built the famed Bent's Fort in Colorado. This trading mart stood midway on the new freighting route between St. Louis and Santa Fe.

William married two different women from a powerful Cheyenne family – first Owl Woman, and after she died, her sister Yellow Woman. His five half-Cheyenne children – Mary, Robert, George, Julia and Charles – were Charlie's second cousins. William sent George and Charles to white schools in the Midwest, but the "inoculation" didn't take – both of them, and Julia and Robert too, opted to live with the still-free Cheyennes, even to fight with them against the whites.

Only Mary abandoned tribal life – she married a white rancher and lived quietly on a land grant in Boggsville, Colorado.

In his biography of Russell, the artist's nephew Austin Russell tells us a significant fact: as a boy in St. Louis, Charlie was powerfully aware of this blended Bent family background of his – it was one of the things that fired him to head for the frontier.

By 1880, however, when 16-year-old Charlie Russell went to Montana for the first time, Bent's Fort was abandoned, a distant memory, and the Cheyennes were battered prisoners of war on reservations. Two of those Bent cousins – Mary and Charles – were already dead. Charles had became a Cheyenne Dog Soldier and died while fighting against the whites.

But George, Julia and Robert were still alive. As 1900 neared and Russell became nationally famous as an artist, the three were living in post-conquest poverty on the Southern Cheyenne reservation in Indian Territory. Julia had married another half-blood Cheyenne, Edmund Guerrier, a noted former scout and trader, and they had two little sons. George Bent's first wife had died, and he had re-married – a Cheyenne woman named Coming Up. They had four children. Robert Bent married a woman named Elk.

Indian children were not welcome in public schools at that time, so the Bent and Guerrier children were sent off to the Carlisle Indian School, founded by Quakers and located in Pennsylvania.

Meanwhile George Bent and Ed Guerrier worked for the Indian Agency at Darlington, trying to mediate with the government for the needs of the People whose fate they'd elected to share to the end. They were pro-active tribal members who tried to help build roads of peacetime survival and economic subsistence for the Cheyennes. George Bent was an intelligent, articulate and sensitive man whose letters to ethnologist George Hyde constitute a unique Cheyenne eyewitness record of those long years of warfare.

Was Russell ever in contact with this raft of part-Cheyenne cousins of his? Two generations of them, in fact? After all, weren't they the living spirit of that red sash he wore? Tribal genealogy considered cousins to be as close a blood relationship as brothers and sisters. Russell may have known this.

Was it politically problematical – even risky – for Russell to establish a personal relationship with George, Julia, Robert and their children? This is a possibility. His wife Nancy, who served as his agent, may have felt that his art career would suffer if he associated openly with former "hostiles," even those who were his own kin.

It's also possible that Russell did quietly attempt to connect with the reservation Bents, but was rebuffed by them for some reason. Or perhaps he was prevented from speaking with them by the Department of Indian Affairs.

In spite of all the anti-Indian bias in the air, it's clear that his relatives the Cheyennes were on Russell's mind. Of the some 4000 works created by Russell, quite a number of them depict Cheyenne Indians. One black and white drawing, "Bent's Fort on the

Arkansas River," was done as a magazine illustration. It shows a family group of Indians sitting their travois horses outside the fort's massive adobe walls, waiting for the gate to open.

In his striking 1899 portrait "Indian Maid at the Stockade," Russell shows us a girl who is likely Cheyenne. She is leaning against the log wall of a trading post – possibly one of the Bent posts. She is decked out in trade finery, notably the broad leather brass-studded belt and knife scabbard and silver ornaments favored by Cheyenne women. With her blouse hanging open, she has been tabbed as an example of Russell's fondness for brown-skinned soft porn. But one detail reveals a deeper, sadder meaning – her hair is worn loose and cut short, an Indian social expression of mourning. Her expression is defiant, and she holds her long Cheyenne quirt ready to lash out. She is definitely not somebody's "fort girl."

Who Was Kee-Oh-Mee?

While historians have never been able to nail Russell's personal relationships with Indian women, he was close enough with the Northwest tribes that he probably could have married into one of them, if he'd chosen to do so. Hence another reason why the red belt might be personally significant for the artist.

The painting "Kee-Oh-Mee" is thought by some to portray a Blood woman with whom he fell in love while visiting Canada in 1890. If she was a real person that he cared about, the luxury of her surroundings and the Medicine Pipe on the ground beside her suggest that she was a person of consequence. The Pipe is a very personal thing, and First Nation people never treated it as a prop – Russell smoked the Pipe himself, so he surely knew this. So the Pipe in the painting has to belong to the woman being portrayed.

But that historical window of time, when it was an attractive option for a white man to marry into the tribes, had closed by the time Russell got to Montana.

When Russell was ready to settle down in the mid-1890s, marrying into the tribes was not only socially dangerous but legally problematical. By the time Charlie married his wife Nancy in 1896, Montana was hardening its heart towards "miscegenation," and in 1906 would outlaw marriages between whites and blacks or

Asians. The politicians stopped short of outlawing white/Indian marriages – probably because they already had so many mixed-blood constituents living in the state. But nationally, there was even talk of amending the U.S. Constitution to outlaw interracial marriages – it was first proposed in 1871, then in 1912-13 and again in 1928. Fortunately Congress quashed this bill.

There may be yet another Indian angle to the Russell family story – one that only professional genealogists and modern DNA research could uncover. It's possible that a direct ancestor of Charlie's had some Native American ancestry that Charlie knew about.

In other words, there may be a good reason why Russell was said by many to "look very Indian."

While we may never know all the facts and hidden heartbreaks in the Russell family story, there is still the inarguable fact of the red sash that the artist wore so persistently in his self-portraits. Whatever the personal reasons for Charlie Russell's wardrobe statement, it was a moment in American history when it took a heap of courage to be saying to the world, "My mother is of the People."

Further reading:

Charles M. Russell: The Life and Legend of America's Cowboy Artist, by John Taliaferro (Red River Books, 2003).

CMR – Charles M. Russell, Cowboy Artist: A Biography, by Austin Russell (Twayne Publishers, 1957).

Life of George Bent: Written From His Letters, by George E. Hyde (University of Oklahoma Press, 1983).

Many Tender Ties: Women in Fur-Trade Society, 1670-1870, by Sylvia Van Kirk (Watson and Dwyer, 1996).

The Bent Family in America: Being Mainly a Genealogy of the Descendants of John Bent, by Allen Herbert Bent (BiblioBazaar, 2009)

The Charles M. Russell Book: The Life and Work of the Cowboy Artist, by Harold McCracken (Doubleday & Co., 1957).

The Melungeons: Resurrection of a Proud People. An Untold Story of Ethnic Cleansing in America, by N. Brent Kennedy (Mercer University Press, 1997).

CITIES

TO LIVE (NOT DIE) IN L.A.

Unpublished commentary written in 1994

After the recent riots, as I watched a rain-storm move in off the Pacific, I remembered my queasy feelings last autumn when I first moved to LA. – an intuition that the city was a human thundercloud about to discharge a mighty bolt.

Now came the lull – a gentle rain that quenched the last embers of the riot fires. It was a hint from Life that healing is possible. The pink lightning did her sword-dance over the freeways. Her blades leaped 50 miles long, bathing the burned-out blocks and the loot-littered streets in a rosy strobe-light glare, all the way from Santa Monica to West Covina. Not nice safe Hollywood lightning, done by special-effects people in a studio. Real lightning.

As the rich and powerful of America watched the TV news scenes of looters in Rodeo Drive boutiques, they must have gotten the shock of their lives. Real human lightning had struck into their "safe" little world.

Lightning kills you if you're standing where she wants to be. But lightning also has the power to infuse nitrogen into the air, so the enriched rain can nourish plants.

In human terms, L.A. is the collective voltage of all the closely packed people, and all the ethnic groups who live here. Depending on how she moves, the L.A. Lightning can nourish and create – or she can kill.

Our modern technology cannot yet direct natural lightning. But we can direct our own human lightning.

I wonder which kind of directing it will be for L.A. Will it be new life? Or death? We all know that "it's not over."

The L.A. human storm touched off hair-raising lightning-strikes in other cities as well. But I wonder if enough of the powerful people who run our cities and our big businesses, and our federal government, realise the seriousness of what just happened. Doubtless the King and Queen of France, when they heard of the first riots in Paris in 1786, knew "it wasn't over." Nor, in 1990, did the Soviet Communists and old-guard KGB think it was "over" just because they had already heard thunder of dissent rumbling underground for decades and tried hard to keep the Lightning in jail.

History shows us that, in every collapsing society, the rich and powerful knew that trouble was coming. But they were always taken by surprise – by the shattering suddenness of the changes when they finally came. Dan Quayle and his advisors, touring L.A. the other day, know it isn't "over." Yet Quayle's remarks about single mothers put him in the same class with Marie Antoinette saying, "Let them eat cake."

No, it's not over. Not for Republicans, or Democrats either. More and more Americans are disgusted at both parties' refusal to be real – at the silly finger-pointing and game-playing that our campaigns have become. Ross Perot swears he is real, yet so far we haven't heard a real plan from him.

Most American voters – those of us who don't live in that remote world of power and perks – know we are not sitting in a comfy auditorium listening to high-school debates. We know that far more than justice for Rodney King is demanded of America. We, at least, know that we are all standing in the open field of destiny, under the advancing storm. How come our "leaders" act as if they don't know this?

Will we the People have the wisdom to be real? Can we craft the kind of lightning-rod that will direct our Lightning into real communication and real agreements, and real plans, and real solutions?

Most of all, will our wealthy honor the real priorities so that the needed funding can be found for positive change? Our nation is still enormously wealthy – even in these harsh times, that wealth has not mysteriously disappeared. On the contrary, too much of our wealth is stored in pork barrels by people who believe that the National Guard can protect their personal warehouses.

History shows that the problems we face – pollution, overpopulation, unemployment, ethnic grievances, the growing injustice and paralysis of our infrastructure – cannot be resolved by martial law, or church sermons about morality. History shows that, when politicians try to make deals with the Lightning, they get zapped. When prayermongers try to convince the Lightning, they too get zapped.

To rephrase Abraham Lincoln, the Lightning can't be fooled – not some of the time, not any of the time. Her experience tells her when creeds part company with real life. She knows what is real. She is that volatile side of people – women, men, children – who have been pushed and pressured to the max by the daily crushing of a society that is losing the power to be real. She is prepared to strike with all her power at what is not real.

L.A. does have her electricians who now are racing against time to re-wire the city with some good lightning-rods. But these dedicated people are still few, and their resources scanty.

"Healing L.A." is now the by-word of this lull time.

But healing L.A., and healing America, will take a tremendous effort and caring by all citizens. The alternative – as those of us know who have really felt the storm coming – is civil war. That will be when the pink lightning arcs all the way from L.A. to Washington D.C., and from Chicago to Austin. I would not want to be standing on the spot where that ultimate Lightning wants to touch down.

A WESTERNER PONDERS NEW ORLEANS

Originally published as a foreword in the anthology *Love, Bourbon Street,* edited by Greg Herren and Paul J. Willis (Alyson Books, 2006)

When I was a little kid in the 1940s, I first met the city of New Orleans as a powerful and mysterious spirit. She had reached all the way into the Pacific Northwest and touched her finger into the cemetery in my Montana hometown.

The Hillcrest Cemetery was located in hayfields and rolling hills west of town, near the county airport. It was "neutral belief territory" – the result of a recognition by the town that things had to get less bigoted on the interment front. The Catholic Church, whose Jesuit missionaries had occupied the ground floor in local history, originally had the only cemetery game in town, but they were sticky about allowing people of other religions, or no religion at all, to be buried in "their" territory. So everybody in town took a deep breath, and relocated Catholic graves out into the ecumenical sweep of agricultural land. There they rested cozily among Baptists, Anglicans, Presbyterians, Mormons, Freemasons, Christian Scientists, and atheists.

Two of the oldest graves belonged to nameless early-day

settlers. Local tradition said they were from New Orleans. How did locals know this? Even though Montana is a semi-desert climate and the water table was deep below ground, these were typical New Orleans burials – the coffins were set above ground with a tomb built over them. One was boxed in by weathered brick, with mortar crumbling out. The other was slabbed in by native porphyry quarried in the mountains long ago.

When my family visited the cemetery on Memorial Day to decorate our plot, I always felt the pull of those two anonymous burials – the mystery of those forgotten lives. I'd slip away from the opulent Victorian part of the cemetery, where my German immigrant great-grandparents and great-uncle and the rest of their generation slumbered beneath massive granite memorials amid the shade of lush cottonwoods and weeping birches.

Out in the hot sun of that oldest part of the cemetery, I'd stand there pondering those two weathered piles. The area around them was bleak, untended – no nice green lawn or planters full of pansies. But Mother Life had gentled the graves in wild baby's breath just coming into bloom – it had seeded itself from florist bouquets across the way. The seeds had probably walked over here on the shoes of previous curious visitors. The cemetery maintenance man had given up trying to battle the baby's breath – it was now considered an ornament, not a weed.

My newborn writer's imagination tried to grasp the enormous journey those two men had made. They may have been of French descent, maybe even Cajun or Creole, and found their way up the Mississippi to St. Louis, and from there laboriously up the Missouri with a boatload of voyageurs. They came at the end of the fur-trade era, just before the Montana gold rush filled the Rockies with greed, insanity and violence.

I already had a sense of myself as being "different," and wondered whom they had loved. Were they straight? Did they marry tribal women, as so many pioneers did? Were their wives buried there somewhere too, amid the baby's breath blowing in the wind, under some of the toppling anonymous wooden crosses or eroded stone markers in that same area? Did they maybe love each other? After the beavers vanished, these men might have made a living as free traders, or perhaps joined the small community of mixed-blood stock raisers in the Deer Lodge valley, dealing in Indian-bred horses and the first tricklings of Spanish and American cattle coming up from the emigrant roads.

I was struck by the cultural stubbornness of these graves – planning for a high water table in a country where rainfall averaged only nine inches a year.

The deed hinted at New Orleans' hold on her children. No matter where they emigrated, they took something of New Orleans with them. She was an urgent spirit, very passionate and possessive of her progeny – so different from the benign post-Christian traditions that had sent so many European and Eastern immigrants to sleep there, whose burials were all framed in a generic conformist Victorian style with brooding stone angels.

When I grew up and left Deer Lodge, New Orleans was one of the many things that stuck to my shoes like some of those tiny baby's breath seeds. She went away with me into my future as a writer.

Every great city has her powerful spirit who guards her walls and tends her public life and her people's destiny. In Athens, she was seen as warlike – Pallas Athena, a battle-maiden armed with shield and spear, driving a chariot and four careening horses. In Rome, she was Juno, stately, motherly, a diva of commerce, her temple guarding the mint where Roman coins were struck. In London, she was Themis, keeper of the law, riding her river on a great barge. In New York City, she is Liberty poised on her Island, balancing a book and torch.

The Spirit of New Orleans might be called a *loa* or a goddess, and given different names, depending on whom you talk to. She is tinged with the color of many peoples, black, brown, and white, who built on that high ground above a swamp, by a great natural port. Her toga may be draped in the same European neoclassic style that inspired many of her older buildings, but it's an African textile. Her necklace is Mardi Gras beads. Her shield luminesces with fish scales. After all, she's a harbor girl.

Today, in these post-Katrina times, she has her work cut out for her.

Whatever her name, she was the American city who sent her children out as carriers of traditions that stuck to their shoes no matter where they went. Early-day black jazz musicians fanned out to Chicago and New York, and took their music with them to create a sound that ultimately defined an entire nation and every skin color in it. New Orleans cuisine went out to the world – all Americans know the taste – gumbo and pralines, and they're learning other dishes too, as Emeril Lagasse celebrates the city's culinary inventiveness on his TV show every day. New Orleans was first to export that decorating trend called "shabby chic," conveying an image of frayed but enduring gentility.

Last but not least, New Orleans writers, whether Tennessee Williams or Anne Rice, Mark Twain or Kalamu ya Salaam, gave a gift to Americans of prose with an urban pungency of narrow old streets where the drains don't work too well, and the gardens are recklessly overgrown. Historically, the city has been a refuge for writers, an inspiration for them.

Many of our more straitlaced American citizens sniff at NOLA, at her festering poverty and feisty decadence, at her year-round calendar of pagan festivals, whether it's the saturnalias of Mardi Gras and Southern Decadence, or the spiritual sensations of Voodoofest, or the Satchmo sounds of Jazz Fest. They brag that they have their roots in a more Puritan and proper and prosperous port somewhere else – in Boston or Philadelphia or Seattle. A few cities can argue that they are the oldest in North America: St. Augustine, Florida, and Santa Fe, New Mexico. The pueblo of Acoma, New Mexico, alleges to be the oldest continual inhabited site, with people living under its beams since B.C.E. and a guardian goddess with corn silk in her headdress. As someone who is part Native American, I can claim a root or two in Acoma. But New Orleans has a richly layered history that is unique – a mingling of languages and bloods and sexualities: even a commercial transcendence, that places it on the short list of the great ports of the world, the ones that almost live forever. She is a peer of Rome, London, Constantinople, Hong Kong, yet nothing like any of them.

There is a little of New Orleans in everything that's America.

For me, New Orleans is the only city in America where I felt that I'd been there already when I finally arrived.

It was the late 1990s when I first visited the City. New Orleans Pride had invited me to be its grand marshal. I stayed with a Pride committee member in his Garden District home and got my first whiff of the storm drains in the Quarter, the noise of Bourbon Street, the bustle of the waterfront, the chicory coffee of the Café du Monde.

I was not surprised to realize that gay people had gathered in New Orleans from the very beginning. The port had drawn them there in wave after wave, on Spanish galleons and French frigates and American square-riggers and modern-day cruise ships of many nations. We have always been numerous among sailors. We always swelled the ranks of travelers, of refugees looking for a new liberal land. Often we carried the coats-of-arms of aristocrats where we were protected from social censure by family wealth and power. It is no accident that the oldest gay bar in the U.S. is Lafitte's on Bourbon Street. It is no accident that there are gay krewes in Mardi Gras. In a very real way, the deepest roots of gay, lesbian, bisexual, and transgendered life and liberty in the United States must be looked for not in New York or San Francisco, but in N'Awlins.

We were cautiously made welcome in New Orleans, I learned, because we brought jobs and dollars and tourism to a city where these were precious. All the grim anti-gay machinations of the Religious Right, who have such power in the South, have failed (so far) to dislodge us from our longtime niche in N'Awlins. Economics creates its own inarguable measure of tolerance.

After the Pride festival ended, I was taken to restaurants, museums, antique galleries, voodoo shops, and, of course, the de rigueur visit to the St. Louis number-one "city of the dead." There I paid my respects to Marie Laveau, and walked around for a long time, reading the names on tombs, feeling that sense of childhood time coming full circle. Lo and behold, on one of the other tombs, I found the Warren surname. A distant relative of mine rested there, bones crumbling just above that murky water table so close to the surface. My Warren forebears were originally from West Virginia, a genetic blend of English Quaker and Melungeon, but they had scattered through the South and West – this was the first I'd known that they'd wandered clear down to New Orleans.

With time I would return to the city several times for Saints & Sinners, the only literary festival I know where the workshops and panel discussions take place in bars.

Attending Mardi Gras a few years ago, I enjoyed an ineffable trip up the river as part of an RSVP cruise aboard the *MS Zuiderdam* – a chance to approach the city the way the Native American canoes and Civil War privateers had done, and now the oil tankers and container ships anchored in the roads approaching the harbor. It's no surprise that today I remember the river trip more vividly than Mardi Gras.

The moment came when I told my friends I was thinking of moving to New Orleans someday, to live there for a few years so I could really get to know the city. I did take note that my New Orleans friends were nervous about the levees. They talked about the "big one" the way people in L.A. talk about the "big one." Only that one in NOLA was going to be a hurricane.

After Katrina, I anxiously tried to keep in touch with my NOLA friends who were now scattered everywhere from Florida to Chicago, refugees again, but not from hate this time – parked here and there with friends and family across the South and Midwest. The Internet was the easiest way to reach them, and, little by little, I found them all. Friends who lived in the Quarter managed to learn that their homes had survived more or less unscathed.

In those first days after Katrina, the Religious Right announced that they knew for sure, beyond a shadow of a doubt, that God had destroyed New Orleans because the city tolerated gays.

"Well, God's aim must be terrible," a friend of mine said. "He destroyed the whole Gulf Coast too, and a lot of straight people."

A year later, as I write this, America still faces our government's lack of care for the countless thousands of people whose health, homes, and businesses were destroyed by Katrina. The Iraq war shows our disregard for people of other countries, but Katrina puts a glaring spotlight on government's apparent inability to meet the urgent human needs of American citizens.

Our government not only forgot about the people and the city of New Orleans – it also shot itself in the foot by forgetting about the Port of New Orleans, fourth busiest in the world and vital to the U.S. economy. After Katrina, the port was dead in the water, cranes toppled, workers vanished. Gary LaGrange, president and CEO of the Port, told *Forbes Magazine*: "Congress has developed a case of amnesia now that the national media has moved out of the city. They have forgotten about New Orleans." Many months later, as I write this, the Port is still struggling to get fully operational again.

Great cities pay a big price for living such long lives – they go through cycles – power and glory, then death and destruction and extreme hardship. In the early centuries of this era, ancient Rome was hammered by invasions and almost became a ghost town, its population reduced from millions to perhaps 50,000 people. It was several centuries before Rome slowly began recovering and rebuilding and repopulating itself. In 1666, most of London was destroyed by the Great Fire, as a direct result of government failure to recognize that the medieval wooden city was a potential firetrap. It took nearly half a century to rebuild London. These are times that test the spirits of not only the people of the city, but even the City Spirit herself.

The Great Lady of New Orleans surely had tears mingled with rain running down her cheeks as she surveyed the devastation of her city and her people after Katrina. While she can't prevent the downturn cycles from happening, she guards the secret of rebirth and new life.

Today New Orleans's most precious export to the rest of the country will not be music or cuisine. It will be a renewed consciousness of America's urgent responsibilities to her own people. Not since the 1960s have such great numbers of American citizens been marching and demonstrating and protesting about urgent human issues. But today, nationwide protest is finally happening everywhere – touched off by the immigrant issues, the Iraq war, the blatant corruption in our public and corporate life, the growing loss of civil liberties, and, most of all, by our country's seeming abandonment of its historic position as a world leader on human rights. Katrina-related protest expresses an outrage against political apathy and blundering, against the greed of insurance companies and land-grabbing developers, against deliberate attempts to disenfranchise the people of color across the North Gulf.

New Orleans has asked America a fateful question. Her spirit is reaching far, far into the American mind, the way she did across thousands of miles into my home town, and she is touching millions of hearts and minds with a horrendous and heartbreaking question about America's future – not only as a democracy, but as a country where every human life is supposedly respected.

Can America answer that question?

Writers hold a key to that wracking question that New Orleans has become. Words are needed, whether the editorials expressing outrage, or the stories touching millions of hearts.

There is no doubt in my mind that New Orleans will rebuild. Even as the flood waters were finally receding, people were stating their intention to go home and rebuild. Among them were events producer Paul Willis and author Greg Herren, my friends, who announced that the Saints & Sinners Literary Festival would happen as usual in May 2006. There is no doubt that the port will be repaired – at enormous expense, of course – for the simple reason that the U.S. can't afford to write off a major port.

With government apathy still so glaringly obvious, citizen activism is stepping in. As I write this, 700 college students who had volunteered for debris removal are in St. Bernard Parish as part of a Habitat for Humanity project. TruthOut's Allie Deger, who went with them, said: "When I asked the students why they chose to spend their spring break gutting out houses in Louisiana rather than lying on the beach, they all shared the same lament: 'We cannot rely on this government, this administration to provide assistance to its citizens.'"

Will the new New Orleans be the warm humanist multicolored pulsating port city that it always was? Will it be a rebirth of the familiar city that dreamed awake all that jazz and wrought-iron balconies and the Jell-O shot? Will the street musicians and shrimp fishermen come back? Will Mardi Gras really be the same as before? I wonder. The new post-1700 London was not the same city as the old medieval London, but it became equally powerful in a new and unique way.

Will the spirit of New Orleans be driven away, so that those who value money more than human lives can build a cold tight-ass anti-ethnic anti-humanist post-millennial hub for big business?

Whatever the future holds for New Orleans, this anthology is part of that rebuilding. Those of us gay people who live in the city, and those of us who don't but who are the city's spiritual, more distant children, are part of that future, whether the Religious Right likes it or not. Our hopes and dreams get quietly tracked everywhere, like baby's breath seeds on people's shoes. We pop up everywhere, in the damnedest places. We're impossible to eradicate, impossible to resist. Like New Orleans, we are an irresistible, indestructible part of America.

There are new stories that only we can tell, and new ways of telling old stories that only we would know how to find.

TRAVELING LIGHT

Originally published in 9/1995 *LifeStyle*

Last year I experienced one of those cruel losses that hardened Angelenos know. To save my valuables from the November '93 Malibu fire, I put them in storage in L.A. There, on January 10, the Northridge earthquake came along and crunched them into oblivion.

To a writer and artist, the hurt was both professional and personal – unsold paintings, irreplaceable unpublished manuscripts and research materials, valuable books, family photographs, 15 years of business records. As I surveyed the rubble, I thought about my lifelong war against the tyranny of material things.

The story starts on a historic Montana ranch, in a 28-room Victorian mansion where a tomboy girl-child frowned as she watched her mother dust the bric-a-brac, bagatelles, horse jewelry, documents, memorabilia.

Swearing that I would spend my life writing, not dusting what-nots, I leaped into marriage and a 3-bedroom house. But, guess what – numerous family treasures stalked my trail.

In 1973, after 13 years of House Beautiful, with marriage gone bad and coming-out urgent, I threw typewriter, manuscript of *The Front Runner*, sleeping bag and a couple pairs of jeans into one of our two VWs, and headed for a Fire Island beachhouse. There, the board floor got cleaned with a broom. There was no dishwasher, no gimcracks or hoo-hahs. I lived on clams, and got to spend almost all my time writing and thinking.

Meanwhile, back in Montana, the National Park Service had termed the wondrously cluttered old ranch a "time capsule of Western history" – bought in 1975 and turned into a national park. Moi – I was now a refugee from artifacts. I figured the true valuables of my heritage were in my heart.

But somehow I edged back into acquisitive insanity–bought my own home in Duchess County, New York in 1976. True, it was only 2 bedrooms. But as I published books, it became the archetypical writer's retreat, bursting with chachkas, papers and electronic office widgets.

In 1980, choking on the clutter, I landed the book contract for *One Is the Sun*, and it needed research travel. With a screech of joy, I headed down the road in a pickup/camper. For two years, I carried my home on my back, like a turtle, and did all my writing on the camper table.

Settling in California in 1982, I sent for the New York kit and kaboodle and stored it in Sacramento, while I built a home in Nevada County. My dream house had just 800 square feet, and one bedroom.

On move-in day, I experienced what bullfighters call "the moment of truth." The old kaboodle wouldn't fit in the new house. Shocked at how much stuff I had, and what I'd spent to store it, I went wild – burned papers, unloaded chachkas on local antiquaries. Problem: a 17th century Flemish monastery cupboard, theoretically worth thousands, that absolutely nobody wanted, not even the local antique dealers. Solution: my brother Conrad helped me haul it to the county dump. As it toppled onto the trash, a spidery old man came scuttling, and loaded the thing into his pickup. Conrad and I watched with astonishment. Inventor, poet, and country boy, Conrad shares my passion for a life as lean as a hunting knife.

In 1991, I moved to Los Angeles County, and skinnied down further. My home is a sunny rented studio room, 450 sq. ft., where the only conversation piece is the Pacific view. Furnishings are sticks that would bring $50 at a yard sale. The only office finery is a PowerBook 170, printer and fax machine. Transport: a dusty Toyota pickup that I call the Silver Pony.

In late 1993, while firestorms consumed the Southland, I thought I was pretty well-prepared – valuables hustled to the L.A. storage, disk backups and a few banker's boxes and an emergency kit in my pickup. Fortunately, the Malibu fire stopped 1/2 mile from my house. Early on the morning of January 10, when the first big tremor hit, all I did was shakily crawl under my desk with the disk backups for my new novel *Harlan's Race* in my hot hand. Fortunately, the house survived the quake.

Two days later, my business partner called from L.A. to report that 20 billion tons of freeway were parked across our storage.

I have dealt with the heartbreak of the lost stuff. Now and then, a twinge does kick in. But lost paintings can be done over, and better too. I have my life, my friends, my PowerBook, and my fistful of backups.

Yet beyond the raw loss, there were still spooky questions of chachkas. In spring 1994, after our father's death, Conrad and I returned to Montana to handle the estate. The Park Service got their pick for the collection, of course. Conrad and I gingerly took a few mementos. Then we held one of the best-attended auctions in Montana history and sold every last damn horse-shoe nail.

"Don't you want any of this?" a family friend asked in distress, looking at the vista of Warren brummagems in the auction tent.

"Nope," we said.

As I used the estate-sale proceeds to start my own small publishing company, Wildcat Press, I felt all that cluttered history come full circle. A century ago, an American family counted itself lucky to live in a cabin, and to bequeath a few quilts and silver spoons to the kids. Today, the average heterosexual or homosexual couple slaves for a lifetime to own a big well-furnished house. They pay rent called "interest," then deed that house back to the bank so they can fund their old age. Dream homes are built outlandishly large; upkeep consumes enormous time and expense. And these post-Versailles mansions must be filled with piles of pinch-becks, and barricaded by burglar alarms.

On top of everything, Americans work like dogs to pay insurance and taxes on these frivolous fortresses. No wonder old people struggle frantically from under the woes of property, and want to spend their sunset in an RV.

When disaster strikes, as so often recently, loss is tremendous. But how much of this heartbreak, these "staggering losses" reported by the TV news, could be eased by less conspicuous consumption?

These days, my whole show fits in the Silver Pony. The Big One? At least I'll go to the Great Round with my backups in my hand. Riots? The looters can have my sticks of furniture. I don't even have a pet.

These are times for surviving. Nobody survives if they stop to grab their knickknacks. Amid our national worry with physical obesity, I ponder how spiritually, emotionally and mentally fat is our culture ... at a time when homeless people haunt our streets, and hunger casts its long shadow across the Earth. At times I wonder if the religious revival sweeping the country, and all those Biblical injunctions against laying up treasures on Earth, will have any effect on the national lunacy for sheer stuff.

In *Platoon*, veteran sergeant Elias helped the new grunts lighten their battle packs. He said: "Shit-can this ... you don't need this ... or this." Stuff went flying into the bushes.

Like Elias, life can teach us the wisdom of traveling light.

GRANDMA'S GARDEN IN MID-WILSHIRE

Originally published in 9/25/1996 *Wilshire Independent*

When my business partner and I moved to our L.A. city neighborhood three months ago, I had no idea that a flower garden would open doors to my new neighbors. It was my first time at city living – I've always been a country kid. City life seemed cold and impersonal. So we expected to be ignored by our neighbors.

The house was located in the Mid-Wilshire area, and was going to double as a business office and a home for myself and my business partner. The landscaping needed a major blast of magic. First, two guys with magic wands called machetes made some masses of roof-high pampas grass disappear so you could actually see the lovely old stucco facade. Then I studied the small front yard, with brick walk curving to the front door. Typical "award-winning California landscaping," with its plants turned into architecture, does not appeal to me. That kind of planting never looks lived in, or enjoyed.

What I wanted was flowers... bountiful bowers of them. Flowers that were accessible, non-architectural, that invited a person to pick a bouquet on the way to the doorbell. Random patches of mixed flowers, like my grandmother's garden had years ago on the ranch where I grew up. Grandma's garden was for actually wandering around in, sniffing fragrances in, and cutting a few stems for an "old fashioned" bouquet in the house. It had vegetables, too – Grandma didn't mind mixing in every vegetable known to humanity.

My business partner got into the magic too – he had a ranch and a grandma's garden in his own past. At Mortigans Nursery on 3rd Ave., we each loaded a cart with personal old-fashioned favorites. He picked phlox, carnations, begonias. I went for salvia, lobelia, fuschias. We agreed on lots of roses (and sniffed them to make sure they were fragrant varieties).

Our first inkling that we were wrong about city unfriendliness came as I toiled with my shovel, planting. Walking was popular on our neighborhood streets, so walkers started giving feedback – young couples with strollers, joggers with Walkmen, old European-born couples walking dogs or just keeping fit. As the boring grass in our yard gave way to a mass of bloom, vibrant with bees and hummingbirds, people started by leaning over the low stucco wall to chat. Even the mail woman and the UPS man couldn't resist taking a sniff at the roses.

"We wondered who was moving into this house."

"Glad you chopped down that awful grass."

"Your garden is so... different."

"Are those ONIONS? I never knew onions had such pretty flowers."

"We live around the corner – come and see us."

Even boys in baseball caps commented: "Cool!"

As we started visiting neighbors, an old-fashioned mixed bouquet or a sackful of squash was a good way to spread the magic. Flowers and produce from the supermarket lack the vibrancy of lovingly tended plants from a personal garden. When I helped with decorating at the Wilshire street fair that year, my bouquet glowed on the neighborhood association's table, and one of the women took it home afterwards.

This experience has got me thinking. In days gone by, yards were for the practical and the personal, not for display. To have a bit of land was precious – you crammed every inch of it with life-giving vegetables and spirit-gladdening flowers, and you shared it around. How much more livable and human would Los Angeles be today, how much more warmly knit our neighborhoods, if more people had grandma's gardens instead of pretentious little plots of grass?

CALIFORNIA DREAMIN' ON

Written in 2003 on assignment for a new California magazine that never got launched

It's no accident that the worst wildfires in state history hit us at the same time as political wildfires of the recall election that replaced Governor Gray Davis (Democrat) with Governor Arnold Schwarzenegger. Thousands of families saw their dreams of the good life swept away in firestorms raging across San Bernardino County. There are 22 dead, hundreds injured, 80,000 evacuees, several towns wiped out, nearly 3600 homes lost. Estimated cost: $2 billion and counting, with fears that the fires might bankrupt the state. Now winter rainstorms loom, threatening mudslides. Angry citizens are asking the usual question, "How can we keep this from happening again?" But few are asking one loaded political question: Why are so many Californians living in these fire-ridden areas to begin with?

Answer to the question: because our state's land-use policy is stupid, uncaring and dangerous to us all.

Californians need to get back to some life-and-death basics about land use that have been slowly forgotten over the last 50 years. Otherwise, like the flooded-out fools who always rebuild their homes on a flood plain, they will set themselves up for the next round of disaster. Land-use policy has to underlie *everything* in the daily life of people living in any state. We need reality about the land herself – the California earth – *how* people use it, *why* they live on it, *where* the land's future is going. As a result of our neglect and unthinking, the land is trying fiercely to get our attention, and the wildfires get worse every year.

I first saw California in 1949 – a breathless 13-year-old Montanan whose ranch family had arrived to spend Christmas with relatives in Orange County. Used to the long bitter Montana winters, I was awed by the orange groves in bloom in December, by the rich black volcanic soil that burgeoned crops year round – alfalfa and lettuce and rice and onions. In Costa Mesa, then a sleepy little post-war development, the endless bean fields surged right up to my aunt's backyard picket fence.

The American dream of "going west and finding gold" ended its historical journey in California. But the real California gold was never that yellow ore. It was the land, and its wonderful climate, and how people used the land for profit. The first Spanish ranchers, the first Anglo miners could make it big because they stole their land from the Indians.

Over the years, some of my own family did good in "Caliprunia," as Montanans called it. After World War II my aunt and ex-Marine uncle, who were general contractors, made it big in the Orange County construction boom. My brother and one of my cousins made it in the engineering and electronics boom, as it sprawled across northern California. You could even make it big as a retiree, spending your final years cozily in Santa Barbara, as my Montana godfather and godmother did. But however you made it big in California, it was always because of land.

In 1980, now age 44, after decades of working in the New York media, I journeyed here to stake my own share of the California dream. But I found a state that seemed to be forgetting the frailty of what that dream was really based on. Californians liked to brag that the state was the #1 agricultural producer and exporter in the United States – and #12 in the world, a powerhouse to feed the hungry. By 1999 production values were still reaching $26.7 billion, with California growing more than Texas and Iowa combined. But if you factored the exploding California population into the math, plus growing U.S. food imports – 60 percent of our produce, 40 percent of our meat – those California brags started looking a little shaky.

The fact is, those rich farmlands and ranchlands that turned

California into a global food market were being chewed up by rampant housing and industrial development. Vistas of orchards and bean fields that I remembered in Orange County were gone – vanished under a concrete desert of tracts, malls and freeways. According to the Agricultural Issues Center of the University of California, between 1988 and 1998 the state lost around half a million acres of farmland to urban development.

True, some wary souls in agriculture did try to shelter farmland by putting it in trust. But this protective effort sent an even hairier trend into motion: developers simply said there wasn't enough farmland to develop, so they pushed their plot-mapping into the wild lands of California. With a seemingly endless supply of "open available frontier" out there, California cities let decay creep into their inner-city real estate. Result: hundreds of businesses relocated, and thousands of upper-and-middle families sought the good life out of town. Those brushy hills and mountains were so beautiful, so inviting, so private, so cheap by the quarter section.

The problem was – those brushy hills and mountains are designed by Mother Nature to burn every 6-7 years.

By contrast, Europe – where I lived for a time in the 1960s – has her teeming millions squashed onto a small outworn continent whose last frontier vanished in the Middle Ages. Europeans have already hit the wall big-time on land-use policy. For decades now, from across the pond, they've watched with astonishment as we ever-more-extravagent-and-wasteful Americans paved over more and more of our agricultural land and let our cities go to decay. At the heart of European Union organizing is intelligent life-and-death reality about land use, including protection of as much farmland as possible.

For California, this growing perilous imbalance between a people's needs and industry's wants are being driven by a hungry construction industry that is also a powerful political lobby. But the voters have been party to this peril too, because the construction industry builds what people want.

Developers' excuse for their building frenzy is that California is now the nation's most populous state (over 34 million people) and the fastest growing. Through the year 2020, the U.S. Census Bureau says that California will grow by the largest percentage of any state. The California Department of Finance projects that

Californians will swell to nearly 59 million people by 2040, mainly in formerly agricultural regions of the state.

But when the buildable farmland is gone – as it will be soon in the Imperial Valley, and in the Central Valley if Sacramento and Bakersfield keep on expanding – Californians will keep on carving deeper and deeper into that wild fire-prone land in their undisciplined, unplanned search for housing space. They will forget the horrible lessons of the San Bernardino fires. And when the next fires come, with those vast smoke plumes towering into the atmosphere and visible hundreds of miles out to sea on satellite photos, the media will go into their usual hysteria and ask, "Why did this happen? How can we prevent it from happening again?"

Yes, the 20 dead people, the hundreds of injured, the 3600 homes lost – these are the price that we've paid for fifty years of unintelligent land-use policy.

For myself, I've found a personal solution to the wildfire danger. From 1991 to 1996 I had lived in Malibu, fabled Malibu with its world-class brushy hills. There I rented studio space in a friend's $5-million custom home atop a ridge. After living through the 1992 Topanga firestorm, and several other world-class fires that burned right up to the next ridge, I finally said nuts to Malibu and moved into West Los Angeles.

I may not be safe from earthquakes here, but at least I'm safe from wildfires and mudslides! My congenial, urban, ethnically diverse neighborhood, built in the 1920s, is a great place to live. It's reviving itself with fixing-upping and curb-appeal jobs. People value it for good schools, for proximity to the Farmer's Market and The Grove. In fact, the residents actually go for walks here. Not only do they walk their dogs, but they can walk to anything you need, whether it's banks or hospitals or one of 3rd Avenue's 40-plus restaurants, or Museum Row on nearby Wilshire Boulevard. People know their neighbors. They look out for one another.

Living in this part of L.A. has made me realize that Californians CAN make their cities work. And if they can make cities livable for human beings, we can leave those brushy dangerous hills to the deer and California quail.

COOKING

DREAM SOUP

Originally published in *Food for Life... and Other Dishes*, edited by Lawrence Schimel (Cleis Press, 1996)

Where food is concerned, nothing is more magical than things that I grow myself.

Partly it's an old ranch thing – I grew up watering and weeding a vast World War II "victory garden" that fed a whole ranch – both family and hired men.

Partly it's a gay thing. Over the years, I've pondered on the love that so many LGBT people feel for good eating, and for making a piece of our planet beautiful and fruitful by having a garden. Maybe the social agony that we experience has left many of us feeling cut off from Life. So we make a super-human effort to get back in touch with the roots of existence. We can do this with food, gardening and a closeness with the Land. In my novel *The Front Runner*, when coach Harlan Brown and runner Billy Sive moved into a house together, they took possession of the yard as well – and planted a garden.

At any rate, home-grown food is far better tasting and less chemically polluted than commercial food. My Native American relatives always had gardens, even the poor ones on the reservation, who ate prairie dogs to stay alive during lean times. Some of the most wonderful stories that they shared with me were about food (including a hundred ways to cook prairie dog).

Dream Soup is a kind of soup/stew that some Western tribes call *posole* (pronounced po-so-lay). You can vary it with what's in the garden, on the shelf, in the fridge or freezer.

Corn is the key ingredient – its very spirit, its *número uno*. To say "corn" in the many languages of the First Nations is to say "mother," because its young juice is like milk. Most Americans eat corn in that baby stage. So they don't have a clue how tasty corn is when it goes starchy on the ear, yet still soft enough to cook in an hour or so.

I learned a lot about corn in the early 1980s, when I was researching my Western historical novel *One Is the Sun*. I visited a friend in the Santo Domingo pueblo on the Rio Grande during the Corn Dances. All of us were eating mature boiled corn, with *posole* on the side, till we almost burst. Every little kid wandered around carrying an ear of corn, gnawing on it. It was their answer to the candy bar. Truly we have lost the ability to enjoy the essence of corn, without butter or other white-man frills.

To be stored indefinitely, corn must be dried hard, like beans. To cook it, you have to soak it overnight, just like beans, and cook it till tender. This "parched corn" (as the anthros call it) is what kept Native Americans alive for thousands of years. Treated with lye water, corn turns to hominy.

Since those *One Is the Sun* years, I always try to grow some corn wherever I live, and carry with me a few dried ears of Golden Bantam for seed. Golden Bantam is a short compact plant with small ears, an old variety that's been around for centuries. It makes a beautiful and ornamental planting in a suburban flowerbed if that's the only place you've got to grow vegetables. And it matures fast – 75 days. Plant a few seeds once a week from last frost until mid-July, and you will have waves of ripening corn for one feast a week through the season. Corn likes sun and rich soil and adequate water. It grows well in wild riotous pagan intermixings with other plants, like squash and beans and tomatoes.

Meat is *número dos* in *posole*, and gives it body. When I was sent to visit a Medicine chief and his family on the Navajo Reservation in the 1980s, they fed me *posole* made with desert-bred mutton. That sheep had lived on the desert for years, nibbling all kinds of tough desert plants, so the meat had a wild sagey taste. The *posole* was served up with a platter of smoking hot fry bread. That meal stands out in my memory as one of the best things I ever ate.

But you can make *posole* with beef, pork, lamb, venison, poultry, rabbit, whatever meat you happen to have on hand. That's what The People did in the old days.

Herbs are important. The old people added whatever herbs were around, so there is no fixed list. Put in the ones you like. Dried or fresh is okay.

There is no "one, single, correct way" to make *posole*, just like there is no one, single correct way to make New England clam chowder. Many different recipes can be found online. Surprise – there is no onion or garlic in this *posole* recipe, which I was given as a gift. I asked one of my Indian aunties why. She said that the old-time cooks didn't always use onions. And garlic, she pointed out, is a European introduction.

"You can get the taste of the meat and corn a lot better," she said, "if you don't smother it in onion."

In short, your own imagination, and knowledge of your own personal and subtle tastes, are challenged by this dish. It's also a dish that gets better with re-heating.

DREAM SOUP (POSOLE)

1 large soup pot
equal amounts of the following: cubes of your favorite meat, cubed potatoes, diced tomatoes and cut fresh corn (or cooked hominy)
fresh or dried herbs (thyme and oregano are good ones)
several cubes of good quality beef extract
spring water to cover
sea salt to taste
pepper to taste
optional: New Mexico hot chilis – whatever kind you've got.

Lightly brown the meat in a heavy skillet without fat, moving it with a fork to keep it from burning. Layer the meat in the kettle alternately with the potatoes, tomatoes and corn. Sprinkle the herbs, spices, salt and crushed beef cubes over the top. Add water till it barely covers the kettle contents and spices. Deglaze the skillet with a little water or broth, and add this liquid to the pot.

Bring slowly to a simmer, cover and simmer over low heat till the meat and corn are tender. Do not stir. This keeps the pieces of meat and vegetable intact. The spices will simmer slowly down to the bottom of the kettle.

Serve in large bowls with big soup spoons, and your favorite hot bread on the side. Recipes for different types of Indian fry bread can be found online.

Note: If you are going all the way and using dried corn, soak it and simmer it separately until close to done, before combining it with the *posole*.

A BOUNTEOUS MEAL

Originally published in *Montana Magazine*, October 1991

It is easy to romanticize about "the good old days," and forget how hard one woman worked to make a family meal in 1869. Today, my great-grandmother's ranch kitchen, her Victorian paraphernalia of cookware, her recipes, and the legacy of her creative thrift, is a national treasure–part of a national park in Montana. There, visitors can see what pioneer ranching and cooking were really like.

I grew up on the ranch there at Deer Lodge, in the 1940s, when my great-grandmother was still alive. Yet, today's culinary age is so radically remote from hers, that I have to fight to understand why Victorian women spent so much time in the kitchen, and why they appreciated food in a way that many people today do not.

Real Victorian food is eclipsed today, because it is so laden with carbohydrates and saturated fats. But the Victorians needed exactly that kind of diet to survive. The hard physical work done by 90 percent of society, especially the Western settlers, meant that fat and cholesterol plagued no one but the rich and idle.

Most importantly, the people who ate Victorian food lived – and ate – much closer to Life.

Butter, for instance.

In the spring of 1869, when 18-year-old Augusta Kruse Kohrs arrived in Montana Territory, there were still millions of buffalo in that vast stretch of wild land–but only a few dozen milk cows in trading forts and gold camps. Therefore, if she was to have a quarter cup of butter for a pan of *Apfelkuchen*, Augusta must conjure cows into her life.

And she would have to learn about cows, for she was a city girl, born in Altona, on the Elbe River in Holstein, then part of Denmark. Daughter of two freethinking and impoverished Germans – a midwife and a composer – she had emigrated to Iowa to escape the repressions of Prussian expansion in northern Europe. She had an education unusual for women of her time, and a keen and creative mind.

After working as a governness, she decided to marry another young German emigrant, Conrad Kohrs. He was visiting relatives in Iowa, and Augusta found him suitably democratic and kind. His stories of the beautiful free West, and his growing cattle trade there, intrigued her.

Now, as Augusta climbed stiffly out of the Daugherty wagon in which she and her new husband had jounced over hundreds of rocky miles, her keen mind was on milk cows.

The Precious Cow

However restrictive on women the Victorian age was, its women had kept a tight hold on cow care. Cows kept children alive. Cow care needed the deep, feminine demand for perfect cleanliness.

The profound 19th century love of the milk cow, and the placing of poetic flower garlands around her horns, is not understood by today's suburbanites and lovers of "country life," who never see the cows whose store-bought milk they drink. In the countryside of 1869, if you had milk, it was from your own cow.

A good milk cow is precious beyond all counting – a goddess of bounty, one of Earth's most wondrous gifts to humans. The death of that cow – from wolves, milk fever, injury or gun shots – was a disaster that impacted the bodies, minds, emotions and spirits of an entire family. It was no wonder that Augusta's Teutonic ancestors regarded the cow as a sacred symbol of Life.

Unlike many pioneer brides, who arrived at a canvas tent or log cabin, my great-grandmother walked into a regular carpentered house – one of the first in the territory.

At that time, Montana was still wild, with many roving Indian camps and only a few gold towns and forts. There were no railroads yet. In fact, there was little communication with "the States" at all, save by slow-moving freight wagon, stagecoach, telegraph, Missouri River steamboat, or travelers on horseback who agreed to carry letters.

The house was a former trading post, dating from 1862, built in Hudson's Bay Company style by a wealthy mixed-blood trader. True, it was unpainted, already horribly weathered. The bare furnishings included a pie-safe, a rosewood dining table and chairs, and an iron cook stove.

South of the house, Augusta's sharp eyes spotted a little pasture with a pole fence around it. The trader, John Grant, had created that marvel of white-man engineering for his own milk cows. In 1866, Grant had sold his home to Kohrs, who turned it into the rough-and-ready headquarters of his young cattle ranch, the CK.

Right now, the pasture enclosed her husband's best horses.

When Augusta Kohrs hiked up her dusty skirts and entered the house, she immediately wrinkled her nose with distaste. For three years, it had been the barbarian lair of bachelors, namely Kohrs and his half-brother John Bielenberg, and a male cook. It was full of unwashed dishes, dogs, horse gear, dust and bedbugs.

Kohrs and Bielenberg, building their business, had never taken the time to eat more than pemmican, or steaks and bannack bread fried in tallow. The only milk they had tasted was at a mountain man's cabin down the valley, where a single cow lived. There, at the blackmail prices of the frontier, the brothers happily traded a quarter of beef for a few cups of milk.

The few Métis (mixed-bloods) remaining in the valley referred to cow milk by the poetic Indian name of "grass-flower juice."

Now Augusta decided that her precious books and sheet music, and a bit of heirloom silver, would stay packed in her trunk as yet. Instead, she unpacked her biggest apron and her oldest everyday dress.

As she started boiling water and killing bedbugs, she briskly issued an order in the best Prussian manner: "*Ich muss eine Kuh bestizen!* I must have a cow! The little pasture will be for my cow. And," she announced to Conrad, "you will dismiss the man cook. I am now the cook."

"*Jawohl!*" replied her husband respectfully.

Augusta, being the young cosmopolitan, was determined to turn this rough ranch into a glowing center of beauty, kindness, comfort and culture. Someday she would even have a piano, so that she could play her favorite Wagnerian arias! And she would have every culinary marvel of the day ... even though, for a time, she'd have to do most of the hard work herself.

For now, just baking a simple pan of *Apfelkuchen* presented a myriad of challenges. Her recipe for *Apfelkuchen*, a dessert that is to Germans what apple pie is to Americans, called for:

3 cups dried or fresh apples
2 cups sugar
1/4 cup butter
6 eggs
1 large cup dry bread crumbs
½ lemon, juice and rind
1 tsp vanilla

For the quarter cup of butter, here is what had to happen:

Mounting his fastest road horse, Kohrs scoured the country, and found someone with two unbranded milk cows to trade. At the blackmail prices prevailing on the frontier, where everything a white person might want was scarce, an ordinary beef steer traded for $100 in gold dust. But these good milk cows cost Kohrs a fortune – maybe closer to $200 a head. This is the equivalent of around $15,000 in buying power today!

Augusta's first cows may have been Guernseys. Their origins were obscure, and one did not ask too many questions. Maybe some migrating Mormons had trailed them in from a farm in Deseret. Or maybe they had been stolen from a mission or an army fort by enterprising Indians, who then traded them to a Métis trader for one of the new repeating rifles.

The CK brand was quietly applied to the cows' sleek golden hides. Then, ceremoniously, with all CK hands assembled for the great event, the milk cows were loosed in the little pasture.

"*Ach du lieber*...how beautiful they are!" Augusta said.

The protective fence was built of lodgepole pines that were cut and traded by the valley's last free Indians and Métis. It enclosed some rich bottom-land along the Deer Lodge River. Stock stealing was rampant, so the ranch always kept a guard posted at night, like an army fort.

Augusta now issued further orders. The cows were to be kept scrupulously clean. Their hindquarters were to be washed every day! There would be no brown flecks in her milk!

So Kohrs built Augusta a little log milking barn. The barn sheltered the milker from Montana blizzards, and the milk from blowing dust. Local wolves were killed, to keep them from killing the precious cows. Twice a day, punctually, the hired man drove them to the barn. Time, tides and milk cows wait for no one. If a cow isn't milked on time, her udder can burst.

At first, Augusta was the one to wrap her city-bred fingers, so skilled at the piano, around the teats of her cows. With time, she trusted the most careful of the men to do this critical job.

Milking done, she heated the milk to pasteurize it (as an educated European, she had heard of Louis Pasteur's discoveries about bacteria in milk). Then she skimmed the cream from the milk. Water was hauled from the spring and heated, and all milking utensils scalded clean. The milk and cream were poured into precious metal cans, and set in the nearby spring to cool.

To heat water, wood had to be split (the hired men did that), and fires tended in the cook stove (Augusta did that).

When the cream was aged a few days, my great-grandmother spent part of a morning churning it to butter in the wooden churn. She saved the buttermilk for drinking and baking. Then she washed the butter in clear spring water, kneaded it to remove the water, molded it in a decorative wooden mold that she had brought with her, and set it to chill.

Finally the churn had to be scalded out and aired.

To all this, veterinary care of the cows must be added. For instance, jars of a wondrous substance called Bag Balm were among the "stateside" goods brought in by freight wagons. Bag Balm contained wool fat, and kept the cows' teats soft.

Since Augusta scoured her plank floors with a holystone and lye, she probably used a lot of Bag Balm on her hands, too.

Because the cows ate whatever was growing in the river-bottoms, their milk shifted hues of taste from season to season – not like today, when cows from New York to Los Angeles are fed the same kind of bagged commercial feed, and their milk tastes the same no matter what time of year it is. But in springtime, when the Montana meadowlarks sang and the wild plants came springing up lushly in the bottoms, the milk of Augusta's cows tasted like bunch grass and wild onions. In summer, it tasted more of clover and yarrow.

The men put up hay for her cows to winter on. Unlike the range cattle, and the cayuses that everyone rode, the gentle Guernseys were not expected to paw into the snow for food.

Augusta's Pantry

By and by, as the ranch grew, the cows proliferated into a small herd that was worth many bars of pure gold. Meanwhile, similar towers of human effort went into building her pantry, so she could assemble other ingredients in that first pan of *Apfelkuchen*.

The six eggs, for instance. Augusta's first chickens were descendants of a few hens and a rooster imported in crates in a bumping wagon, by John Grant's trader father, clear from Fort Hall, Idaho. A rooster and hen, at the get-rich-quick prices, went for $75, or about $5,000 in today's buying power.

As for the bread-crumbs, she made her own by drying bread leftovers in her oven, and crushing them with a rolling pin. The crumbs were kept in a tin.

Yeast starter for bread? She got it from a Métis woman neighbor. On cold winter nights, she had to remember to take it to bed with her, or it would freeze.

The dried apples? They voyaged in wooden crates all the way from northern California, or Washington.

The flour and sugar? These came from Salt Lake City in Mormon freight wagons, and sold for $12 a hundredweight. At one point, speculation had driven flour prices up to $80 a hundredweight, causing riots in the Montana camps. Vigilante groups seized flour from speculators, and distributed it to the people.

The single lemon? It came all the way from California by express stagecoach, and probably cost $5 – if Augusta could get it. As a measure, a common horse or a rifle cost $50 in 1870. Today, an average kind of gun costs $500, which would make that lemon worth $50 in today's supermarkets.

Augusta regarded that lemon as an extravagance, and she did without it until the Kohrses were wealthy. A poorer woman couldn't have afforded it at all.

Vanilla beans? Those fragrant seed-pods of a tropical orchid wended all the way north from the Yucatan, where they were harvested by Mexican slave labor. A single bean cost $2 by the time it got to Montana.

Sometime in the fall of 1869, that first fragrant pan of *Apfelkuchen* came from the oven.

The hungry women and men, assembled at the battered old rosewood table, surely must have watched with shining eyes as Augusta served the steaming delicacy onto their few precious china plates, using one of the prized coin-silver spoons brought from Altona. Then – oh, most incredible marvel of all – Augusta topped the *Apfelkuchen* with spoonfuls of ... whipped cream!

How can a person of today, accustomed to casually squirting anemic supermarket whippo out of aerosol cans, possibly understand what this homemade luxury meant to Augusta's table guests?

The wondrous dessert followed a main course that was usually beef, of course.

Coming from tiny Europe, where pastures are small and cattle belong mainly to the well-to-do, Augusta must have been stunned at the growing Montana opulence of millions of cattle, that ranged across millions of square miles of open grass country.

However, she recovered quickly, and adapted some of her favorite Prussian recipes for American beef and veal.

Good pork came to her from a local packing plant started by her husband's brother Henry Kohrs. Thousands of squealing porkers lost their lives on the Emigrant Road – killed by wolves, bears, Indians, overturned wagons, kicking horses, hunger and thirst – before enough survived to stock the first Northwest ranches.

But game meat? No. By the time she came West, the game had been devastated in vast areas, by millions of hungry emigrants who picked the deer bones like army ants.

On the back of her stove, a huge pot-au-feu was kept simmering. Thrifty Augusta tossed every knuckle bone and peeling into it, with precious Jamaica peppercorns, and herbs gathered from the meadows. According to German custom, the evening meal was always light, and it was often soup – beef broth with rice, or barley soup, or black bean soup.

Augusta's Garden

That very first year of 1869, she began the creation of her kitchen garden.

In this, she was helped by a CK man with a borrowed plow, and a tall picket fence to keep out cattle and whitetail deer. A "cattle-boy" on a fast cayuse was sent speeding to the trading post at Hell Gate, 50 miles away, to get vegetable and flower seeds. The joy of eating the first crunchy young cabbages, delicate lettuce, sweet carrots and peas and peppery turnips can hardly be described.

Her garden herbs included medicinals. Like many emigrant women, she knew the arts of healing teas, and had brought packets of tea seeds from Germany. Among them was mullein, known to her as *Koenigskerze.*

Trading with some neighbor woman, she got a few roots of that indestructible frontier delicacy – rhubarb, known to pioneers as "pie plant."

For sweets, she and her three growing children – and her German governess, when she could afford one – gathered the wild fruits of the hills. In season, there were wild huckleberries, Oregon grape, tiny strawberries, gooseberries. Precious glass jars, and wax for air-tight seals, provided them with preserves. The chokecherries that ripened on small trees along the river made a delicious syrup for pancakes.

But cultivated fruits needed a lot more time and patience to get into Montana.

Fresh apples, for instance. Wagonloads of baby orchard trees, carefully watered along the way, came jouncing in from Washington and Oregon, to start the fine orchards in the mild valleys around Flathead Lake, which still produce today. But the Deer Lodge Valley was too high and cold for growing all but crabapples. Not until those imported trees bore their first fruit was Augusta able to bake *Apfelkuchen* with her own fresh apples.

Augusta's creativity provided good eating for the ranch hands of the growing ranch, as well as her growing family.

Some cow outfits fed their men poorly, and were infamous for it – even shunned by cowboys looking for work. But Augusta put out bounteous meals for CK cowboys. She wouldn't have it said that she didn't take care of her people. In later years, the CK bunkhouse had male cooks again – Chinese, Irish, German. Whatever their nationality, they had to meet her German standards of *putzig* and cleanliness.

During those years, the Kohrses grew wealthy, and returned from trips to New York and Europe with beautiful china, tableware, paintings and sculptures – even a piano – to beautify their home. And they obtained a set of brass Swiss cow bells, the finest available. The bells were beautifully engraved with rococo flowers and leaves. Each bell had a different tone – some high, and others low. Each cow had her bell song. At milking time, when the cows headed determinedly up the road to the milking barn, heads swinging, they sounded like a Wagnerian opera chorus.

By 1889, with 12,000 steers a year going to the Chicago markets, the Kohrses were wealthy enough to add a brick wing to the old clapboard trading post. Central to the brick addition, Augusta designed a huge new state-of-the-art kitchen, a butler's pantry, and a big oak-paneled dining room that could seat up to 30 people.

Beneath the new wing, in the deep-dug rock-walled basement, she wanted a whole plant for food processing and storage – mechanical milk separator, big sinks for scalding, root cellar, wine cellar, and a shelved commissary for storing bags and boxes. A walk-in cooler held a whole beef and dozens of cans of milk and cream. It operated with native ice, sawed in blocks from the frozen river every winter, and stored in a pit under sawdust.

On the sunny south side of the brick wing was a structure that Augusta had dreamed of having ever since she came to Montana. Her dream was a natural one, in a land where cold weather lasts for nine months of the year. Walled in glass, heated by a woodstove, the greenhouse delighted her with flowers through the winter, and pots of parsley and other fresh herbs.

Amid all this food creation, Augusta Kohrs found time to raise three children, help manage the ranch, educate and care for dozens of frontier orphans, read Schiller and Goethe, bring opera to Montana's capital, build a wing on the capital's only hospital, help Theodore Roosevelt campaign for president in Montana – and agitate for the vote for Montana women. Often, too, she embroidered sumptuous tablecloths, to add more beauty to her bountiful meals. In the center of the table, her own flowers always fountained from a sparkling bowl of cut crystal.

With time, as her husband took a seat in the state legislature, she had her "salon," entertaining leading lawmakers and artists at her table. If food was music at the CK, then Augusta Kohrs was the composer and the conductor, with all the Wagnerian grandeur of her time.

When I was born in 1936, Augusta was still alive – a stately old lady of nearly 90. Husband long dead, wealthy and independent, she no longer put in the endless hours of work in order to eat. She and her housekeeper shared simple meals every day – but she still loved to spread vast banquets for her family. And the meals still used good Guernsey milk and butter.

Like Queen Thusnelda

I remember being a small child at these Germanic feasts, at which she presided like Queen Thusnelda of ancient times, whose portrait hung in the sitting room. I was awed, craning my neck to see her over the roast turkey.

Over the years, Augusta's thrift infected us, too. Little of her cookware was ever thrown out. Even her most battered coin-silver spoons and paring knives, dating from those early years, survived to become "historical artifacts," along with her gilt-edged cow bells, and her favorite cut-glass bowl, twin to one now in the Metropolitan Museum.

In 1945, she died – a spirit whose cup in Valhalla surely had a dash of vanilla in it.

In 1977, the National Park Service purchased the oldest CK buildings, and opened them to the public. As a tribute to the importance of food at the CK, the GKRO staff brought life and "authenticity" to the house by having fresh bread on the kitchen table for visitors to see. They keep the greenhouse lush with flowers and pots of herbs. In the old garden, the original "pie plants" still brandish their crimson stalks. The stately golden spikes of mullein, descendants of escapees from her garden, grow wild along the railroad tracks near Augusta's old house.

Today, as Americans buy butter in a supermarket, how many people think of the life of a cow?

DELIGHT AND DANGER OF CHILE PEPPERS

Part of a "Victory Garden" series originally published in 2009 at Bilerico Project (www.bilerico.com)

The fiery colors of autumn come to the garden a little early... in the form of peppers getting ripe. With the Labor Day holiday hitting America, many of us are going to be doing family feasts or cookouts, and the menu is sure to include chile peppers in some form. I have a mad, wild love for these giant berries, especially the hot variety. They are easy to grow, as colorful as flowers, fascinating to look at – not to mention the adventure of eating them.

Did you know that people have been chowing down on chiles for 7000 years? That the hot pepper is multi-purpose – staple, spice, disinfectant, preservative, health food, medicine, even a weapon? Neither did I, till some years ago, when I was introduced to chile growing by Arizona writer/book reviewer Ken Furtado, who wrote for *Echo Magazine* for many years.

Around 8 or 9 years ago, I met Ken while on visit to Phoenix on book tour. Ken invited me to his home, where he had cooked a whole spread of traditional Hispanic dishes. It was another of the best meals I ever ate in my life. As we toured his herb garden, Ken proudly showed me his splendid jalapeño plant, which was big as a rosebush. He explained that it was five years old already. Every Southwest family – including his own Hispanic ancestors, who'd been living there for a couple of centuries – once kept a collection of pepper plants going in their home garden, he said.

Back at my own L.A. home, I planted my first jalapeños and learned that pepper plants do indeed live for many years in milder climates. Today I have a dozen and a half varieties going – more than I can eat or even give away. From the purple-brown poblanos to the lemon-yellow banana peppers, they're like an edible flower garden. Especially the sweet bell peppers, a group that evolved to the biggest size, but without the hot kick – they come in literally every color of the rainbow.

In short, I grow chile peppers partly for the hell of it. I can't help myself.

Unique History of Peppers

All varieties come from the genus *Capsicum*. Peppers are one of the Americas' great food gifts to the world...along with corn, squash, tomatoes, potatoes, avocados, pineapples, peanuts and two dozen other food plants that were domesticated by First Nation peoples of Central and South America. Archeologists have found traces of chile use going back for nearly 7000 years.

From American shores, via the Spanish and Portuguese, peppers spread like culinary wildfire around the world, to be adopted hungrily into cuisines on every continent, from China to Western Europe. There, the local agronomists developed new varieties. In Hungary, meat stew becomes "goulash" with the addition of paprika, a spice made from a mix of bell peppers and wax peppers. In Italy, chile pepper seeds are sprinkled as a garnish. In Spain, cooks do all kinds of things with big red pimientos, like stuff them with *bacalao* (codfish).

A pepper's intensity can actually be measured by a scientific yardstick called Scoville heat units. According to Wikipedia, "Bell peppers rank at 0 SHU, jalapeños at 3,000-6,000 SHU, and habaneros at 300,000 SHU. The record for the hottest chili pepper was assigned by the *Guinness Book of Records* to the Naga Jolokia, measuring over 1,000,000 SHU." The near-lethal Naga was developed in Dorset, England, from a variety popular in Bangladesh.

That active ingredient, capsaicin, is what makes your eyes tear, your nose run, your heart pound and your body break an explosive sweat when you bite into a habanero. Which is why pure capsaicin, at 16 million SHU, is used in pepper spray and can incapacitate a mugger instantly. It also kills bacteria...which is why cooks rub chile powder on meats.

Growing Peppers Is Easy

In my space-conscious city garden in West L.A., chiles do well in window boxes or big pots. They prefer full sun, but also thrive in bright dappled shade – in fact, it's surprising how much shade they can tolerate. Requirements: a well-drained fertile soil. Regular watering when they need it. Don't let them sit in soggy soil, though, or they develop root rot. And they appreciate being fertilized.

Do I have a favorite? It's an heirloom variety, the balloon pepper. I found a baby plant at my local garden center. It grows into a woody shrub about 3 feet tall, the size of a smallish hybrid-tea rose. Every summer and fall, it stays so covered with deep-red peppers that visitors often mistake it for a flowering rosebush. The fruit is shaped like a pouch about an inch and a half wide. It has a bit more heat than wax peppers, but not much, and a mellow fruity flavor that I'd describe as kinda mango.

In a mild climate like California, pepper plants will live through the winter outdoors. My oldest sweet bells and hot chiles are five-six years old and still going strong. In spring, I just prune them like rosebushes, and give them a shot of steer manure, and off they go. Once they start popping those distinctive star-like flowers, they continue fruiting for the rest of the season...which is well into winter in California. At Thanksgiving, I harvest the last of the balloon peppers for a favorite stuffing recipe.

In a more frigid climate, you can try bringing your chile plants indoors for the winter, and keep them in a sunny window.

They don't transplant well, so start them in the pots that you plan to bring indoors.

Health Do's and Don'ts

Chile peppers are loaded with Vitamins A & C. These helped ancient American peoples to eyesight health, as well as scurvy prevention in a part of the world where citrus-fruit culture was unknown. Capsaicin was also known to be a natural anesthetic, and is still used that way today. A gay male friend of mine who was living with AIDS told me how he managed the intense pain of neuropathy in his feet by using a salve containing capsaicin. His doctor felt this was a better choice than the standard painkillers like codeine, which are addicting.

A word of caution: when you clean the hot chiles, wear kitchen gloves. The insides of the hot peppers – juices, pulp, seeds – can actually burn your hands. And once you cut a hot pepper open, that capsaicin vaporizes into the air, so it can make your eyes and lungs burn if you bend over the peppers and breathe that air. Wash your hands right after handling them, and don't touch your eyes before washing.

Don't ask me what a thousand generations of Indian cooks did before they had rubber gloves. But they must have had a technique for protecting their hands from burning.

Once peppers are cleaned for cooking, I never discard the seeds – just throw them back into the garden, and get quite a few volunteers the next spring.

Cooking With Peppers

An encyclopedia can be written on this subject. Peppers can go into everything, and with everything – soups, stews, salads, garnishes, cheese spreads, appetizers, jams and jellies, even desserts. Dessert? Oh yeah. In my favorite *Fanny Farmer Cookbook* recipe for old-fashioned gingerbread, a teaspoonful of cayenne powder goes into the batter along with ginger and other spices. Kicks it up a notch, as Emeril says.

Peppers have spawned a global trade in hot sauces – from the "fire oil" of China and Thailand, to the jerk sauces of Jamaica. And there's America's own Tabasco Sauce – invented in 1868 by the McIlhenny family of Louisiana from tabasco peppers that they grew locally. Anyone with a love of culinary risk can find websites where these bottled sauces from all over the world can be purchased – thousands of brands, mostly made by small family-owned companies.

In another Victory Garden episode, I talked about preserving fruit. Well, peppers are fruits. To keep your surplus through the winter, you can do what Indian and Hispanic families have done for centuries – get a big needle and some stout string, and make strings of peppers, and hang them in a cool shady place to dry. They reconstitute easily when you soak them in water or throw them into soup.

I've also made a type of confit with Hungarian wax peppers. They need to be ripe and bright red. Here's how to make it:

Take a couple dozen peppers, cut them in half, and clean these strips of inner pulp and seeds. Put 2 cups of good olive oil into a deep skillet, and sautee the halves very gently in the oil, together with 2 cups of pearl onions and a little salt and garlic. Move the vegetables around constantly and don't let them brown. When they're just tender, cool them and pack them in a clean jar or plastic container with all the oil. Store them in the refrigerator.

These strips of red pepper confit make a tasty garnish for steaks, burgers, potato salads, etc.

Getting Started

For the post-millennial gardener who wants to get acquainted with this amazing family of plants, I suggest seven types to start with. They can be found in most garden centers as small starter plants:

- bell peppers – the garden isn't complete without them
- banana peppers and Hungarian wax peppers (pretty mild)
- anaheims and chili de arbols (medium hot)
- jalapeños and habaneros (very hot to blow-your-head-off hot)

Once you fall in love with peppers, there are specialty seed companies that you can find online, where you can buy seed of just about any variety that is available. Even the Dorset Naga, if you want to live dangerously.

As America moves deeper into an age of environmental stress, when victory gardening will be ever more vital for individual Americans, one of the most important plant groups in our backyards will be those eternal, irrepressible pepper plants.

GENDER

TWO-SPIRIT PEOPLE...
AND ASSUMPTIONS ABOUT THE SO-CALLED "BERDACHE"

Condensed version of an article originally published in *Whosoever*, November/December 1998

Many people ask what I know about the "berdache" – that sacred person in the native world who is said to be "Two Hearted" or "Two Spirited" – both female and male. The questioners have read my historical novel *One Is the Sun*, which is a story about 19th-century native Medicine women in the Northwest. They have also noted the thread of First Nation people through my gay novels.

The word "berdache" is a pejorative Old World word for "catamite," misapplied by anthropologists to a New World social figure that Europeans didn't understand. Different Native American cultures had their own words for such a unique individual – *winkte* among the Lakota, *hwame* among Mojave people, and *lhamana* in Zuni.

Centuries ago, I'm told, these persons were the essence of deity and prayer. They were usually accepted in the native world, and viewed as having mystical powers. They were colorfully portrayed in the 19th-century art of George Catlin and other artists. Today some in the gay community feel a great connectedness with the Two Spirit, and a yearning to be similarly powerful and accepted in American society. Walter Williams has written feelingly of the "berdache" in his book *The Spirit and the Flesh: Sexual Diversity in American Indian Culture*. GLBT youth like to hear about Two Spirits.

Through the 1980s, as I wrote *One Is the Sun*, I searched for my Native-American family roots, and found some relatives who were learned people. They shared some amazing information that is not found in books. The information forced me to unlearn my assumptions about many things, including the "berdache."

To understand how a Two Spirit saw himself/herself, and how others in the tribe or band saw this person as well, a 20th-century American has to put aside all the traditional Judaeo-Christian beliefs about sexuality, and even the western European non-Christian humanistic notions of sexuality. We have to step through the looking glass, into a different world.

The fact is, Christianity's perspective on personal and sexual identity is radically different than those of many Native American cultures and spiritual systems. So the Christianized person has a hard time getting a fix on any of the different non-Christian social types in the native world – not only the Two Spirit, but the peace chief, war chief, Medicine person, sacred clown, male and female warrior, buffalo caller, Sun Dancer, Dog Soldier, sorcerer, storyteller, camp crier, healer, keeper of a Medicine Lodge, marriage go-between, and First Nation-style prophet. These have no functional counterparts in today's American society.

Christian European assumptions about cultures and people go so deep in the minds of many Americans that we even have a hard time understanding the historical traditions and what we call "folk tales" of Native American people...what the symbols mean, what the stories are really talking about. At first I stumbled in my attempts to step through the looking glass – struggling to see how women healers of the mid-1800s lived and saw the world. My book was eventually published in 1991.

To open up the question about Two Spirits, I'm going to follow a looping round-about trail, over hills and through valleys – like my native grannies often did when I asked a question!

The prophet is a good place to start, because prophets are so familiar to Americans from the pages of the Bible.

Many non-native Americans insist on seeing the native prophet/preacher as a male – as an Indian Jesus or "Christ-like" figure. Some anthropologists insist that native spiritual traditions are really pre-figurations of Christianity. This is because some classical anthropology operates off a Western European belief that all human spirituality evolves towards monotheism – namely, the Judaeo-belief in one male God, and the Judaeo-Christian belief in God's redeemer named Jesus Christ, that are the foundation of today's Western civilization.

This belief assumes that monotheism is "better," "more civilized," "the only truth." Whereas systems that honor a God and Goddess, or many gods and goddesses, are viewed as primitive, barbaric and untrue. Stories of native prophets are often included in the category of "redemptive allegories" by anthropologists because they attempt to find similarities between Christian and non-Christian prophets. Way back in their minds, they associate the idea of a prophet with John the Baptist, whom Christianity views as a herald of its coming Redeemer, i.e. Christ.

Peter Powell, a noted anthropologist of the early-to-mid-1900s who was also an Episcopal missionary, made his reputation looking for Jesus and prophets and "redemptive allegories" among the Cheyennes. In the 1980s, when I first started feeling my way towards Medicine women and my *One Is the Sun* story, I studied Powell's works, *Sweet Medicine* and *People of the Sacred Mountain*. In Powell's view, much in the old Cheyenne way was a preparation for Christianity.

A case in point was Powell's interpretation of the Cheyenne "culture figure" Sweet Medicine as a Jesus-like prophet. According to the Cheyennes, Sweet Medicine came to them and gave them their tradition of law and government. Powell meant well, and was trying to give the Cheyennes some political protection during that awful and painful period (from the 1880s till the 1970s) when the federal government still criminalized all Native American beliefs and ceremonies. Powell wanted to destroy the historical stereotype of Indians as painted devil-worshippers – creating in its place a dignified and positive image of the Cheyennes as a deeply spiritual people. I can't fault him there.

But Powell also failed to convey the bitter philosophical and political disagreements among the Northern Cheyennes at that time. He talked mainly to one faction...the one that was closest to his own viewpoint, naturally. Part of the disagreement was over the role of women in the tribe. Could women be Keepers of sacred Medicine things, or not? Predictably, as a typical patriarchal-minded Christian, Powell evidently talked to many more Cheyenne men than he did women. So he missed the boat on things that women could have told him.

In Volume II of his work *Sweet Medicine*, Powell actually wrote, "Traditions of women chiefs exist, as well as accounts of women possessing great supernatural powers." Then, having whetted the reader's curiosity, he proceeded to say nothing more about these great Cheyenne women chiefs and spiritual leaders!

Only in passing did Powell mention that "sweet medicine" is a Cheyenne name for a medicinal root that makes women's milk flow better. Through this symbol, the very name of Sweet Medicine tells us that women had an important role in the tribe's spiritual life and the development of its laws and government.

So an anthropologist who believes in a male God and a male Saviour and a male priesthood, has a hard time making sense of a culture where women were priestesses, chiefs, fighters, great legal minds, prophets, magicians and healers! Generally, U.S. anthropology during that period – from anthropology's infancy in the late 1800s till after World War II – was oblivious to information about women's power in the native traditions. This was because white women couldn't be ministers, medical doctors, judges, lawyers, soldiers, politicians.

When Sweet Medicine people first encountered Christianity (I was told), they found the missionaries' story of Christ's torture and death on the cross to be revolting and incomprehensible. They felt the same way about God's alleged willingness to sacrifice his son. The influence of this tradition among the Cheyennes was what steeled many of them to resist Christianity for such a long time. To this day, in spite of long-time missionary presence among the Cheyennes, a significant percentage of the tribe still follow the Old Ways.

"Redemptive allegory" was injected into native traditions after first contact with whites. This process started five centuries ago. By the 1500s, the Spanish took over South and Central America and the American Southwest, while northern Europeans began invading the rest of North America in the 1600s. So when we read old native traditions that were first written down in English a mere 100 or 150 years ago, and notice the presence of "Christian-like material" there, most likely it was injected into those traditions in post-contact times.

As my tribal cousins said, "We read the same *National Geographic* articles about Indians as everybody else."

Along with redemptive allegory, there are other assumptions that some anthropologistics make, about the meaning of key native words and symbols. This need to better understand symbols is very fundamental to seeing what native spiritual or sexual tradition really means – including the Two-Spirit Person. If you can unlock the symbols, you can crack the walnut of meaning.

Book of the Hopi tells of one such misunderstood symbol. In the early 1980s, I spent some research time with its author Frank Waters and his wife at Taos and talked with them about this. Decades before, the Hopi elders had asked Waters to write the book because they were fed up with all the white academics' misinterpretations of Hopi tradition.

In the book, Frank relates a key Hopi story of how the tribe "lived with the Ants" for a while. Most white anthropologists dismiss this story as a "childish fable." How could a tribe of humans possibly go live in an anthill?

After I read this book, I suddenly began to understand how an animal symbol, in a First Nation history, has a clear meaning and a biological explanation, as created by people who observed life closely. What do ants do? They live in highly organized societies, with armies and slaves and intensive food culture. And they build complex architecture shaped like.... pyramids. Oh...the light dawned for me! The Hopi story was talking about the pyramid cultures of Central America, who were fiercely militaristic and practiced slavery and had sophisticated agriculture. So, what the story really means, is that the Hopi People lived in Mexico for a while, before moving north to their present territory in the U.S. Southwest.

All the things I've mentioned have some bearing on what a "berdache" is, or isn't. What does the name "Two Spirit" mean?

According to my family teachers, many spiritual systems of the Americas taught that all being, including Deity, is twinned in nature – both male and female. The symbol of the Sacred Twins is found throughout the native American world. In some traditions, the twins became two males. But the symbol in its purest and most ancient form is a pair of female and male twins.

My teachers pointed out that this philosophy of dualism used to be found everywhere in the world. For male and female to exist in the Deity's creation, these two powers have to co-exist in the Deity, who is creation's source. Even the very word "deity" in English comes from a root word related to *duo*, that means "two," according to the *American Heritage Dictionary of the English Language.* The teachers compared it to similar twinnings of Goddesses and Gods that were celebrated everywhere in the pagan Mediterranean world – Juno and Jupiter, Cupid and Psyche, etc. But conventional Christianity took the "two" out of Deity and taught that it was only "one," meaning male. So-called monotheism doesn't really refer to one God vs. many Gods – it really means "God minus His mate and female partner, the Goddess."

In this view, all human beings are dual in nature as well – male and female. Humans are seen as relatives of the Goddesses and Gods, while animals and plants do not live on this same plane of duality. When a human person is born, only one or the other twin usually comes into substance, into life on Earth – the other half remains in the spirit world as a higher self. A woman living on Earth has a male higher self, while a man on Earth has a female higher self.

The higher self is still part of the "total beingness" that each of us have. The higher self helps to protect and possess the library of spirit knowledge and learning that each individual person has accumulated through many lives. It can influence us and communicate with us. It can also be hurt, and its powers even diminished, by hatred and non-acceptance coming from the twin who is in substance. Men who hate women and war on them, or women who hate men, are really warring on their own higher selves.

Some First Nation people have a concept similar to what Eastern philosophies call "karma," meaning the long-term consequences of our actions through many lifetimes, through our struggle to learn and grow and discover what it means to be human. Each time we die, our twin selves are reunited in the spirit world. The etymology of the word "die" has its root in the word for "two" also. When we die, we become "two" again – only to separate upon rebirth in another life. That is the real meaning of the word "death," which even today – despite Christianity's effort to purge ancient meanings out of every dictionary – shows clearly that Western language had an ancient understanding of duality in all things.

However, all laws of nature allow for variance and change. Now and then, a person's karma dictates that both male and female are coming into substance together. These are the Two Spirit people.

Sometimes a Two Spirit's dual nature is actually visible in the genitalia, which may express both male and female characteristics. In other cases, the influence of the spirit-world twin is simply felt as an overriding influence coming from the world of the invisible. This explains the urgency with which some transgendered people wear clothing of the opposite gender, or seek sex-change surgery. They are not imagining things when they feel that they are "a woman in a man's body," or "a man in a woman's body."

In Deity, two are mysteriously also one. Thus the forked tree – a key symbol of the Sun Dance – expresses that way in which all beingness is one. A woman may have her hidden male side, and a man may have his female side, and a Two-Spirit person may express both genders openly, but each of them are a single Person.

In pre-contact times, according to what I was told, many Native American people had a great reverence for these Two-Spirit people.

Quite naturally they viewed Two-Spirits as extraordinary sources of information about human nature. Two-Spirits were healers, artists, prophets – whatever their personal vision impelled them to be. The native world had great respect for personal vision. If you were born a male, but came back from your first vision quest and said that the

Medicines were telling you to live as a woman, your vision was honored. You even got a new name celebrating your choice! Likewise the woman who said she wanted to live as a man, love as a man, even fight as a man, was able to do that freely.

Few cultures in the native world had a central authority, as in Christianity, that purported to know what was "right" and commanded each person to follow its dictates without question. There was no Bible-type dictate against cross-dressing.

Some Two-Spirit people (I was told) took the role of sacred clown, or "Contrary." The Contrary's job was to keep a camp's social dynamics balanced. If the people were laughing too much over something, the Contrary cried. If the people were crying too much, the Contrary laughed. So Contraries were indispensable at major ceremonies, because the community's feelings and experiences could get so intense that somebody needed to move in and lighten things up.

Some Contraries were such artists at social commentary that they played an important role at law councils. According to my teachers, they might raise issues, or introduce important questions of law into the debating circle – much as legislators introduce bills today. The Contraries helped this process along with great artistry and humor, acting out scenarios that got people laughing about issues that had burdened them or terrified them. Or the Contraries made people cry about questions that needed to be taken with more deadly seriousness. In this way the Contraries helped the whole tribe understand why an old law was bad, or why a new law was needed.

This acting-out was called "mirroring," and it was important as a kind of tribal "media." The mirroring included a cutting-edge humor and social comment that survived in the great humorist Will Rogers, who was part Cherokee and brought it to the white man's Broadway stage.

Often the old-time Contraries lived as the opposite gender, or simply wore clothing of the opposite sex. Some made a show of doing everything backwards – walking backwards, riding horses seated backwards, in order to be a living symbol that reminded people of the need for balance on a daily basis. Some Contraries were healers. Some Two Spirits, known as *winktes* among the

Lakotah people, functioned as go-betweens when marriages were to be made.

Some Contraries (I was told) were what we might call transgendered or intersex" people today. It was recognized that they were born with variations in their genitalia that made them different from most people. These differences were accepted without hostility – they were considered a Medicine thing. Other Contraries were what we might call "gay," "lesbian" or "bisexual" – although we can't equate our 1990s political and social concepts of sexual orientation to those of the 1890s, from other cultures and a more bygone day.

Now and then a person simply crossed over, and lived as the opposite gender, but weren't true Two Spirit people. Such a one may have been the Blackfoot woman who is the subject of Benjamin Capps' *Woman Chief*, a historical book that fascinated me as a child. She lived and fought as a man in the late 1800s, and took a woman as her wife.

Not surprisingly, European and American missionaries were shocked out of their minds by the Two-Spirit people. Priests and preachers did everything they could to wipe out all shadings of native sexual diversity. Today's fierce U.S. biases against transgendered and intersex people have their roots in Old Testament teachings, but they were honed even sharper by these missionary purges of the tribes.

These are only a few of my thoughts on that Person known to anthropologists as the "berdache." Human spirituality and human civilization reveals an unending quest to know the nature of Deity, and the nature of human destiny – to know what is true, and to ask what truth really is. Today the Two Spirit person is here once again to tell us that U.S. laws and social customs outlawing sexual diversity are bad laws, and ought to be changed. The Person With Two Hearts ought to be not merely accepted, but celebrated as in those days of old.

That experience of twoness as "one" is a key stage of our karmic journey to learn what it means to be truly human. Maybe the Two Spirit Person is that much closer to human than the rest of us.

CALAMITY JANE:
"THAT AWFUL GIRL"

From a longer article "Cowgirl Revolution," originally published in 2008 at Outsports.com

Like many sports, professional rodeo is still obsessed with the ruggedly masculine, in everything from image to income. From 1929 onwards, the sport began relegating women to the rhinestone brigade – rodeo queen and trick riding, as well as "non-dangerous" events like barrel racing. Yet it wasn't always so. Rodeo is the only American sport where women actually enjoyed equal status at the beginning – along with a little room for unconventional gender profiles like that of Calamity Jane.

Rodeo grew out of the vast livestock industry that once flourished west of the Mississippi, from Mexico north to Canada. But cowgirls had a different role in that industry than cowboys did. "The boys" were employees – working stiffs who populated ranches by the countless thousands. "Boy" referred to your lowly and possibly non-white social status. "Cowboys" did the dangerous dirty horseback work that the "cowman" or owner needed done.

But "cowgirls" didn't figure among these galloping grunts. A ranch might hire a woman to cook or do bookkeeping, but it didn't pay women to do the rough jobs. Instead, "cowgirls" reflected the owner and better-heeled side of ranching. My dad set me straight on the social innuendo of this term, when I was a young teen and he was educating me to run the ranch some day.

"You're not a cow *girl*," he said pointedly. "You're a cow *woman*."

Being a cow woman was about the land you owned. In the Spanish-speaking areas of colonial America, especially in California during the 1697-1848 period, ranches were created out of vast land grants given by the crown to families brave enough to rough it in the New World. Wives co-owned land with their husbands. Under Spanish law, when a man died, the inheritance went to his widow, not to his oldest son as in English law. A Spanish *ranchera* or cow woman was titled the Doña; her husband was the Don. These terms are the Spanish equivalent of lady and lord.

Spanish California women virtually lived on horseback, since equestrian skills were part of upper-class social life. Even on the bigger ranches, a whole crew of well-born *rancheras* might turn out at round-up time to help brand and ship the beef cattle. Historian Kathy Hughart relates: "Foreign visitors marveled at California women's horseback riding skills and expertise with the lasso." Californians also turned out on horseback for annual fiesta-type affairs that evolved out of the annual fall cattle rodeos, or roundups. At these fiestas, everybody competed in ranch-based skills and horseback games.

These practices prevailed even after the United States grabbed California and the Southwest away from Mexico in 1848.

In the U.S. itself, whose laws and customs traced back to England, things developed differently for ranch women.

After the American Revolution, the new state constitutions tied property ownership to the right to vote, and limited voting rights to white Christian males. Women's freedom to own land didn't start till the Homestead Act of 1862, which the federal government passed in order to speed American occupation of vast areas that might still be grabbed by the British or Russians. Instead of favoring the upper class by going the land-grant route, the U.S. opted to favor the little guy, because they wanted instant population density all over livable areas of the West. Signed into law by Abraham Lincoln, this Act put millions of low-income owners on 270 million acres by the early 1900s. To claim a 160-acre parcel of land, a homesteader had only to be a head of household and 21 years old. So, for the first time in our history, an unmarried woman or widow could stake out a homestead – build a house and barns, make other improvements, and live there for 5 years before "proving up" and getting title.

Sudden land ownership shot new life into the women's suffrage movement, which had stalled since colonial times. Not surprisingly, the first states to legalize the female vote were Western states – Wyoming being first in 1869. In turn, land and suffrage touched deeply into other areas of women's sensibilities – including gender identity and sexual orientation. We can only guess how many of these female homesteaders were closet cases of the Victorian era – women who were looking to escape the church-driven strictures of life "back in the states." The vigor and independence promised by Western life would surely have drawn lesbian and bi women by the wagonload. Women's westward spirit was movingly, if quietly, expressed by closeted lesbian novelist Willa Cather in her novels *O Pioneers!* and *My Antonia.*

A ranch woman of more modest means couldn't afford to hire a bunch of cowboys. At most she might hire a hand or two at roundup time. The rest of the year, she (and her daughters too) had to get their own work done – harness and drive a team, rope steers, cut cows or calves out of the herd, do branding, and sit a bucking horse on a cold morning. In short, the Western livestock business prompted some of the first stirrings of women's liberation in the workplace.

Some Western women did crash the male job world – but they did it by wearing men's clothes, adopting male mannerisms and passing as men. Western history is full of stories about these gutsy individuals, some of whom were evidently lesbian or bi women or FTM transgendered people.

To fight the trend in some localities, Bible-thumping moralists cited the Old Testament prohibition of cross-dressing, and passed laws making it illegal for women to wear trousers and other men's clothes. But these prohibitions never made it to state law, probably because Western lawmakers knew that such laws would have kept the poorer rural women from getting work done.

That's Entertainment

Through the late 1800s, ranches and communities started getting together for the first informal celebrations of ranch sport.

At first these were called "stampedes" or "roundups." Eventually everybody opted for the Spanish word for roundup – *rodeo*. And the *rancheras* were there for the big party. Their liberated participation in early-day rodeo meant that some of its early figures would fall hazily into the LGBT category, though we can't put a nice neat label on them today. And it guaranteed a huge controversy over "feminine appearance" in the arena.

Rodeo, and women's role in it, got its biggest push from the Wild West shows. In 1883 frontiersman-turned-producer William "Buffalo Bill" Cody brought international popularity to ranch sport when he added it to his historic show, the biggest and most successful traveling entertainment enterprise in American history. With the Indian wars finally over, the "old West" was now sufficiently tamed that it could – along with surviving celebrities like Chief Sitting Bull and Liver Eatin' Johnson – be recycled as circus for city people.

Cody was a shrewd promoter, but also a forward-looking man who aimed to inject authenticity and diversity into his shows. Along with the choreographed stagecoach robberies and re-enactments of battles, Buffalo Bill created sport exhibitions and competitions based on ranch skills, showing how women as well as men lived the frontier spirit. The "cow girls" roped steers, topped broncs, did relay races and trick riding, often competing directly with men. Out of respect for Victorian dress code, they often rode sidesaddle. If they rode astride, they wore voluminous skirts or circusy costumes that were actually a safety hazard.

Other Wild West shows followed Cody's formula. Some of these shows were still touring the U.S. into the mid-1900s.

The term "cow girl" had a less respectful ring than *ranchera* or "cow woman." In those days, the social establishment looked down on entertainers of all kinds – circus acts, vaudeville and burlesque performers, early film stars, etc. – considering them to be bohemian types who led irregular and immoral lives. Plus the Wild West performers were employees. So, despite their efforts to look ladylike, the rootin' tootin' females who worked for the shows were called "girls" and grouped as bohemians along with the "boys." This old show-biz terminology still survives today in Broadway and casino shows, where the chorus line was (and still is) called "boys" and "girls."

Between 1884 and 1901, one of the West's most notorious gender-bending women was a cowgirl star in Wild West shows. She would cast a long shadow down the history of rodeo – one that still looms there today.

"That Awful Girl"

Born in 1856 to struggling pioneer parents, Martha Jane Canary was orphaned at age 13. Though her life was later aggrandized by legend, it was actually "a bleak story of poverty and alcoholism," according to historian James McLaird, who spent many years sifting patiently through frontier records so he could write her definitive biography. But we know one fact for sure: Martha lived to defy convention on the gender frontier. A strikingly pretty but tough-as-nails brunette girl with grey eyes, who started fending for herself and wearing men's clothes at age 15, she was dubbed Calamity Jane.

For 30 years, Calamity led a transient life around the boom towns of the West. Her favorite hangout was Deadwood, in Dakota Territory.

In 1875, when she was 19, the U.S. Army was still fighting the Plains tribes and making expeditions into the Black Hills and eastern Montana. For a couple of years, Calamity put on uniform and smuggled herself into army expeditions as a camp follower. There she was the soldiers' pet, and mastered skills that would later be important in the arena – riding well, shooting a rifle well, and driving a big wagon team so expertly that she could reportedly knock a fly off a mule's ear with her long bullwhip. Invariably the commanding officer learned of her presence in the train, and wrathfully sent her back.

Calamity loved to make a grand entrance into Deadwood, riding down the main street in plainsman's clothes – fringed buckskin jacket and breeches, with her wide hat tipped at a rakish angle, her hair all windblown and a Winchester rifle across her saddle bow. For many astonished pioneers, she was the first woman they'd ever seen ride astride. Already a heavy drinker as a teen, she became a familiar figure in saloons west of the Missouri, where she loved to treat everyone in the house. Far from resenting her invasion of their domain, most of the male drinkers liked her – she was entertaining, funny, generous and kind (when she wasn't pissed off). So they put up with her fiery temper and her fondness for brawling.

As her reputation spread, newspapers started logging her movements around the West. It got to be big news when Calamity Jane rolled into town. One newspaper editor called her "that awful girl." It's a wonder she was never lynched. But she did have her friends in high places, plus civic good will that she'd built by nursing sick people during the West's frequent epidemics. Former johns may have left her in peace for fear she'd yell their names to the press. The worst punishment she usually suffered was a few days in jail, or being asked to leave town.

From local headlines, Calamity moved to national icon status with author Edward Wheeler in his popular dime novels about the West. He made her one of the first pulp-fiction heroines – beautiful, daring, with long streaming hair – and he never paid her a nickel of royalties for his exploitation of her name and image.

Meanwhile, the real Calamity's boozing often left her borderline broke.

Yet she worked hard at making a living – first as a prostitute and dance-hall girl, later as a teamster, gambler, faro dealer, bartender, nurse, cook, waitress, laundress. A couple of times, she made an abortive try at running a small business – madam, saloon keeper, hotelier, roadhouse and restaurant owner. Her two tries at marriage and her several cohabitations with men may have been efforts to get a roof over her head when she needed one – including a stint with a rancher co-habitant in Montana. Later in life, she capitalized on her celebrity by publishing a short autobiography and doing lecture tours, where she told entertaining tales about her life, and sold the book and photos of herself in buckskins with her trademark rifle.

But in the end, most every dollar she made went into drinking.

Calamity's Orientation

Where in the LGBT acronym can today's historians pigeonhole her? We don't know.

Certainly the Westerners of her time knew she was "different." Cross-dressing alone was viewed as unnatural by the Victorians. Was she a lesbian? One 19th century newspaper writer called her a "queer freak of nature." Another called her "a pupil of the Oscar Wilde school of esthetics," which skated close to saying she was gay, since British playwright/poet Wilde had made no secret of his homosexuality. For a year during her camp-follower time, Calamity had a teen female companion named Little Frankie O'Dare, who may or may not have been a lover. Other female sidekicks appear in her life later, but briefly.

On the other hand, her long string of relationships with men could mean that she was bisexual. When she was young, she often arrived at a dance-hall in bowler hat, black tie and tails, and danced some wild reels with the girls for part of the evening, then returned in women's evening wear, complete with feather boa and fancy hat, to dance with the men.

But Calamity was a lone wolf – never with anybody, male or female, for very long. In his 1990 novel *Buffalo Girls*, Larry McMurtry (co-author of the *Brokeback Mountain* screenplay) portrays Calamity as a "hermaphrodite." I doubt she was intersex, since it's medically recognized that intersex people are unable to have children. According to historian McLaird, Calamity had a daughter and son that she farmed out to be raised by others, since the life she led could seldom support a child.

In my opinion, her intense identification with men – notably her handsome drinking buddy Wild Bill Hickok, who is thought by some to have been gay himself, and was shot to death in a Deadwood saloon in 1876 – may send the message of a gender-identity issue. While she never tried to "pass" as a man, Calamity embraced all the frontiersman's habits – hard drinking, cigar smoking, colorful swearing, loudmouth bragging, card playing, gun slinging, show-off feats, fist fights and general mayhem. She celebrated these habits even in women's clothes. If Calamity lived today, with access to the counseling and medical resources for sexual realignment, she might decide to cross all the way over.

We do know a second fact about Calamity. The press of the day built her into such a celebrity that Wild West show producers saw her box-office potential. This is how the "awful girl" became one of the ancestors of women's rodeo. Indeed, Calamity sought jobs with the shows because the pay was good, and she invented more colorful stories about herself to hype her image. One of her legends says she toured with Buffalo Bill's show, but there's no evidence for this. Buffalo Bill gave himself top billing in his own production, so he may have feared that Calamity would upstage him.

But Calamity did tour with other shows. Starting in 1884, at age 28, when she still had her good looks, she joined Tom Hardwick's Great Rocky Mountain Show. The show toured across the West and Midwest to Chicago, and society paid good money to see the infamous loudmouth frontierswoman come charging into the arena. They said "ewww" as they watched her riding astride in those men's buckskin breeches. They hyperventilated as she showed them her skills with rifle and bullwhip. Essentially they saw Calamity as a freak show. The other big female headliner, shooter Annie Oakley, also wowed the crowds with a masculine skill – but she did it in feminine clothing, with a bonafide husband on display and a gracious, retiring manner that "proved" her "womanliness."

In 1901, age 45, Calamity made her last and most dazzling cowgirl grand entries at the Pan-American Exposition in Buffalo, New York, in an arena that drew 25,000 spectators a day. There, in the Fred Cummins Show, she shared top billing with Chief Geronimo and was lionized by high society. For a time the show managed to curb her drinking, and she wowed the crowds with her riding and rifle handling. On July 31, in the parade down Buffalo's main drag, she provided a unique spectacle as she drove a 100-mule team pulling a big water wagon. An Exposition photo caught her in a backstage moment in the show's tent area. It's a poignant image – the bronzed woman with the haggard boozer face, sitting a horse in her buckskin trousers and show-time regalia – looking far older than her years.

Then Calamity fell off the wagon, spent a night in jail, and quit the show. Broke and stranded, she touched Buffalo Bill Cody for enough money to get home.

By late 1902, Calamity was back in Deadwood, suffering the terminal effects of lifelong alcoholism. Despite the efforts of friends who looked after her, she died in July 1903. At her request, she was buried in a man's shirt in the Deadwood cemetery, right next to Wild Bill Hickok.

She was only 47.

Damsel Doggers

Calamity may have gone to the great arena in the sky, but her reputation – and the issue of appearing "womanly" and feminine – stayed around to haunt rodeo cowgirls for the next hundred years.

During the 1884-1920s heyday of the Wild West shows, more than 100 women contestants a year were still competing directly with men in the most bone-busting events – saddle bronc riding, steer roping, bull riding. This at a time when the Olympic Games were just beginning to ouchily allow female participation, and only in "ladylike non-strenuous" sports.

After 1920, rodeo parted company with the Wild West shows, and started establishing its own identity. But rodeo still kept the circus MO – the grand entry, the spangles and glitter, the trick riding and fancy roping, the target shooting from horseback – and the attitude about "girls." Major Western cities had their own annual rodeo. A circuit grew up around the country, with championship finals in Madison Square Garden in New York. Since ranch life still had a lot of hard-riding, hard-working women, few people had major objections to females competing with men. Indeed, rodeo cowgirls were not at a athletic disadvantage with cowboys, because the riding events favor qualities that both genders can have – a lean light build, good balance and quick reflexes.

With the public hungry for variety, a new event called steer wrestling (aka chute dogging) had been invented. You slid off a galloping horse onto the back of a galloping steer, grabbed his horns while braking him to a stop with your feet, then twisted him to the ground. Successful male doggers tended to be beefy linebacker types.

But inevitably women were going to try dogging too. One of the first and best damsel doggers was Fox Hastings. She had run away from home at age 14 and got her start in the Irwin Brothers' Wild West Show, doing bronc riding and trick riding. After she married bulldogging star Mike Hastings, she switched over to competitive rodeo. In 1924 she made her dogger debut at the Houston rodeo and set a new record.

By the 1920s, however, rodeo management was pressuring cowgirls to appear more "womanly." With safety in mind, the women had succeeded in shedding those long Victorian skirts. But men's trousers were not an option for the arena. Instead, the women rode in split skirts or bloomers, and knocked themselves out to look as feminine as the trendy "Gibson girls" in the popular magazine ads. Not till well into the 1920s did cowgirls start wearing pants in the arena – but never men's trousers or blue jeans. Instead they wore Western-style dress pants tailored to fit the female body.

But even as the rest of the country was going off the deep end with bathtub gin and Jazz Age sexual liberation, male rodeo organizers were going ever more conservative… wanting to spin the cowgirl image away from the gender-bending Calamity Jane model. It was now risky for a rodeo woman to be visibly unmarried as she traveled the circuit. The most diligent historian of women's rodeo, Texas author Mary Lou LeCompte, mentions the Wild West shows but bends over backwards to avoid mentioning Calamity Jane. LeCompte does briefly discuss today's homophobia towards lesbians in other sports, but asserts that almost all the old-time rodeo cowgirls were married and genuinely womanly (translation: heterosexual). It's that same old refrain of "no lesbians here" that we often hear from women's basketball.

The Rodeo Cowboys Association had been compelled to deal with discrimination against black, Hispanic and Indian cowboys, but they grew a big blind spot on women's equality. After Eastern promoters started staging indoor rodeos in places like Madison Square Garden, women began to be excluded from the shows.

Hobbled Stirrups

Through the 1920s, national women's bronc-riding champion Bonnie McCarroll of Idaho did manage to make herself the brightest cowgirl star. She also signalled the striving for greater "femininity" in her image. Rodeo organizers were now pressuring women bronc riders to avoid the unseemly spectacle of being thrown. Many rodeos prohibited women from riding "slick" (with loose stirrups) and made them tie the stirrups down. Supposedly this was safer. Actually it was more dangerous, as cowgirls learned the hard way. But organizers ignored the risk.

Then at the 1929 Pendleton Roundup, Bonnie came out of the chute on a bronc named Black Cat, with her stirrups hobbled. As the horse somersaulted, Bonnie's foot got caught in the tied-down stirrup. Black Cat scrambled up and ran, dragging and kicking the rider in full view of the horrified crowd. Bonnie died in the hospital of massive head injuries.

McCarroll's tragic death provided the excuse that the rodeo establishment was looking for. Instead of accepting responsibility for having imposed the hobbled-stirrup rule, pro rodeos simply began barring women from "dangerous" competition.

The Fifties and Sixties would be called the Golden Age of Rodeo, as the sport went heavily professional and sponsor-driven, with rich prize money and major advertising exposure now available. Women's barrel racing became a standard event, with the support of the Women's Professional Rodeo Association. To this day, WPRA is the oldest organization of female pro athletes in the U.S… thus opening the way for women's battle for equality in all other sports, and the only one that is controlled entirely by women.

But its members were still fighting the old Calamity Jane battle of "looking feminine." Texas old-timer Eileen Tidwell, who helped organize the women's Texas Barrel Racing Association in the 1950s, remembers, "It was agreed that we needed to be glamorous and well dressed. Therefore among the first rules of the TBRA was the dress code, which mandated long sleeves, hat, boots and dress pants ... not jeans."

Today Calamity Jane's legend has established her as an enduring American symbol for feisty female independence. She has been the subject of as many movies as Joan of Arc. As I was finishing this piece, I happened to watch the 2007 Tournament of Roses Parade, and there, among the horseback entries was a group called "Men and Women of the Old West." Among them was Calamity Jane herself, complete with the plainsman's hat, the fringed buckskins and the windblown hair.

But pro rodeo today has little in common with Buffalo Bill's Wild West. Today the top contestants, both women and men, can win $250,000 a year in prize money, with a few individuals topping $1 million. Rodeo women do enjoy some degree of income parity with men – top barrel racer Charmayne James Rodman was the first "million dollar cowgirl."

In mainstream pro rodeo, cowgirl contestants enjoy the spotlight once again in the biggest national shows…but they're still relegated to "gender appropriate" competition – meaning the timed riding events like barrel racing and team roping. Most rodeos don't offer as many women's events as men's events. Cowgirls do compete in all events at all-girl rodeos, as well as in a broader range of events in high-school and college rodeos. But these shows get little national visibility, especially on TV. Even on the college rodeo circuit, Title IX has only a partial effect – college cowgirls compete against men only in barrel racing and roping events.

The men's dress code has loosened a little – enough to adopt any country-music fashions that don't endanger safety or macho image.

The National Pro Rodeo Association actually launched a "Tough Enough to Wear Pink?" campaign in 2007…but they weren't trying to take pink away from gays. They just wanted to do fundraising for breast cancer.

In women's pro rodeo, however, dress code still rules supreme. The code's defenders insist that it's still important to sell that glamorous, dignified and conventional image to sponsors. But on another level, the code pays lip service to that old notion still cherished by many conservatives, that "lesbians are, by their very nature, not feminine, womanly or glamorous." In other words, if enough cowgirls run the drums in stunning County Music Awards outfits, none of them can possibly be dykes.

Lately, however, some rebels are flouting the dress code. Historian Mary Lou LeCompte tsk-tsks about feminist barrel racers. She says, "Few wear the dashing outfits promised by their publicity. Few even bother to wear the western attire required by the WPRA rules. Instead they compete in rugby sweaters and the like." LeCompte thumps the WPRA for failing to enforce its own rules, and adds, "As long as athletes must depend on sponsors and television to provide their prize money, they will have to take appearances into account."

In the last analysis, though, that cherished belt buckle is not just about the right to ride bucking bulls. It's about the freedom to look like – and act like – who you really are. Calamity Jane would approve.

Further reading:

Calamity Jane: The Woman and the Legend, by James D. McLaird (University of Oklahoma Press, 2005).

Buffalo Girls, by Larry McMurtry (Simon & Schuster, 2001)

Cowgirls of the Rodeo: Pioneer Professional Athletes, revised edition by Mary Lou LeCompte (Illini Books, 2000).

"Home on the Range: Women in Professional Rodeo – 1929-1947," by Mary Lou LeCompte, *Journal of Sport History*, Winter 1990

HISTORY

WHEN RESEARCH GETS REAL

In the early 1980s, I began to research my fifth novel, *One Is the Sun*. This was a historical novel about native American women of the mid-1800s. Already I'd learned that a great deal of writing about those times was more academic than real. But I wasn't sure how real until I researched the travois – a simple, everyday tool of those times.

The word "travois" is French, from *travaille*, meaning work. It came into the English language through the fur-trading and buffalo-hunting Métis (mixed-bloods). This implement was the equivalent of today's family van – a wheelless vehicle used for hauling families and goods around. It is described by the *American Heritage Dictionary* as a "primitive sledge." The art of Charles M. Russell portrays countless travel scenes with tribal people using their travois. During the mop-up wars in the late 1800s, as the U.S. Army herded remnants of tribes onto the reservations, many frontier photographers documented the travois. A used-up pony usually posed for the picture, with a tired woman on board, maybe a couple of exhausted sad-faced little kids staring at the white-man photog – their faces mirroring shell-shock at the killing and terror they'd been through. Indian men were pointedly issued buckboard wagons by the U.S. government. Missionaries sermonized against the travois, condemning it along with the Sun Dance and dog soup.

But the travois didn't obediently vanish. By the 1950s, many Western native people still hauled stuff around the "rez" in battered pickups. Yet the "primitive sledge" survived in the back hills, among Old Ones who were too poor to own a truck. They used it to haul firewood. Often, too, the travois made its state appearance at Western powwows and historical pageants, all fancied up – pulled grandly down Main Street by a well-fed horse and a girl in her beaded best, with the band playing up ahead.

While interviewing people, I met a middle-aged learned Montana-born mixed-blood woman who was then living in California. She turned out to be a walking archive of knowledge on the travois. Her real name does not matter – there are still political problems with publishing the names of reservation-born people who give out "real" information. At her request, I will call her Old Lady Library.

When Old Lady Library was young, she said, an aged Medicine Woman often took her into the Big Horn Mountains for teaching and ceremony. Quietly the two women loaded a few necessities onto two small travois, and headed their ponies into remote canyons where snoopy missionaries and BIA officials would not find them doing their "pagan" things.

"Even a four-wheel-drive can't go where my teacher and I went!" my informant laughed.

In the spring of 1987, she outlined my research. "First of all," she said, "you will pull a travois around, and learn about this thing. Yes. Uh-uh. Not a horse. You."

"Huh?" I said.

"The first travois were designed for people to pull."

I was always ready to be the argumentative academic. "But the early peoples had dogs to do the pulling."

"Supposing your dog died? Or ran away? Hm? Or maybe somebody stole your dog. Before the good old days of horse-stealing, people stole dogs. Did you ever think of that?"

I hadn't.

My informant was relentless. "You will build a space-age travois, and pull it around, and live with it every day like I did. If you do this, you will begin to understand."

"And," she added, "don't run around like a dumb-ass anthropologist looking for 'authentic' materials. Get your brain in gear. Hunt for the best materials at hand, in your own world. That's what those old-time women did. "

Swiftly, on paper, Old Lady Library sketched the people-pulled travois. The two slender poles had to stand as high as the owner/puller could reach with one hand – in my case, about 7 feet. They were joined by a simple harness that would fit around my body.

"By the way, go study the fulcrum," she added. "You can't know the travois without knowing a bit about Archimedes."

From Charlie Russell to ancient Greece was a long leap.

Everything I learned from this experiment would fly in the face of much sacrosanct academic theory about how and why old-time Indians did things.

What kind of wood? My brain went into first gear. Softwood. Hardwood would hold up better, but it was too heavy for a person to haul around. And Montana didn't have serviceable hardwood trees. The best would be tough lodgepole pine – I knew its toughness from the hundreds of miles of pole fence on our Montana ranch. But in a pinch regular pine would do also. At the local lumberyard, for 15 cents a foot, I purchased a pair of 2-inch pine dowels that were seven feet long.

At the hardware store, I got professional-grade duck tape and stout twine. These would replace rawhide thongs. At the feed store, I obtained two clean gunny-sacks, free.

What would be the strongest, most modern harness-type materials? At the army-navy surplus store, I found two khaki web-belts.

Arriving home, I dug my back-pack out of storage. Inspecting its stout aluminum-tube frame, I was sure it could function as the main load-carrying cross-brace of the travois. The indigenous peoples knew the back-pack, which was framed using willow or cottonwood. Aluminum, with its light weight, would be the perfect substitute. Old Lady Library had told me how reservation people would quickly slap a backpack onto poles, creating an instant travois.

"Remember," the old woman cautioned, "the load has to be minimal. Every foot soldier knows that. Even a horse can carry only so much."

In the shade of a cottonwood tree, my materials and work-tools were arranged on the tailgate of my pickup. I experimented, grumbled with frustration. My brain ground into second gear... barely.

Translating the old lady's drawing into the actual vehicle was not so simple. The twine and duck-tape fastenings, securing the harness and load-carrying parts to the poles, had to be stout, else they would tear loose. Then, on a trial run around the yard, I realized that I had positioned the back pack too low – it could not clear minor rocks.

With library books, I reviewed Archimedes. The laws governing the movement of weight by levers were known to ancient Mediterranean thinkers. The fulcrum is the balance-point on which a lever lifts, and turns, a weight. A travois, then, is a movable lever, used to shift weights along a continual line of travel. So the ancient First Americans must have had the knowledge of levers in order to design the travois. The "primitive sledge" was not so "primitive" after all.

"Well, you've got the right idea," Old Lady Library said, inspecting my work. "But the structure needs to be more loose-jointed."

She explained that a travois, like an airplane wing, will tear itself apart if it is a rigid structure. It has to be limber, so it can flex its way over rocks, sagebrush, prairie-dog hills, creek-beds.

Two neighbor boys came to visit – Shane, 8, and Gage, 7. They hovered with intense curiosity. "Indian stuff!" they said. "Cool! Can we help?"

Their arrival addressed something I'd wondered about – children.

"Sure," I said. "You can be my research assistants."

"You gonna pay us?" they asked slyly.

"Same rate as raking leaves. Fifty cents an hour."

"Deal," they said.

Travois had hauled children, and sick people too. How? Between the poles, above the back-pack brace, I secured one of the gunny sacks like a bucket-seat. The travois now looked like a stretcher (which is, in fact, one of its relatives). In an emergency, the bucket-seat could carry a baby's cradleboard, or a sick child.

One spring morning, the boys and I were ready for our first journey.

"You and the boys will imagine that you are the last survivors of your camp," Old Lady Library said. "Everyone else has been killed. All your horses stolen. You and your two grandchildren are traveling alone, afoot. You are heading for a river about 20 sleeps away, where a friendly camp has always located in the autumn. Lucky for you, it is summer. But winter is ahead."

Our expedition would be more like "one sleep" – down the dirt road, across the pasture and back – a distance of about a mile.

That morning, I strapped on my "possible belt." This carried my Al Mar knife and a Bic lighter, modern version of the coal-carrying pouch. Old Lady Library had emphasized how the old-time women wore knives. To the knife belt, I added an antique Navy Colt cap-and-ball pistol my dad had given me – a valuable trade-item in those days. Meanwhile, the boys piled up the load:

1 hatchet

1 set of reloading tools for the pistol, including a little bar of lead

5 pounds of jerky

1 dome tent – equivalent to hide shelters of dog-travois days.

3 blankets

Three extra pairs of sneakers – equivalent of a bundle of moccasins

1 cast-iron kettle from my camping equipment, similar to the trade kettles popular with 1850s Indians

Three sets of winter clothes

The travois groaned, almost buckled under this load. Old Lady Library looked grimly at it through her aviator sunglasses.

"Uh-uh," she said thoughtfully. "Take out half of that jerky. Remember that you are all good hunters. So you will be killing grouse and prairie dogs along the way."

"Prairie dogs?" The boys wrinkled their noses. "Yuk! We'll eat buffalo meat!"

"Prairie dogs are delicious," the old lady growled. "I grew up eating stuffed baked prairie dogs on the rez. And how will you pups and your grandma hunt even one buffalo? Get rid of those damn winter clothes too."

"But ... winter is coming! I argued.

"Only rich people with a lot of horses hauled their winter clothes around with them," the old lady stated patiently. "You and the boys are poor. When autumn comes, and the animals have their thick coats, you'll kill a lot of rabbits. Rabbit-skins are warm. You'll sew and sew! Then you'll put those winter clothes right on, and wear them till spring. And then you'll throw them away."

The lightened load, including blankets and kettle, came to slightly over 90 pounds.

Old Lady Library helped me adjust the harness around my upper body, so it didn't interfere with the Possible Belt. I shrugged at it uncomfortably – the harness cut into the muscles supporting my breasts.

We started off.

While the boys foraged ahead, Old Lady Library strode beside me. "Don't walk upright," she said. "It's hard on your back. *Lean* into the harness. Let your body weight, and the gravity of Mother Earth, do the pulling for you."

I obeyed. Suddenly the load sprang along more lightly behind me. The harness stopped cutting my breasts. My hands, each of them holding a pole, did no more than guide.

"If you are attacked," she pointed out, "you can let go the poles, and use both your hands to fight – and you can also keep moving forward."

Drawing my unloaded pistol, I turned and dry-fired at an imaginary enemy. The travois flexed and turned with me – pivoting smoothly on one leg, drawing a circle with the other leg, like a compass in geometry class. Not bad. My mind jolted excitedly into third gear.

"You can also drop the harness, and run for your life," said Lady Library.

Pretty soon I got tired, and jettisoned the 15-pound tent. This lightened the load to 75 pounds.

"We can build little shelters out of our blankets and branches," I told my teacher. " And leave the branches behind."

"Uh-uh. Yes," she nodded.

"Hey!" The boys were running toward me. "We caught four prairie dogs!"

They were waving the "meat" in the air – their four socks.

"That's exactly the way it happened," laughed Old Lady Library. "Mama hauled the load, and kids brought home the bacon.

Now... what if one of your pups has a hunting accident? Hm? Sprains his ankle?"

This was the big crisis – the one that I'd worried about.

I yanked the bundle of blankets out of the burlap "bucket seat." Gage slipped his arms through the bundle's ties, and carried it like a back pack. Then I plopped Shane into the bucket seat. He sat comfortably, legs dangling over the back pack. When we moved on, 50 pounds of boy had upped my load to around 125 pounds.

I struggled, feeling like a goddamned plow-horse. Sweat trickled down my face. I had to lean into the harness with every ounce of weight. Some soft padding on the web-belts would be good, I thought, so they wouldn't chafe my chest.

"Pretty soon I'll be played out," I panted.

"I know," said Old Lady Library calmly.

"We'll have to lay up somewhere, and hide, till Shane can walk," I groaned.

"No. You've got to find that camp," insisted my teacher. "Winter is coming. You might get caught in an early snowstorm."

The life-and-death reality of travois times loomed clear. I pondered what to throw away next.

"The blankets? No. The iron kettle? We need to eat ... "

"The kettle?" she said coldly. "You can roast a prairie dog on a stick over a fire! Better get your mind in gear, or you're going to be dead."

There was a long beat. Then I tossed the heavy cast-iron kettle into the grass.

Old Lady Library grinned.

"Uh-uh," she said. "I think you are starting to understand."

Over ensuing weeks, I pared the load to 60 pounds.

A travois had a short life, like a rainbow. On grassy prairie, a travois might last for half a season. But dragged over rough ground, like the weathered lava of the Snake River plains, or the granite passes across the Rockies, a travois wore down in a week or so. It was speedily replaced, its stumps fed into the campfire.

The travois also shaped other technology.

"Before the Spirit Dogs (horses) came," said Old Lady Library, "our people did know iron. That metal that some of us called *Miss-squa-ea-meah*, Red Earth Woman. But we weren't dumb about iron, like the anthros think."

The rare knife of meteorite iron was a status symbol, she said. For long centuries, in northern Canada, a great meteorite boulder provided chipped-off blades of "star iron," before white men hauled it off to the Smithsonian. But the peoples' need to minimize weight biased them against iron. No wonder so many pursued a sophisticated technology based on lightweight materials. For blades, they preferred obsidian, which is lightweight and doesn't rust. Portable teepees were tiny, made from a few hides. For containers, they stuck to water-tight baskets – pottery was too heavy, and breakable. The birchbark canoes, snowshoes, dog-sleds, kayaks, back-packs, toboggans, willow back-rests – all light as feathers. Kettles? Leather ones made of a buffalo's paunch.

Overland trade-goods also had to be light. Feathers, plant drugs, seeds, beads, little copper bells, arrows, textiles, abalone and cowrie shell. A single back-pack load of parrot feathers, coming up from Mexico, could make a native trader richer than J. Paul Getty.

Only with the arrival of Spirit Dog did heavy freighting and metal use become reasonable for the tribes. Teepees ballooned in size. The travois got bigger, too. It took one stout horse just to drag the new-model lodgeskin weighing around a quarter-ton. And it took several horses to haul the dozen longer, heavier poles. A wealthy woman needed quite a few travois, pack-horses and helpers to schlep her family from camp to camp. She could now transport iron luxuries like kettles, fry-pans and hatchets.

According to Nick Eggenhofer in *Wagons, Mules and Men*, the average "prairie schooner" wagon, with a team of horses, hauled only 2,500 pounds or less. The one-horse travois with its 500-pound load could go almost anywhere except up a cliff.

Today, while some historians still talk condescendingly about the "primitivity" of the early Indians, that modified travois is still in use among us – whether as medical stretchers, or as the wheeled suitcases that are pulled through airports by airline crews.

In 1991, when *One Is the Sun* was finally published, the travois provided me with some wonderful book-tour show-and-tell. One day in Gualala, CA, the mall in front of the Gualala Bookstore became a sea of delighted shrieks as kids and parents hauled each other around in the one I'd built. As I watched the loaded travois disappear down the crowded mall, with everybody staring at it, I knew that Old Lady Library was smiling like a coyote somewhere.

I was finally understanding what she'd meant about Archimedes. The old Greek had said he could build a lever that would move the Earth. The one I'd built had moved my mind.

LIBERTY IS A PAGAN GODDESS
American Truths as Revealed By That Symbol on Our Coins

"Every coin has a story to tell," a Chicago collector said recently. "Money is history that you can hold in your hands."

This is the standard philosophy about coins. But it was my mother, a ranch wife who grew into a historian and serious coin collector, who pointed out to me an extraordinary fact. For almost two centuries, a pagan goddess got top billing on U.S. coins. How – she asked me – could this happen when the brand-new United States supposedly clung so fiercely to established Protestant religion?

Nellie Bradford Warren never got to attend college. During the Great Depression, after she finished high school, she went to work to help support the family. But she was passionately self-educated, with an abiding interest in history, especially American history, and ancient Greek and Roman history. She got interested in numismatics by poring over a motley collection of old coins that had collected in the safe at our Montana ranch – everything from an 1855 octagonal California gold piece and some Civil War cents, to late 1800s Eagles. From there Nellie branched out to Greek and Roman coins. She saved every penny she could from the "house money," bought reference books, pored over coin catalogs.

She even studied some Greek and Latin so she could read the inscriptions on ancient coins. Now and then, drawing a deep breath when she saw a bargain, she ordered something and waited with bated breath till it came in the mail. With reverent care, she'd install it in one of her fattening coin albums. Now and then, too, she'd take the profit on something that had gone up in value, and trade it for an item that was rarer.

My dad, focused on keeping the ranch afloat, looked the other way when she spent her "pin" money on coins – it made her happy.

Needless to say, my mother's passion for history rubbed off on me, the way human fingerprints get left on coins. One day when I was visiting her in the 1960s, Mom had me flip through her cherished *Guide Book of United States Coins*. She pointed at various early coins that showed the Goddess of Liberty seated or standing, splendidly draped in her Roman toga, holding up a pair of scales or a liberty cap. The motto of one 1786 Massachusetts coin clearly identified her as "Goddess Liberty."

"Good grief," my mother said, raising her eyebrows. She was a Presbyterian who had played the organ at her church, and felt a certain pride in her Puritan ancestors, the Bradfords. But she also found pagan deities to be fascinating – especially Liberty. "I thought they didn't like pagans in Massachusetts. But they went and put Liberty on their coins. How in the world did *that* happen?"

My mother died in 1979, but her question stuck in my mind, like a tiny spine from a prickly pear that gets buried in a finger. The slightest move, and you feel that buried pain. Through the 1980s, as American right-wingers started getting ever louder with their claims that 1960s liberalizing was a betrayal of our national destiny and that America had been "founded under God," I realized that my mother's question is a devastating one.

The story of why Liberty was put on our coins in the first place, and the battle that was launched by fundamentalist church people to get Her taken off, is one of our nation's most important – and least told – epic stories. Symbols are highly charged, and vital for any nation's public positioning. Like ideas, symbols tend to have long lives; they can also be constantly readopted and reinvented, even manipulated. For thousands of years, empires and nations have put their most important symbols and their most vital positioning on their currency. The United States of America was – and is – no different.

Today most Americans react with deep emotion to our national symbols, exactly as they're supposed to do... but many have no idea what these emblems really mean, or where they came from.

A Paradox of History

The battle over the Goddess of Liberty shows how a fundamental shift in our national consciousness took place between around 1850 and the Second World War – a move away from our founders' original positioning. The re-positioning radically altered how we see our history and express our symbols. Yet our founding coins are still there on the record, dotted along our time-line. They're forensic evidence of the starkest sort, like an unmistakable trail of fossilized footprints along an ancient Western riverbed, that tell us whether it was a mammoth or saber-tooth tiger that once walked there. The time-line of coins, and the images on them, tells the real story of where we started, and where we went.

During the 1776-1783 American Revolution, our concept of "liberty" evolved slowly and creakily to include freedom from church rule as well as freedom from overseas rule by kings. Colonial American governments had been little dictatorships of established religion, with church and state functioning as one organic complex, and all persons except white male Protestant property-owners barred from voting and office-holding. Yet change was unfurling on the wind. In Europe, the revolutions that erupted between 1581 and 1850 – in Netherlands, France, Italy, Spain, German-speaking countries – were driven as much by hatred of clergy as by hatred of monarchy. Absolute rule by churches was now seen as conflicting with the emerging concept of "human rights."

Inevitably these anti-church feelings filtered west across the Atlantic. After the American Revolution, founders who were concerned about human rights began advocating amendments to the new U.,S. Constitution, to be called the Bill of Rights. Abuses listed in the Bill of Rights had been perpetrated not just by and in

Britain – they had been perpetrated by established religion right in the American colonies. Proof of this can be found in the Massachusetts Body of Liberties adopted by the colony's government in 1641. This almost forgotten document – in spite of its theocratic foundation and its grim list of Old Testament death penalities – was a response to growing questions over absolute church authority in the Massachusetts Bay Colony. The Body of Liberties was actually the first "declaration of rights" in American history, because it compelled the Puritan churchmen running the colony's government to establish a general court, and to grant due process to anyone accused of a crime, including the right to a trial. It also put an end to the use of torture.

As the "free" United States was born, most of the new state constitutions and state statutes clung to the old religious establishments in that state. Ministers were on the state payroll. To hold office, an electee had to swear publicly on the Bible that he believed in the key tenets of Protestantism, including the Trinity (which barred Unitarians from office, in effect). But, on the emerging federal level, the Bible was no longer in the driver's seat. It was the classical pagan tradition of Roman Republic that was being revived. Many of our founders were educated in ancient history, so they were very familiar with the Roman Republic.

It was this tradition that determined much of our national structure of government – as well as the symbols placed on our coinage.

Roman Rigor

In the pre-Christian Mediterranean world, culture started with questions. Intelligent questions enabled the ancients to make their amazing advances in science, philosophy, medicine, engineering and government. One of the most urgent questions was this: do a people have the right to demand accountability from tyrannical rulers? Out of this question came the city republics of Greece and Rome.

In 509 B.C. the confederated Roman tribes answered this question by dethroning their cruel king.

The word "republic" roughly translates as "returning to the people" (Latin *populus*). Dictionaries loosely define a republic as any form of government that is not a monarchy. But it's vital to be more specific. The Roman republic was definitely not a democracy as we understand democracy today. The *demos*, or "common people," weren't deemed a legal part of the *populus*. The new Rome, with its growing urban center on the famous seven hills, continued to be ruled by an oligarchy of powerful wealthy patricians, or aristocratic families. They controlled the Senate, a legislative body of elders (*sen* means old) that already existed during Rome's monarchy. Roman women had greater legal, economic and social independence than Greek women, but still lived "under the power" of Roman men.

The Roman republic did evolve in a democratic direction for a time, as the monarchy fell and the tribes' non-aristocrat population angrily demanded certain rights. They wanted to be considered part of the *populus*. They wanted the laws to be written down and made public. They wanted their interests to be safeguarded from patrician abuse by tribal officials, or *tribuni*, that their designated assemblies would elect. So a constitutional body of law, the Twelve Tables, was written and posted on bronze tablets in the Forum – a code that endured for the next 900 years. Tribunes and consuls effectively formed a new branch of plebian government to balance that of the aristocrats. Officials were not elected directly by the people, but by a body of electors that supposedly comprised the Republic's best minds.

The Republic also established a judicial system to try wrongdoers and settle disputes. Hence a system of "checks and balances" emerged in Roman civic life.

Unfortunately, at an early date, the Republic began turning itself into an empire by annexing nearby towns and cities. By 235 B.C.E., it controlled all of Italy south of the Po valley, and went on to engulf the entire Mediterranean rim and part of Europe. In 65 C.E., the Republic died officially when Augustus Caesar proclaimed himself emperor. He insisted that he ruled that empire by "divine right" in the name of Jupiter, Rome's chief God, and he made it stick because he controlled the army.

For the next three centuries, Rome was a dictatorship, with the emperor insisting that he ruled at the will of Jupiter. Succeeding emperors took away the tribunes' power, crushed the

Senate, forbade elections, and amended the Twelve Tables by personal edict. This religious cult of "divinely mandated" imperial rule was headed by Rome's high priest, or *pontifex maximus*, and centered around the temple of Jupiter. Diocletian upped the ante by forbidding Roman citizens to move their domicile, so they couldn't escape the tax collectors.

During the imperial period, as Christianity percolated into the Roman aristocracy, high-born Christians saw the advantage of hijacking this centralized pagan government for its own "divinely mandated" purposes. After 395 C.E., when Emperor Constantine became a nominal Christian, the old regime transmogrified into the Roman Catholic church's government. Tribunals vanished (the church had no use for "people's representation") while the Senate became the Roman Curia of the Church. To drive that message home, the old bronze doors of the Senate were re-installed in Rome's first cathedral, St. John Lateran. Christian patrician families wielded the same enormous power that pagan patricians had once wielded, and supplied candidates for candidates, bishops and popes. The office of *pontifex maximus* morphed into the Roman Catholic office of pontiff, or Pope. The old electors now became the College of Cardinals, who elected the Pope. In 529 Emperor Justinian did a Christian update of Roman law. Roman imperial taxes became tithes demanded from outlying territories of the Church.

In other words, the Roman Empire didn't fall. It just became Christian.

After the "Fall"

After this "fall," as Charlemagne unified most of Europe under a dictatorial Christianity and was crowned Holy Roman Emperor in 800, the old pagan electors were revived as a body that now elected the Christian Emperor. And that Emperor ruled by that old adopted Roman idea of "divine right."

Meanwhile, the Republic ideal survived only in isolated pockets – in the city of Venice, for example. In the 700s, Venice boldly reverted to that type of government with the election of a central executive figure, called the Doge, by its Grand Council.

While nominally Catholic, the Venetian republic was independent of Holy Roman rule and lasted for more than 1000 years.

But by the 1500s, that centralized Catholic control had become a major irritant in the Holy Roman Empire. In England, coming on top of Henry VIII's desire to divorce his wife, that old irritant helped to drive the country's noisy departure from the Catholic fold. The same irritant also drove the Protestant Reformation in German-speaking areas of Europe. Many Anglicans and Protestants continued to extol the idea of an all-controlling absolute monarchy that ruled a single nation in God's name.

But with nationalism surging everywhere, the Republic concept did re-emerge more powerfully during the 14th century, thanks to the Renaissance revival of interest in classical thought and tradition. City-state republics started popping up all over Europe. Europe's discovery of something called "Parliament" was actually a post-medieval reinvention of that two-pronged Roman government – the Senate and the branch representing the people. Under Edward I, England decided to adopt the two-house system – the House of Lords and the House of Commons.

A key event, the Dutch revolution, took rebirth a step farther. In the 16th century, as the Dutch threw off Spanish Catholic monarchy, they re-created a Parliament called the Staten-Generaal, with semi-autonomous status for their 17 provinces. In 1548, the Dutch northern provinces formed their own Republic of the Seven United Netherlands. The republic had a central executive figure, the *stadtholder*, who was elected by the Parliament. Though it established a Calvinist state church, the Dutch did evolve a policy of limited toleration for Catholics, other Protestants, and Jews.

In the 17th century, the revived Republic idea started taking root in North America, where some of the colonial governments began operating off written constitutions rather than royal charters granted by the British crown. Even while the American Revolution was being fought, the two-house model was adopted for new state legislatures, and later (after adoption of the U.S. Constitution) for the U.S. Senate and House of Representatives. Old "checks and balances" of executive, legislative and judiciary were re-created. American founders were inspired enough by the

Dutch example that they borrowed the Dutch unity symbol, a bundle of arrows, and put it on our Great Seal.

In short, the old Roman Republic idea provided a handy model for dethroning of post-medieval monarchy, including the British in America. The fiercely Calvinistic Bible-believing males among our founders may have seen the Republic idea differently than founders like George Washington and Thomas Jefferson, who were deists, meaning they rejected reliance on faith, and used reason only to find evidence of a Supreme Being. But both factions were in evident agreement about one thing: Roman republican government had worked for a long time – why not revive it in the New World?

But the new United States took a step farther than the Dutch model, which had still accepted the political primacy of one religion. Many American founders now looked back at the Holy Roman Empire, and at Cromwell's England, which resembled what Jefferson called a "Protestant Popedom," and they saw the danger of putting any one religion in charge of a government. They felt that a people should be free from the control of any one religion – from the abuses that a ruling religion inevitably committed.

So it was not surprising that our founders chose a non-Christian symbol of liberty – one that reached all the way back to the very origins of Republics, in order to express the aims of their new nation.

This was how the old Roman Goddess of Liberty emerged on our shiny new national coinage as the principal ikon of change.

The Liberty Cap

Where did Liberty herself come from? Many Americans are conditioned by academia to think of ancient Goddesses only in connection with "fertility rites." Yet throughout pre-Christian history, there is an archetype Goddess who embodies the highest powers of law, justice and government. She is found in many Western cultures, under names and guises that emblemize different dynamics of society, from the military to the commercial. I call her the Great Goddess of Government. Because coinage and fiscal policy is a vital duty of any government, it follows that She became a popular image on many ancient Greek and Roman coins.

This Goddess is always easy to identify. Ancient art clearly identified the different Gods and Goddesses by visible attributes – actions, clothing, items they hold. In case the visual bona-fides were not enough for an uneducated Roman, Latin mottos on the coins usually identified a deity by name. In the great city of Rome, the Government Goddess took many forms. As the maiden warrioress/protector of the city, she was Minerva, armed with spear, helmet and shield. In another form, she was Roma, the spirit of the city itself. In yet another guise, she was Justitia. There, she embodied the severity of justice by wielding a sword, the weapon of choice for death penalties meted out to Roman citizens.

A more matronly and down-to-earth form of Government Goddess captured the hearts of Romans as well. This was Juno, mother of Minerva; she was was the wife of Jupiter, ruler of all Roman Gods. As such, Juno was not only the patroness of marriage and family, but the guardian of the Roman state, especially its fiscal business. Her temple stood on the Roman equivalent of Wall Street, namely on Capitoline Hill right near the Senate, which was empowered to order up coinage. The Roman mint operated at Juno's temple. As Juno Moneta she was the emblem of commerce, identified by the pair of scales she carried. In fact, Latin *moneta* meant "mint," from which comes our "money." Our word "office" comes from Latin *officina*, meaning the mint's workshops, where coins were struck.

Roman women, while legally viewed as being "in the power" of family men, did have some say about money and property, running the household, managing slaves, etc. Various powerful Roman women – wives of emperors, Senators, consuls – made their mark on Roman history. After passage of one unpopular sumptuary law limiting the amount of gold and possessions a woman could hold, an extraordinary thing happened. For days, thousands of women poured into the streets and staged a massive demonstration, stopping traffic and buttonholing every Senator and consul who came along. The government finally caved, and repealed the law.

This social and economic leverage of Roman women probably

explains why Rome put a Goddess, not a God, in charge of the mint.

Last and most important of their government deities, Romans loved the Goddess of freedom, Libertas (Latin for "liberty"). Her temple on the Aventine Hill was historically important to Romans because she embodied the Republic's victory over monarchy.

Liberty's image was a popular one on coins – several emperors, including Galba (who helped rid Rome of the cruel Nero), celebrated her copiously on their issues. She could be identified by her long scepter, symbolizing her authority over herself, and the pileus, or "cap of liberty," that she either wore or held. This cap was worn by slaves when they were freed during a ceremony at Libertas' temple. Covering your head was a right reserved to freemen, especially the upper class. An important feature of Roman culture was this upward mobility that it allowed. One could move from slavery to full Roman citizenship, and be rewarded for your industriousness and brilliance.

In the New World, the image of Libertas was so loved by our founders that she made her debut on the obverse (face) of U.S. coins even before the American Revolution.

Coins Made in Private

American-made coins were already struck in the earliest colonies. The first Virginia charter of 1607 said that the colonial government "lawfullie may establishe and cawse to be made a coine, to passe currant there betwene the people of those severall Colonies for the more ease of trafiique and bargaining betweene and amongest them and the natives there." But in the beginning, coins were scarce, not standardized or centrally minted. For legal tender, colonists had used tobacco or Native American wampum (strings of valuable shell), along with a motley assortment of stray foreign coins – British shillings and pence, Irish coppers, Dutch dollars, trading-company tokens. Silver Spanish milled dollars were popular.

During and after the Revolution, as American-made coins appeared in larger numbers, they were stamped by small private mints or individual engravers, often from dies made in Britain. So these private coins, though allowed to circulate by state statute, didn't represent "state religious policy." Clearly their designs suggest that Age of Enlightenment sympathies – and a familiarity with ancient Roman coins – prevailed among some individual engravers, many of whose names we know.

For example, George Wyon of Birmingham, England may have designed the beautiful "Immunis Columbia" coins of 1785-87. Some of the last privately minted coins to be circulated in northern states, the Immunis Columbias were struck in both gold and copper, portraying the Goddess in elegant detail. The motto calls her "Columbia," a new goddess name for the Americas created from the surname Columbus. She is a fusion of Liberty and Juno Moneta, holding a pair of scales in one hand, and a scepter and liberty cap in the other. Commercial freedom – freedom from royal taxes, freedom to trade with whomever they pleased, buy and sell whatever goods they chose – was as important to the American colonists as was political freedom.

In 1787, the new U.S. Constitution – written in that tradition stretching back to the Roman Twelve Tables – took coinage out of private hands, vested it in the federal government and established the dollar as our unit of currency. When Congress started centralized minting at the Philadelphia Mint, there was a hot debate about what symbol to put on the coins. According to *A Guidebook of United States Coins*:

"Many members of the House favored a representation of the President's head on the obverse of each coin. Others considered the idea a monarchic practice. Washington is believed to have expressed disapproval of the use of his portrait on our coins. The majority considered a figure emblematic of Liberty more appropriate and the Senate finally concurred in this opinion."

So engraver Robert Birch was hired by Congress, and came up with a buxom Liberty with thick wavy locks. She was identified in the Roman manner by the motto LIBERTY PARENT OF SCIENCE AND INDUSTRY. These were coined in 1792. Shortly the motto was shortened to one word: LIBERTY. Sometimes she wore the liberty cap. Sometimes the cap simply hung on the end of her scepter.

In other words – though state government continued to establish an official Bible-based Protestant religion, the majority vote among the framers and ratifiers of the U.S. Constitution had clearly not favored established religion. Two years after Liberty appeared on the first federal coins, the adoption of the 1789 Bill of Rights actually barred Congress from establishing religion. A later U.S. Supreme Court decision made it clear that the First Amendment applied to the states as well.

Our American founders drew their concerns about religion from Europe as well. In 1789, as the lid of revolution blew off in France and wicker baskets heaped high with severed heads, some of those heads belonged to churchmen. A fierce anticlerical spirit drove that explosion. If the newborn United States of America did not make religious liberty into a national policy, the nation might dissolve back into competing states, each with its established church. Without unity on this issue, the United States might perish in religious wars as horrible as the ones that wracked Europe for centuries. By the late 1780s, Congress was already realizing that potential new territories to the west were populated with many unbelieving refugees from the States, who now hesitated to enter the union without guarantees of religious liberty.

So Liberty became to America what Juno/Roma was to Rome – the personification of our new republic's spirit.

In the early 1800s, designers began putting her head or bust on the coins, rather than using her whole figure. Sometimes, as on the 1839 cent pieces, Liberty is young and pert, with a Greek antique look (large nose and eyes, as on Greek vase art). Other times she looks European and matronly, almost dowdy, as on the 1816 large cent. Sometimes her bosom is pushed high and half-bared, as a nod to high-waisted ladies' fashion of the Napoleonic period. Often she wears the aristocrat's diadem associated with Juno in Roman coins. In the 1833 half-cent piece, the motto is right on the diadem. But always the motto stresses who she is: LIBERTY.

Not surprisingly, Goddess images even spun off onto some state seals. Inevitably, they found their way into civic architecture across the country – courthouses, city halls, government buildings, museums, even schools and public libraries – any that were built in the neo-classic style. Right on top of the Capitol building in Washington D.C., in 1863, Congress installed a magnificent 19-

foot bronze Liberty created by Masonic artist Thomas Crawford. Indeed, on the heels of Liberty, other pagan Roman symbols flooded into the architecture of our capitol – like the fasces, or bundle of sticks that symbolized the old Roman unity of tribes.

This trend gained speed as the frontier rolled West. In Austin, Texas, for example, the Great Goddess took her stance on behalf of "Texas justice" on top of the state Capitol dome, holding a sword in one hand and the Lone Star in the other. A similar Liberty went up on the Kansas Capitol in Topeka. Murals, sculptured friezes, posters of the period – all show her busy with the frontier business of America, striding along with swirling robes, or hovering protectively in the air over pioneers with their covered wagons. On the state seal of California, designed in 1849, she appears in her guise as the fighting city goddess Minerva, with helmet, armor and shield, and a bear at her feet.

Growing Dissent

But while Congress was busy stamping a pagan Liberty on our coins, many of our Protestant Bible-believing citizens were simmering with discontent.

They saw themselves as latter-day descendants of the Israelites standing on the threshold of a new Zion. They believed that God had given this continent to them, in exchange for their agreement to abide by Bible-based law. In their minds, "God's gift of the land to them" automatically extinguished all Native American title to land and tribal sovereignty, as well as any territorial claims by other religions. It gave them a perceived right to determine the nation's course through legislation and social pressure "in God's name." The Bible brims with accounts of atrocities and massacres, telling how entire non-believing populations were put to the sword. Some conservative American Protestants felt justified in doing likewise to America's pagan enemies, notably the Native American tribes. The Old Testament also gave Protestants what they perceived to be the "God-given right" to own slaves.

For many decades after 1789, as new states and territories entered the U.S., evangelical Protestants mounted huge efforts to missionize the large populations of "unbelieving" pioneers and native peoples living to the West. This westward movement of belief, called "The Great Awakening," kept stride with westward flowings of the frontier. That emerging national belief in "eminent domain" was a perceived God-given "right"of the United States to wipe out not only the land rights of American Indian nations, but also the property rights of Catholics who had settled in the West when it belonged to Spain and Mexico. That drive to occupy the entire continent had a strong Protestant and Biblical hue. Denied their empire in Europe, where Catholicism still had a strong hold, the Protestants would now establish their Bible-based empire in America.

Through the 1850s, in spite of this strong Christianizing movement, our national civic heraldry continued to feature a pagan Liberty on our coins. But, despite growing federal pressure to privatize religion at the state level, many states only paid lip service to the idea of "liberty for all Christians" and clung to their established churches. Thomas Jefferson referred to Connecticut as a "Protestant Popedom." Massachusetts didn't privatize its state church till 1833.

Paradoxically, not all American Christians were in agreement that this approach was what "liberty" should mean in America. Some church members were liberals who agonized at all the human-rights abuses being committed in the name of the new Zion.

Colonial Puritan persecutions of Quakers and other sects had caused widespread revulsion – had fueled powerful dissenters like William Penn to go out on a limb with demands that all forms of Christianity be tolerated. Thomas Jefferson and Roger Williams went a step farther, demanding tolerance for Jews, Muslims and pagans. Slavery was already becoming a hot issue among the more progressive Christians. The Underground Railroad, a network of safe houses and sympathizers, started operating even before the Revolution and continued till the Civil War, ultimately helping over a hundred thousand escaped slaves to reach freedom. Also festering were the issues growing around women's rights, child labor and a need for voting rights to be expanded beyond the ranks of property holders.

These "heresies" by liberal Protestants didn't stop conservative Protestants from pushing their own aims. The word "liberal" entered their political language as an unflattering epithet. After all, a "liberal" was devoted to liberty as personified by a pagan goddess. That was viewed as a bad thing by believers.

Ironically, through this whole period, while many Christian Americans advocated the removal and extermination of the pagan native tribes, the pagan goddess on our money had adopted a Native American look – complete with feathers in her hair.

The "Indian Queen"

One of the forgotten facts about America's founding is that pagan native tribes with democratic governments were helping from the sidelines. The northeast tribes had confederated into the Six Nations governed by a elected council of men and women, the Haudenosaunee. Benjamin Franklin is known to have had his liaison among the Seneca chiefs. When Iroquois chiefs visited the Continental Congress on July 11, 1776, they were received with great demonstrations of respect by the white delegates. Congressional secretary Charles Thomson carefully wrote this event into the Congressional Record. The chiefs were told by the Congress that Americans and Iroquois would hopefully act "as one people."

Learning from the North American tribal confederacies made perfect sense. After all, our founders were painfully aware that Europe had no living, working democracies to serve as a model.

Long before the American Revolution, European artists had become romantically infatuated with what they termed "noble savages" in the New World. Following an ancient tradition that personified continents as Goddesses, the Age of Enlightenment created a new symbol – the Goddess of the New World. She had various names – America, Columbia, etc. On maps and in book illustrations, She was splendidly crowned with a headdress of feathers that stood straight up, after the manner of some tribes throughout the Americas. She was carrying a bow in one hand and a tomahawk in the other, wearing Europeanized versions of Native American dress. Accompanying her were New World sacred animals like llamas or rattlesnakes.

The choice of weapons was not an artist's whim – there were actual reports that some native tribes had their New World amazons who were expert with the bow. These amazons inspired Spanish explorers to create the name California, whose shores they explored at an early date; Califa was the name of the original Amazon queen who fought in the Trojan War, as mentioned by Greek historian Herodotus.

At first this Native American Goddess was portrayed as voluptuous and wild-looking, sitting naked on an armadillo, as per the famed European engraving by Adrien Collaert II after Marten de Vos, "Personification of America," 1765-1775. Later she grew more dignified and matronly, wearing a toga-like robe with tribal fringes and ornaments. Because monarchy ruled the Americas in those times, she was known as the Indian Queen or the Indian Princess.

However, once the American colonists had thrown off British monarchy, our coin designers radically repositioned the Indian Queen. She was now considered to symbolize the United States only. And she morphed into a classical mode, albeit with recognizable Indian details, suggesting a human woman chief wearing the feather headdress that denoted leadership, honor and respect by her people. In 1787-88, in the Commonwealth of Massachusetts, Joshua Witherle designed cent and half-cent coins with a standing figure on the obverse. On the figure's head is a little pouf of feathers. She wears a Roman-looking kilt and sandals, and holds a bow in one hand and an arrow in the other. The figure is minimal and geometric, suggesting that the designer may have copied it from a wampum belt or other tribal work.

New York State coins also doted on the Indian Woman Chief. In New York State in 1787, a coin showed the same minimalist figure holding a tomahawk (symbol of war) in one hand and an unstrung bow (symbol of peace) in the other. Another New York State issue, the so-called Nova Eborac series, portrays a wonderful hybrid figure – a splendid robed Liberty crowned with big feathers, seated in the Roman fashion with her scepter, shield and liberty cap.

A Confederatio copper, believed to be struck from dies made by George Wyon of England, has the Woman Chief on its obverse. She is identifiable by her bow and quiver of arrows, and the motto AMERICANA INIMICA TYRANNIS. In other words, the Native American Liberty was styled as the "enemy of tyranny."

In 1792, for one of the first Congressional issues, Robert Birch designed a silver cent with an unusual Liberty head. Her streaming hair and her big Native American disc earrings frame a distinctive Native American profile with a high-bridged nose. As late as the mid-1800s, there were gold dollar and 3-dollar pieces with Liberty crowned by a chief's feather headdress. For the 1854 dollar, James Longacre designed the headdress as a hybrid: it's the Juno diadem with feathers. In the 1865 dollar, the headdress looks more authentic. In both versions, the feathers stand up straight and stiff, as was common among Eastern, Mexican and South American tribes, instead of trailing back over the shoulders as worn on the High Plains. On the reverse of these Indian Queen dollars is a wreath of Native American plants – corn and tobacco and cotton.

Clearly, by the 1850s, persistent portraying of Liberty in a chief's feather headdress suggests that some in Congress remembered dimly how women had held high political leadership in the Haudenosaunee.

Yet in a manner that looks hypocritical to many of us today, Congress approved designs for these Indian Liberties even as the United States ended its era of friendly trade with the tribes and was launching an all-out war in order to capture the tribes' lands across the continent. A brown-skinned Libertas meant little to vanquished tribes who were dispossessed and forcibly Christianized.

Significantly, by the late 1800s, as the last of the free Western tribes were herded into prisoner-of-war camps called "reservations," Native American Liberty was vanishing from our coins by then – replaced by the familiar male "Indian-head" issues. These were minted in the early 1900s; a few of the Indian-head nickels still circulate today. The chief's bonnet has just a few feathers trailing down. His expression is sad, somber. On the reverse a buffalo stands with head lowered in submission. Both images reflect defeat.

North vs. South

Liberty also meant little to black slaves, who had seen her as a symbol brandished by their white Southern owners before and during the Civil War. Southern history tells one horrible story of a Liberty monument in a Southern city that was used to hang black men during a lynching. Our country's now-habitual use of the

Liberty symbol was becoming more and more at odds with the injustices committed against blacks.

As the United States lurched towards the Civil War, coin designers' use of that liberty cap started stirring some hot debate. How could the U.S. display this symbol when our country permitted slavery?

Ironically, the Southern Confederacy was laying its own claim to the liberty cap. To them, it represented states' rights, not the rights of slaves. In 1861, when rebel forces took over the Southern federal mint at Dahlonega, GA, the Confederacy used captured dies and bullion to coin thousands of gold dollars with capped Liberty heads on them. That same year, the South also commissioned a half-dollar that displayed a classic seated Liberty holding the cap. The reverse showed the cap as a crest for the Confederate arms. In 1861, 500 of these half-dollars were coined by a New Orleans mint. But the Northern blockade, which cut the South off from a steady supply of bullion, made it impossible for the Confederacy to launch its own coinage. The half-dollar dies were found gathering dust in private hands after the Civil War.

A similar fate met Confederate designs for a cent, commissioned to a Philadelphia engraver named Robert Lovett. Fearing that he'd be prosecuted for treason by the U.S. government, Lovett decided not to deliver the job. Instead he hid the coins and dies in his basement. Ironically, this Confederate cent also featured the Goddess wearing that controversial cap.

In other arts, the North/South struggle over the symbol continued. The South plastered Liberty on several of its state republic flags, notably Alabama's. In the North, the Copperheads – Northern members of the Democratic Party who opposed Lincoln and wanted peace – wore buttons cut from copper coins depicting Liberty. On both sides, war memorials to fallen soldiers sprang up everywhere, including Gettysburg, with the Goddess of Liberty standing stark against many skylines, along those many fields and forests where so many millions of men died.

Even individual soldiers fought with the Goddess's name on their lips.

On Sept 1st, 1864, one W.R. Clack wrote a letter to his family filled with the fulsome prose of the times: "It is hard to conceive of the great joy that will animate and enliven the hearts of the people when this cruel slaughter of Americans by Americans are ended... When spears are turned into pruning hooks and swords into plowshares, and the Goddess of Liberty folding away forever the bloodstained banner of Civil War wares upon her wounded bosom the healing olives branch of peace."

In Congress, meanwhile, as the Civil War rumbled onwards, a political tug of war was developing over our national motto on the coins. As Christian religious sentiments flared around this horrendous conflict that was leaving a quarter of the nation devastated, and both sides went to church to pray for victory, the motto "In God We Trust" suddenly appeared for the first time – on our 1864 quarter dollar.

After the Civil War ended, the two mottoes continued to see-saw back and forth in an atmosphere of growing controversy.

Changes in the Wind

It had taken almost a century – from 1776 till 1862 – for the conservative Puritan-type Protestants to recover that leverage at the federal level that they had lost during the Revolutionary era. But by the end of the Civil War, they had made big inroads in the grassroots everywhere, and were poised to take over that religious groundswell that liberal Christian abolitionists had created around slavery. Their goal was to reshape what they viewed as a "godless" American Republic into a Christianized Protestant American Empire. In 1864, the thunderclap appearance of "In God We Trust" on the coins signaled the re-emergence of a politically powerful conservative Christianity, and a church cultural repositioning that went to war on the old Enlightenment.

On a parallel track, other political demographics in the United States continued to struggle towards a more democratic expression of that Republican government. Once again the *populus* were speaking out, angry, confronting the aristocrats. They wanted voting suffrage for former slaves and women – for Native Americans on reservations, for 18-year-olds, for people who didn't own property. They wanted an end to child labor, decent working conditions, the right to form unions, fair treatment for immigrants and a host of other things.

Meanwhile, as cities and communities reverberated with these issues, their local pageants often featured Goddess Liberty. When the 15th Amendment was passed in 1870, granting the vote to blacks, communities celebrated all over the country. Typical was the stirring scene in Oberlin, Illinois, as the town turned out for a huge parade. According to the local paper, it featured "a large band-wagon, in which were thirty-seven young ladies, representing the thirty-seven States of the re-constructed Union, and another representing the Goddess of Liberty–all dressed in white.....Banners, with appropriate mottoes, were displayed ..... Some of them were, *We want civil rights*; *Oberlin foremost in the battle for freedom*."

Yet clearly a growing number of church people felt that the pagan Goddess on our legal tender was ungodly. It was time for Her to go.

By the time the Statue of Liberty's bronze colossus was inaugurated in New York Harbor in 1887, Her engraved image on coins was already going through a sea-change. It was not only disappearing, but showing a curious de-dignifying. On his 1880 gold dollar, George T. Morgan did a Liberty who looked like a frumpy housewife, with her hair in a bun. In 1892, Charles Barber's half-dollar Liberty looked strangely masculine, with short hair. In 1917, there was a public scandal over Hermon A. MacNeil's new quarter with its Standing Liberty holding a shield and olive branch. Her toga exposed one breast. Newspapers filled with angry editorials about this "obscenity." Congress hastily ordered the offending mammary gland to be covered up.

Efforts of the Leviticus lobby to get Liberty off our money were so stealthy that most of the public probably didn't compute what was really happening. She had already vanished from the cent by 1857. From 1837 till 1897, the dime had carried a seated Roman-style Liberty holding a liberty cap on her scepter. But suddenly, in 1897, she vanished off the dime as well. She was off the nickel by 1912.

Meanwhile the tug-of-war over mottoes continued. In 1908 President Theodore Roosevelt removed "In God We Trust" on grounds that the First Amendment prohibited use of God's name on our coins. But Congress overrode him, and put IGWT back. Nevertheless, a few designers managed to have their own way with coin ideology. In 1916, Adolf Weinman got the old motto LIBERTY back onto his new silver dime, along with a Goddess wearing a distinctive winged helmet. It was no accident that women's suffrage was being hotly debated at that time.

Between 1900 and World War II, like a colorful sunset that ends a fine day, several of the last beautiful coin Liberties were issued. Famed American sculptor Augustus Saint-Gaudens, whose works showed so much sensitivity about women, designed what many collectors consider to be the most magnificent American coin ever. In 1907 this $20 gold piece was minted in dramatic high relief, with Liberty surging dramatically out of a burst of sun rays. Saint-Gaudens also did the last of the feathered Liberties on his 1907-33 gold eagle, and colluded with President Roosevelt on getting the motto IN GOD WE TRUST briefly removed. Adolf A. Weinman did his own dynamic "Walking Liberty" on the 1916-1947 half dollar.

Last but not least, Anthony De Francisci's silver "peace dollar" of 1921-35 featured a young Liberty crowned with rays of light. Her poignant, melancholy expression and parted lips suggested that She was saying something profound about the First World War that had just shredded Europe.

These Liberties were jeered as feminist propaganda by church people opposing women's suffrage. H.L. Mencken was so disgusted at these jeers that he wrote: "It would surprise no independent observer if ... the goddess of liberty were taken off the silver dollars to make room for a bas relief of a policeman in a spiked helmet."

The 19th Amendment was finally adopted in 1920, and my great-grandmother and grandmother finally got to vote.

But despite this victory for women, Liberty was off the quarter by 1930. By 1935, the last of the Liberty dollars were minted for circulation.

An Ungrateful Nation

Ironically, it was World War II, and the "crusade against fascism," that struck a huge blow at our official affection for pagan Liberty.

By then, church repositioning of American history had made many American citizens and historians unable to see that European fascist movements were nothing more than extremist versions of that Christian Imperial fundamentalism which had already been running Europe for many long centuries. Americans who hated Hitler failed to compute the fact that German fascism had enjoyed broad popular support from conservative clergy and lay people in both the Catholic and Protestant regions of Germany.

As a symbol, Liberty did see us through World War II. Wearing Her liberty cap, She was still on the dime till 1945. As the beautiful Walking Liberty, She was on the half dollar till 1947. But our government and our most conservative citizens were evidently not grateful to Her for leading us to victory over Germany and Japan. After 1947 – poof! She was gone from our money entirely – replaced by heads of male Presidents.

By 1950, with the cold war gearing up and Radio Liberty beaming political messages to people behind the Iron Curtain, the pre-Christian Goddess who had always been the American embodiment of liberty was not seen as a symbol that would help oppose "godless communism" around the world.

Starting in 1971, the dollar went all-male – Eisenhower's head on the obverse, and the Apollo 11 moon-landing insignia on the reverse.

Changes in monetary policy were also removing Liberty's image from public view on a broader level. The U.S. government had already ended circulation of gold coins in 1934, when President Roosevelt took the country off the gold standard. For a time, federal law prohibited U.S. citizens from owning any gold at all. My mother hid the ranch's little collection of antique gold pieces, in fear and trembling that the government would show up at the front door and want to confiscate them. Now Washington D.C. started taking the .900-pure silver coins out of circulation as well. Many old coins were melted down, while others disappeared into private collections. The result: new generations of Americans grew up without seeing and handling those female images of Liberty that had coursed daily through American commerce and family life for almost 200 years.

Coins are intimate and tactile and deeply human to the people who use them. Given to kids as allowance, carried in pockets as lucky pieces, saved in children's piggy banks or housewives' cookie jars, hoarded during wars, buried in the back yard during times of danger, kept in desk drawers as keepsakes of past generations, coins get worn smooth by the warm fingers and sweat and cares of living people.

But my generation was the last to finger the winged helmet on that 1916 dime as we paid five dimes to get into a movie. I loved the heavy clink of silver dollars in my jeans pockets, and wondered why the Liberty on that 1921 dollar looked so sad. In 1955, when I left the ranch and rode the train east to college, I tipped the Pullman porters with silver dollars... and arrived in New York City to be shocked by the discovery that "pilgrims" (as Montanans called Easterners) didn't use silver dollars any more. Manhattan cabbies didn't want my silver cartwheels – they barked at me to pay them in greenbacks.

Mom lived to see the federal government re-legalize private gold ownership in the 1970s. Now suffering from what may have been multiple sclerosis, Nellie loved getting out her coins and looking at them, though her shaky fingers now had a hard time holding them. Eventually Mom's condition became so bad that my dad placed her in a convalescent home in Great Falls. She left her beloved coins behind in the ranch safe.

After my mother died in 1979, my father sold her coin collection to pay her accumulated medical bills. It brought over $100,000.

"She did good with her pin money," Dad said.

Today's Attacks on Liberty

Today the old Liberty coins are a hobby, albeit one that can run into seven digits. On December 1, 1999, the best surviving example of that "scandalous" quarter dollar – the one showing Liberty with a bare breast – went on the auction block to raise money for cancer research. It was part of a collection that brought almost $1 million total.

Today, in recognition to our true history, lovers of Liberty at the U.S. Mint and in Congress have staged a comeback for the Goddess on some new coins. In 2007 the Statue of Liberty was a feature symbol in the rollout of commemorative Presidential dollars. In an interesting positioning shift, the motto IN GOD WE TRUST was moved to the side of the coin, where it was incised around the edge. These Presidential dollars wouldn't be popular with anyone except collectors

– most Americans preferred paper dollars by then. (In a minting error, some were missing the motto on the side – these were dubbed "the godless dollars" by some church people, and snapped up by collectors.)

Far more dramatic, in 1986, was Liberty's grand entrance onto our bullion coins, called Eagles. Bullion is not circulated – it is traded, stored in Fort Knox, and serves as an investment medium for IRAs and 401(k)s. Weinman's 1916 Walking Liberty re-emerged on the silver Eagle, and Saint-Gaudens' magnificent Liberty on the gold Eagle. They were followed in 1997 by the platinum Eagle, with a modern design of the Statue of Liberty's head. In recent years, the supply of these striking U.S. bullion coins has been limited by a surge of buying precious metals as a hedge against inflation.

Who authorizes coin designs today– especially those that signal political shifts? The U.S. Mint is an independent agency, under jurisdiction of the Department of the Treasury. The Federal Research Bank tells us, on its website, that "the Director of the Mint selects designs for U.S. coins with the approval of the Secretary of the Treasury, although Congress may prescribe a coin design. A design may not be changed more often than every 25 years unless Congress determines otherwise." Congress has been involved in coin-design approval since virtually the beginning of U.S. history. Clearly it was a quiet majority vote in Congress that put Liberty back on our bullion coins.

Away from the investment market and the art world, however, the Liberty symbol keeps only a fragile hold on our national conscience.

Today even many liberals are lacking in a sense of Liberty's relevance to national and world issues. The Statue of Liberty is often positioned as a relic of the past, a dated symbol of 19th-century aspirations of European immigrants, rather than a symbol that might be meaningful for the non-European immigrants piling into the U.S. today. Some liberals take a politically correct view that Liberty represents only the aspirations of white people – that she has nothing to say to blacks, Latinos, Asians, Pacific Islanders. Few liberal Americans refer to the Statue of Liberty as a Goddess, showing that most aren't even aware of Her classical roots. She is commonly called "Miss Liberty" or "Lady Liberty," or just "The Statue."

Meanwhile, as part of what they call a new "Awakening," the religious right have gone to war on the actual Statue in New York

Harbor. One group started a drive (which has failed so far) to replace the historic torch with a cross. The Internet bristles with slanders of our erstwhile national symbol. A website for the Society for the Practical Establishment and Perpetuation of the Ten Commandments states: "What the heathen Statue of Liberty really means [is] ...Freedom to practice homosexuality or lesbianism ...Freedom to murder innocent human embryos and fetuses...Freedom to publicly blaspheme God." Another website rants: "You probably didn't realize it but America is steeped in Idols! The Statue of Liberty is actually a replica of the Babylonian goddess 'Ishtar,' the Mother of Harlots."

Americans who were shocked at the Taliban's destruction of ancient Buddha statues in Afghanistan need to realize that the Christian brand of this fundamentalist iconoclasm would happily blow up the Statue of Liberty in New York Harbor. These institutions are actually run by the type of person who fought tooth and nail to get the Goddess of Liberty off our coins. Today they fight to erase the very separation of church and state that the Goddess Liberty stands for. Self-styled historical "experts" like the Rev. Peter Marshall want to restore America "to its Bible-based foundations through preaching, teaching, and writing on America's Christian heritage and on Christian discipleship and revival." Clearly Marshall has no clue about our real history.

In the most recent coin kerfuffle, Sarah Palin weighed in on the Presidential dollars during a speech in early 2010. She was upset about the God motto being bumped to the rim of the coin. "Who calls these shots?" Palin demanded to know. "It's a disturbing trend."

Religious righters were busy firing off angry blogs and emails, blaming this alleged "trend" on the Obama administration. Finally research-minded reporters at Newsminer.com and other publications pointed out that the "disturbing" deed had been done by the Bush administration. In 2005 Congress had passed the Presidential $1 Coin Act, which stipulated that "In God We Trust" be moved to the edge, and President Bush had signed the bill.

For me, all these feverish efforts to rewrite our history only serve to throw my mother's question into sharper relief today.

American history has taken Libertas on a long journey, retooling Her and re-expressing Her. As my mother's daughter, I still have high hopes for Liberty. The country She symbolized in the 1700s was not perfect then – witness slavery, and witness repression of women and native peoples. And this country is not perfect today either – witness the teeming human-rights problems we face in 2010. Yet Liberty has always served as an inspiration to change. Proof of Her potential for new power, Her ability to be alloyed into any culture, anywhere in the world, can be seen in the Liberty put up in Tiananmen Square by Chinese dissident students. This statue was destroyed by the People's Republic of China's government, but the demands for democratization by many of China's people go on.

Today it amuses me to see certain fundamentalist Congress-members rise in the House and Senate and make loud speeches about "America being founded under God," when they're standing under that great dome that is topped by a statue of pagan Liberty.

Over thousands of years of world history, one thing has not changed – that, for a civilization to have any lasting worth, a high value must be put on the individual human life. As globalization swallows the globe, and money and free trade become the reason why so many things are done politically by so many governments, it behooves us to remember that money is best used to meet basic human needs, not to exploit or limit these needs.

In this republic now alleged to be founded "under God," there is one inalienable fact: the pagan Goddess of Liberty did preside over the birth and growing pangs of the United States of America. It is also a fact that there's no mention of Liberty in the Bible.

Further readings:

A Guide Book of United States Coins, 34th Revised Edition, by R.S. Yeoman (Western Publishing Company, 1981).

Exemplar of Liberty: Native America and the Evolution of Democracy, by Donald A. Grinde, Jr. and Bruce E. Johansen (American Indian Studies Center, Los Angeles, 1991).

"An Appreciation of Thomas Crawford's Statue of Freedom," by Katya Miller (U.S. Capitol Historical Society, 2007)
http://www.ladyfreedom.net/history.htm

MANY CLOSET DOORS: Mixed Ethnicity and Sexual Orientation in Montana History

From a speech at the Myrna Loy Cutural Center in Helena during Montana Pride, June 10, 2000

Thank you. This is a very meaningful day for me, and I know it is for all of us – the fun and learning, the sharing – the stories that so many of you tell about civil-rights progress made in Montana during the last five years.

Tonight I want to share a little bit with you about the meaningfulness of this day for me, not only because of my family connections with Helena and with Montana, but because of the history that connects me. I come from a family that is drenched in an awareness of history. I grew up with stories told at the dinner table about all kinds of things that had happened a century before. What the stories bred in me is an awareness of this fact: if we can't understand and respect the past, we will not understand and respect our present. We will continue to make the same mistakes, and we will not have a future.

The day before yesterday, I was interviewing with a woman from the Helena media and she said, "Oh, I didn't know there were gay people in Montana before now." Like we all somehow have landed on the latest shuttle from Mars. Yet we've been here from the start – and our families have been here.

Every time I come back to Montana, I find myself in conversations with lesbians and gay men and bisexuals and transgendered people. Inevitably we start comparing notes on family and somebody says, "Oh, my gosh, my greatgrandfather knew your greatgrandfather way back when and they did such and such together." What fascinates me is – how often these LGBT Montanans that I meet are mixed-bloods like myself.

So this fact extends our horizon not just back to 1862, when white men discovered gold in Montana. It extends our horizon back 1,000, 5,000, 10,000 years to when human beings first were into Montana. Because if you have Native American blood, that means that all of that history is part of you, and part of us.

There has been a great deal of fundamental dishonesty in Montana about ethnic blending. It's a closet, a big one. There are families who cannot acknowledge that their great-grandmother was a Crow woman or a Blackfoot woman ...or that their great-grandmother was a black woman, or an Asian woman. This family may also be unable to acknowledge their gay or lesbian or bisexual or transgendered children because they are lacking an understanding of how diversity is so much a part of life.

When I began writing the novel *One is the Sun* in 1980, it came to me very profoundly that there was a major horizon that I still had to cross in my life, in terms of understanding who I am as a woman and as a human being – where I come from and what is my present and where am I going. That path had led me back to Montana to find Native American relatives that I knew were here somewhere. I knew that the closet had existed in my own family. I knew that there were ancestors, relatives that were no longer mentioned, and I wanted to find these people.

The bottom line is I did find some of them – people who were able to tell me things I'd never known before. For example, I asked them, "Where did the name Deer Lodge come from?" Because in the Native world you have to ask the right questions or you don't get the information. The conventional history in Powell County has always said, "Well, there were a lot of deer in the valley in the old days, so they named it Deer Lodge."

And where does the word "lodge" come from? If you look at the map, you find the map of Montana and Wyoming sprinkled with names that suggest institutions in the Native world. There is Grass Lodge and Red Lodge and Bear Lodge and so forth. Who were the people of the Deer Lodge?

My Indian relatives said, " Well, the people of the Deer Lodge were Earth Thunder's people. She was a great woman... Medicine chief, healer, teacher of people, especially young people who lived in the Deer Lodge Valley right before the gold rush. And she was a mixed blood."

You have to imagine how my hair was standing on end when I heard this. The human faces of the real history began to be visible to me.

Let me give you another example. I come over here to the Montana Historical Society and was looking through the library for early materials about the Deer Lodge Valley when I come across a little book called *The Deer Lodge Pioneers*. It was published in the late 1880s sometime, as I remember. The photographer went over to the Deer Lodge Valley with a camera. Now remember that in those days, you're talking about a horse and buggy and a tripod camera and those awkward glass plates. He traveled all over the valley and took pictures of all of the families. There they were, husband, wife, children, log cabin, horses, dogs, whatever they had. And almost every single woman in those pictures was not white. There were women who looked Mexican, women who looked to be pure Native American of some tribe, and women who looked mixed.

The *History of Montana* that was published in 1881, even before the territory became a state, was already beginning to put the boilerplate of history in place. It was quite clear from this book that the "history" had all started with the wonderful white man who found gold and built the railroads and built the mines and so forth. One volume was full of biographies where we got the head-shot photos of the wonderful individual pioneers – Mr. So and So who was born in Boston or born in Germany, who came to Montana in such and such a year and did such and such wonderful things. And in due course he had children and all of the children were listed, along with mention of what the children did. But no mention of the wife. Why? Because she wasn't white.

This morning, at the march, we were chanting about "no more silence, no more lies." But there's also the lie in Montana about the mixed-blood people who were here even before the gold rush – the children of all those French and Spanish and Portuguese and British and German trappers and traders who came in here and married into the tribes in order to do business here or just because they liked it out here.

Now what does this have to do with gay rights? Well, in my opinion it has very much to do with gay rights.

If in my own family I couldn't talk about my Indian relatives – if it was a tricky thing to talk about my own grandfather's Cherokee ancestry, how was I going to talk about Uncle so and so who never got married and probably was gay? How can any family talk about Great-aunt so and so and her lady friend from Boston who came out here and started a business in Helena and obviously were an item?

If we can't talk about the ethnic secrets in the family, we can't talk about *any* of the secrets. Secrets are not good, are they? Secrets are kept secret because they damage this conventional picture of Montana – what Montana is and where Montana has been and where Montana has wanted to be going. And so we have the silence about the secrets.

When I finally came out – not only about being gay but about the ethnic things in the family – some of my family members were just as upset that I had opened the door of the ethnic closet as they were that I had opened the door of the sexual closet.

So this weekend I've already had conversations with some of you – "Oh, yeah, I go back to the McDonalds," or "I go back to this or I go back to that." One gay man told me, "My great-great-grandfather was one of the mountain men that settled in the Deer Lodge Valley, and he married a Shoshoni woman." It turned out that my great-grandfather knew his great-great-grandfather, and now here we are at the Gay Pride festival and we're talking about it.

Montana is not unique. Every state has its historical fakery, its closets full of pain and lies. It's time, as we said this morning, to end the silence, to end the lies.

We are all part of families. We are all part of a state where diversity needs to be not only tolerated, as one of the speakers said this morning, but celebrated in all its aspects. And Montanans will never celebrate gay people if they can't even celebrate their own family trees, their skin colors, their DNA.

Today we've talked about the media and the legislature in this State, and their responsibilities to humanize the laws and to cover the news in a more honest way. But I also want to see the educators, and the historical people who are in charge of the information, get busy humanizing what they do also. I was shocked to learn that here in Montana they no longer require teaching our children about Native American history. How embarrassing – in a state where we have all of these tribes, all of these languages – to have an English-only law. Officials would not get away with that in Los Angeles, where I live right now, because close to 50 percent of the city now speaks Spanish.

If we cannot be honest about our past – if we continue to live in these delusions about what our state is and who we are – we will not be honest about our present – and we will not have much of a future

So, in closing. I want to say how much I appreciate being here with all of you this weekend. There is a lot to do, as we have heard from Christine Kaufmann and other speakers this morning at the rally. But I am very hopeful, that if we deal with other closets in Montana, that we will get our own closet door open once and for all.

Thank you.

POLITICS

FRONTIER JUSTICE IN THE NINETIES

Originally published in
***The Ethical Spectacle*, December 1996**

I used to think that Dan White's sentence was the benchmark for holding a human life cheap. This elected official loaded a handgun and went to San Francisco city hall with a *High Noon* kind of murder in his heart. He shot to death not one but two fellow politicians: gay supervisor Harvey Milk and San Francisco mayor George Moscone. For two killings, White got 7 years, and was out in five.

But the other day, in Tennessee, Judge Doug Meyer opened a new frontier in the cheapening of life. He sentenced Adriana Blair Butler to 30 days in jail for shooting her mother's lover in the head. Thirty days...count them. The judge opted for leniency because, he said, there had been provocation. (After all, the mother's lover was a lesbian.)

These bargain-basement reductions on the price of life are affecting many Americans equally.

Today there is a widening gap between actual sentencing and what might be called punishment appropriate for the crime. Somehow, our whole system of justice has gotten dangerously twisted. Legislators, law officers, judges and juries don't just downsize penalties when it suits them (especially when it gets a white man off). They upsize penalties as well. In the last decade, there are whole rafts of new federal, state and local laws that criminalize actions once legal.

Misdemeanors can be upgraded to felonies. Counts are compounded, adding up to lots of time. While both political parties make loud speeches about putting away serial killers and sexual predators, legislators are quietly putting away ordinary people and first-time offenders for things like driving without a license. The criminalization of smoking and being HIV positive will be a windfall for the prison system. In several states, new "three strikes" laws propose to make crimes like prostitution a reason for life behind bars without parole.

Unthinking citizens who cheer "get tough" crime policy are simply not noticing the growing erosion of American life by this broaded definition of "crime" – in, say, the low-income West Virginia family who must pay a staggering $5000 fine because their kid got caught doing one graffiti.

In the territories of the Old West, people were commonly hung for stealing a horse. If you were black or Chinese or Native American, you could be hung for the fun of it. Life was cheap on the frontier. Stakes were high, with vast land and wealth for the taking. Law and order was thin, and often operated freely off personal bigotry and greed.

Today, with our country so overcrowded and overheated, with a punitive spirit riding high, life is cheap again and we're sliding back into frontier justice. There are not only the old bigotries and greeds to contend with, like those which sentence people of color to more time for the same crime. There is also a spooky new bureaucratic drive to monitor and control people's every action and punish them harshly for all kinds of minor offenses. The U.S. has the largest prison population on Earth, with 1 million people behind bars, and this is due as much to first offenses and victimless crime as it is to serial killers and drug dealers.

Murder and manslaughter sentences are a good way to measure the falling value of human life. With killer Butler's 30 days in mind, I pondered these sentences in the recent news right in California where I live:

Item: a grandmother in her 60s was arrested, handcuffed and booked for helpfully putting money in somebody's meter that had expired. She had no idea that this is illegal. Grandma got a $500 fine.

Item: In Los Angeles, a homeless person now gets six months in jail for sleeping on the sidewalk, and another six months for taking aluminum cans and other valuable recyclables from trash. Similar new laws target homeless all over the country.

Item: six months in jail for killing and eating a dog – a California law that targets Asian immigrants with different culinary traditions.

Kids are dirt cheap, as the lynch-mob mentality rides ever higher. Kids are subject to new criminalizations that would drive adults to riot – from suspicionless drug-testing to repressive curfew laws. In Camden, N.J., kids age 6-17 are arrested if they're found on the street during school hours. Minors are more prosecuted as adults, with those who kill being targeted for life sentences. Minors are jailed merely on the parents' request, or by a judge, to "teach them a lesson." Parents are held cheap, too – California parents can be jailed for a year and fined $2500 for failing to control their children. Statistics already reveal the stark fact that "getting tough" often turns a youthful offender into a hardened, angry adult repeater.

The question must be asked: Why is frontier justice in the saddle again?

More than misguided demands for "more morality," it is "more money" that is driving this trend. "Gold in them thar hills" translates into prisons as the hot new growth industry. Job-hungry communities lure new prisons the way they used to lure industry. Massive fines, lawyer's fees, jail and prison costs per inmate, the privatizing of prison construction and operation, the growing power of prison guards' unions – all are creating new funding, cash flow and pork in a starved economy. Just as the Old West suffered serious damage from out-of-control mining and logging, so our spiritual and economic landscape is eroding seriously in the New

West of today, as more and more ordinary citizens are caught in the toils of sentencing inequities, and their living is destroyed, and their rage and cynicism builds.

It is no wonder that more and more Americans have less and less respect for the law.

As for Adriana Butler, she is lucky that she put a bullet in somebody's head. If she had put a quarter in somebody's parking meter, she might have done 4 times the time.

Update in 2011

Sad to say, the U.S. penal problem continues to clank out of control. According to the most recent statistics published by the Bureau of Justice, the U.S. adult prison and jail population stood at 2,284,913 by the end of 2009. Add in a shadow population of those Americans who are on probation or parole, and the BOJ total reached a staggering 7,225,800.

MLK DAY IN CHOTEAU, MT

Originally published 1/21/2008 at The Bilerico Project (www.bilerico.com)

It may seem odd that I'm talking about global warming on Martin Luther King Day. But if Dr. King were alive today, I'll bet he would be concerned at how this threat has some terrifying implications for civil rights. In any case, I can't resist commenting on an event that happened in my home state the other day, that shows how deep some Americans still have their heads buried.

In Choteau, Montana, the school board pressured the high-school principal to cancel a speech on global warming by a Nobel laureate. They felt that the message to their farming and ranching community would be "anti agriculture." The speaker, University of Montana scientist Steve Running, who had worked with the UN science panel sharing the Nobel Prize with Al Gore, was shocked at this tragic tic of shortsightedness.

As a ranch-born Montanan, I share Steve Running's shock. With global warming kicking in, agriculture will be one of the first sectors to be devastated. In fact, farmers and ranchers are already being bankrupted as chronic and unprecedented drought ravaged large regions across the U.S. during the last year.

I wouldn't dare to guess how Dr. King might mention global warming in his "I have a dream" speech. But it would probably be in there somewhere. Something along the line of how little black kids and brown kids and white kids need more than schools where they can learn in equality – they need food to eat and a world to grow up in that isn't devastated by war and natural disaster. All the civil rights in the world will not help much if Earth heads into one of the periodic convulsions that has marked Her history. The complete breakdown of societies and governments, of law and order, that would follow a global catastrophe – or even a widespread famine – would be horrific from a human-rights standpoint. All the different civil-rights communities who are fighting right now for justice would experience the horrors along with everybody else.

Choteau is a small town (pop. 1800) that sits just east of the Rockies' front range, amid a vast sweep of wheat farms and cattle range. And this isn't the first time that Choteau has been in the news for climate shortsightness. In late 2001, David Letterman, who owns a big vacation ranch nearby, took a poke at the town on the "Late Show." Choteau had done a fundraiser and sent money to the 9/11 families in New York. Letterman pointed out that Choteau forgot about rural families right in their area who were suffering from drought. I imagine that some in the town missed the point and called Letterman "a goddam pilgrim" who had no right to criticize Montanans.

But the other day, the Choteau school board found itself the target of a whole heap of criticism...from other locals and from people around the state. High-school students and some townspeople raised enough of a ruckus that the media came to town again.

Steve Running commented sadly to the AP, "I think there's a faction of society that is willfully ignorant."

If my dad were still alive, he'd have a thing or two to say to the Choteau school board. Con Warren ranched in Montana all his life, from the early '30s till he retired in the '80s. In his later years, he became passionately convinced that a big climate change was afoot. He died in 1993, before the alarming recent figures on polar ice melt were in. But he spent his final years sitting hunched in his kitchen, rolling his handmade cigarettes and talking to anybody who would listen about the alarming things he'd noticed. The trend to drier, open winters with little snow pack. The changes in native vegetation. A creeping desertification across the whole West, which he compared to what's happening in the Sahel of central Africa.

Dad was even convinced that the rampant clear-cutting of timber in the Rockies was adding into a drier climate.

"Trees make weather," he said. "They bring water."

The fact is, my dad was that rare bird – a Republican who wasn't brain-dead about global warming. In order to make a living, he'd learned to pay attention to Mother Earth, so he couldn't deny the evidence that was right in front of his eyes. My dad never got a Nobel Prize, of course. His only public recognition was being named to the National Cowboy Hall of Fame as recognition of his pioneering work in rangeland replanting after the big 1930s drought.

I often encouraged him to do public speaking and help raise American consciousness on global warming, especially around the state.

But Dad shrugged me off. "Nobody's going to listen to a cranky old cowboy," he said.

Maybe this new ruckus in Choteau will spark a change in local thinking. Like every other issue, global warming has to be dealt with on a community level, not just on a global-policy level. People will be deeply affected at the community level...like all those islanders in the South Pacific who are making plans to move because they're already experiencing the awful effects of rising ocean levels. Surely there are farmers and ranchers in that big-sky country who share my dad's creepy feeling about what's ahead.

Hopefully they will be cranky enough to make their voices heard.

CENSORSHIP:
BURNING CHARLIE RUSSELL AT THE STAKE

Letter faxed to Montana state senators in 1995

February 28, 1995

Dear Senator:

As a born Montanan of pioneer stock and a recognized writer with three bestsellers to my credit, I am deeply concerned to see HB 83 so close to establishing statewide censorship in Montana.

I can say a thing or two about books in Montana. My family gave Montana the Grant-Kohrs Ranch National Historic Site at Deer Lodge, including its library of priceless documents and rare first editions of Western classics. My pioneer greatgrandparents built the William Kohrs Memorial Library in Deer Lodge. I graduated from the Powell County school system. For 17 years I condensed books for the *Reader's Digest*, a publication read in most Montana homes and schools. I belong to the Montana Authors Coalition. While I need to live and work in California today, my heart is never far from bunchgrass and cottonwood trees.

Yet I am among a few Montana authors listed as "dangerous" by the American Booksellers Assn. in their *Banned Books 1994*. I feel honored to be in such "dangerous" company as Mark Twain, Margaret Mitchell, Noel Coward, Rudyard Kipling, Sylvia Plath, Alexander Solzhenitsyn, Frank Baum, Edgar Rice Burroughs, Charles Dickens, George Eliot, Ernest Hemingway, Walt Whitman. All these writers are being yanked from bookshelves in the censorship frenzy now sweeping the U.S.

In the Big Sky state, that namesake novel *The Big Sky* has actually been challenged by bluenoses in Montana schools! A.B. Guthrie must be turning over in his grave.

In my conservative '50s Montana schools, many of the works banned today were taught without batting an eyelash. These included *The Grapes of Wrath, The Wizard of Oz, Silas Marner, Diary of Ann Frank, The Ox-Bow Incident, My Friend Flicka, Huckleberry Finn, All Quiet on the Western Front* and Shakespeare. Believe it or not, all these books are now "dangerous" – recently challenged and listed by the American Booksellers Assn. in their *Banned Books 1994*.

Four decades later, in 1995, the new breed of religious extremists make my old high-school librarian look like a wild-eyed liberal. They advocate the strictest censorship since colonial days. They don't just want to get rid of gay novels and tracts on evolution. They want to sweep U.S. bookshelves clear of the classics too. Oz, Huck Finn, fairies, fantasy, folklore, anthropology, Native American and other non-Christian philosophy – all are currently under heavy attack. Yet all these subjects were acceptable in those stuffy schools of my childhood.

Today's American censorship steps miles beyond "uplifting literature vs. pornography." A long shadow is falling across our freedom to explore books and printed information of any kind – including classics that have reposed on family and school bookshelves for well over a century.

How far is the insanity going to go? How pathetically small is the Big Sky going to get?

Will Charlie Russell's paintings be dragged off Helena and Great Falls museum walls, and burned? Russell's art is grittily "pagan." Nationwide, how far will extremists pursue their attempt to control every citizen's thinking? Dr. Seuss's *The Lorax* became "dangerous" in northern California when local timber interests objected to a children's book about loving trees. *Tarzan of the Apes* was banned because "Tarzan was living in sin with Jane."

Anyone who hates trees or extramarital sex can personally refrain from reading such books. But deny them to all?

Banned Books 1994 reveals a startling fact: most book challenges come from just one person, or a tiny handful of people.

Why are the rest of us putting up with this?

As a Montanan who traveled far from bunchgrass country, I lived and worked as a journalist in fascist Spain of the 1960s. Unlike most Americans, I have real experience with total censorship, and it isn't pretty. In Spain, not a word got in print unless approved by both the government and the Catholic Church. Offenders – writers, editors, printers – disappeared into Carabanchel Prison in Madrid. Repression was so total that Spanish letters virtually suffocated for lack of fresh air, and most Spaniards privately regarded their media as a joke.

Is this the kind of country that we want?

In 1975, when General Franco finally died, Spain was so sick of censorship and religious control that the Catholic Church fell from its all-controlling position and democracy came in. Can't we profit from such stark lessons of history? Principles that are put in place by force will inevitably be removed by force, by an indignant and long-suffering citizenry.

Please oppose HB 83 – if you don't want to see the "last best place" become the first state to legalize Franco-style censorship.

Sincerely yours,
Patricia Nell Warren

Note:

HB 83 was written and introduced by the Montana chapter of Citizens for Decency Through Law. Founded in 1956, the CDL was one of the first major anti-pornography organizations to emerge in the U.S. The Montana bill was intended to expand the state's existing obscenity laws by making it a crime to display obscene material to anyone, not just minors.

HB 83 did pass the Montana State House of Representatives. But the Montana State Senate version of the bill was voted down 32-18 by the Senate judiciary committee.

ANATOMY OF A SHORT SALE, OR, A WESTERNER LOOKS AT THE FORECLOSURE WAR

Originally published 5/23/2010 at The Bilerico Project (www.bilerico.com)

While the world was going to hell in a hand basket, I was moving. On April 30, 2010, escrow closed on the short sale of the West L.A. house where my business partner and I had operated Wildcat Press for 14 years. While Tyler and his partner moved to a nearby apartment, I moved to a private-home rental with friends in Glendale, in the San Fernando Valley. We continued operating the LLC from two separate, smaller offices.

As I packed personal and business effects, I was unable to boo-hoo about our fate. The fact is, we have lots of company. For three years now, a nationwide financial and economic war is being waged by the lending industry, as it refuses to help most of the 1 in every 4 homeowners who are underwater on their mortgages. So millions of us are refugees. President Obama and his soft-on-big-business administration are letting the lending industry get away it (as did President Bush and his soft-on-big-business administration).

The experts saw it coming. As more and more Americans

plowed deeper into personal debt, lenders plowed deeper into granting subprime mortgages to these Americans – and approximately 80% of these were the bloodsucking adjustable-rate ARM variety. In 2009, *Bloomberg* reported, "More than $750 billion of option ARMs were originated in the U.S. between 2004 and 2008...California accounted for 58 percent of option ARMs."

Lenders knew exactly what they were doing. Many homeowners were desperate to make up for decreasing income and rising costs of living, education, healthcare, running a small business. They rushed to re-fi so they could use some or all of their home equity for these purposes. If all they could get was an ARM loan, they (like me) signed on the dotted line. Then, as the rising rates (including my own) bumped that monthly payment upwards, horrified homeowners began to find themselves unable to pay it.

That was when the fiscal fire-bombing started to fall on our lives.

Latest (in mid-2010) figures from the Mortgage Bankers Assn.: 14.4 percent of American homeowner/borrowers were delinquent or in foreclosure on their mortgage. It was hard to find 2010 figures on exactly how many people have mortgages, but U.S. statistics for 2005 show 48,394,000 home loans on the books. So today's figures might be closer to 50 million. At the massacre rate of 14.4 %, that is probably more than 7 million mortgages hitting the wall.

But a gritty close-up on these numbers reveals that each imploding mortgage affects more than one person. It shatters a family with children, or an elderly couple, or a single professional with a small business. Not to mention a town or city or county that will no longer collect the taxes that the homeowner pays, nor enjoy the local purchasing power of that small business and household.

How Loan Modifications Don't Work

When homeowners first start fighting their personal mortgage battle, they're always astonished when a lender refuses to accept partial payments. I certainly was. Even the high-interest-hungry credit-card companies have no problem working out a payment plan with a cardholder who is falling behind. But when it comes to real estate, the deck is stacked differently.

Next, the homeowner wistfully believes all the advertising propaganda on TV and the Internet. The ads allege that our government and the lenders are ready to "help homeowners" and rescue our country. To achieve that, they have created so-called "programs" for loan modifications. For a few weeks, I believed the propaganda myself. After all, I voted for Obama. I grew up in the aftermath of the Great Depression, when people had voted another Democratic President into office in hopes that Franklin D. Roosevelt would create programs to help many Americans save their homes, find jobs and survive.

So the hopeful homeowner slogs through some rounds of application for a loan modification. What you hope for is a fixed rate, a reduced monthly payment – perhaps even a reduction of principal. Eventually Tyler and I piled up enough paperwork to cram a banker's file box. But in the end, the homeowner is informed – as we were – by a cursory form letter sent by snail mail, that the LM application has been turned down.

The fact is – the lender has done the arithmetic and knows that they will make more short-term money on your loan by seizing your house. So the underwriters look down at you from their lofty, unassailable, anonymous, non-accountable Olympian heights, and they say no.

In our dealings with the lender, we never got assigned to a case manager till late in the game, when we complained that our case was being mismanaged. One application had been turned down because of our alleged failure to provide requested documents. Yet we *had* supplied the documents before the deadline, and could prove it with office fax records. We also knew that the lender's representative had verbally acknowledged receipt of the docs in a phone conversation that was surely recorded. So we screamed for a re-review, and got it.

But the re-review came to nothing. We never got to talk to the underwriters directly. Most of the time, we found ourselves talking to some peon wearing a headset – a different one every time we called – who sat in a little cubicle somewhere on the planet and stared at our file on a computer screen, and was uninformed about our case.

Throughout the whole process, we got a close-up look at how disorganized and slipshod these big corporations are. Different departments weren't communicating with each other. Paperwork was "lost." Vital information supplied by a homeowner could be ignored. Yet these are the giant businesses to whom our government entrusts the nation's fiscal fortunes.

In the end, my business partner and I figured out what the media and the lender weren't telling us – that many homeowners don't even qualify for the now-famous "programs." Most apply to low-income homeowners who have Fannie Mae or Freddie Mac loans. Even with these, the lenders are picky about requirements, so it's hard to qualify.

Later came Obama's much-touted HAMP program. But the loan ceiling for HAMP is $729,000. So... if you have a loan bigger than $729K – and many Americans do – the White House and the federal government are telling you to "go jump in the creek" (a favorite expression of my dad, who was too old-school to use the "f" word in public). In our West L.A. neighborhood, which is lined with single-family homes and duplexes in stately 1920s Spanish Revival style, probably not a single property would qualify for HAMP.

To cloak their own guilt, the lending industry's PR peons cooked up an urban myth about homeowners with larger-than-HAMP loans. They allege that it was all our fault – that we were greedy and signed onto a high-risk loan in order to get a house we couldn't afford.

The major media, who don't do much questioning or investigative reporting these days, mostly bought the urban myth. So they have little sympathy for the many homeowners like us who actually afforded their homes for years. My business partner and I bought that house in 1996 and were never late with a mortgage payment for 12 years. Like many, we saw the value of our home triple over 10 or 15 years. It's likely that most of us who re-fi'ed with an ARM did so to finance a dire need. In our personal case, it was to raise new financing for our business. Others likely did so for equally valid reasons: perhaps a kid's college education, or unexpected medical bills.

Bottom line of the programs: my business partner and I didn't qualify for government help. So our lender processed us as a "regular in-house loan modification."

How many Americans are actually helped by these programs? How many actually bob and weave their way through the tortuous process of a "trial modification" (which can last for six months) before they are finally green-lighted for a "permanent modification?" I went and looked for the figures. By December 2009, out of more than 700,000 Americans who had applied, *only 31,382 borrowers* had run that gauntlet to get permanent modified status. This shocking stat comes straight from the Treasury Department.

And some of those 31,382 folks found themselves modified to a larger monthly payment, not a smaller one.

So the Democratic President for whom I voted has hung me and my business partner out to dry – along with 7 million other Americans. Obama's administration has given billions of bailout dollars to these big corporations, but has not compelled them to do the right thing by his long-suffering home-owning constituents. The lenders know they are free to ride rough-shod over the top of us.

Ironically, the Republicans who now swing Congress are not a better choice. They talk loud about their ideological issues, like Obama's "socialism" and the need to outlaw abortion, but they aren't any more interested in battling the lending industry than the Democrats are.

How a Short Sale Works

From that point on, my business partner and I were launching a frantic search for a reliable L.A. realtor who specializes in short sales.

A short sale, we had learned, is preferable to foreclosure. Sure, you lose any shreds of equity you might still have in your property. You hand over the keys and walk away without a penny (though some lenders will give you "moving money" to make sure you don't trash the place on the way out). But the lender does agree to accept a lower-than-market sale price as full repayment of the loan. So a short sale puts less of a black splat on your credit record than a foreclosure does.

For a short sale to be watertight, the lender must also agree not to sue you later for the unpaid balance. This is possible in the 26 states that have "non-judicial foreclosure" laws. Lucky for us, California is a non-judicial state.

Eventually we settled on a local realtor firm whose staff included a sharp lawyer. They specialized in short sales in Los Angeles County. By then, our county was one of the hardest-hit counties in the U.S. In April alone, the month that our short sale went ahead, it had 3,245 repossessed properties being sold at auction. Even Hollywood celebrities were losing their homes.

Our realtor made this painful process as painless as possible. We paid them no fee – all the fees would be paid by the lender. The first thing they did was get our lender to agree to stop the clock on foreclosure, meaning that the sheriff's sale was formally postponed. Then they started advertising. Property values in our neighborhood had slumped somewhat – our house had lost perhaps $400,000 in appraised value in the last couple of years. But even in "as is" condition, without cosmetic fix-ups, our building got attention – families with children were very interested in its 4 bedrooms and 4 baths.

Within the month, a buyer came along whose offer was not too far under current appraisal value. So our lender agreed to the sale, and threw in some moving money to boot. Otherwise we would have become L.A. County's foreclosure # 3246 of the month.

On April 30th, we packed the last of our stuff and turned over the keys.

Once foreclosed, some Americans are able to move in with friends or family. Or maybe they can afford a minimal rent somewhere. At the age of 74, I count myself one of the lucky ones. While the publishing business is impacted by the general downturn in retail sales, my own little imprint is soldiering along on cost-cutting and reduced income. My business partner and myself have found other sources of income, which help us keep the rent and bills paid. Several friends of mine, who also went through short sales, went a similar route, and are hanging in there.

Many others, however, have not been so lucky.

2011 Update – The West at Risk

A year later, how do I view this disturbing experience?

Three quarters of a century ago, my dad enlarged our Montana ranch by buying up some homesteads that had gone through bank foreclosure as a result of Depression bankrupcy. Today, ironically, I have completed the circle by losing my own home, along with the corner lot on which it stood.

More irony: the American West, once so bright with promises of "free homestead land" and "real-estate booms," is now living in a dark time of land being wrenched away from people. The West is even becoming a metaphor for the disaster. According to Assistant Attorney General for the Civil Rights Division Thomas Perez in a speech last year, the over-the-top subprime scene was "the Wild Wild West for all too many years."

Indeed, the West is the major battleground of the national mortgage war. According to a RealtyTrac end-of-2010 report, six of the top ten foreclosure-wracked states were Western states: Colorado, Idaho, Utah, California, Arizona. And the #1 state is Nevada, where one in every 84 homes went on the auctioneer's block.

Nor is this a recent trend. In January 2008, *Forbes* was already listening to the gunfire of financial skirmishes, and reported that the hardest-hit ten counties were mostly located in the West. California already had four counties on that top-10 list. By January 2010, the *Wall Street Journal* was reporting, "The 20 cities with the highest rates of foreclosure notices were all in California, Florida, Nevada and Arizona."

Most likely the West's top billing in foreclosure fiasco is owing to its undeveloped areas, much vaster than those found in the Midwest, South or East. Cheap land made for speculation bubbles – the "boom or bust" syndrome that has always been a thick vein in the motherlode of Western attitude. Today some Western homes sold at sheriff's sales hadn't even been lived in yet.

Major media are curiously reluctant to put a human face on the statistics. The growing numbers of homeless, which include entire families with children and seniors. The epidemic of tent cities and shanty towns everywhere, along with the spike in crimes and health problems resulting from these disruptions. The public is given incomplete figures on unemployment and homelessness so we will hopefully believe announcements that "the economy is improving."

The astronomical human cost gouges even deeper – the neighborhoods blighted by empty houses, the loss of value due to their being vandalized. Indeed, a recent report by the Mortgage Bankers Assn. compares these emptied neighborhoods to Old West type "ghost towns" and predicts that some of them will never be re-inhabited.

Americans have always been told that bankers and lenders are smart and know what they're doing. One would think they'd be smart enough to try keeping hard-up homeowners *in* homes, so properties would be secure and kept up. But evidently not.

Some pundits compare these losses to those of the Great Depression of the 1930s, when around 2.4 million farms and urban homes went into foreclosure. But, even allowing for today's U.S. population, which is double that of the Thirties, today's foreclosures dwarf what happened in the 1930s. According to an estimate by *Seeking Alpha's* real-estate expert John Lounsbury, around 7 million foreclosures will be completed. Not to mention that our Thirties government finally felt obliged to deliver real help. An agency launched in 1933, the Home Owners' Loan Corporation, did admittedly exhibited some racist attitudes – but the 1 million homes it saved from foreclosure form a stark contrast to the paltry totals of loan modifications granted today.

Indeed, what makes today's economy radically different from that of the Thirties is our now-pervasive habit of living in extreme debt – not only home mortgages but credit cards, student loans, payday loans, even so-called "military loans" preying on people in uniform. Many Americans find – too late – that they have signed themselves over to a lifetime of indentured servitude to interest payments. Rates for poor credit can soar to 40 percent, which is tantamount to loan-sharking. As I write this, the latest instrument of economic unfreedom is a so-called "subprime credit card," with interest at 79.9 APR.

Waking Up from the "American Dream"

The "American dream" was what down-on-their-luck Europeans and Asians came here for. In the colonial era and the early states, it was done through land grants. Later the U.S. government passed the Homestead Acts of 1862 and 1909 and gave away 270 million acres across the West and Alaska. By 1934, 1.6 million homesteaders had applied. We have to be honest and admit that most of this U.S. land had been taken away from tribes who lived there for eons. The southwest quadrant of the continental U.S. was taken away from Mexico, who had taken it away from Spain, who took it away from the tribes.

But today that same government is helping to strip its citizens of land by its pathetic failure to curb the cut-throat lending and investment practices that led to this disaster.

Some will say that the wheels of karma are turning – that land is now being torn away from descendants of those Europeans who seized land from the indigenous tribes. But this "sins of the father" notion is too simplistic and PC to explain what's happening. Why? Because many Americans have some First Nation ancestry, but they don't live on reservations, and some are surely figuring among the homeless. Indeed, a woman friend of mine who is part Shoshoni is valiantly battling to hang onto her little one-story frame home in Sherman Oaks, not far from where I live. She was two months behind on mortgage payments, but fiercely took on more jobs and has caught up on her payments.

In my lifetime, I haven't seen any other event so directly impact the personal lives of Americans across our entire population – not even 9/11. Only World War II compares – it battered the nation in every way, from the 1,500,000 soldiers who were killed, wounded or missing, to the hardworking and thrifty civilians, both male and female, who toiled to support our military in winning that war. Since World War II was "something that somebody else did to us," it was a popular cause – allowed into full political visibility by our government, and fully exploited by our media.

The mortgage massacre is War too – and a big one. But it is being done to the American people by its own government, and by an out-of-control financial industry that has its home base within our borders. Our Foreclosure War is part of a larger global war on peoples in other countries as well – a titanic struggle for power over trade, and currencies, and access to markets, in the course of which the big powers have apparently lost sight of the value of ordinary people's lives. Yet it's the buying power of billions of ordinary people that is intended to keep the global economy afloat. Free trade is everybody buying everybody else's stuff. But if most people are too broke to buy, what happens to global trade?

Dare I call it World War III, even though it's being waged with dollars, not drones?

In the United States, this Foreclosure War may prove to be far more destructive to the principles for which our nation supposedly stands, than anything done to us on 9/11 by foreign terrorists.

I leave it to historians who come after me, to quibble about how and why the Foreclosure War was allowed to happen, and what the real motive was, for those so-called Americans who are profiting from it. Is it their aim to crush us enough that we'll accept some new ideology? Or did things veer out of control because many business leaders and politicians are simply greedy and stupid? Whatever the motive, I can't imagine why it is in our national interest for so many middle- and lower-income Americans to be so broken.

For another generation, at least, the economic and political bombing rubble of this war will be starkly visible across our country – as were the burnt chimneys and bomb-pocked streets of European cities after World War II. But as we rebuild, hopefully more and more Americans will reject state-subsidized debt, and embrace the thrift that made things work for our ancestors.

SEXUALITY

GIRL GRASSROOTS

Originally published in *Lesbian News*, June 1994

When I was 8 years old, I fell in love with Eleanor Roosevelt. During the 1944 presidential campaign, Eleanor and Franklin D. Roosevelt rode their campaign train through my Montana town. I didn't care about him – I wanted to see *her*. I was squeezed in the crowd, waving wildly, being trampled by adults. Finally my dad got me up on his shoulders so I could see.

There she was, on the platform of the last car, with her funny hat, her buck teeth and shy brave eyes. She was standing beside FDR in his wheelchair. She waved back.

Surely she was waving at me.

Even on the playground, kids argued for Roosevelt or Dewey. When they laughed at Eleanor's buck teeth, I slugged them in the mouth. My parents were surprisingly tolerant of my tomboy exploits – even though I broke lances for Eleanor and they broke them for Dewey.

My parents were humanist Republicans who owned as many miles of bookshelves as barbed-wire fences, They sent me to Presbyterian Sunday school, but never propagandized me about church. The family tree was loaded with Irish rebels and democracy-minded Germans. Our Native American branch was tinier, starting with Cherokees in colonial times.

I was surrounded by big animals, tractors, guns, leather and men – my dad, my Marine uncle, my brother Conrad, cowboys, veterinarians, hunters, livestock auctioneers. The women I knew best were my mother and a few ranch girls like myself.

Conrad and I were loners but never lonely – roaming around with a .22 rifle, plinking at tin cans, listening to curlews running in the grasses. The curlew, a long-billed speckled bird of the Western prairies, isn't a melodious bird. But she is gifted at running, and so well camouflaged in the grasses that you don't see her until she flushes from under your horse. Then she wings off with a fading cry that seems to leave a long story on the wind. Conrad's cry was being a pilot someday. Mine was being a writer. We were two curlew chicks, at one with the grass.

There was no TV in my world. Nothing to hold a child's imagination hostage, as electronic empires do today. In the Powell County grade school, every student had to read a book a week. One day, English teacher Jane Jordan held up *Robinson Crusoe* and talked about something called "verisimilitude." Mr. Defoe helped pioneer verisimilitude, she said. It is a writer's trick, she said, that makes the book seem real.

I was fascinated by this idea, and put it to work in my next short story.

By the time I was 13, some of my favorite authors were Willa Cather, Mari Sandoz, Margaret Mitchell, Frank Baum, Winston Churchill, Oscar Wilde, Mark Twain, Frank Bird Linderman, T.E. Lawrence, and, of course, Eleanor Roosevelt. My reading showed me that many different galaxies of human feeling shine within the far-flung universe of humanity.

Those pre-TV heroes were freedom fighter types. Today's children cause pacifists to weep as they idolize fighters. But children need to love fighters. Kids are so easily bashed that they need to know they can fight back. Eleanor's *This is My Story* told of her shy, tortured girlhood, and her growth into a fighter for human rights.

In 1946, when *Gone With the Wind* came back on a re-run, every girl in town dug her mom's 1920s chiffon flapper dresses out of the trunk in the basement. At slumber parties, we got ourselves up in Civil War drag, and the prettiest girls fought to be Scarlett O'Hara. But my broad-shouldered frame simply burst those wispy dresses. Somebody had to play Rhett Butler, so that was me. I put on a man's jacket and carried my girlfriends up the stairs.

Those very muscles made me a speedy curlew, a good sprinter, and I could beat most boys at playground running. But '40s' girls were banned from high-school track.

Yet I had my goals. If Eleanor could triumph over homeliness, I could damn well do the same.

"No one can be made to feel inferior without their consent," she said in *My Story*.

Books and movies and radio were silent about beings called "lesbians." The doughty female pioneers of the valley surely numbered some of those, but they weren't called that in Deer Lodge. I never heard the word "lesbian" until college. Nor would I know until years later that my Eleanor was alleged to be "one of those."

Yet, without a clue that we were doing "femme" and "dyke," something to be labeled "role-playing" in the future, my favorite girlfriend and I had our first romance. We were 13.

I Was Her Girl Gunslinger

She was from the wrong side of the tracks, willowy in those chiffon dresses, reputedly fast with the boys – a real-life Scarlett. But boys weren't kind to her, so she turned to me. I was her girl gunslinger, and beat up any boy who teased her. We carried on passionately for a year, under cover of "sleeping over" at each other's houses. Our parents didn't have a clue.

It was a book – T.E. Lawrence's *Seven Pillars of Wisdom* – that told me men have these same feelings. T.E.'s memoirs were those of a young British officer, and, right on page 2, he got down to brass tacks about "gays in the military." As I cried over *Seven Pillars*, with the power that children have to vibe into the collective mind of humanity, Lawrence and his lover S.A. became part of my world.

After a year, my chiffon sweetheart and I drifted apart. Each of us were determined to deal with those monsters called boys.

My mother helped me try. It would be years before I would fully appreciate my mother. She headed me quietly toward career and independence, out of her society where a woman's path through the wild grasses was as clearly trodden as a cattle trail to water. Unfailingly, she praised my high school writings, corrected my English, provided me with my own typewriter. Mom had her own dreams. She'd never gone to college, yet eventually she would make her mark as a Montana historian.

But surely she had burning questions about where my lack of interest in "ladylike behavior" was going to lead.

Tulle Ball Gowns

In the late '40s and early '50s, there were many burning questions. Most of them didn't flare in the headlines yet, only in people's minds. Sexuality, for example. When the children I knew ran afoul of the moral system, they didn't get their day in court, or their bites on the evening news, like today. They simply disappeared – pulled under and swallowed, like swimmers eaten by sharks. One day a boy – honor student, popular athlete – didn't show up at school. A cold whisper ran through the school that he had raped a little girl. It was never written up in the town paper, and we never saw him again.

In 1953, I went away to Stephens College in Missouri. During freshman year, I met my first female couple. Boys' haircuts were in fashion, and these two were the perfect butches in their D.A. (duck ass) cuts that were popular then, complete with the rebel curl at the back of the head. They were rooming together, carrying on right under the nose of the house mother. I wore a D.A., too, and had another more bittersweet affair. This time it was a girl in my dorm who wrote riveting poetry.

At this Southern school, I kept trying. Vast tulle ball gowns were the rule for formal campus dances. I poured myself into one of those, and knew I looked ridiculous. I dated boys from "Mizzou" (U. of Missouri) and the Army base at Fort Leonard Wood. For a time, I became a Catholic.

The last two years, I transferred to "the" Catholic women's college of the day – Manhattanville College of the Sacred Heart in Purchase, New York. Here the curlew tried kissing Ivy League boys, and pouring herself into the little black cocktail dress favored by Manhattanites. I didn't have a girlfriend there, though I was best friends with a homely, brainy foreign student from Germany. By senior year, I no longer believed that any religion has a monopoly on truth.

Burning questions of the '50s were in the headlines now. The Nixon/McCarthy hearings. Hints that Hollywood and Washington D.C. were "infiltrated" by homosexuals. The attempts to censor unruly new writers called "beatniks." My favorite was Allen Ginsberg, who painted homosexuals as apocalyptic and hair-raising.

After graduation in 1957 came marriage to a Ukrainian émigré poet whose family had fled communism. I had found – I thought – my real-life Rhett Butler.

The Solid-Gold Salt Mine

By 1959, I was deep into writing and a career in publishing. *Reader's Digest* had its corporate headquarters in Pleasantville, one hour north of Manhattan. To the world, it was the biggest most popular magazine. To us staffers, it was "the solid-gold salt mine."

I had blossomed, lost 40 pounds. My curlew camouflage was now a Chanel-style business suit and hair in a tight bun. The media world of those days was a handful of magazines and book houses, not the crowded scene of today (in fact, no one used the word "news media" until sometime in the '60s). My job was to condense non-fiction books. To find "usable" books, I read 300 or 400 a year. Our idea of what to do on vacation was not reading a good book.

This conservative magazine was an odd meadow for a fledgling pagan libertarian curlew to light in. Yet I learned a great deal there, and joined a little group of editors who tried hard to liberalize the magazine.

Working at the *Digest* in the '60s and '70s was a good place to see the bank-vault door of American myth being blown open. Our corporate office's location in the countryside made for a remoteness from messy civil-rights wars at lunch-counters and universities. So some liberal editors devoted their vacations to wading through the mud of reality somewhere. Between '62 and '71, I spent time in fascist Spain, as liaison with our Madrid office on some book projects. The reality of living under a right-wing dictatorship affected me deeply.

For a time, while Jimi Hendrix died and Coretta King cried, *Digest* liberals tried. I tried to publish pieces about discrimination against native peoples. Young staffers who smoked pot tried to soften the magazine's noisy position on marijuana. Major battles were fought over whether the magazine would acknowledge growing criticism of the Vietnam War.

Now and then, events shook us. Issue editor Bill Hard always had a radio going in his office. One day I happened to be standing in the typists' bull-pen when Bill stuck his head out the door and shouted in a broken voice: "My god! President Kennedy was just shot!"

Lawsuit Against Reader's Digest

I remember where I was on June 28, 1969 when I learned that drag queens had gone to war with vice cops. It was around 9 a.m. and I was at my solid-gold *Digest* desk, reading the *New York Times*, as every staffer was supposed to do. According to the *Times*, the riot happened the day before at a notorious downtown bar called the Stonewall Inn.

To young lesbians and gay men today, in an America where "gay" makes the network news every day, it's hard to convey how mysterious the gay world was then – especially if you were still on the outside of it trying to find your way in. For me, the sexual part was never the hard part. What was hard was the courage to let family and friends see the consciousness of a gay writer that I hid inside – a personal galaxy of my own that carried both women and men on its starry rim.

My Ukrainian friends, artists and writers who lived on the lower East Side, spent time in Greenwich Village. Strolls led us past bars and movie theaters where gay men and lesbians hung out. I saw lesbians going into Fedora's, and yearned to follow. For a time, I was interested in a couple of Ukrainian women, one a well-known poet. In Ukrainian society, lesbian openness was quasi-accepted among the educated émigrés that I knew in New York.

But my own personal Rhett Butler didn't like homosexuals. So I conformed and wrote some Ukrainian poetry where curlews of homosexual theme wore a camouflage of allegory.

In 1971, Dial Press published my first novel, *The Last Centennial.* It sold 2,500 copies and sank without a trace. No matter – my next novel wouldn't be another *Titanic*. I scanned the different theaters of civil-rights war to see which one needed a new correspondent.

Women's rights, for one. In 1972, 17 other *Digest* women and myself filed charges against the company in federal district court. Staff conservatives were shocked: those distant wars had finally come to their solid-gold doorstep.

Athletes' rights, for another.

In 1968, I had finally gotten back to the old curlew love: running. My husband and I weren't getting along, and jogging together was a last stab at "togetherness." Inevitably, we found ourselves at our first long-distance race. Women's distance running was new then, and U.S. women were limited to 2 ½ miles – the Amateur Athletic Union insisted that women would drop dead if they ran any farther than that. Some of us intended to show the AAU that they were full of it. In 1969, I was one of 12 women crashing the Boston Marathon and other races, running "illegally" without official numbers. No women fell over dead.

Running Past Barriers

My personal best was a 4:20 marathon – a time that didn't destine me for Olympic gold. But I jumped into the fray, becoming a member of the N.Y. Metropolitan AAU long-distance committee as well as national publicity director for the Road Runners Club of America. Within a few years, hundreds of women were running marathons. Eventually, the AAU conceded defeat, and cleared women for the same distances as men.

About this time, activism made me see that I was a failure as Scarlett O'Hara. I needed to be me. For others, there might be the inching out of the closet into their first gay sexual experiences. For me, there was the locked bottom drawer, where I kept my first gay writings. For example, a novel started in Spain in the mid '60s titled *The Burning Bull.*

Now, in the winter of 1972-73, I pondered gay men and lesbians whose hidden presence could be divined in my sport. Running 50 miles a week, I'd sleeked down to 125 pounds. Road races were their own kind of dating scene, and a few women hit on me. I wasn't ready to respond, but it was secretly exhilarating.

One night at a party in Manhattan, a young runner confided in me. Why he trusted me, in those closety times, I'll never know. But he had been a top college miler. He talked about the terror and heartbreak of passing for straight so he could stay on the team. Finally he'd left serious competition, and became a model.

A novel about gay runners, I thought, might make a helluva story. Briefly, I considered a plot line about two lesbian runners. Then I decided against it. Conservative bacon-and-eggs Americans believed that all women athletes are "unnatural." A novel about dykes in track suits wouldn't tell them anything they didn't already "know."

Rethinking the Plot

But the conversation with that gay miler haunted me. Conservative America believed the opposite about gay men – that they couldn't hack he-man sports. The subject was a media bomb waiting to go off. So I started rethinking the plot. What if a gifted gay-male runner made the Olympic team? What if his coach fell in love with him?

The manuscript was written on lunch hours, and kept in a locked desk drawer at the *Digest*, where my spouse wouldn't find it.

Reading 400 titles a year gave me an overview of trends. A few books such as *Best Little Boy in the World* were out, and trade experts talked about the "emerging gay market." My book had to be frank enough to capture gay readers, who were probably (judging by the "all-male" theaters now advertised in my *NY Times*) hungry for a more dignified eroticism. But not too explicitly – otherwise it would scare straights away.

Some old grassroots literary lessons came up. The two lovers had to be fighters. I had not forgotten T.E. Lawrence's story – love under fire is the strongest kind. And I would tell the story with

Miss Jordan's "verisimilitude." The book had to read like the better autobiographies that crossed my desk at work.

My narrator, track coach Harlan Brown, quickly found his prose voice. He was blunt, vernacular – a peculiar blend of sensitive and crude. He was also the epitome of male values I'd grown up with. I had gleeful fun running down the checklist – Republican, church-going, middle-class, blue-collar, crew-cut, patriotic, ex-Marine. Even though I was suing the Digest for discrimination, I let Harlan be a "male chauvinist" – at least in his early years. My main character needed to grow and mature, just like we real-life people get to do.

Compassion for Men

At that time, I was not clear why this macho archetype was springing fully armed from my brow, at a time when I was struggling towards renewal of myself as a woman.

Later, I could see how I needed to heal myself. When the marriage finally exploded, I wasn't feeling all that friendly toward the male sex. To avoid sliding over the edge of hate, I needed compassion for men. To become a woman of power, I had to end my own myth that men have power because they hold those macho values. For a man, the ultimate slavery is his belief that being a "he-man" gives him power and makes him free.

Oh, and one more thing. If I published this book, the whole world would know where my head was at.

On days when I worked at *RD*'s New York City office, the curlew poked her beak timidly into gay life. I didn't have the courage to scope out any bars. But I did call a hotline, and made my first contact with the Mattachine Society.

One day in April 1973, while in Manhattan on *Digest* business, I quietly dropped by my agent's office and gave him the typescript. I was nervous about my financial future. Divorce would be messy, and demand taking a leave from work. My husband had lost our savings in the stock market. But I wouldn't have asked for alimony anyway.

Ten days later, William Morrow bought *The Front Runner* for $7,500.

Celebrating Freedom on Fire Island

The money funded my freedom, and a summer on Fire Island. One Saturday midnight, I stood in the doorway of the Ice Palace in Cherry Grove, and stared inside, fascinated at the smoky spectacle of men dancing with men, women with women. I had never been in a disco in my life, and was ripe with cowgirl innocence for that heady experience.

When I returned to the *Digest* office in October 1973, *The Front Runner* was in galley proofs. I was divorced and 37. I arrived at work wearing a halter top, platform shoes and no bra.

Coming out at the *Reader's Digest* was its own peculiar kind of piquant. Once a month, our book scouts had lunch with trade editors and agents, and filed reports on upcoming books. Sometime early in 1974, one of our scouts woke up to the fact that Morrow's hot new gay novel was written by a *Digest* employee.

When the page-proofs arrived in the office, to be rated for "usability," my colleagues passed them around avidly. One by one, they stuck their heads in my door to ask in a stagey whisper:

"Pat – you really did write this?"

"I did."

Among themselves: "Gawd, she did write it."

When TFR made the best-seller list, the company swallowed hard, especially when I mentioned in a *New York Post* interview that I'd had relationships with women.

Needless to say, TFR was rated "unusable." Since I was already suing the company for discrimination against women, and since they couldn't fire me because federal law protected me from reprisals, the *Digest* did not bash me. In fact, the company magazine actually ran an article about my bestseller. Maybe they'd decided to make the best of a bad thing.

By 1975, I was being inundated with fan letters from gay men, but I had no idea that the book would never go out of print, or that it would garner a surprising number of women readers. For now, a few lesbians and gay men on the staff quietly identified themselves to me. One lady Digester and I got drunk together at lunch, and shared our till-then secret stories and gossip about sodomites in the solid-gold salt mine. We laughed ourselves silly, and became close friends.

For me, the first great blessing of coming out was not the great leap into bed – it was simple human companionship with my own kind.

I spread my wings, and flew the last few yards of grass into freedom.

WHAT MY MOTHER DID AFTER SHE READ MY GAY NOVEL

Author's Foreword to the 1996 edition of *The Fancy Dancer*

Sometime in 1977, I nervously went home to Deer Lodge, Montana – that ranch-country town that served as the real life model for Cottonwood in *The Fancy Dancer*. There, I visited my mother in the convalescent home where she now languished, far from her ranch home. She lived in her bed or wheelchair now, in the last stages of what the doctors thought might be muscular dystrophy.

A few months before, I had sent my parents a first-edition copy of *The Fancy Dancer*. Mom had been mining through it, glasses perched on nose, like the self-educated housewife/historian that she'd always been. She was always reading up on things – Julius Caesar, Eleanor of Aquitaine, Winston Churchill. Now she was catching up on her daughter's literary doings. By then I had outed myself to my parents, by publishing *The Front Runner* in 1974. Evidently, back in the 1940s, my parents had already got an inkling that their tomboy daughter was not going to grow up to be Betty Grable. So they'd been accepting, but hesitantly – inclined to let their town friends and their colleagues in the cattle business know that blood is thicker than water and a better glue than belief.

But ... what would my mother say about *The Fancy Dancer*? The story trod so relentlessly, knee-deep, like a mustang fording a creek, through the rich spiritual and religious mud of that town where she had grown up, gotten her first job, married my dad. Maybe it waded a little too deep for her.

Unlike my dad, a cowboy pagan who could read the teaching in buffalo bones strewn through the grass, my mother had strong ties to the ancient civilizations of the Mediterranean. As a teen, Nellie Bradford Flinn was a Jazz Age amazon who loved dancing the Charleston, but loved sports even more. Her high-school girls' basketball team had scandalized everyone by being the first in Montana history to take the floor wearing shorts and T-shirts, instead of bloomers and middy blouses! She was a dead shot with an orangewood bow or a .410 shotgun. And even more than sports, she loved history.

In 1936, as she gave birth to me, churches were what moved the trembling needle of the Deer Lodge social compass. In my fuzzy baby vision, the town's many church steeples slowly came clear, dominating the skyline of stately cottonwoods. Even though the town's population was only 6,000 people, those churches were packed on Sundays. Collection plates brimmed – silver dollars clinking into them. The ladies' apparel shop stayed afloat on steady sales of hats and white gloves. The kind of Easter bonnet that today is a drag queen's delight was favored in 1948 by the stuffiest president of the Women's Club.

Yet the valley's oldest spirit of prayer called to me not from churches, but from ancient earthen mounds on the ranch, built by forgotten native healers. There I loved to sit in the blowing grasses, holding my cow-pony by the reins, and wondering what ceremonies had happened there.

I knew that some of the valley's last native people had been massacred near that spot in the 1860s – the site of a mass grave was known to the family. After that, the churches had come – each one in its time – Catholic, Methodist, Presbyterian, Seventh Day Adventist – to lay down its own archeological layer of belief. A splinter group of Mormons had fled there from Deseret. Sturdy Swedish and German immigrants built the plain Lutheran building, while well-heeled Episcopalians raised a gothic marvel with stained glass windows. Deer Lodge's First Baptists tended to be redneck descendants of Civil War refugees, while Christian Scientists were town intelligentsia, keeping a low profile in their reading room on a side street.

For me, in grade school, "church" began with the squat brick building of the Presbyterian church on Milwaukee Ave. This was my mother's chosen church – she played the organ there. With other tots I mindlessly sang "A Sunbeam for Jesus" in Sunday school.

Noticing that I was bored stiff by the long sermons, my mother said firmly:

"Religion is something you should know. When you grow up, you will make up your own mind about what you believe."

Those were the days when Catholics still ate fish on Fridays, when a word spelled "ecumenical" wasn't in the American language yet. America's "Bible-thumpers" had no use for "mackerel snappers," and vice versa. Atop a hill overlooking the town was St. Mary's parish church and St. Mary's Academy. From the parish tower, an hourly carillon of bells floated down over the cottonwood groves to grate on the ears of every Bible-thumper in town. My mom and dad were liberal enough that they didn't mind my best friend Shirley Sexton being a fish-eater. Shirley and her large family lived next door to our ranch; she and I grew up on horseback together. I, the stubby Protestant tomboy, shriveled with envy as Shirley was chosen to crown Mother Mary with roses on the first day of May. It was a mackerel-snapping cod-crunching shrimp-licking rite that had the town Bible-thumpers viewing it as a pagan goddess ritual and muttering with disgust.

My mother had only one thing to teach me about all that town emotion centered around the churches.

"Never argue with anybody," she said, "about politics or religion."

Through high school, I was faithful to the family Protestant rites. My family was full of Freemasons, and my mother belonged to the Order of the Eastern Star; ergo, I joined the Order of the Rainbow for Girls, and rose to worthy advisor before I left high school. More legends of atrocities came my way, more layers laid down, as I heard tell of Templars burned at the stake.

After graduation in 1953, I followed Mother's advice to the point where I never dared to debate religion with her. After all, she knew more about it than I did.

Drawn by the goddess glow of Mary, I became a Catholic convert during my first college year – only to abandon Catholicism in 1956 after I started analyzing some of the other beliefs that I had accepted with such emotion.

My mom and dad weren't thrilled that I'd become a holy-water hustler. But they couldn't protest.

"You taught me to make up my own mind," I reminded them.

"Well, I sure did," admitted my mother.

From 1957 to 1973, there was abortive marriage, and years of more wondering, sitting on this and that ancient mound of thought – reading Hinduism and Buddhism and Islam and other -isms, until my path through the waving grasses of questioning finally brought me full circle to the native mounds, to my growing understanding that the pull of Mary was real and deep – that she was Mara to Europeans, Morelah to some of my native ancestors.

Now my snow-haired mother peered up at me from her wheelchair. Here I was, ready for that long-delayed discussion.

How was I going to open the conversation?

"What did you think of the book?"

Or, "Do you have any questions?" Or ...

The minute I sat beside her wheelchair, she pulled a pile of clippings out of her bedside drawer. Her veined hands fumblingly sorted through them. They had been torn out of church publications and Northwest newspapers.

"Well," she said as briskly as her advancing speech impediment would allow, "I've been reading up on ... er ... homosexuals."

"You ... have?" I was speechless, eyes fixed on the clippings.

"My church is ... discussing what to do about ... them."

Until that moment, Nellie Bradford Flinn Warren had never willingly pronounced the dreaded H word out loud in her life. She'd read *The Front Runner* with a certain detachment, considering what an athlete she'd been, and kept her thoughts to herself. But now, once the clippings came out, we could talk.

"You taught me to make up my own mind," I reminded her.

"I certainly succeeded, didn't I?" she said drily.

Naturally, we didn't talk about sex. My mother had never talked openly about sex. Though she'd spent most of her life in a ranch world where men and women talked frankly about the private parts of animals, my mother maintained a certain Victorian discretion. The greatest daring of a 1950s mother had been hers. She had given her teenage tomboy daughter one of those newfangled sex-education books – the kind that started being published after World War II, with all the coy drawings of human private parts – and she let the book do the talking.

What we did talk about was the Bible, and whether or not Presbyterians were going to let a gay minister preach. We talked of Sappho's poetry, and Alexander's empire. We discussed the Roman emperors who had their – ahem! – certain young men for "close friends."

In 1978, as I published yet another novel about gay life and religion, my organ-playing Presbyterian mother had a last word to say about the growing noises from a new movement called "the Jesus freaks," later to be known as "the religious right" – led by a young preacher named Lou Sheldon and a former Miss America, Anita Bryant.

"Well," she said, "they do hate homosexuals, don't they?"

Visit after visit, as she grew more stooped, I don't remember a lot of words. What I do remember is holding hands with her, and the long silences, and the growing pile of clippings. She lived another two years, in her own growing fuzziness, as the keen blue eyes dimmed and the clippings were harder for her to read. Now emaciated and crippled before her time, the erstwhile amazon finally died in 1979, at the age of 68.

Of all the things she said, I remember most fondly the way she chuckled, tapping *The Fancy Dancer* with one bunioned finger.

"I suppose everybody in town is running around trying to find a copy of your darn book ... to see if they're in it," she said.

A COMING-OUT TALE OF OLD MONTANA

Originally published 10/9/2008 at The Bilerico Project (www.bilerico.com)

One coming-out in one small town can move the hearts of a lot of people for a long time after. Whenever I go home to Deer Lodge, Montana, and enjoy the acceptance, or at least tolerance, of a certain percentage of the population, I know that I owe it to a man named Jan Stewart. Deer Lodge is the 2nd oldest community in the state – it goes back before the 1860s gold rush, before the mixed-blood ranchers who settled there in the 1850s, into the last days of the fur trade and the First Nation peoples living there in the valley. Jan made that history even more colorful.

I didn't meet Jan till after I came out myself. In 1976, I published my third gay-themed novel, *The Fancy Dancer*, and it became a national bestseller. While the story focused on the travails of a young closeted Catholic priest, it was really about the secrets of a small town – my own home town, in fact, thinly disguised under the fictional name Cottonwood. By then I was living in New York, but often traveled home to visit my parents, who still lived on the ranch north of Deer Lodge.

There, a cousin, Dean Tavenner, who owned the book shop in town told me that he was doing a brisk business selling *Fancy Dancer*.

My mother had already read the copy I'd given her. She had put out the word to her women friends in bridge club, Eastern Star, the Women's Club and the Presbyterian Church, creating a small tidal wave of book sales for my cuz.

As a novelist, I thought I'd done a good job of indicating hot spots of valley life where certain secrets lay buried in the lives of both closeted men and women. But some time after the book was published, a reader's letter was forwarded to me by the publisher, William Morrow. It was a masterpiece of elegant old-school handwriting in fountain pen, informing me that the writer was gay and lived in Deer Lodge. He suggested we meet next time I was in town.

Jan was a stocky silver-haired man in his 60s, who loved to camp and tease while smoking the kind of cigar I would expect from a banker eating lunch at the Montana Club in Helena. In a town where most men stuck to cowboy shirts and jeans, Jan stuck to slacks and leather sandals and California-style short-sleeve sports shirts (in summer, anyway). He didn't make any speeches about gay liberation. He didn't need to. In a town where he was unique, all he had to do was walk down the street with his cigar and his sports shirt and wave hello at his friends. That alone was a statement.

It turned out that Jan's ancestors had arrived in Montana before the gold rush, as had mine. One of his greatgrandfathers was an eastern Ojibway who had migrated to the territory with the voyageurs, to make a dollar in the fur trade. Once there, he married into the Stewarts, one of the many Scottish families that pioneered into the territory's early trading networks. Jan had grown up on a little ranch in southwest Montana.

As we were having coffee at the Four B's Cafe, and Jan's stogie polluted the air in our part of the restaurant, I asked him, "We're practically related. Why in the world didn't we ever meet before?"

"Because I wasn't here," he said. "I went through high school ahead of you. Then I left Montana in the Fifties and went to California ...and became a Buddhist."

The lure of Beat Generation questioning had reached the questioning ranch kid, who heard about Jack Kerouac, and probably read an outlaw copy of Allen Ginsberg's *Howl* that drifted through town. Jan followed the well-worn trail of Montana ex-pats that led to the Golden State, where he eventually headed for one of the many

Buddhist monasteries tucked away in the hills. Along the way, he had figured out what attracted him sexually. Turned off by Christianity, Jan became a for-real Buddhist. Most Buddhists have no ideological problem with same-sex orientation, so Jan could proceed on to other questions about life, such as reincarnation and why we have to come back to the planet so many times to figure out a few things. He learned Chinese so he could study Chinese Buddhism. Seeing his enthusiasm, his order assigned him to translate some ancient Chinese texts that had never been done into English.

Customarily (Jan told me) a monk was supposed to do translations on a long-term retreat. But Jan's idea of a retreat was to return to Deer Lodge. In a state that had always harbored pockets of religious nonconformism, from a rebel group of Mormons through communities of Mennonites and Hutterites, to Elizabeth Clare Prophet's Church Universal, Jan's choice of a spiritual path didn't raise many eyebrows.

The small late-Victorian frame house he'd bought was right near Cottonwood Creek, which wended through the oldest, most historic – if slightly shabby – part of town. Inside, the place was monkishly neat, with the smell of cigars and sandalwood incense mingling in the air. In the living room, his altar was the focus, with Buddhist scrolls hanging on the wall behind it. Half a dozen Siamese cats dozed on his meditation cushion, or superintended as he sat at his oak desk translating...working in the Victorian handwriting I'd first seen in his letters. His modest living costs were covered by a stipend from his order.

Every gay man has his straight woman sidekick. Jan's was none other than Vivian Stuart Kemp, who lived next door in the elegantly weathered Victorian where she'd spent much of her life. Vivian was in her early 90s, the town's dowager "daughter of a pioneer" – the only one alive who could actually remember things that the rest of us had to read about in history books. Vivian's son had died, so she had adopted Jan as a surrogate. He spent time with her every day, helped her with business and errands.

Whenever I visited Jan, we'd go next door for tea. As Vivian got out the good china cups and a plate of sugar cookies, her black eyes always sparkled with impish humor as she told the latest story making the rounds. She and Jan kidding around together were funnier than "Saturday Night Live." Vivian too was a mixed-blood – her pioneer father, Tom Stuart, had married a half-Blackfoot woman and homesteaded a little ranch on the Deer Lodge River, just south of my family's own ranch. (Stuart – Stewart – different spellings of the same name, so the two families' Scottish ancestors were probably related somehow back in the Auld Sod.) Vivian's family and mine had known each other since she was born, and Vivian was a good friend of my mom's.

Since Vivian was the mega-matriarch of Deer Lodge society, not a single homophobe in town dared to say a word against Jan.

Now and then, as we munched cookies and talked history, Vivian would get out her shoe box of early-day photos. They were taken during her dad's time, and showed Deer Lodge as it was in the early 1860s. Along Cottonwood Creek, log cabins stood with teepees next door, and dogs and horses roaming around, and wagons or carts parked. There were Victorian studio portraits of tribal women in Victorian gowns whose names I had heard a million times but whose pictures I'd never seen, who had married white or mixed-blood traders in the valley.

Leafing through them with Jan, I always felt amazed at having discovered this knitting circle, which had existed right under my nose in Deer Lodge for so many years without my knowing it.

"I wish I'd met you in time to put you in *The Fancy Dancer*," I told Jan.

"Just as well you didn't," he grinned. "Nobody would believe that a gay cigar-smoking Buddhist lives in Deer Lodge."

And so the Eighties passed, with me going off on my own retreat – massive research on *One Is the Sun*, a historical novel about Montana. Now and then Jan and I exchanged letters, and I saw him and Vivian whenever I was in town. He was politically aware and supportive of the first gay-rights efforts in Montana, which were fiercely opposed by stirrings of extremism that would bring the Montana Militia briefly to power in the 90s. Local rednecks would arm themselves right there in the county.

But Jan wasn't worried. "If they shoot me," he said, "they'll be sorry when they meet me in my next life."

As time went on, my research showed me how deeply LGBT people were braided into Montana history. The braid is a powerful

First Nation symbol – it grows in strength with every new thread plaited into it. In the old days, people braided everything in their daily lives – stories, hair, lariats, horse's manes, even switches of sweetgrass for incense.

Today, we try to braid politically and socially. At Montana Pride I would meet other LGBT descendants of those old-time families, some of whom had lived right in the Deer Lodge valley. There was the gay greatgrandson of Robert Dempsey, mountain man who opened the first roadhouse near town. There was the lesbian granddaughter of an elderly retired cowboy that my family knew. There were transgendered people whose eyes lit up at the mention of Two Spirits. We were all braided into the great Montana rope, for sure – no effort could ever tear our thread out, no matter how hard it got yanked.

Jan's translation project was coming to an end – time to move back to the monastery in California. But his health was not good. One day there were no more letters inked by a post-Victorian who loved Chinese calligraphy, and I learned that Jan had died.

Vivian lingered a few years, then followed him. That shoebox of photos is out there somewhere, with her heirs – I hope it finds its way into an archive, because the images in it have not been preserved anywhere else. Those Buddhist texts are out there too, probably being read right now by Americans who rediscover the achievements of ancient China. Unless they meet Jan's spirit in another life, they'll never know about the man – and the six Siamese cats – who got those texts into English.

Today, when I visit Deer Lodge, I always remember that I'm part of that local braid first started by Jan and Vivian – with some threads added by Vivian's group of liberal-thinking women friends who backed them up. Women like Thelma Shaw, who served on the library board and made sure my books and certain other books weren't censored. Women like my mom, who played the organ in church and thought that *The Fancy Dancer* was a fair picture of life in Cottonwood. When Montana's governor finally had the courage to veto a bill passed by the state legislature that made homosexuality a crime, it was thanks in part to small-town changes of heart like the one in Deer Lodge.

In early 2008, when I went back to Montana for the first gay-themed Library Week events ever held in the state – including one in the Deer Lodge public library – it was clear that the braid was growing longer, and more magnificent.

Today, we're trying to plait ourselves more deeply into national American life. We may win or lose political battles like ENDA and Prop 8. But history teaches that time is on our side. Every coming-out, every support of a coming-out by some loving ally, is a thread in the ever-growing strength.

ORANGE COUNTY ODYSSEY

Originally published 9/1994 *Orange County Blade*

I first saw Orange County in the winter of 1949, when I was 13 and thought the word "gay" meant "gay '90s." My California aunt and uncle had invited us for Christmas. So we made the long drive – endlessly long for a kid – from our Montana ranch.

In those post-war days, as everyone my age can remember, any car trip was an epic expedition. The first motels were popping up at the edges of towns, so you didn't have to drive all the way into town to overnight at some seedy old brick hotel near the railroad depot. We followed an icy highway that was two-lane all the way across the reaches of Idaho and Nevada, as vast and strange to me as Outer Mongolia. I stared out the window of our lumbering Buick, and missed my girlfriend, so secretly loved.

Then my jaw dropped as the snow magically faded before that first hot orange California dawn. Palm trees and oil derricks stood stark against the sky, just like in the movie posters I'd seen. My dad almost got us killed as he blundered up the off-ramp of the first freeway we'd ever seen in our lives. After he did a fierce screeching U-turn (more like a stunt driver than a cowboy), we stayed off the freeways and found another safe country two-laner that led us south into Orange County. There was no smog then – nothing but black earth and orange groves and bean fields, and Mexicans who worked them.

My aunt and uncle lived on the outskirts of a small town called Costa Mesa, with bean leaves brushing their back fence. We visited the Marine Corps Air Station at El Toro, where Uncle John, a Marine lieutenant, flew a new-fangled kind of plane, the first fighter jet we'd seen outside the Movietone newsreels. My girlfriend was very femme, and she would have sniffed at the jets. But I got a wild butch thrill from watching them scream over.

The family stopped several days at the Laguna Hotel, where my great-grandparents used to winter in the gay '90s. Beaches were strange to a kid who was more used to prairie thunderclouds piling like surf against the Rockies. But I liked those beaches. For some reason, I liked the bean-fields. I identified with the brown Mexican faces, because I'm *mestiza* myself. The fact was, I felt at home in that hot-orange dawn, and wondered if I'd live in California one day.

Before we went back to Montana, the family got personally acquainted with something called a television set. We'd already read about TV in *Life Magazine*. I was profoundly impressed with the thing, and wrote a postcard to my girlfriend, telling her about this miracle. Television wouldn't edge over the Rockies into Montana until 1954.

I dwell on this kid memory because so much of it would change. America's post-war uniforms already hid the first gay and lesbian activists. TV would turn into an acronym for "transvestite." Those rich black fields would vanish under concrete foundations of America's most stolid suburbia. Above these, in the hot air, would rear invisible ramparts of ideology, flags waving, as the name Orange County became synonymous for ultra-conservative attitude. For a time, my aunt and uncle stopped speaking to us Warrens, as they turned John Bircher and argued with my liberal Republican parents, and with me, the prodigal niece. The Laguna Hotel would overlook a changing town, one that became the gay thorn in Orange County's side.

It was 1981 before I finally moved to California.

By then, my aunt and uncle had mellowed, so we mended fences, and I lived with them for a while. From their patio, I heard the traffic roar on the Newport Freeway. The bean fields and orange groves were vanishing under slabs of concrete malls and parking lots. El Toro was still out there, but it too would later vanish. I was a published author by then, with a controversial book called *The Front Runner*. My aunt and uncle had actually read it, and they had the questions about being gay. Uncle John, who was out of the Corps by then, may have wondered if he'd helped inspire my ex-Marine narrator. But both of them merely remarked that the book had helped them see the humanity of being gay. Hearing it from family gave me a wild thrill. I swallowed tears and told them I was glad to hear it.

No wonder that 45 years later, being grand marshal at Orange County Gay Pride has special meaning for me.

As thousands of homosexuals march the Irvine streets for the first time, triumphant waving arms will mimic the wind-waves through those bygone bean-fields. We gay people bring back a greenness, a black-earth honesty, that confront those glowering bastions of denial. We revive a naturalness of those unforgotten orange groves. We add missing colors to the American flag. Black and white thinking is a concept – but, in real life, all the colors are found in white ... and black, too. Every painter knows that.

Today, with the gay and the anti-gay movements growing in Orange County, its homophobic haunts are synonymous with ultra-closet. As hatred spews ever stronger from pulpits and radio stations, the ultras believe they can make us disappear by forcing us out of sight. But we know otherwise. Gay, lesbian, bisexual and transgender children will go on being born from those conservative families.

It's a paradox of gay life: those who repress us actually do our "recruiting" for us. When they force us into heterosexual conformity, they merely amp the numbers of our next generation. No wonder the "family values" crowd deny that gay has any genetic basis. For 2,000 years, the ultras have tried to chainsaw the orange grove of gay life, but we always grow back from the roots. We are still here, like the black earth is still here, deep beneath those malls and freeways – needing only the earthquakes of freedom to crack the concrete.

When I ride in the Orange County Pride parade, waving at the hands waving back at me, I remember that long-ago hot coppery dawn, those breezes over the bean-fields, and know I'm coming home.

"IT'S MY HISTORY TOO"

Originally published 12/10/2009 at The Bilerico Project (www.bilerico.com)

In August 2009, I reported on a historic event at The Autry National Center of the American West in Los Angeles. As I stood in the crowd with L.A. press, museum staff and Stetson-topped members of the International Gay Rodeo Association (IGRA), the two iconic cowboy shirts worn by Heath Ledger and Jake Gyllenhaal in *Brokeback Mountain* were installed in the museum's showcase on classic Contemporary Westerns. Just yards away was another exhibit featuring cowboy wear and horse gear that belonged to founder and famed actor Gene Autry himself. The two shirts, tucked together on their wire hanger as in the film, had been put on loan by vintage Westerniana collector Tom Gregory.

That event sparked the planning of "Out West," a series of upcoming lectures at The Autry, which will explore – for the first time ever – the LGBT side of Western history – from gunfighters to women ranchers and Native American healers, and of course that provocative male figure, the cowboy.

This coming Sunday, December 13, "Out West" will offer its first program from 3:00 p.m. to 5 p.m.

Panelists: William Handley, USC professor of English; Peter Nardi, Pitzer professor of sociology; and Kenneth Turan, Los Angeles Times film critic. With support from moderator Virginia Scharff, professor of history at the University of New Mexico, the three will dig deep into the canyon walls of contemporary Western life, to excavate some answers to that question: "What Ever Happened to Ennis del Mar?"

The film left that question hanging in the air.

Though many Americans today think of the West as that phalanx of "red states" on the TV map during election night, the West can surprise with its sudden shiftings of spiritual sunlight and shadow, its social landslides that can reveal unsuspected layerings of raw experience and ideological challenge. In fact, the West's essential quirkiness has enabled all kinds of LGBT people to find something out here – from hiding places to homes. At times, we have not only survived here, but thrived here.

Arrival of the two shirts inspired the Autry's staff to decide that they wanted to explore those centuries of hidden LGBT lives. In so doing, The Autry became the first major American museum to recognize the contribution of LGBT people to the American West.

Sponsors of the series have been generous with their support – Tom Gregory, HBO, the Gill Foundation, and the Small Change Foundation, in association with GLAAD, HRC, the Courage Campaign, and the Gay and Lesbian Rodeo Heritage Foundation.

Looking Back

Creator and consulting producer of the series is Montana, Wyoming, Colorado-raised author and filmmaker Gregory Hinton, the man who brought Tom Gregory and the shirts to The Autry.

In Los Angeles the other day, at a little French eatery on 3rd Avenue, I sat with Gregory over brunch and we "chewed the rag," as my rancher dad used to say, about growing up gay in the West. There we were in the West's vastest city, geographically far from our childhood haunts, yet spiritually still close to – and making our peace with – those powerful influences of land and weather and people and conquest that shaped us both.

I asked Gregory how and why, after writing books and making films, he took an unexpected trail to planning these historic history lectures.

"It started with my dad," he told me, "– with going back to Cody, Wyoming, where I grew up as a boy."

Kip Hinton had been editor of the *Cody Enterprise*, founded by Buffalo Bill. A fire had destroyed an archive of the newspaper's original copies, but the Autry Library arranged to borrow microfilm of the complete set from 1956-1962, when Gregory lived in Cody. Rediscovering all the wonderful columns that his dad had written, with their small-town humor and skill at saying a lot with few words, Gregory found himself reconnecting with his home state as a grown man, in a way that he had never dared to do as a kid.

"And the sole reason for not being there before," he told me, "was because I was gay."

Early this year, while working on his latest novel *Night Rodeo*, Gregory discovered The Autry and started going there to write. Setting up his laptop in a quiet corner of the sunny patio, he sometimes took a break to wander through the galleries so richly crammed with arts and artifacts and memorabilia – with The Autry's original Museum of the American West made even vaster by addition of the Southwest Museum of the American Indian, and the Institute for Study of the American West.

"It was enormously comforting," Gregory said, "like walking through my childhood. The staff got used to having me around. I've probably been there a hundred times this year."

Looking at the Charlie Russell paintings and Remington bronzes and Indian arts, and hearing all the talk of "Western history," Gregory suddenly had another powerful sense of reconnection – of ownership in something that he'd never felt was his before.

"It's my history too," he told me.

Surrounded by all that movie memorabilia, Gregory started wondering what had happened to the two shirts worn in *Brokeback Mountain*. More than anything else in the film, they symbolize the dangerous journey that two cowboys made to a secret place in the Wyoming landscape that only they could know and understand. Doing some research, he learned that Tom Gregory had won the shirts at a charity auction, so he looked the collector up.

"Our community had so many disappointments this year," Gregory commented, referring to the same-sex marriage battles in many states, in particular Prop 8 in California. "That's why what's happening at The

Autry is a wonderful anomaly – something we should support and reinforce."

I agree – it's our history too.

Recognition Coming

For his part in creating these events, the IGRA is awarding Gregory with their President's Award for 2009. The Autry Library has also accepted the IRGA archives into their permanent rodeo collection, also facilitated by Hinton.

Meanwhile, *Rolling Stone* has cited *Brokeback Mountain* among the 10 Best Films of the Decade. The magazine's Peter Travers says: "Ledger gave the film its soul. He didn't just know how Ennis moved, spoke and listened; he knew how he breathed. Seeing him inhale the scent of that shirt hanging in Jack's closet is a scene that pierced your heart."

That reality of the film's most powerful and enigmatic character, and the questions about Ennis that remain to be answered, are the focus of the upcoming program on December 13.

For anyone in the L.A. area who wants to attend an "Out West" event, it's an easy drive into the Valley. The Autry's magnificent facility, complete with restaurant and shop, is located on the Griffith Park Campus at 4700 Western Heritage Way, Los Angeles, CA, 90027-1462. Admission to the event is free.

SPIRITUALITY

THE RIGHT TO BE SPIRITUAL

Originally published in *The Ethical Spectacle*, 6/7/1996

The other day, a young lesbian sent me an email about her struggle to reconcile her love of God with her love of women. She feels lost, totally confused. The only "spiritual people" that she knows are church folks who hate homosexuals.

After I answered, I got to thinking about all the "rights" being argued today. The right to marry. The right to attend school in safety. The right to express yourself. The right to have rights. But how about the right to be spiritual?

In college in the 1950s, as an intensely spiritual kid, I had my own struggle with her question. It started with Catholicism: how would I reconcile my own dawning truths with the Pope's self- appointed right to be "right?" Why do some religions have Goddesses, and others only Gods?

After I came out in 1974 and published my first novels about gay life, the questions rankled deeper yet. Why do same-sex attractions persist, in spite of the efforts by some religions to stamp out homosexuals? I became convinced that religion as jury-rigged by homophobic Western males would never meet my spiritual needs. Religion didn't matter anyway. I was out, wasn't I? My new self-honesty was enough, wasn't it?

So I buried that young spiritual part of myself... only to discover, as the 80s neared, that it was still there. Worse, it had gotten strangely sad and sick. Writing was hard, and I didn't have much to say.

The discovery shocked me into re-confronting the old questions.

Alone on a California mountaintop one night in the 1980s, I built a little fire. My native aunties call the fire Cheemah. I sat watching the many fantastic shapes that Cheemah shaped with Her flames. Were these not the myriad possibilities that lay before the human spirit? As I prayed with my fire, I found that I had to give myself the RIGHT to be there – to be spiritual in my own way, to be who my vision tells me that I am. So many people had tried to dictate to me about what "spiritual" is, that I wasn't even sure I had this right.

Unfortunately, our notions of what is "spiritual" are shaped by culture, politics, and what we see in the media. In the 50s, "spiritual" was radio broadcasts by Bishop Fulton J. Sheen, and bestselling books of Dr. Norman Vincent Peale. By the late '60s, "spirit" wore beads and peace buttons, in pop music and film. By the '70s and 80s, news shows and cable made their big break into power – "spirit" was either on the news as a Jesus freak being dragged out of a cult, or as New Agers reading *Seven Arrows*.

Today, as TV virtually rules our lives, the most muscular TV spiritual presence is the born-again variety. You have to have money and good publicists to command TV, and evangelical Protestantism has both – it dominates the news, and controls several major channels. On Sunday afternoons, you can have your choice of Dr. Gene Scott, Benny Hinn, or the Crouches telling you what the proper parameters of spirituality are. Even Catholicism takes a back seat to EP these days. An Italian friend reminds me, "The United States has always been a Protestant country. Look what happened to our only Catholic president."

"Spiritual" is even sharply and crassly defined by our penal system. Outside of prison, citizens may technically enjoy the right to pray as they wish. But one million Americans behind bars do not have the same right. The "get tough on criminals" movement wants to end the diversity of religious expression allowed in our jails and prisons. Yet evangelical missionizing is ever more present in our prisons. Indeed, some kinds of protection from jailhouse violence, even parole, are sometimes not available to inmates unless they jump through hoops for the chaplain. Some prisoners feel forced to pretend "penitence." Others, unwilling to lie, may have a genuine desire to change their lives, but their search for spirituality may take them into the proscribed areas.

These days, for many Americans, the bottom line is: "spiritual" is more and more identified with a strident, controlling brand of media Protestantism. Many, like my young correspondent, feel forced to deny their need for spiritual healing, because of this scary association.

Yet ultra-right-wing Protestants are not the only ones who would say that we must pray their way, if it at all. The sermonizing spirit of our times has infected other belief systems as well. In recent years, some gay, lesbian, bisexual and transgendered people have felt unwelcome in so many different churches, that they investigated the spiritual ways of native peoples. Some native cultures are more open-minded about homosexuality.

Yet even here we sometimes encounter an ouchiness about "who decides who has the right to what." As a mixed-blood, seeking in the Native American world, I encountered some people who teach that they alone can give permission to a person to carry a Sacred Pipe. I sat alone by a few more prayer fires, and pondered the story of White Buffalo Woman carefully. To me, the story says that She gave the Pipe to all humans, not just one tribe, as a way to pray. Why should anyone's immortal destiny depend on permission from some mortal, whether it's the Pope or a Medicine man?

Historically, in the West, many gay people have ravenous spirits, because so many religions rejected them. They responded to these rejections by creating their own churches and spiritual practices. In the early 70s, I remember feeling very moved when I visited the Church of the Beloved Disciple, a tiny Gothic marvel with stained-glass windows in downtown New York City. I could feel the hunger that created this place of prayer, and the rage that gay people could not pray openly in "real" cathedrals. Gay-created spiritual movements are many – global growth of the Metropolitan Community Church has been parallelled by growing gay New Ageism, complete with gay men pounding on drums and lesbians working with crystals.

In a Northwestern U.S. town, I felt equally moved when visiting the home of a Buddhist gay man who was translating ancient Chinese texts. The vibrant quiet of contemplation around him, the spartan simplicity of his life, brightened by his puckish sense of humor, were outward signs of the spiritual home that he'd had the courage to to build, after long years of heartbroken drifting. For him, the challenge was going beyond coming out – daring to give up the sexual freedom prized by so many gay men, in order to follow Prince Gotama towards personal enlightenment.

Yet another emotional moment came to me while hearing a pagan lesbian tell of the powerful healing that she experienced, when she finally made her first spiritual journey to the ancient sacred places of Britain, and prayed for the first time at a thousand-year-old holy well in Cornwall. She left a blossom floating that would spread ripples of her prayer after she was gone, and for as long as it stayed afloat. The questions about "fairy people" of old, and their link to us despised "fairies" of today, are questions that veer beyond academic research, into the realm of personal vision.

In gay literature, few scenes of spiritual awakening are as intense as the one in T.E. Lawrence's memoir *Seven Pillars of Wisdom*, as he tells of that moment in the Middle Eastern desert, when he met an old Bedouin praying at a tiny mountain spring. Exhausted by the carnage and hardships of desert war, by the spiritual denial and devastation that he had experienced as a well-born closet case in British society, Colonel Lawrence heard the old man's words with searing clarity, "The love is of God, and from God, and towards God."

Yet, however deeply we gay people may feel our spiritual challenges, we have a severe image problem. TV never shows us at prayer! If it did, the public would have a radically different perception of us! Indeed, we are the only minority in America who are perceived by the media as having no spiritual life whatever. Other than the rare news scene of parents, lovers and friends grieving at the AIDS Quilt, most TV and movie images of gay people still tweak the negative and the sexual. I wish news cameras would catch the glow on the lesbian ex-nun's face as she speaks of Mary, whom she still loves and holds high as a luminous ideal of powerful woman.

On TV talk shows, gay, lesbian, bisexual and transgendered youth are squeezed for the purely sensational, as hosts insist on discussing their sex life. If only a nationwide TV audience had a closeup on a 16-year-old Latina lesbian's earnest eyes as she told me, "It was my faith in God that helped me get out of gang life, and stop drinking and doing drugs." I wish they could see a 17-year-old prostitute, a Thai immigrant, express his yearning for self-respect and healing by painting golden Buddhas. I wish they could see the 15-year-old drag queen, dressed in her best, drawing herself up to her full height (which included 6-inch platform shoes) and telling me with great dignity, "I've realized that I am a very sacred thing."

Despite right-wing allegations of the gay community's affluence, gay people don't command the money to buy our way into the same kind of prime-time acceptance and visibility that Pat Robertson, for example, has bought. With a single telethon, the 700 Club can raise a pile of money that GLAAD or HRC would need a year of hard work to scratch together.

Indeed, Robertson and other TV church cultists have succeeded in upstaging the whole gamut of U.S. spiritualities – whether American-born Muslims praying towards Mecca from Chicago, or Mexican immigrants praying with their departed loved ones on the Day of the Dead. Even the Interfaith Alliance, that new coalition of churches who oppose the radical right, still has a low profile in the media.

In the November election, religious-right Republicans tried to allege "illegal campaign contributions" made by a Buddhist Temple in California that Vice President Gore visited. The uproar around other such donations, like the one made by Gandhi's grandson, showed clearly that bias against non-Christians was the real motive here. Yet the Christian Coalition saw nothing improper or illegal in their own political fund-raising, or in the 25 million voters' guides that they handed out.

No wonder my young correspondent feels "lost."

A dangerous journey faces her, as she struggles to separate what is "spiritual" from what is "political." But she has a right to make that journey.

A spirit is standard equipment for every human, along with a body, emotions and a mind. That spirit hungers to be nourished as much as body, mind and emotion do. Vision isn't a special gift given to an elite few. Nor is it something that you automatically get by joining a church or going through a sweat lodge. Young people hunger for spiritual growth as much as they do for sexual growth. This is how the cultists of every variety get their hooks into kids – by pandering to kids' need to belong, to feel the first rushes of vision.

Having rights may be a collective concept, but each of us gets – or doesn't get – our rights as an individual. Like snowflakes, no two human spirits are alike; and, like a snowflake, each spirit follows its own unique course as it rides the winds of storm. Spiritual challenge is terrifying precisely because it is personal and lonely. Yet we homosexuals have a right even to this stark and extreme testing, because it can tell us – more than any night in bed – who we really are.

Today every human spirit faces the challenge of breaking through that wall of media images that money and politics have built around each of us. Beyond that wall is a vast vista of possibility. Prayer can heal anyone, regardless of gender, race, ethnic background or sexual orientation. Even atheists talk to themselves about their lives; their very denial that a Deity exists must be ringed round by a sacred fire of protection for their right to deny. No one achieves anything positive in life without some kind of conviction about one's own destiny.

I hope the young woman who wrote me can give herself that right to celebrate and heal her own spirit. Isn't that what "life, liberty and the pursuit of happiness" really means?

EAGLE FEATHERS OF THOUGHT

From a 1999 dialogue at *Bridges Across the Divide* with an emerging young Christian leader

The young man asked me about something I mentioned once on Bridges, about praying with eagle feathers. "Do you do that?" he commented. "Without being disrespectful, can I ask why?"

My answer was this:

There is nothing disrespectful about a good question. I'll share some Eagle Feathers of thought.

Once upon a time in the 1980s, I watched a Medicine Woman working on somebody with an Eagle feather. She worked that feather up and down the person's body, flapping it vigorously and rhythmically against the person, from head to toe, all through the person's aura. Afterwards I asked her why she did that.

She smiled and talked about energies, and how real they are. She said that the living Eagle had been way up there, high above the Earth, at one with the thunderclouds and the lightning. She said that the feather still held the living bird's energy of being exposed to that thunderclap power of storm change, lightning change, rain change. She wanted to bring that energy into the sick person's aura, which is the body's magnetic field, and influence the changes going on in the sick person in that powerful way.

Call it a placebo, or whatever you will...but that sick person got well.

Once upon a time I also learned that I don't need to have an Eagle feather in my hand to pray with one. I can close my eyes and remember my encounters with living Eagles.

Like the Eagle that came to me when I was sitting on a rimrock high above the Rio Grande River in pueblo country.

For a while she circled slowly right in front of me, at eye level, out over the abyss. At the closest point of her circle, I could have reached out and touched her wingtip as she went by. Each time she went by, she fixed me with her powerful golden eye and listened while I sang a Medicine song to her. Maybe the message of that experience was that I was a lot closer to Vision than I'd thought.

The Christian mystics inherited an old tradition of the sacredness of Eagles, from pre-Christian peoples who had been observing life and animals for thousands of years, and creating all the natural sciences as they were in ancient times. So they had the Great Understanding about what an Eagle's power is.

I think that the meaning of all symbols comes direct from Life, and observing Life. A symbol doesn't have some arbitrary meaning assigned to it by some long-ago academic or functionary. I finally figured this out after staring at Life for a long time, in new ways, during the 1980s. You can't imagine how excited I was to finally begin to understand what symbols really mean – they are very important to writers! How can we use them powerfully if we don't understand them even a little?

So... the Eagle has a power to see all things from high up. The Eagle symbol says something about vision. It opens the power to sit within ourselves on a Vision Quest, and see our life and the world clearly but from far away, with everything seen in relationship with everything else in the great circle of our horizon.

How can the Eagle do this? The bird has parallax vision that is among the most powerful on Earth. From 5000 feet above the Earth, through his closing dive on his prey, the bird can adjust his vision so he never loses sight of his goal. That is how we ideally can translate our Visions into the realities of daily life.

But there's more. The Eagle is also a war symbol, important to great fighters and generals. Why? Because to win, you must have a good strategy, and you can't do that without the power to pull back in your mind. You have to look at the battlefield from "far away" before you even set foot on it, and see everything that's there with relentless clarity, in relationship to everything else. The Eagle's powerful sight enables it to power straight in on its prey – a symbol of putting the perfect strategy into action.

So the Eagle relates to politics as well as spirituality.

Down through history, different peoples adopted animals as the symbols of entire tribes and peoples, even of ruling dynasties. They put these symbols on their banners, shields, crowns, buildings. The tribe of Judah were the people of the Lion, while the Benjamites were the people of the Bee. In Egypt, you had two great peoples united under one crown – the people of the Cobra (Lower Nile) with the people of the Vulture (Upper Nile). The Vulture was always regarded as a "bird of peace," because vultures don't kill – they eat only carrion. Whereas the Eagle is a killer, hence a war bird.

The people of the Eagle appear in the Middle East, migrating out of Central Asia, around eight thousand years BCE. They leave very clear footprints in the archeological remains of those times. They were very warlike, sweeping everything before them and conquering many tribes, building a great empire and consolidating their power by marrying the conquered royalties. They were also an intensely patriarchal people – their god was male, represented as a king with eagle wings. This is why many of the Middle Eastern animal symbols suddenly sprout wings. The winged bulls, winged horses, etc. represent dynasties (including the Jews, who were taken captive by these people, hence the winged lions) that fused these patriarchal conquerors with older traditions.

At a certain point the Eagle moves into Greek history and tradition as symbol of the god Zeus – evidence that these warlike people must have merged with the Greeks. About this time, the Eagle god also is portrayed as a god of lightning and thunder, because that is the energy that ancient peoples associate with eagles.

From there the Eagle flew onwards to the west, into the Roman tradition – as symbol of the thunderbolt god Jupiter and the Roman imperial family. Eagles were also carried on the standards of the Roman army and its legions.

And from there, as early Christianity absorbed Greek tradition and Roman tradition, the Eagle became a Christian symbol. It emerges as the symbol of Christian emperors right down through the Holy Roman Empire, with ruling families like the Hohenzollerns and Hapsburgs.

Church authorities also designated this bird as the symbol of the Apostle John.

You might think that John's eagle symbol relates to this Apostle's powers of vision, as in *Revelation* and so on. Maybe so. But the Gospel of John is also the one that puts a big emphasis on Christianity's new direction – the Greek/Roman direction of declaring Christ to be a ruling god, rather than the Hebrew direction, in which the Messiah was seen as a human being, a great leader. At that point in its history, Christianity was parting company with traditional Judaism. So it was appropriate to garnish the Gospel of John with the imperial eagle symbol of ruling gods.

In my opinion the symbols of the four Evangelists – the eagle (John), the lion (Mark), the bull (Luke) and the winged human (Matthew) – represent four separate Middle Eastern/Mediterranean traditions of spiritual and political thought, that were brought together under one book cover by the early church. Each of the four Gospels emphasizes something different. If you study those gospels closely, and you get to understand the symbols and their history more deeply, you can see the logic of why each animal symbol was attached to each particular Gospel.

After the Eagle ruled Europe for a long time, it ultimately flew to North America, where it became a symbol of the new Republic.

Those of our founders who saw the new U.S. as the spiritual descendant of the Roman Republic had a vested interest in choosing the Eagle as our country's symbol. Their choice says something about their attitude towards central government, authoritarian rule, church power in the New World. Whereas our more liberal, less traditionally Christian founders (like Thomas Jefferson, who was a Unitarian and didn't believe that Christ is God) had a problem with such an authoritarian churchy concept. Americans have been disagreeing about this ever since!

Today the Eagle is still the symbol of American warriors. He shows up on patches and insigniae of our best Special Forces fighters. We're looking at a symbol that has been on record around the globe for around 10,000 years!

But beyond the symbol, there is the living bird – who has nothing to do with our human politics and prejudices.

The one I saw in the Rio Grande canyon lives beyond belief, in her world of winds and storms and thunderclouds...a magnificent creature.

THE DAY THE DEER TOLD ME THINGS

Originally published in Fall 1996 *Roundup*

It was a luminous July dawn at Mesa Verde – dew heavy on the grasses and leaves – when I spotted the doe deer standing a few yards from my camping spot. Inside the truck-camper, my journey companion was still asleep. No one else stirred in the many RVs parked around the campground. Dying fires sent up wisps of smoke. The air smelled of wet ashes and wet sage. All across those rocky mountainsides were blurs of blue in the green – patches of blue lupines in bloom. The only movement was flitting songbirds... and deer.

Dozens of blacktail does with growing fawns, yearlings, bucks with horns in the velvet – seemingly fearless of the smells and sights of humans.

Not far away were the famous cliff dwellings. The deer tribe had held this area for countless centuries. They had been sacred to the now-vanished human tribes, giving them food and tools, as well as inspiration for graceful images on that amazing pottery so prized by museums.

The doe lifted her head, jaws grinding as she munched on willow leaves.

"Walk with me," she said.

It was 1981, and I was finally daring to accept the fact that I could really hear animals talk. It had first happened a year before, near my

New York State home, when I pulled onto the shoulder to help a big snapping turtle that some heedless driver had injured as it crossed the road. As I bent over the agonized creature, seeing her crushed shell and glistening innards, she stared up at me and I heard a tiny voice screaming right in my head.

"Look at me!" she cried. "I am the Earth! There is not much time!"

Yes, time was urgent. I'd made my social coming-out as a gay person more important than my spiritual questioning. It was time to get more real... put aside novels about gay life for a while, and write of the native Medicine Women who were in my mixed-blood ancestry, in my Montana roots. So I sold my home, bought the truck-camper and headed west.

On that morning in Mesa Verde, I was well into a research journey around the West. The research was for a historical novel, *One Is the Sun*, that Random House had just signed me to write. But this research was not the library variety, squinting at microfilms, poring over old artifacts, pawing into dusty museum file drawers. This research had me trudging the raw road of life, trying to walk out of my European/Judaeo/Christian high-tech thinking, and into the everyday thinking of native people who see all forms of life as conscious spirit. This way, I could write more honestly of my central character – Earth Thunder, a real-life native woman healer of two centuries ago, who saw the world that way.

To understand Earth Thunder, I needed new knowledge. About animals, for instance.

What about "animal spirit guides," as anthropologists called them? One animal I needed to know was the deer. Earth Thunder was teacher and healer to a group of people called the Deer Lodge. Why were deer important to Earth Thunder? To women healers? What "spirit guidance" could a deer give?

Since childhood, I had "known" that animals communicate with one another, and with humans. I grew up on a ranch, did wildlife conservation work, lived close with all kinds of animals. But actually hearing them talk, the way I could now, was an unsettling new thing.

A few of my native relatives, whom I had tracked down, were people educated in the Old Ways. They told me, "Animals are the keepers of all knowledge and wisdom. And each animal is the keeper of a particular power of knowledge. Each animal is important, from the earthworm to the eagle."

At first, this statement made no sense to me. "Anthros," as my kin called anthropologists, are sometimes given real information by so-called primitives. But most anthros' understanding of this information is limited, because they insist on filtering it through a religious viewpoint that scorns animals as lesser beings. Rarely do academics – as the young biologist in the film *Cry Wolf* – manage to tear through the data curtain, and venture into the mysterious realms of real animals, and their real relationships with us.

So I was learning to go to Life itself (aka "biology", "ecology") to figure out where the native peoples might have gotten these ideas. My *vihio* (Cheyenne for white person) mind struggled for a new perspective on old beliefs, imparted to me by a culture that has divorced itself mentally, spiritually and emotionally from the life cycles of its Mother Planet.

One person who told me many things was Old Lady Library.

Speaking with the rhythms of one who had grown up speaking only "Indian," she told me that the badger is the keeper of the roots of all things, while the cats are keepers of balances in the universe. Roots made sense, because badgers den in the earth. Cats as balancers made sense too, because as predators they prune the populations of plant eaters, and keep their numbers in natural balance with the plants. But deer keeping was less obvious for me.

"What are deer the keepers of?" I asked.

"The deer," Old Lady Library responded with dignity, "are the keepers of all magic."

"Why magic?"

She chuckled. "That is an excellent question. Excellent! Uh-huh. Yes! Go ask the deer."

"Go and ask the deer," I had repeated numbly. "How?"

"The deer will tell you when you travel the Salt Road ... just like they told the First People. And you must travel the Salt Road, all the way from Canada to Mexico, or you won't understand anything about your story. The Salt Road is the old north-south trading road that everybody used. It was a good route too. The interstate highways follow it today."

OK.

"You will do a lot of praying along the Salt Road," the old woman ordered me further. "No journey is any good without prayer.

Even the old salt-traders prayed their way from Mexico to the northern tundra, and back. I want you to pray morning, noon and evening, every day. This way, you will stay out of that white-person thinking of yours. There is the magic of prayer, too. Go to the feed store and buy many plenty of those little blocks of salt that ranchers buy. Here and there, when you pray along the Salt Road, you will leave some salt for the deer. And they'll show up, and tell you things. Uh-huh. Yes. You'll see."

Right.

With a young friend named Lisa Sweetgrass, and a map supplied by Old Lady Library, I set out along the Salt Road, following it south from Great Salt Lake toward Mexico. Sweetgrass was a mixed-blood seeker like me. So we were both having experiences with animals that shocked us into new questionings. Lizards parked themselves in our laps. Eagles perched near us. Faithfully, but a little disbelievingly, Sweetgrass and 1 had left a block of salt at every important prayer spot. But nothing had happened ... until now.

The doe was already walking away. She glanced at me over her smoothly sliding tan shoulder. Blacktails are among the smallest of North American deer, but this one had a commanding presence that made her seem big as a mule deer. She was older, yet glossy with health. It was odd that she had no fawn.

Every grouping of mammals has its matriarch – perhaps she was the deer chief of this community.

"Walk with me," she said. "I know of your question about magic."

Now I was embarrassed that I had doubted. So I followed the deer at a respectful distance, perhaps 20 feet behind her.

She led me on a meandering path, into the thickets of brush along the rocky hillsides. The well-marked deer-trails were everywhere, clear as freeways, stamped out by tiny hooves, marked with droppings. They crossed with one another richly – a galaxy of interchanges more complex than any in Los Angeles. She stopped now and then, to scratch behind an ear with a hind hoof, or urinate, or snatch a bite of vegetation, but she seemed to know just where she was going.

"We Deer People make our existence easy for the plants to bear," she said to me, "by eating a little bit of many different things. This way, there can be many of us around here, without harming the land."

I could hear the doe's words clearly in my head, as I slid through the brush behind her, feeling the leaves stroke me the way they stroked her.

Definitely her voice was not something I heard with my ears. Mosquitoes whined everywhere – those I could hear. We emerged into the sunlight, where a little dewy clearing was blue with juicy lupines. She buried her nose in them, then raised her head, munching a stalk. Dew winked on the deep-blue blossoms. She stared into my eyes with her wise brown eyes that held a distance of millions of light years and millions of cycles of life.

"What do you remember about lupines from your childhood?" she asked.

The memory lit my mind like lightning. Lupines, found everywhere in the Rockies, are poisonous to domestic livestock. Every Western livestock-owner lives through lupine time with a worry in the back of the mind, hoping not to find a favorite horse down and dying. Some range-owners go to great lengths to eradicate lupine from their land. But here was this deer, calmly chowing down on lupines.

Next, she stretched her neck to nibble a leaf of jimsonweed – another poisoner of domestic stock. Jimson can kill humans too, as New Age druggies experimenting with hallucinogenic plants had found out.

The doe was still staring into my eyes, the leaf disappearing between her lips. Steam curled up from her tender black muzzle. The delicacy of that breath of hers, in the cold dawn, was wondrous to see. The steam iridesced with colors as it vanished in the cold air. Suddenly I was reminded of the little curl-like scroll symbol that ancient Indian art often placed beside the mouths of animals and people. Did it stand for speaking, teaching? For the breath of life that carries speech?

"My rumen," she said, "has the power to transform the poisons in these plants, so they nourish me instead of killing me. Is that not a magic power?"

"Yes, that is ... very magical." I let my own silent words go back to her.

I was remembering how I'd helped Old Lady Library butcher a deer for food – the children pitching in so they could learn too, all of us respectful, singing a quiet Giveaway Song as we worked. We cut open the deer's rumen, and found it packed with a fragrant changing mass of vegetation that the deer had eaten that day. Each sprig of plant, each leaf, was still identifiable.

Some of those plants were poisonous to humans and livestock. The stomach holds the power of change – transforming one being into another – grasses, leaves and flowers into bone, sinew and nerve cells. Could the deer have inspired native peoples to process dangerous plants so they'd be safe for food or drug use – plants like camas, cassava, potatoes (whose foliage is poisonous) – even jimson, which is still used in some native dream-ceremonies involving drugs? Could those images of deer on the ancient pottery be a celebration of this plant wisdom?

My Teacher was looking at me fixedly. Deer don't smile, yet she almost seemed to grin.

"You are beginning to understand," she said.

For perhaps an hour, the deer chief and I wandered together, over the hillcrest and away from the campground full of RVs. I lost track of time. On the summit nearby, I glimpsed a lonely ruined stone tower from the time of the Cliff-Dwellers. She told me to stay away from it. The past was of no consequence, she said. What counted was now.

The morning grew hotter. Most of the other deer had vanished. It was time to lay up in some cool nook, to chew cuds and do plant-magic. Finally, in a deep thicket against a hillside, the deer chief found a dome-like opening, a kiva of leaves. In the glowing mottled shade, she turned to face me.

"Thank you for the things you told me," I said.

Again she seemed to smile. Deer amusement is subtle, like their presence. "Now," she said, "I will show you another reason why deer are known for their magic."

And she vanished before my eyes.

No, she did not slide away into the brush. She was simply gone... in an eye blink, like that swirl of breath of hers, vanishing in the morning sun. I was left alone in the brush, suddenly aware of dogs barking and children's voices at the campground.

When I got back to the camper, Sweetgrass was up and making coffee. I told her of my adventure.

"Wow!" said Sweetgrass with 19-year-old energy. "Cool."

I have waited many years to tell this story.

One Is the Sun was published in 1991. The story of Earth

Thunder, leader of the Deer Lodge, wove a little deer wisdom into the story line. Women, as child-care specialists, have needed to know how to doctor sick babies and ailing women since the beginning of time–to understand and cultivate drugs that regulate the woman's moon-cycle, that ease the pains of birth, that make the uterus contract, milk flow or dry up, that banish pain and fever. All were known to the native peoples. Indeed, some of these drugs are still in use today, from willow (aspirin) to coca (Novocain), under fancy chemical names fixed by the FDA.

My new novel got no big blasts of publicity, but slowly it found its readership. There are those who prefer it to *The Front Runner* and think it is my best book. Even in the gay community, *Sun* has its fervent fans – men and women both.

In that same year, 1991, I ended the 10 years of vision quest with my relatives, and returned to a closeness with urban life, settling in Malibu, 30 minutes from Los Angeles.

But I've waited to share this story.

It is not the kind of story that is generally welcome in contemporary American life, especially while a narrow kind of religious feeling is sweeping the country – a feeling that is suspicious of Earth, of anything called "wisdom" that can't be found in church doctrine. Who would believe that the deer, or any other animal, can tell us things? On TV my tale would be relegated to *The X Files*, or some other series about "the paranormal." People are taught to believe that magic is bad and scary, known only to sorcerers who worship Satan, as in Stephen King novels and Hollywood films. Who wants to know that real magic has its source in the Earth? Molten lava turning into rich earth, or lupine blossoms turning into baby fawns? Who wants to hear that magic is every power to balance destruction with creation?

When Mike Benda of *Roundup* came out of the blue, asking me to write about animal spirit guides, I heard the voice of the old Deer Chief in my mind.

"It's time to tell the story," she said.

Yes, the Deer Chief kept her promise. The day I met her was 15 years ago, and her granddaughters are now grazing on Mesa Verde. But her spirit comes to me still. I can always feel when the Deer

People are around, even before I see them. When I was living in Malibu, I could be driving up Latigo Canyon toward my rented home, and I'd get this sudden gut feeling, with clear images of deer flooding into my mind. "They send you pictures, just like the TV does," Old Lady Library always said. And when my truck rounded the next shoulder, a deer or two would be standing in the chaparral near the road, staring at me. I always slowed down when I got those feelings, so I have never hit a deer.

In Malibu, many were the Magic Ones who came to plunder my corn-patch and rose-garden. I let them harvest rosebuds, always left corn-ears for them. They came, bringing their babies, to graze scant yards from my patio chair, letting me see that they were willing to eat every kind of exotic ornamental flower sold in the local nursery. They also pruned my oleanders, yet another poisonous plant. One morning early, a grizzled old buck stood motionless on my garden path, and held up the clouds with his big rack of horns while I sang to him in the wordless chants that I'd learned.

It was in Malibu, with deer munching outside my window, that I returned to stories of gay life, and found new maturity and insight to continue *The Front Runner* series.

"It's time," said the deer chief, "for Harlan Brown to be older and wiser." So I wrote *Harlan's Race*, sequel to *The Front Runner*.

And the magic of prayer? I think that we get what we ask for. If we wish for war, we get it. If we wish for healing, we get it. The prayer of a single human is strong enough. But the collective prayers of an entire community, a whole nation, a planet full of humans, are hair-raisingly powerful. Do we pray to be wise? To be revoltingly wealthy? To be victims? To have political revenge on our enemies? To control others?

The human imagination eats everywhere, like the deer, swallowing poison and non- poison alike. Prayer changes every poison, every nutrient, into some kind of reality. As America tightens up and grows ever more reactionary, I often think about the gay community's growing challenges and wonder if we pray enough. Our enemies pray a lot. Will both gays and anti-gays get what they pray for? Will either side's prayers prevail? The deer know where it's all heading, I think.

In mid-1996, I moved into the heart of Los Angeles. Instead of a sweep of mesa, I would now be keeper of a corner lot, with 300 square feet of front lawn.

The day I moved out of my Malibu rental, I took that last drive down the canyon with boxes filling my pickup. Two deer were waiting, in a little hollow right by the road.

"You will find plenty of magic in Los Angeles," they said. "Right on Wilshire Boulevard you are going to find it."

"Thanks for reminding me," I said.

They smiled.

"Plant many roses in that little front yard of yours," they said. "That way, our spirits can come and munch."

WOMEN

REMEMBERING QUARRA GRANT: FIRST "FIRST LADY" OF MONTANA TERRITORY

Quarra Grant looms as a beloved and gentle ghost of my blended-heritage childhood. She was the first woman to live in the 1860s ranch house where I grew up. When I was a kid, I heard her name mentioned hundreds of times – mostly in connection with what a great cook she was. Yet she was mysterious. Till recently I knew next to nothing about her life, let alone what she looked like.

Stories like Quarra's are becoming more crucial than ever. As I write these lines, the Texas Board of Education is moving to impose a more reactionary slant on textbook content – which they have the leverage to do, since Texas buys a lion's share of the textbooks purchased each year in the U.S. The new guidelines are pushback against liberalized history of the last 40 years – meaning that the Texas Board would bulldoze towards little or no mention of contributions by women, racial minorities, LGBT people, liberal Christians, and non-Christians. If these reactionaries have their way, many groups of Americans will become Ghosts of History Past – like Quarra almost did.

The magnificence of the ranch house itself is a doorway into this story.

In 1862, the region was known as Montana Territory to its few hundred white and Métis settlers; to its thousands of Shoshoni Indians, it was known as Toyabe Shok Up, "land of the mountains." Till then, those inhabitants had lived in log cabins or skin lodges. This house was to be the first actual framed dwelling in the territory's history – built for Quarra and her Canadian-born Métis husband, Johnny Grant, the territory's wealthiest, most powerful trader.

The spot chosen was a little rise overlooking grassy meadows and cottonwood groves along the Deer Lodge River. A nearby spring provided water. On every side, the broad valley was rimmed by snow-streaked ranges of the high Rockies.

Quarra was then around 20 – one of the hundreds of women from prominent tribal families who had married traders, scouts, explorers and stockmen. The traders were dubbed Relatives of the Rolling Wheels by the tribes, according to my own Métis relatives. They were careful to make these dynastic marriages in order to ensure protection for their business.

Quarra was a choice catch – said to be a granddaughter of the great Shoshoni chief Washakie, known for his friendliness towards white settlers. A younger Shoshoni chief, Tendoy, was Quarra's brother. It's true that food was to be a garnish on Quarra's history. The different bands of Shoshonis were known by staple foods – Salmon Eaters, Pine Nut Eaters, Bison Eaters, etc. Her mother was from the Tukudeka band, known as the Mountain Sheep Eaters. Her father, Kontakayak, belonged to the tribe called Bannocks by the whites because they made a type of bread from pounded chokecherries – it resembled the traditional Scottish bannock.

Quarra had first caught Grant's eye in Idaho, when the Bannocks were living near Fort Hall. This was the Hudson's Bay trading post where Grant's father was chief trader – Johnny had come there from Canada as a boy and grown up there. He himself was Métis – his mother's family, the Brelands, were old-time traders and wove themselves deeply into the Canadian tribes.

Quarra had already distinguished herself as a cook. Grant had been married previously, with several children by that first Shoshoni wife. He loved good women, good horses and good eating. So he was impressed with Quarra. "She was a thorough

Indian woman," he wrote of her later, "and not handsome, but a better and more clever woman without education could not be found. She showed a wonderful skill in taking up all the ways of white women."

Most of all, Grant loved her lively personality. He said, "She was bright and merry as a lark."

So in 1855, Quarra married her Rolling Wheels man "after the custom of the country" (meaning no ceremony in a white man's church). She left her Idaho band and made the journey into southwest Montana. Her mother, whom Quarra loved very much, came with her, and made camp wherever her daughter lived, pitching a couple of teepees there. One of Quarra's sisters, Margaret, had married another prominent trader, Robert Dempsey, an Irishman who also lived near the Grants.

Her brother, Tendoy, with whom she was also close, was in and out, protecting his Rolling Wheels brother-in-law's business. Horse-stealing was rampant – to the tribes it was a sport. But Johnny's Shoshoni and Bannock relatives put out the word that stealing from Grant was a no-no. Tendoy made sure that any horses stolen from Johnny were returned.

At first the couple lived in an unpretentious log home on the Little Blackfoot River at the foot of the Deer Lodge valley. He let his herds of cattle and horses grow.

Those years were the last gasp of fur-trade-type business in Montana, and at first there was little market for cattle. But Grant knew that gold was to be found in Montana. When the gold rush started, he would be ready to sell a lot of beef. And indeed, as the first nuggets were panned out of creeks in the Deer Lodge valley and elsewhere, and miners started flooding into the country, Grant started getting rich – very rich, the granddaddy of all traders.

So a big new home would send the appropriate social message. The house "cost me a pretty penny," Johnny wrote later in his memoirs.

In spring 1862, Grant hired a crew of French Métis carpenters and workmen. Materials came from all over, with enormous effort. Lumber was hauled a hundred miles from the Flathead Reserve, which was forest in northwest Montana ceded in a 1855 treaty by the confederation of Salish, Pend d'Oreille and.Kootenai tribes. Lime for the plaster came from limestone freighted out of the nearby mountains. Crates of glass panes for the 28 sash windows were ordered from St. Louis and brought up the Missouri River by steamboat, and thence overland from Fort Benton in freight wagons. In this region where even one small glass window in a cabin was almost unheard of, these sash windows were extravagent – the financial equivalent of bringing rocks from the Moon.

Amid the hammering and sawing, Quarra and Johnny and their children and several adopted children lived right nearby. They were crowded into a railroad-style line of cabins that also sheltered John's trade goods. Quarra and Johnny both adored children, so they'd taken in a couple of waifs.

In late 1862, the house was still not finished, but Quarra and the noisy brood of children impatiently moved in. While the family took over the upstairs, the spacious ground floor functioned as trading post, entertainment area and kitchen. Across the lane, the line of cabins became a bunkhouse where Grant's Métis workers and teamsters now stayed.

"My wife was very proud of our new house," Grant wrote later.

Quarra learned how to use the cast-iron cook-stove and went to work.

At first their furniture – beds with hay mattresses, etc. – was rough and hand-made. They were both used to sitting cross-legged on the ground, Indian style, so they had to get used to chairs. Later Johnny acquired some elegant stuff that came upriver on steamboats – a Belter type rosewood sofa, a set of chairs with horsehair seats, a big round dining table. Last but not least, an Eastern-made pie safe, where Quarra stored the bread and pies for which she was becoming famous.

Not far away, along Cottonwood Creek, other cabins had popped up – homes of other mixed-blood families, including the Dempseys. Grant had persuaded them to settle there.

The little community among the cottonwoods would shortly be platted and grow into the town of Deer Lodge. But from the start, it was dominated by the big Grant house on its rise above the river. It looked foreign and imposing, styled as it was after grand clapboard homes and Hudson's Bay trading posts in eastern Canada. True, it had no lawn or shade trees, so it just sat grandly in the dirt. Dogs and horses and Spanish steers with big horns roamed loose around it, and Johnny's freight wagons were parked nearby at random. Quarra's mother's camp with its cooking fire sat right nearby – it can clearly be seen in two drawings of the period that survive.

So the Big House became the heart of the community's social life. Weekly dances were held there, with merry French fiddle music and moccasined feet dancing the quadrilles. When the traveling Catholic priest from the Flathead mission came through, Mass was celebrated there. There was horse racing, gambling and other sporting stuff beloved by whites, Indians and Métis alike. Most important, the Grants maintained the Indian-style hospitality that kept them popular with the tribes. Chief Big Nose of the Blackfeet, who lived to the north, was another friend and protector.

"When we go to his place, he feeds us to the eyes," the chief said.

The Grant period of the Big House also saw comings and goings of white men whose names later studded "Montana state history" – from gold discoverer Granville Stuart, to banker A. J. Davis, to my own greatgrandfather Conrad Kohrs, who arrived in the valley with $25 in his pocket. Grant took a liking to young Kohrs and staked him to a start in cattle trading.

So, with the region still a territory, with no government to speak of, the Big House was functioning like a motley mix of governor's mansion, chamber of commerce, parish hall and sporting matrix. If Grant was the First Gentleman of Montana, Quarra was his First Lady. It was Camelot, cottonwood style. She was not just cook but "hostess with the mostes' " – working hard to take care of all these visitors to her husband's trading business. Her personality lit the house up. Grant noted that she was "gay in her moods, and friendly with every one regardless of nationality or color. She could speak several Indian languages as well as English and French."

When Grant went away on business trips, which he often did, Quarra ran the show.

At some point, though Grant was not particularly religious,

Quarra was baptized a Catholic. But it couldn't have been easy for her – once a girl born into a life where the People lived in skin lodges and hunted for their food and prayed to the Great Spirit.

Quarra was to live that fantastic life in the Big House for a little over three years.

With the gold rush now going full blast since 1864, her husband was now the wealthiest man in that part of the West – probably the wealthiest trader since William Bent of the Bent's Fort days. Bancroft's *History of Montana* would credit him with owning some 4000 head of cattle and 5-6000 Indian horses. He also owned a freighting business – 28 wagons that rolled in with every kind of goods, from flour to fancy French mirrors – from Salt Lake City, to the south, and Fort Benton on the Missouri River to the north. With his trade overflowing the Big House, he opened a store in town, as well as a restaurant, saloon and grist mill. He amassed a heap of gold from trading with miners, giving him a net worth of nearly half a million dollars – making him the Montana J. P. Morgan.

But that Cottonwood Camelot was coming to an end.

Quarra's energy, her health was suddenly flagging. She was coughing a lot – developing what the Victorians called "consumption," i.e. tuberculosis. This imported European disease was one to which First Nation peoples had little natural resistance, and it killed them by the hundreds of thousands.

The territory was changing too – things going dark. A shattering end had come to the old trading era, which had started with furs in the late 1700s, and with live-and-let-live arrangements between Indian, Métis and white. Outlaw elements migrating to the gold camps brought violence and crime, not only against other whites but also against Indians and Métis. An uncle of Quarra's, Chief Snag, had been brutally murdered in the nearby mining town of Bannack as he was visiting a daughter of his. As the wealthiest "half breed," Johnny Grant became a target of white resentments and racial bigotry. When he built a livery stable in Deer Lodge, it had barely opened for business when an arsonist burned it to the ground.

Reluctantly, in 1866, Grant decided to go back to Canada – perhaps the Three Rivers country in Manitoba, where he had grown up. Con Kohrs had now established himself as a successful cattleman and wanted to buy Grant's ranch.

So Grant made the deal – the Big House, its furnishings and nearby buildings, and 350 cattle for $19,200. Grant moved his family temporarily to another, smaller home in the area.

Since Quarra was ailing, the move must have been hard on her. Sometime in 1866, she gave birth to one last child, their fifth. Apparently Grant pondered with dread the idea of taking her to Canada. Not only would the long trip in a wagon train be hard on her health, but she would be separated – perhaps forever – from the family members that she loved so much. So he counseled with his wife.

According to his memoirs, he told her, "Quarra, I am going to the Red River to see some relations and some friends. If the country suits me, I am going to move there. Will you leave your people to come with me?"

Quarra's reaction was extreme anxiety. Indian women who married out of the tribes had learned to fear a moment like this. Many were the white husbands who dumped their country wives to take a white wife in church. On top of this, the man often took away his children, and the Indian mother never saw them again.

So Grant's memoirs reveal that she looked at her husband "with fear in her eyes."

"She said, 'If you will take me, I will go to the end of the world with you to be with you and my children. Will you take me?' she asked, in her pleasant way, but with trouble in her voice too for she was afraid to be left. I assured her I would take her."

So Grant went off for a winter of fact-finding, taking his oldest daughter, Mary Agnes, 14, by the previous marriage. Quarra and the rest of the children remained in the care of friends, possibly her sister Margaret Dempsey. The support network included my greatgrandfather Kohrs, who promised to keep them supplied with beef.

First Grant took a boat downriver to St. Louis, where he put Mary Agnes into a convent school. This was the custom with Rolling Wheels families who were Catholic, intending that their mixed-blood daughters be able to assimilate easily into white society. Then he headed north for Canada, where he spent the winter. As the months passed, he determined that Three Rivers was still a peaceable country where his children could grow up unharmed.

But when he returned to Deer Lodge in spring 1867, there was bad news.

Quarra had died in February. From witnesses of her last days, he heard heartbreaking stories about how she had asked for him – how she worried about leaving her children orphaned – how she had held her baby tight as she died.

The *Montana Post* obituary reported, "Her funeral was attended by both whites and natives, who mourned her untimely departure. She was much respected by the former, and her memory will be fondly cherished by her countrymen and women."

The local Catholics had taken charge of her rites. Instead of burial in a cave in a rock cliff, as the Shoshonis had always done, Washakie's granddaughter had been put in the earth, Christian style, beside the new little Catholic church in town.

Grant grieved hard. He wrote later: "My first thought was the great loss our children sustained. She had been such a good mother. My own loss I realized more and more as time passed."

As a final blow, the new baby died shortly after.

Grant wound up his affairs, took the four other children, and a couple of the adopted waifs, and moved to the Métis community in Canada. There he married again, so his children would have a mother. He never again achieved the wealth he'd gained in Montana, but spent the rest of his life providing for his raft of children by getting them "scrip," i.e. Canadian certificates that enabled mixed-bloods to claim small grants of land.

In my childhood world of the mid-1900s, I actually lived in the Big House for a while.

By then, thanks to my German great-grandparents' many years in the house, the place was bigger, more modernized, more opulently post-Victorian. Its décor was an archeology of periods layered one on the other, from the heavy ornate pre-Civil War styles up to post-1900 Art Nouveau. Amazingly, Quarra's things were still there – proof of the respect in which Con Kohrs had held the Grants.

More to the point, the feeling of her was still there in the house.

In the sitting room, I often sat on her rosewood sofa, with its slippery original horsehair covering, and felt her presence. I wondered about her as I lifted the stove lids to stick more wood in the old cast-iron cook stove, which had been moved into the bunkhouse, where our own men lived. In its place was a more state-of-the-art 1890s range that the Kohrses had installed. But her pie-safe still stood in the Big House kitchen, and we still used it for storing baked goods. When I touched its beautiful doors, with their insets of tin sheeting punched in geometric designs, it made me feel closer to Quarra than anything else in the house. She felt like family to me.

You could almost smell the warm aroma of her pies, made with imported dried apples or local berries picked in season. From Métis relatives of my own, I would learn how passionately some First Nation women adopted the European pie – and put their own magic into it. The great Indian cultures that invented the tortilla and the tamale, not to mention bannocks made with chokecherry meal, surely knew a thing or two about what to do with a pie.

Other family members had the same feeling about Quarra. My aunt Charlotte, my mother's sister, who lived in the Big House with her husband and children for several years in the late 1940s, swore that she had seen Quarra's ghost. Indeed, all of us – at one time or another – saw things and felt things around the place that were spirit nudges of one sort or another. These presences were never malevolent or scary – just gentle, sometimes puckish and very persistent.

My brother, ranging along the creek one day in the area where Quarra's mother had camped, found an old stone mortar half-buried in the dirt. Quarra's mother might have used it for her own chokecherry grinding – maybe with Quarra sitting crosslegged and chatting with her.

What did Quarra look like?

Historical archives had their photographs of Johnny Grant. Even Tendoy's portrait was around, dating from 1880, with the old chief now living on the Fort Hall reservation and wearing a white-man jacket and tie. But there were no portraits of Quarra. Was it possible that white-man history could put such a low value on the life of the woman who had helped turn that house into the social center of Montana for a time?

Forty years later, the ghost of Quarra reached out and touched my hand, leaving in it a photograph of herself.

Right there in Deer Lodge, in one of the oldest cottonwood-shaded frame houses, that photo had been hiding all that time. It was in a cache of snapshots and daguerrotypes that once belonged to Granville Stuart. An early immigrant from Virginia, he was one of those who had married into the ranks of Shoshoni women. Now the cache was in the keeping of his niece Vivian Stuart Kemp. Vivian was the town matriarch – in her 90s then, daughter of a half-Blackfoot woman and Granville's brother Tom Stuart.

It gave me delightful chills to have tea with Vivian, and laugh with her, and ask her about the old days. She could remember all those people that were just names on a page to me. Came the day, sometime in the late 1980s, when Vivian pulled out that box of Uncle Granville's photos. Among the black-and-white images of early Deer Lodge – cabins here and there, parked wagons, loose dogs and horses, there were a few pictures of dark-skinned women – the tribal wives of those long-ago traders.

Then Vivian said, "And here, dear, is one of Quarra."

I was thunderstruck as I took the photograph in my hand.

It must have been taken around 1865. Quarra was posed, stately and unsmiling, in front of a typical Victorian painted studio backdrop. One hand rested on the back of a fancy parlor chair. She wore a dark velvety dress with a high collar and elaborate bustle and bits of Victorian jewelry, including tasteful ear-drops. Her sturdy waist looked cinched by a corset. Under the flounces, she probably wore high-buttoned shoes. Her dark springy Indian hair was twisted into a fanciful coif that might have been copied from *Godey's Ladies Book*. In short, she looked every inch a First Lady.

Her husband had said she was "not handsome," yet her face was astonishingly good-looking. She resembled her brother Tendoy – broad cheekbones, dark expressive eyes, high-bridged nose. But it was her expression, not her features, that struck hardest. She stared directly into the camera with an embattled kind of dignity. Her mouth was set in decision. Around the house she may often have been "merry as a lark," but at that moment, in front of the white man's shadow box, her face said it all. No, it hadn't been easy for her.

What had it cost Quarra to lace her free waist into that tight corset? To part company with her People's ceremonies and start attending Catholic mass? To make bread and pies with white-man wheat flour? To think of her children going off to convent school? To ask desperately whether she could move to a far-off place called Canada, there to be safe from white outlaws who murdered Indians?

In time, Quarra's photograph vanished again, like one of those brief rainbows that trail after a fast-moving Rockies thunderstorm. When Vivian Kemp died, a relative of hers inherited her estate and moved to the West Coast, taking the collection of photographs. I had managed to obtain a copy of Quarra's portrait… but my copy was lost in 1994 when my California storage was destroyed by the Northridge earthquake.

But today her mixed-blood descendants, and those of other Grant and Shoshoni relatives, form an enormous clan. Some still live at the Fort Hall reservation. Others are sprinkled across the U.S. and Canada. Members of this proud clan, including my friend Anita Grant Steele, genealogist and descendant of Johnny Grant's brother, Richard, have been patiently patching their family history back together – figuring out who was the child of whom, who was married to whom, from diaries and reservation rolls and church registers and scrip records. Along the way, they've gathered a sizeable archive of old photos, putting faces of loving remembrance on many of those forgotten Indian and Métis women – the human timbers of early Montana society.

When Johnny Grant's memoirs were finally published in 2008 in their entirety, after drifting around in different manuscripts for over a century, further poignant details of Quarra's life and character emerged from the blur of oblivion.

After my family's ranch became the Grant-Kohrs Ranch National Historic Site in 1977, we started hearing from those many Grants and other descendants, some of whom visited the ranch for family reunions. There they can go in the Big House and see Quarra's pie safe in the kitchen, her cookstove in the bunkhouse.

Her things belong to the American people now. Her Big House belongs to the American people. And now that she is being remembered, so does she.

I have always felt deeply that the spirits of those who went before us *want* to be remembered. Whether they be white or black or brown, whether they be Christian or pagan, whether they be gay or straight, they want us to know. They have their own way of making sure that truth wins out.

Further reading:

A Son of the Fur Trade: The Memoirs of Johnny Grant, ed. Gerhard J. Ens (University of Alberta Press, 2008)

Bancroft Works, Volume 31, History Of Washington, Idaho, and Montana, 1845-1889, by Hubert H. Bancroft (The History Company, Publishers, San Francisco, 1890)

Feathers in the Wind, by Patricia Kutch Beatty (genealogy and history of the Grant and LaVatta families, privately printed by Outlook Graphics in 2002).

Many Tender Ties: Women in Fur-Trade Society, 1670-1870, by Sylvia Van Kirk (Watson and Dwyer, 1996)

ALICE GREENOUGH: WOMEN'S RODEO PIONEER

Excerpted from "Cowgirl Revolution," originally published at Outsports.com in 2008

After women were barred from competing in professional rodeo in the 1930s, rodeo cowgirls were stuck with the "safe" stuff like trick riding and rodeo queen. They became the rhinestone hatband on the Stetson of rodeo life. During World War II, some out-of-work cowgirls went to work in the defense industry, building fighter planes and helping run the country while the men were soldiering overseas.

When the war was over, cowgirls were in no mood to continue sitting on the fence. By 1948, they had declared war on the male-dominated establishment by organizing the Girls Rodeo Association. They fanned out across the country, promoting a new sport called women's barrel racing, aiming to get back in the competitive arena. GRA also staged all-women rodeos where "ladies" competed boldly in all the standard events.

The most celebrated of these post-war activists was Alice Greenough, women's world champion bronc rider.

She was definitely a throwback to the Wild West cowgirls of old. Alice and her sister Margie – along with their brothers Turk and Deb, also champions – were the second generation of a Montana rodeo dynasty that is still going strong today. The Greenough kids had actually been to that fabled place called Hollywood, where Turk married the famous fan dancer Sally Rand and Alice did stunt riding for the movies. Alice may have toed the line on the rule that cowgirls should be glamorous, but to Western teens of my generation, she was a heroine of a new order. In a time when most women's careers were limited to secretary, nurse, teacher and housewife, Alice lived a fast and exciting life that we could only dream about.

In fact, our mothers were tsk-tsking that Alice had been married and divorced not once, but twice. Dear, dear! The very mention of her name gave us small-town girls some delightful bohemian shivers.

Home-Town Rodeo Gals

Around 1949 or 1950, when I was a young teen, Alice Greenough made an unforgettable appearance at my home-town rodeo. She had retired from active competition by then, but had formed a rodeo production company with her old cowboy friend, Joe Orr, and still did exhibition rides.

Deer Lodge (pop. 6000 then) sat in the heart of Montana pioneer cattle country, and had held a rodeo every year for almost half a century. Local promoter Tony Sneberger, who owned the Corner Bar in town, was also chairman of the Powell County fair board. As such Tony produced the big combined event in August – county fair, livestock show, race meet and a world-championship rodeo sanctioned by the Rodeo Cowboys Assn. When the Girls Rodeo Association lobbied Tony about putting a GRA event on his program, they found him to be an open-minded guy. He also owned racehorses and had just hired Janet Thomson, one of the first female racing trainers in American history.

So Tony saw the box-office value of a little cowgirl controversy, and contracted the Greenough-Orr outfit for his show.

The Deer Lodge fairgrounds sat amid stately cottonwood groves alongside the state highway north of town. On opening night, the grandstand was packed, with the smell of hamburgers and beer drifting from concessions under the stands, mingling with the earthy odor of horse and cow manure from the brightly floodlit arena. All the big names in rodeo were there – Deer Lodge was the next stop on the world-championship circuit so everybody was gunning for points. As men saddled broncs in the row of chutes, it was time for Alice's exhibition ride – with stirrups hobbled.

The announcer's circusy drawl echoed around the fairgrounds: "And noooow, ladieees and gentlemen, coming out of chute number 4, we have Alice Greenough of Rrrrred Lodge, Montanaaaa, world champeeen ladeez bronc riderrrrrrr.....!"

Sitting in the grandstand, my girlfriends and I were beside ourselves with excitement. We represented several local ranch families and horsy town families, and were dressed to kill in our best Stetsons and dress pants. Our hand-embroidered cowgirl shirts – the fashion rage then – were made for us by our mothers. Our eyes were fixed on Alice's big cowboy hat, which was barely visible over the top of the chute gate.

Then Alice yelled, "Outside!" and the gate swung open.

The bronc burst out in a frenzy of sunfishing and corkscrewing. Alice rode him easily for the eight seconds in her Hollywood outfit, fancy shirt and tailored pants with sequins and beading. She was a flaming, flashing spectacle in the floodlights. Her hat didn't even fly off. We girls cheered ourselves cross-eyed.

Later in the program, Alice was back with a bunch of mounted cowgirls, for the first GRA barrel race that anybody in town had ever seen. The arena crew set up three 50-gallon drums in the arena. One by one, the girls took a run at those barrels, riding wildly against the stopwatch, making tight turns around the barrels in a cloverleaf course, with their hot little Quarter Horses leaning over at a 45-degree angle as they "pocketed" a barrel in explosions of flying dirt. It was new and spectacular, and the crowd loved it.

Those three days were heady stuff for little old Deer Lodge. In the evenings, every bar and restaurant filled up with hard-drinking contestants and fans. The local "chippies" worked on getting a rodeo cowboy in bed before the end of the night.

My star-struck girl posse and I were allowed by our parents to hang out at a popular family steakhouse, the 4-B's Café. The place was more crowded than a Hollywood red carpet, the air chokey with cigarette smoke. Couples were slow-dancing by the jukebox with

Patti Page wailing "Tennessee Waltz." It was easy to rub elbows with the rodeo greats – they weren't walled off behind bodyguards and publicists, like celebrities are today. I vividly remember a moment, as I sat at the counter, when the legendary Jim Shoulders, all-around world champion, slid onto the red leather stool next to me and solemnly ordered a hamburger.

Nearby Alice and her sister Margie were talking to some people, dressed in cowgirl formal wear for evening. I was too shy to ask them for an autograph.

Barrel Racing at the Grassroots

As barrel racing became popular, we local ranch girls had no idea that we were seeing sports history happen. But most of my girl posse grabbed our horses and started practicing.

My best friend, Shirley Sexton, and I had a friendly competition going. She was feminine, petite, the town beauty – rodeo queen, prom queen, cheerleader, etc. – and also an excellent rider on her half-Thoroughbred mare Fancyfoot. I was the rugged unpetite tomboy who loved grungy men's ranch wear. Mom was always battling to get me into dresses, so I grudgingly compromised and went the Alice Greenough route of "proper" cowgirl wear.

At the championship rodeo, the barrel race was reserved for members of the GRA, so we couldn't enter. But Tony Sneberger, ever the forward thinker, had reserved the first day of the fair for another new thing – the 4-H or high-school amateur rodeo. Most rural kids in the county belonged to 4-H, and I was president of my own club, the Powell Champs. So girls and boys turned out for a watered-down version of adult rodeo. It was boys only in the bareback bronc riding and steer riding – and the animals weren't very big or rank. For the barrel race, it was girls only. In the rest of the events, like breakaway calf roping and o-mok-see (American Indian-style equestrian games), the males and females went head to head.

So we girls got half a chance to beat the crap out of the boys, and we made the most of it.

Dress code was less strict at the 4-H rodeos – but we tried to look as flashy as our Hollywood heroines. My favorite outfit was a turquoise suede fringed jacket and matching turquoise Stetson, plus Justin boots and those tailored Western pants. I yearned to wear jeans in the arena but they would have to be girls' jeans – the kind that zipped up the side. In those days, it was considered shocking for a girl to wear men's jeans with the zippered crotch.

I was typical of those first amateur barrel racers, starting out on my Palomino cow horse, Gold Dust. My dad set up practice barrels in a corral that wasn't used much. Then – because Gold Dust wasn't fast enough – I appropriated the ranch's bay Quarter Horse mare, Molasses. She'd been bought for working cattle but she was fast and game. Pop grumbled when I hijacked Molasses. But he was proud when the little mare carried me to the first and only belt buckle of my lifetime as Best All-Around Cowgirl of the Powell County 4-H Rodeo. This was around 1951.

Then Molasses was injured, and I was serious enough about barrel racing that I needed a new mount. I had my eye on the state 4-H and high-school rodeo circuit. Tony Sneberger had a well-bred young Quarter Horse stallion for sale, who hadn't made the grade on the racetrack but was fast enough to blitz any competition I'd find in the Northwest. My dad fancied Quarter Horses, and was prepared to buy this one for me – provided I'd let the ranch use him for breeding.

But my mother put her foot down.

"My daughter is not going to ride a stallion," she said. Translation: I was pushing the tomboy thing too far.

Besides, I was going "back to the states" to college soon. What I really wanted to do was work in publishing and be a writer.

Influential People

The Fifties and Sixties would be called the Golden Age of Rodeo, as the sport went heavily professional and sponsor-driven, with rich prize money and major advertising exposure now available. Women's barrel racing became a standard event, with the GRA giving way to the Women's Professional Rodeo Association. To this day, WPRA is the oldest organization of female pro athletes in the U.S... and the only one that is controlled entirely by women. Thus it helped to open the battle for women's equality across the whole sports world.

Among the star racers of the Sixties was Florida's Donna Alverson, whom I would meet in the early 1970s after I became a Reader's Digest book editor. Donna came to the Digest with a vivid fiction manuscript titled *Drum Runnin' Fool* that drew on her personal career in the sport. I helped her get the novel in publishable shape, and it was condensed by the Digest and published at full length by their Readers Digest Press in 1976.

Donna later retired to breed Thoroughbreds in Florida and edit a horse magazine. Her novel is still viewed by many as the best book about barrel racing.

When Alice Greenough died in 1995 at the age of 93, she was declared one of Montana's 100 Most Influential People. The Montana *Missoulian* wrote: "She is credited with clearing a path for other women to become professional horse trainers and rodeo competitors."

Further reading:

Drum Runnin' Fool, by Donna Alverson (Reader's Digest Press, 1976)

JANET THOMSON: RACEHORSE TRAINER

Originally published 3/19/2008 at The Bilerico Project (www.bilerico.com)

"Women's history" is still such a new concept that many of us, as kids, knew a woman who dared to make female footprints across some male planet. For me, in the sports world, trainer Janet Thomson was one of those. In my memory, I can still see her during the works at the local track, looming out of the mist on a big Thoroughbred as he galloped steadily forward across the long shadows of dawn. His flared nostrils blasted rhythmic jets of steam into the cold air. She was standing high in the irons, talking to him quietly, keeping him in hand at a careful pace.

As she passed the old railbirds who always watched the works, their unfriendly eyes followed her with an unspoken "What in sam hill is a wummin doin' on that horse?"

In the late 1940s and 1950s, horse racing was still a man's game. Women were not welcome around the barns, even as grooms. They were relegated to being the occasional wealthy owner like Elizabeth Arden.

In my corner of Montana, a two-day race meet came to Deer Lodge once a year as a feature of the Powell County Fair. Montana was part of a Western circuit of bush tracks that had sprung up in frontier times. In fact, my greatgrandparents were among the first to import Thoroughbreds into the Northwest in the 1870s, and had bred and raced as a sideline to their range-cattle operation. Montana had two or three mile tracks in cities like Helena and Great Falls, plus a few of the half-mile tracks called "bullrings" scattered through smaller towns.

In Deer Lodge, our bullring was located just north of town, right across the state highway from our ranch headquarters. The half-mile track, and its grandstand and barns shaded by stately cottonwood trees, had been built in the 1890s, relics of more elegant Victorian days. My own family's horses had crossed that highway for their works and races, under the watchful eye of my greatgranduncle Johnny Bielenberg, the patriarch sporting man of our clan.

In the late 1940s my best school chum and I were crazy about racing. While other girls pored over *Modern Screen* magazine and wrote to Hollywood for head shots of movie stars, Shirley Sexton and I devoured *The Blood Horse*, and wrote to Kentucky for 8 x 10s of turf stars. In our bursting scrapbooks, the pics were autographed by male owners or trainers. We oh'ed and ah'ed over Elizabeth Taylor as the girl jockey in *National Velvet*, but girls got to be race riders only in the movies.

The class of racing that rolled into our town every August was minor-league. Some owner-trainers were known as gypsies, "gyps" for short. Few were ethnic gypsies. They were men who owned one horse and spent spring, summer and fall roving from meet to meet around the West, sleeping in the stall with their horse and trying for 3rd place winnings at small meets. The bigger nomadic stables rolled back to California for the winter, where the climate allowed them to go on racing and training at southland tracks like Del Mar and Santa Anita.

Every August, a couple of days before the meet, dusty vans and gooseneck trailers started pulling into our fairgrounds. The empty "backside" area with its weathered barns would suddenly bustle with life. Horses were unloaded and walked around to stretch their legs. Stalls were bedded with straw. Tack and other equipment was set up in a spare stall. While the better-heeled owners and trainers, and their wives, had trailers to sleep in, the workers had cots or sleeping bags in the stalls. There was no track kitchen, so people cooked over campfires or ate at cafés in town.

Most horses on the bush circuit were battered claimers with undistinguished pedigrees, that couldn't get near a stakes race at the big tracks. But here and there, you saw a horse that was well-bred and sound – like the ones owned by our present-day local sporting patriarch, Tony Sneberger. A rodeo producer and owner of a popular bar, Tony also owned one of those itinerant stables based in California. He had enough money, and enough of an eye for good horses, that he usually monopolized the local winner's circle.

The minute Tony's horses unloaded, Shirley and I showed up at the track. Because Tony was chairman of the fair board, he always got the best stalls for himself. Plus he had the best horses and best tack, so he was the class act at the meet.

We were eager to make ourselves useful – anything to be near a racehorse! Tony was respectful of our aim to be groupies, because we were good around horses, plus we were children of prominent local families that he didn't want to offend. So he hired us to muck stalls or walk hots or clean tack. Pay: a dollar an hour, in the clinking silver cartwheels that still circulated in the West.

In August 1949, Shirley and I got to the track and learned that Tony had hired a woman trainer.

From the horse magazines, we knew about trainers. They were cranky cigar-smoking men from Kentucky who wore paddy hats. At our own meet, they were often Hispanic men from California who wore straw cowboy hats. A woman trainer was unheard of.

We were beside ourselves with excitement. Oh, the glamour of it!

Janet Thomson was in her early 20s, short and slight, with curly brown hair under her straw cowboy hat, along with a freckled nose and a shy grin. Born and raised near Winnipeg, Canada, she had first come to the U.S. with a Canadian stable that raced on both sides of the border, and she had decided to stay on this side. She lived in jeans and lumberjack shirts and jockey boots.

We learned that she had started out as that equally-unheard-of thing, an exercise girl. Janet had thought about trying for apprentice jockey. However, hell was going to freeze over before she'd be allowed to do that. But Tony Sneberger happened to be forward-looking on female liberation – his rodeo already included that new sport, women's barrel racing. He had spotted Janet's horse-training gifts. So he put her in charge of his "bang tails."

Janet spent every waking hour with those horses, was careful and protective of them, and often didn't trust them to a hired exercise boy, so she did the works herself. Sleep was on a cot in the tack stall, with the door latched from the inside at night. The night watchman kept a special eye on her safety. She had a pitchfork handy to deal with anybody who bothered her or tried to steal Tony's tack.

The dirt track, which had grown a crop of tumbleweeds since last year, was cleaned up and freshly harrowed. The rail was newly repaired. Shirley and I were two of the railbirds now, watching with starry eyes and open mouths as Janet breezed Sunny One, or Major Hardtack, or Tony's new star, Montana Count. He was a son of 1940 Kentucky Derby winner Count Fleet – a big sorrel gelding with a blazed face, four or five years old. The Count was glossy and perfect, not a blemish on him. Helping out around such a horse made us feel like we were close to the Holy Grail.

So Janet adopted Shirley and me as her track workers. For the four or five days that Tony's stable was at the track, we could hardly be dragged away, except during school hours. Shirley, who was 5'2" and weighed maybe 100 pounds, was granted the mind-blowing privilege of working the Count a couple of times.

On Sunday afternoon the Count went to the post for our local classic – the Powell County Derby. Purse: $500.

I marched to the betting window and plunked two of my hard-earned silver dollars on the Count to win. He went off at 7 to 1. Since breeding tells in horses, the Count destroyed his competition without hardly breaking a sweat. He won going away, while Shirley and I screamed our heads off.

I collected my $14 winnings and we headed over to the backside to hot-walk our Derby winner. Later we blew my winnings on hamburgers and milkshakes.

On Monday or Tuesday, the gyps loaded up and moved on.

For the next few summers, as Shirley and I went through high school and showed up at the race meet every August, our notions of turf glamour faded. Janet's rare position came at a cost. Behind that grin of hers lived a daily grind of effort and fatigue. Racehorses demand backbreaking work, seven days a week. She had already spent many years low on the employment ladder, so her legs were knotted with varicose veins from stress. Plus the usual muscle strains, which she treated with the same Absorbine that she rubbed on the horses.

For both horses and humans, racing is marked by routine breakdown, and occasional catastrophe. Every year, more people are killed or injured in horse racing than any other sport – including motor sports. Unlike racecars, racehorses don't come equipped with roll bars. When a horse goes down with you at top gear, your unprotected body takes the full force of the crash. Janet had had her share of wrecks.

On top of that, Janet allowed that she wasn't paid much. After all, underpaying women was what everybody did in those days. But she was happy to have the job.

In August 1953, we helped Janet for the last time. Tony was expanding into Quarter Horse racing, and Janet was working a well-bred colt from the King Ranch. After the fair, I left town for college.

The day came when bush tracks began vanishing into the mist of a new morning – victims of inflation and waning rural interest in racing. Today they're almost a lost chapter of American sport and social history, briefly glimpsed in the book and movie *Seabiscuit*.

Many years later, around 1992, Janet's path crossed mine again. Through Shirley, who now lived in Oklahoma and had stayed in touch with both of us, Janet learned that I was living in southern California. She had settled in West Covina, not far from Santa Anita. So she looked me up, and we got together for a visit.

As an update on her life, she related that after leaving Sneberger, she had trained for a big stable in Portland, run by the well-known Northwest racing magnate E. A. "Sleepy" Armstrong. Sleepy was a colorful character. Like Sneberger, he knew how to spot talent – he had once taken a chance on a young unknown jockey named Johnny Longden.

"Sleepy put me in charge of the barn when he was away," Janet told me. "He used to call me Daughter, and I called him Pappy. He treated me very well...paid me well too."

Eventually Janet had retired from the racing game to raise a family. "Racing was too hard," she told me.

To my surprise, she was now partnered up with a childhood buddy of mine, Buck Fisk, who grew up at Deer Lodge on our Upper Ranch (his dad was our ranch foreman). Buck went off to work at logging and truck driving. He and Janet had met when he drove the big horse rig for Sneberger. Now both Janet and Buck were walking on canes. Her curly hair was grey, and her legs gave her more trouble than ever.

As I studied the quiet steady look of enduring in her eyes, it occurred to me that Janet had been one of the first women racehorse trainers in American history. She wasn't the first, for sure, but definitely she was one of the first away from the gate. But she had come along too early to think of her rugged independence as "feminist," and she worked too far out at the bush meets to be noticed by historians. Which is why I'm writing about her now.

Today there are hundreds of girl grooms and exercise girls around the tracks. There are a few dozen women jockeys, even a few women veterinarians. But many owners remain hostile to the idea of giving females that kind of responsibility for their multi-million-dollar horses. The good news is – women trainers can now be found in some of the big stables, saddling horses for the Triple Crown. They get their moment on TV at the Breeders Cup.

British trainer Gay Kellaway said recently, "Racing is still a sexist industry, but it's getting better." As in every sport, the trickle of females into the Hall of Fame has been slow and painful.

Often the truest champions can be found not at the top of the pyramid, but farther down in the broader, vaster, more grassroots levels – which is where change has to leave its hoofprints in the dirt if it's really going to count.

PAT QUILLEN: CARING FOR THE SMALL WILDCATS

Originally published in *Cat Fanciers' Almanac*, June 1993

In the quiet mountainsides of San Diego County, amidst the pungent odor of chaparral and the deep greens of avocado groves, an Arabian sand cat contentedly licks her two babies in her den. The hot still air vibrates with the deep yowls of African black-footed cats, and the bird-like calls of Brazilian and Colombian tigrinas.

Anomalies? No. This potpourri of species lives at the facility of S.O.S. Care, an internationally recognized non-profit foundation for the conservation of small wildcats.

Founder and director Pat Quillen is one of the world's premier cat specialists. As part of a global task force racing against time to save the world's wildcats from extinction, this dedicated woman excels at the husbandry of some of the rarest small felines today.

Her goal: "We need to increase the numbers of these species, for release back into the wild," she says.

A World of Wildcats

The world's wildcats total 36 species – and 28 of these are small cats. They are found on every continent save Australia and Antarctica. Sad to say, the little cats have received scant media attention. Because of their size and their elusive ways, they don't lend themselves to the spectacular image-making that big cats do. Yet they include some of the most fascinating, beautiful and highly specialized small animals on Earth.

As superb hunters, the small cats are important to ecologies of desert and grassland and forest. Together with the big cats, they comprise a key family that evolved to help Earth maintain critical balances between plant-eaters and plants. They range from North America's own bobcat and lynx, to the sand cats and desert cats of the Middle East – from the fishing cat and clouded leopard of Asia, or the chaus and serval of Africa, to the margay and Geoffroy's cat of South America.

Indigenous arts of Eurasia, Africa and the Americas show that the small cats were widely loved and appreciated. Ancient artifacts celebrate the little cats of the Americas. Tomb murals of ancient Egypt portray people hunting in the papyrus swamps side by side with small cats that may have been trained to hunt for humans.

By valuing small wildcats as rodent-controllers in the vicinity of grain-fields and grain storage, ancient farmers actually made it possible for certain small wildcats to become domesticated. Several of S.O.S. Care's rare desert species, while they are clearly wild, reveal in their DNA that they may be among ancestors of our domestic cats.

Qualified private wildlife breeders like Pat Quillen are a conservation phenomenon of the last few decades. Many people think "zoo" when they think of successful captive-breeding programs, like those of the San Diego Zoo, which are helping to spearhead the return of Mongolian wild horses and Arabian oryx to their native lands. And it is true that many of today's captive wildcats do live and breed in zoos and wild-animal parks.

However, quite a few small cats are delicate, nervous beings who don't breed well in exhibit environments. The answer: a quiet private facility like S.O.S. Care.

Beginning of a Trend

Back in 1968, Pat Quillen had worked as model and ski instructor – a striking athletic woman with intense green eyes and wind-blown blonde hair, and no inkling of a future in wildlife work that was about to waylay her. One day she happened to spot a leopard cat (*Felis bengalensis*) in an animal dealer's cage. She was shocked at its condition. This tiny species is native to Southeast Asia. The one she saw was clearly suffering from malnutrition, and had a broken jaw. Wrathfully, she rescued it.

In the course of nursing the leopard cat back to health, Pat began to study wildcats, and realized how little is known about the small ones. Few of them have ever been intensively studied in the wild. This passionate experience of healing one cat became the driving force of Pat's career change – to heal an entire family of species.

Pat worked hard, with challenges along the way that every domestic-cat breeder knows intimately – the hard-to-get-but-necessary permits, the long hours, the every-two-hour feedings for hand-reared kittens, the search for clean and affordable meat. At one low point, Pat sold her car to buy food for the cats.

In the early years, S.O.S. Care dedicated itself to the leopard cat, producing 9 outbred generations. Then Quillen took on the rare tigrinas (*Felis tigrina*) of Central and South America and raised 6 generations of these. With time, other species were added to her program. "In our facility, we are never responsible for any cats being taken out of the wild," she says.

Quillen's responsibilities are compounded by the fact that some small cats have become extremely rare. The tigrinas, for instance. At the time I wrote this article, only 25 were known to exist in captivity – and 17 of these lived at S.O.S. Care. The Geoffroy's cat (*Felis geoffroyi*), once deemed "common," was eventually added to the international endangered-species list.

As Pat acquired more hands-on credentials, her breeding successes and dedication began to bring recognition. Within the American Association of Zoological Parks and Aquariums (AAZPA), Pat became one of 12 working members of the Felid Taxon Advisory Group.

Internationally, Pat moved into a global wildcat-specialist network, operating under CITES treaty regulations. These conservationists – zoos, institutes and individuals – coordinate their work through the International Union for Conservation of

Nature (IUCN), which is also referred to as the "world conservation union." Eventually Pat belonged to the IUCN's Species Survival Commission, as a member of the Cat Specialist Group and the Captive Breeding Specialist Group (CBSG). Many taxa of animals – antelopes, primates, etc. – have their own specialty groups.

In 1989, recognition started to come. Pat Quillen was nominated for the Chevron International Conservation Award. She has assisted CNN, BBC and the National Geographic Society on film projects featuring wildcats.

Individual conservationists like Pat have helped create grass-roots programs in cooperation with wildlife officials of many countries, and lightened the financial burden for zoos and government.

"Every person can make a difference," Pat says.

In 1991, as a tribute to her reputation, the Saudi Arabian government gave Pat two pair of their rare sand cats (*Felis margarita*). These animals thrived at S.O.S. Care, and have already produced kittens. Their fox-like beauty and their mercurial movements, designed for camouflage amidst mirages and windblown sand, have made them a popular favorite with lovers of small wildcats.

Kittens Come First

Pat's work was two-pronged. Prong No. 1 was the breeding program itself.

Because of the mother cats' need for quiet and privacy, S.O.S. Care is not open to the public. At this writing, 48 cats lived at the facility. Pat was assisted by a professional keeper and veterinary assistant, as well as a young volunteer or two. An S.O.S. Care trainee had a precious opportunity to work side-by-side with a world conservation figure and learn about wild-animal husbandry.

Pat's breeding program was highly focused. Litters were planned, so that each kitten would have a "good home" somewhere in the international feline action-plan. Under CITES treaty regulations, sales of endangered animals are permitted but these are highly regulated and happen only after extensive U.S. Fish &

Wildlife review; however, it is S.O.S. Care's policy to never sell animals. Cats leave the facility only through breeding loans or gifts (which are also regulated). At its peak, S.O.S. Care's breeding program included tigrinas, sand cats, desert cats, Geoffroy's cats, margays, leopard cats and African black-footed cats.

Pat's policies are deeply humane. Unlike some facilities, that quietly put down their old animals, S.O.S. Care keeps its pensioners in every comfort until they die. *Grande dame* of the facility's cats was Gensie, a Colombian tigrina, age 16, who still raced to nibble rose petals (a favorite tigrina treat) from Pat's fingers.

Kittens were raised by the wildcat mothers, whenever possible. Only if things were not going well did Pat step in and hand-raise the babies.

The cats must be manageable enough that they can be put in a carrier and taken to the vet or evacuated in case of emergency. However, they are not treated like pets. The need to protect and preserve their wildness is urgent, because release into the wild demands extensive "rehabilitation" for captive-bred cats who have lived near humans for several generations. These animals have never been taught to hunt by a wild mother, nor have they hunted for themselves. They may be too familiar with humans for their own good.

People Matter Too

Prong No. 2 of Pat's work is consulting and teaching, on both the national and international level.

Her 24 years of intensive hands-on experience has given her a wealth of valuable information on small-cat housing, husbandry, behavior, nutrition, hand-rearing, infant and neonate nutrition, and basic care. In the early 1990s, with donor support, a new building and outdoor runs went up at S.O.S. Care, making it a state-of-the-art facility, with a video-monitoring system that can add to our knowledge of small-cat behavior. Pat's growing library of video footage captured behaviors that had never been photographed in the wild.

Because of her unique knowledge, Pat has been sought out by conservation-minded individuals, groups and governments in many countries. These include Argentina, Australia, Borneo, Brazil, Chile, Guyana, Indonesia, Malaysia, Poland, Singapore, Spain, Thailand,

Trinidad, as well as a number of other countries in Western and Eastern Europe and Central America. Brazil was a long-term project, where she worked with people involved in rescue and rehabilitation of wild species and co-hosted workshops there for felid specialists. In July 1992, Pat went to the People's Republic of China for the first time, for a meeting on the rare cat species that are indigenous to that nation. Another of Pat's trips, made with well-known wildlife photographer Art Wolfe, was to Borneo in support of Wolfe's aim to get the first known photos of that rare and elusive little rain-forest felid, the Borneo bay cat.

In the early '90s, Pat also started hosting the annual educational International Small Felid Workshops right in the U.S. Held mostly in Las Vegas, these events were typically attended by wildlife workers flocking from at least 10 countries to learn from Pat's hands-on knowledge and experience. She has also helped to provide material support to overseas groups as well, with everything from reference books to veterinary supplies.

In a word, Pat's work focuses on people as well as cats. The illegal wild-animal trade is rooted in developing countries, because the wild regions there often offer a potential "cash crop" of wild animals. Poor people in those rural areas rely on being able to harvest this "crop," in the form of cat pelts, for part of their annual income. Pat hopes that income alternatives can be found for these families, so they will learn to see the small cats as allies in agriculture.

As she points out, "The small cats will survive only if all of us, in every country, take pride in our wildlife, and value it."

Why the Small Cats Matter

For people who care about wildlife, there is beauty and magic in simply knowing that wildcats are still "out there." But there are also some profoundly practical reasons for saving the small wildcats:

1. Help with disease control

Over 30 diseases can be transmitted from animals to humans; quite a few of these can be intercepted by small wildcats.

As world population swells, epidemic disease is a growing threat. The recent resurgence of cholera reminds us that age-old plagues still wait in the wings. Bubonic plague has its natural reservoir in wild rodents of Asia and the Western U.S. (Medieval cat-haters and witch-haters evidently stopped their persecutions of cats when they realized the animal's vital role in plague control). The dread Lassa fever of Africa, whose first known U.S. outbreak was frantically nipped in the bud by health workers in the 1960s, is caused by a virus carried by wild West African rodents.

2. Assistance with "pest control"

Most agriculturists today have forgotten that ancient farmers domesticated small wildcats precisely because of their life-and-death role in protecting crops.

At the recent Rio summit, with other nations signing a treaty to protect bio-diversity, the U.S. government embarrassed its green-minded citizens by not signing. One reason is that some agricultural vested interests still have a lot of clout in Washington. "Bio-diversity" includes bobcats and mountain lions, that many agriculturists would prefer to exterminate.

With cyanide baits and traps, the U.S. federal government's Animal Damage Program has wiped out beneficial predators like the bobcat from wide stretches of the United States. Carpet-bombing of farmlands with pesticides has compounded the environmental damage that we must now live with.

Today, some small wildcats – though undomesticated – can still thrive on the fringes of pastures and farmlands. There they could benefit the ranchers and farmers who are willing to tolerate their presence. Gophers, ground squirrels, mice, wood rats, rabbits, grasshoppers and other crop-destroying animals are all food for hungry little wildcats. On the Pacific Rim, for example, some rubber and palm-oil plantations invite the leopard cat to live among their trees, because this little felid is an efficient killer of palm rats.

In short – wildcat "pest control" is non-toxic, low-tech and free. The small wildcats are a valuable renewable resource. If they disappear, we will have no 100-percent green way to replace what they do.

Clear and Present Danger

As I wrote this piece, the outlook for the little cats was not looking good if the current trends were going to continue.

Together with the gloomy prospects facing the great cats, the future was warning us that we are hurtling toward the extinction of not just individual species, but the entire family of wild felines.

Thanks to the CITES treaty, and to growing public sensitivity, the biggest boom in the small-cat pelt trade is over – the day when (as CITES figures show) a single South American village could market 250,000 pelts.

But despite the CITES treaty, the illicit destruction of wild animals is still a huge international business whose annual profits run into the billions. One example of the impact: For just a few years, the rare Andean mountain cat surfaced in the pelt export statistics, and has been little seen in the wild since then. Wild populations of more common small cats have crashed everywhere. Yet the remaining small cats are still the objects of a relentless illicit fur trade. Pelts are shipped to countries where endangered furs are still openly sold. Kittens still move on the illicit pet trade. In some countries, small cats are viewed as gourmet cuisine.

Finally, the small cats are being hurt everywhere by needless destruction of their habitats.

"But with more intelligent planning," Pat told me, "it will be possible to care for humans *and* for wildlife."

Update in the Year 2010

Sad to say, the intensive global effort to save a wide range of small wildcat species has run into trouble. Too much of their habitat was being destroyed, leaving nowhere for the animals to live. As the global recession deepened, the work was costing too much money, and adequate fundraising was getting harder and harder to do.

Starting in 2007, the IUCN's Cat Specialist Group was confronted with the heartbreaking reality that all the wild felids continue to be at serious risk. Tigers looked to be disappearing in the next decade. Even African lions, which used to be thought of as common, are now sparse enough in numbers that their decline is viewed with concern. Some key financial supporters were wanting conservationists to focus efforts on the high-profile big cats.

On October 23, 2003, this global catastrophe was suddenly echoed in Pat's personal life. When she arrived home from a European trip, she made a devastating discovery. In her absence, the S.O.S. Care facility, and most of the rural township where she lived, had been overrun by one of those world-famous wildfires that sear southern California. Her dedicated volunteers had managed to evacuate all the cats. But her home and almost all the buildings had burned to the ground – along with 40 years of irreplaceable research records, correspondence, photographs and video footage. Nothing was left but the brick chimney sticking up from smoking ashes.

"Other than the cats," she told me on the phone, "everything I own in the world is now in the suitcase I carried on the plane."

Afterwards, Pat's insurance company fought her claim every step of the way and refused to cover the whole cost of rebuilding the facility. Eventually she had to settle for a partial rebuild.

"Dealing with FEMA was another nightmare," she told me.

With this blow coming on top of all the fund-raising challenges, Pat decided it was time to wind things down.

Today, she is no longer breeding – just maintaining a shrinking population as the oldest cats pass on. Gensie is long gone, as are Milagre and a few others I knew. At the moment, just 12 animals are living out their lives in comfort and care in their shaded runs. Politically, however, Pat is still active on behalf of both big cats and little cats. Frequently she is sought out for advice and counsel by programs around the world – notably the recent efforts in Spain to save the Iberian lynx (*Lynx pardinus*). She still cares intensely about the importance of paw-prints around the globe – and human footprints as well.

Looking back on a lifetime of care, Quillen recently summed it up with this simple and stark comment: "Many people ask me how and why, and I have very often responded that it is hard to find the courage to take your own path, to follow your heart… and do no harm."

Pat is also careful to point out: "I couldn't have done it alone. Conservation work takes a lot of people, cooperating intensely on an international plane. I could never have done this without all the people who have been there for me over the years – from the volunteers who cared for the cats when I was away, to a generous few who were always there with a little money when S.O.S. Care was most in need."

Further reading:

International Zoo Yearbook: Vol. 35 (Zoological Society of London, 1997).

Noted wildlife photographer Art Wolfe included photographs of S.O.S. Care small cats in a magnificent book:
Wild Cats of the World, by Art Wolfe and Barbara Sleeper (Crown, 1995).

EARTH THUNDER: MEDICINE WOMAN WORKING FOR OUR PLANET

Originally published 3/25/2008 at The Bilerico Project (www.bilerico.com)

Like many Americans, I have some First Nation ancestry braided with the European ancestry in my family roots. When I connected with a few tribal cousins, I started hearing stories about family groups back in the late 1800s who had never surrendered to the U.S. Army, who had never become prisoners of war on the reservations. Instead they slipped off into the wildest, most rugged regions of the West. For several generations, the Wild Ones managed to stay hidden – never leaving a trace for hikers or forest rangers to find, keeping fires tiny and only lit at night. By the 1930s, logging and recreational development of public lands was making it harder to keep their secret. Yet a few families held on till the 1950s.

I thrilled at those stories, and never dreamed that I would ever meet someone who had been born a Wild One... till I met EarthThunder.

Around 2002, she emailed me from Idaho to say she'd read my Western historical novel *One Is the Sun*. Not long after, when I visited Boise to be grand marshal of Pride, EarthThunder and I met, and she told me the story of her childhood.

Listening to the Wolves

"After the Trail of Tears," EarthThunder told me, "some Cherokees dispersed in different directions, so they could stay off the reservations. My family stealthed their way into Idaho. About 40 of us were in hiding in the Sawtooth Mountains south of here. I think I was born around January 1947. My parents had gone out...they were indentured and working on a ranch. They were murdered because they had a child. Somehow they had stashed me and a local sheriff found me. My grandmother heard from the Wild Wolves that I was alive, so she went and found the sheriff, and took me back into the mountains.

"I was raised by my grandfather and his four grandfathers, and my grandmother and 3 of her grandmothers. In summer we camped at 8000 feet, hunting and getting ready for winter. In fall, we made a 100-mile trek along a little trail over the mountains, down into the Malad Gorge at 3000+ feet, where we spent the winter in the caves there, with plenty of dried rabbit and deer. From birth to age 11, I grew up speaking only Cherokee. I didn't know there were other humans living on our big planet."

EarthThunder and I jumped into her pickup, and she took me high into the Sawtooths. Today the area is a 2.1-million-acre national forest, still one of the wildest and most magnificent regions left in the U.S. As we walked along the mountain slopes, through the silence of a summer afternoon, past groves of gnarled old aspens that were thinking about their autumn colors, I imagined a large family living up there without any technical support from the rest of the planet, never reading a newspaper or listening to a radio.

As we watched the little rivers rushing, EarthThunder said sadly, "The salmon and steelheads are mostly gone now. There used to be so many, I could catch them with my hands."

When EarthThunder first left the mountains, her encounters with the outside world were shocking to her. She went to school, learned English and got used to technology. By sixth grade, she already knew she loved other women – her teacher was shocked when she innocently wrote an essay about women hunters marrying each other. Till age 19, she was still going back into the mountains to spend time with her wild family.

What Is "Medicine"?

Eventually EarthThunder found her life-trail as a Medicine Woman. She retains full enrollment as a Cherokee. Her clan elders gave her the name, which is a traditional one.

She says: "I am a Tsalagi, a vessel of dreams of those who walked before, and empowered by Elders' repository of Teachings, 35th generation." She talks about the Thread Peoples, meaning those like herself who hold living threads that link to a pre-industrial consciousness, when humans had more clarity about living in balance with Wildness.

What is a Medicine Woman, anyway?

As the conquered Peoples learned English, they saw the word "medicine" as a handy translation for their idea of the sacred, of personal power – meaning the ability to direct human energies or natural energies at will. In the Peoples' world, there was none of the Christian split into "sacred" and "secular." To First Peoples, everything is Medicine. Everything is one with everything else.

Mainstream white historians have usually blown off First Nation women, often portraying them as servile, pathetic figures. Yet the First Nation world had – and still has – its great women of power. The bronze statue of Freedom that tops the Capitol dome in Washington D.C., is crowned with an eagle headdress. In part the statue is a tribute to those women chiefs who governed equal to men in the Six Nations confederacy. This tribal democracy was friendly to America's founders, attending the Constitutional Convention and sharing some ideas about good government. Later, the ancient trading routes through deserts and across mountain ranges were sometimes shown to whites by influential women like Sacajawea, who belonged to a powerful Shoshoni family and led the Lewis and Clark expedition across the West. Today's highways often follow these old routes.

As for Medicine Women, most white historians have managed to ignore them too – though some of these women left their trail across the mountains of mainstream written history. Examples: Pretty Shield of the Crows and Josephine Headswift Limpy of the Northern Cheyennes. Medicine Women have been political figures, war leaders, clan chiefs, healers, prophets, teachers, artists. While some tribes had patriarchal hostility towards females of power, other tribes held women in awe and great regard.

Important to History

Why would these women be important to our history? After all, according to conservative historians, America is supposedly founded on Biblical teachings that leave no room for other ways of looking at life.

Yet the contribution of Medicine Women who were healers, for example, is braided gently through our national heritage – in the medical arts. In the U.S. Pharmacopeia today, 220 North American medicinal plants are listed. They found their way into usage with colonists and pioneer settlers because tribal women doctors shared with these newcomers the secrets of how to prepare and use these plant drugs.

When First Peoples were pushed into the prison camps called "reservations," they came under fierce pressure from Christian missionaries. They were forced to attend church and send their children to government schools. Gradually the new generations lost much of the knowledge that their traditions had cherished through thousands of years. Since the Bible says that women are forbidden to speak, missionaries took extra steps to silence Medicine Women.

Only in the underground on reservations, or in isolated pockets like the one where EarthThunder grew up in, was any old knowledge and wisdom preserved.

Few Americans today realize that the First Amendment didn't apply to the tribes till just recently. Federal law outlawed the old ceremonies and prohibited healers from practicing the old medical arts, like herbal and crystal healing. If you got caught, you were sent to prison for "practicing medicine without a license."

By the late 1970s, however, when EarthThunder was in her 30s, court decisions struck down many of these bans.

At that time, the New Age movement was getting under way, and there was new interest in the spiritual ways of First Peoples all over the world. A number of Medicine Women and Medicine Men decided to share the old teachings with any non-Indians who came seeking with a "good heart." Today, that decision remains controversial with some in the First Nation world, who feel strongly that traditional information should not be shared with outsiders.

EarthThunder's position is this: "I do not speak for other First Nation Peoples or my reservation. I only speak of my families' stories."

Our Wild Planet

Now around 61, EarthThunder doesn't live in the past. Her daily life is a living bridge between that wild ancient world where she grew up, where people were one with Mother Earth, and the post-millennial world where Earth is being slammed by global climate change and human disruption. She works at renewing that Tsalagi consciousness into the present, and putting it to work here.

"I am in privilege to work for our wild planet," she says.

Deeply involved in the green movement, EarthThunder is also helping to save America's wild wolves, in gratitude for the Wolf Medicine that touched her life at birth. As the wolves do, she travels long distances – but to speak at international conferences. She has visited First Peoples in Australia, who have their own history of wild bands surviving in the outback.

At her Idaho home base, EarthThunder does counseling on wellness, relationships, prosperity and death, as well as wilderness teachings – all drawn from her learnings with her wild family. She's also involved in LGBT activism.

Like so many today, EarthThunder does her work with a website and e-list. Her emails start with a cheery "*O si yo*" (Cherokee for hello). They share information about everything from healthy diet to ceremonies that anyone can do for themselves, to activist alerts on legislation that needs support. Phone calls are punctuated with her chuckles and howls of laughter – humor is important.

When EarthThunder talks about her wild childhood, some Idahoans scoff and say there's no way that a family could have trekked over those rugged mountains into the Malad Gorge.

"But a year ago," she told me, "a pilot flew me over the Sawtooths in a small plane. I looked down there... I looked and looked, and finally spotted that tiny trail that we always followed. It's still there."

ZEST

HAPPY 65TH BIRTHDAY TO ME

Originally published at Gaywired.com, 7/05/2001

The big 65 has finally come, and I've decided not to conform to custom. No gold watch for me. I have no intention of retiring from anything I love. My comment to a journalist was that I'm going to keep writing till I fall over dead on my keyboard.

As I look back over 65 years, 1936 was a good time to get born. As a kid, I got to see the United States before it became as over-technologized and dehumanized as it is now. I can remember when large rural areas had no electricity – at our Upper Ranch, we milked cows and cooked supper by kerosene lamplight.

There were no credit cards, no computers, no email, no jet planes, no frozen food – and no television. Space travel was still science fiction. Large areas of the world were at war, and large areas of the U.S. experienced hardship, yet we hoped to end all wars and all poverty one day. Pollution was still spotty – a clean river for a tomboy girl-kid to fish in, or splash her cowpony through, was taken for granted by me.

The American Dream seemed more reachable then. And what is the American Dream? For me, it meant the power to have a committed and creative life as a writer, and the right to be myself.

It's true that those times were dark with what people call "human rights violations" today. There was little liberty or dignity for people of color, women, seniors and some other minorities...and none at all for gay people.

Yet there were bright things in those times too. For instance, a sense of what I'd call "continuity" was strong in the country. For better or worse, traditions got handed down to the kids. In my own family, I had a strong sense of all those Dog Soldiers and Irish freedom fighters in my blood. The family stories about them drummed in my ears, and made me want to write my own stories.

Looking back, I'm amazed that I survived – the closet, the bad marriage, a few near-fatal wrecks with cars and horses, drinking, poor health, spiritual despair, thoughts of suicide, and the challenge to reinvent myself quite a few times. At 65 I feel like I just finished boot camp. The survival skills I learned ought to get me through the next 40 or 50 years – and there's always more to learn. Old dogs learn new tricks quicker than young dogs.

Today our country talks the talk, but seldom walks the walk, of the American Dream. The United States has got masses of human-rights legislation in place now, yet it's growing harder to get compliance, and the country is gridlocked in litigation. There's an eerie atmosphere – that sultry hush that you feel on a prairie afternoon when tornados might touch down.

No matter what our political views are, I think that most Americans are feeling a collective loss of humanization, a collective dread at the growing corruption in government and law enforcement, at the human-rights abuses being more tolerated. The nation that my generation felt so patriotic about, is now considered a rogue nation by many other countries (some of them erstwhile allies of ours) because we are so at angles with our long-stated Dream. Large areas of the world are still at war, and large areas of the U.S. still experience economic hardship.

Today the loss of family continuity is huge – I wonder how we will replace it. It can't be restored by laws making divorce harder. It has little to do with "traditional marriage" and "values" and "partnerships" and all those things that both conservatives and liberals talk about.

All in all, this is a star-crossed time we live in – but it's also a great time for a writer to be alive. Writers, artists, filmmakers and other creative people have the challenge to be the "mirror, mirror on the wall" – to reflect society's diseases with clear intent, and inspire the will for healing.

So I don't plan anything special on my 65th birthday. Pull a few weeds in the garden, cut a few roses for my desk, write a new editorial, maybe have dinner with a few colleagues and friends. The big 65 ought to be business as usual, not a point of no return.

The kids in my 65-year-old world do give me new hope for the American Dream. The ones I know don't operate off rhetoric. They're too busy trying to survive, to make a living with their own creativity. I pray they survive long enough to look back on today and see it as I see my own life – not as a labyrinth of nostalgia to get lost in, but as a long line of navigational markers that always point to a clouded but alluring horizon – the future.

So this essay is my birthday present to myself. Many happy returns.

MOMENTS OF STILLNESS

Originally published in *Echo*, December 6, 2001

Not long ago, as winter approached, I visited Albuquerque on book tour, and was put up at a charming bed and breakfast in a quiet neighborhood on the edge of town. The building was a 19th century adobe that had been renovated. Surprise: no TV, no radio, no Internet, no telephone. I was looking at four days of no news about the war and the terrorist crisis! Four days of no e-mail!

SCW (severe communications withdrawal) is my term for what I experienced. It's a syndrome not yet studied by Western medicine – but it does exist. Many of us live with multiple TVs in our homes; television even invades our cars now, where it compounds the uproar from radios, cell phones and CDs. Many of us spend the day with phone headsets on, or walk around with cell phones glued to our ears. We're suffering from CA (communications addiction).

The B&B owner was away for the weekend, so I couldn't even use his phone. It was off-season and I was the only guest. I don't own a cell phone, so if I wanted to talk to my office in L.A., I had to hike four blocks to a public phone booth. After two days of acute yearning to read e-mail, I realized how addicted I was to "being in touch."

By Day 3, the quiet started to kick in. The whir of hummingbirds in the patio got louder than the imagined roar of Afghani gunfire inside my head. When a storm moved in, I actually could hear the wind, and the rain on the tile roof at night. The war looked different – sharper edges around the issues and the suffering when I viewed them through those blue wintry shadows under the desert trees in the garden.

Even in wartime, people need to find those moments of stillness. In the film *Platoon*, there is the moment when the young soldier regains consciousness after a hellish night firefight in Vietnam. He finds himself laying there in silence, staring into the eyes of a tiny deer that came stealing out of the jungle. For the moment, amid mangled corpses and blasted trees, it seems like he and that deer are the last living things on the planet. He has a moment of searing clarity about what he just lived through, and that is the defining moment of the film.

That communications cacophony where Americans live today is something that prevents us from having those moments of stillness. The aggressive demands on our attention, the constant clamor of advertising and breaking news, the information overload: they actually make us less clear – not more clear – about who we are and what's going on in the world. Indeed, the communications industry is constantly inventing more and better ways to keep us "connected," meaning addicted. If we don't punctuate this blitz with the occasional healing hiatus, we are in danger of losing touch with real reality.

Holiday time, especially, is a critical time for moments of stillness. The communications clamor intensifies, with all the stuff we're supposed to buy and the staggering social obligations. So it's a must to step away from it, into what T.S. Eliot called "the still point of the turning world."

Out there in the real world, for me in Albuquerque, the winter trees and animals and the beautiful New Mexico land were in a time-out, telling me that I needed a time-out, too. I took it, and lived on.

VICTORY GARDENS, AND STARTING OVER

Originally published 6/26/2010 at The Bilerico Project (www.bilerico.com)

It was sad to leave behind a lot of things – a neighborhood I like, some favorite neighbors, the fruit trees I planted. The new owner of my former home is doing a remodel – the building is already gutted and undergoing a complete transformation.

On moving day, I made the resettlement journey with my laptop and my cat, from West Los Angeles over "the Hill" to Glendale. As the truck and trailer roared along the 2 Freeway north, I thought about the millions of Americans who are going through the same rupture I'd just experienced – short sales or foreclosures on their homes or condos. In my own personal circle, several other people were experiencing that extreme imperative to migrate – even if it's just for a few city miles.

In the best Western tradition, I had packed my covered wagon, and moved on towards the next camp.

But starting over has its bright side. Among other things, I took my Victory Garden with me – most of it anyway.

Into the moving truck went a window box of alpine strawberries, a collection of perennial kitchen herbs in big pots, along with cherished varieties of chile peppers. Plus random volunteers I had spotted – like the cocky little pepper basil seedling that was popping up in a corner. And two loquat seedlings from the now-mature fruit tree that I had planted in 1996 – itself a seedling that I had carted into L.A. from a previous home in Malibu.

Best of all – I dug up my favorite rosebush, "Surprise." Pruned hard so she could migrate without transplant shock, she temporarily became a bare-root migrant in her own right, wrapped in wet towels.

My new landlord and landlady are old friends – Dennis DuVall and Elizabeth, his daughter. Dennis and I went through school together in Deer Lodge, and reconnected years later after he retired from engineering and settled in Los Angeles County with Elizabeth. The two of them are enthusiastic about the idea of communal and environmentally responsible gardening and eating. They have a compost pile ready to go, and we are launching a joint garden.

In short, my Garden Goddess made the migration over the Hollywood Hills with me. She is rooting Her shrine in a new land.

This has been the pattern with me – ever since 1955, when I left behind the childhood family garden that I helped to tend in Montana, and moved to New York State to go to college. There, through long years of education, closet marriage, career and coming out, I left behind some footprints of gardens in cities and towns where I lived – Yorktown Heights, White Plains, Bedford Hills, Pawling. In 1980 I moved back out west and left a few more gardens up and down California – in Nevada County, Mendocino County and Malibu, before moving into Los Angeles.

That's the thing about gardens – you don't really leave them behind – you can always take something with you.

Edible plants have always leapfrogged around the planet with immigrants. And usually those past immigrants moved because they had to.

Examples: Ancient sea passages spread the sweet potato across the Pacific Ocean, on an arc between Southeast Asia and

South America. When my First Nation greatgrannies trekked anywhere, they always took seeds with them...which was probably how a Central American tropical plant like pumpkin reached the tribes in North America.

As Europeans shuffled around their own continent, they did the same thing. Case in point: a humble green called chard, aka silverbeet or seabeet. The most ancient varieties can be traced to Sicily. But chard migrated into northern Europe, maybe with the Romans, and today it's best known as "Swiss chard." When Europeans took ship for the New World, they took chard seeds with them – along with seeds for favorite varieties of other vegetables and fruits known to Europeans. Next, chard went west in the seed packets of pioneer women. For all I know, it reached California with the Forty Niners.

In May, when I moved into my rental space at the DuVall place, they had a healthy crop of Swiss chard coming along in their garden. We plundered it for a big pot of soup, which we shared along with some laughs and stories. It was a special moment.

By then, "Surprise" was basking in new soil in a big pot, beside an unused trellis that was waiting for her to explode with new canes. My breath was bated till I saw those first green shoots popping out.

Yes, starting over can actually be planted and tended. The new garden is going to be bigger and better than the old one – and I intend that my new life will be bigger and better too. Even at 74 (my birthday was last week), anybody can start over and grow back towards Victory.

And if circumstances tell us we *have* to start over, we'd better make the most of it.

PATRICIA NELL WARREN

Photo By Tyler St. Mark

ACKNOWLEDGMENTS

Grateful thanks to these publications for permission on specific articles:

1. *Montana Magazine*
"A Bounteous Meal" – October 1991.
"A Gift of Pheasants" – August 1989
"Grasses: The Graceful Dancers" – August 1993

Reprinted with permission from *Montana Magazine*, a division of Lee Enterprises, 317 Cruse, Helena MT 59604 – 1-888-666-8624 www.montanamagazine.com

2. *Denver Post*
"An Oriental Love Affair" – *Contemporary,* January 12, 1969

3. *Acres U.S.A.*
"Bobcats as Pest Controllers" – November 1992
"Esperseth: A Little-Known Forage Plant" – March 1992

Reprinted with permission from Acres U.S.A., P.O. Box 91299, Austin, Texas 78709 (512) 892-4400, Subscriptions: $27/year. For a sample copy of *Acres U.S.A.* call 1-800-355-5313. www.acresusa.com

4. *CFA Yearbook & Cat Fanciers' Almanac*
"The Gentle Being" – Cat Fanciers' Almanac, September 1992
"Jewelry of Heyoehkah Merrifield" – CFA Yearbook, 1983
"Pat Quillen: Caring for the Small Wildcats" – Cat Fanciers' Almanac, June 1993

Reprinted with permission from The Cat Fanciers' Association, Inc., 1805 Atlantic Avenue, Manasquan, NJ 08736 – (732) 528-9797

5. *Lesbian News*
"Girl Grassroots" – *Lesbian News*, June 1994

Reprinted with permission from LN Publishing Inc., P. O. Box 55, Torrance, CA 90507, 310/548-9888.

Most articles in this book are works for which the author retained all rights. Some articles were previously unpublished and are now © Patricia Nell Warren. A few publications whose permission might have been needed are now defunct. Best efforts were made to locate a surviving entity to which a permission request could be directed. Those particular works are reprinted here with a full credit for the original publication.

Permission questions can be directed to wildcatpress@aol.com.

Special Thanks:

To the Wildcat Press production team:

Tyler St. Mark, Wildcat business partner, for his support – especially creative contribution in developing the cover.

John Selig, nationally recognized gay activist and gifted photographer, for his wonderful cover photo. An archive of John's work can be found at www.johnselig.com

Renne Rhae, California artist, who did beautiful graphics for the mailer pieces in my 2007 West Hollywood city-council campaign. Naturally we went back to her for the *My West* cover. www.ebsqart.com/Artist/Renne-Rhae/6960/

Linda B. Jones, old cat-fancy friend and retired businesswoman, for patiently transforming dozens of yellowed tearsheets and old Xeroxes of articles into Word files ready for typesetting.

James Stelzer, also our webmaster, for his typesetting job.

Shirley Ashford, Wildcat accounting chief, for keeping the wheels turning.

David Daniels for proofreading, as well as for all-around being there while we were moving to new offices during pre-production of this book.

To family:

Conrad Warren, bro supreme, for sharing with me that childhood at the Grant-Kohrs. And for helping me remember so many things about those days in the course of innumerable phone conversations between Glendale and the Oklahoma hinterlands. Which is why I'm dedicating this book to him.

To others who contributed in some way:

The Autry National Center for the American West, for inviting me to speak there and share some of my Western stories in this book. In fact, it was The Autry's initial support for Gregory Hinton's "Out West" program series that first inspired me to start thinking of collecting my own Western writings under one book cover.

Gregory Hinton for his foreword, as well as "Out West" support and counsel on the publishing and promotion of this book.

D. Gregory Smith, Montana activist, for producing the launch of *My West* at the 2011 Montana Pride in Bozeman.

Montana Pride and Bozeman Public Library for their enthusiastic organizing of launch events for this book.

Joseph Cotropia and Paul Fellegy of BioClonetics, for material support for this publishing project.

EarthThunder, for counsel on First Nation history and spirituality.

Laura Rotegard, superintendent of the Grant-Kohrs Ranch National Historic Site, and her staff, for caring about Western history and how important it is to living communities today.

Chris Ford, curator at the GKRO, who looked up things for me, and found photographs.

Cyd Ziegler and Jim Buzinski, co-publishers of Outsports.com, for their enthusiasm over my sports-history series – which included "women in rodeo" material in this book.

Bil Browning at Bilerico.com, for encouraging the writing of history pieces for that blogsite, several of which are included here.

Greg Herren, editor of *Love, Bourbon Street*, for giving me the opportunity to write about New Orleans for his anthology.

Scott Shabel Esq. for legal perspectives.

Cat White, for help with business-related errands.

Larry Rhodes for encouragement and deep love of the West.

Jim Toevs for publishing "Gates" in *Hot Springs Little Baldy Press.*

Anita Grant Steele, descendant of John Grant's brother, for her counsel on Native American and Métis genealogies of the U.S. and Canada.

Dennis DuVall and his daughter Elizabeth DuVall, long-time

friends, for computer and Internet tech support, and what Elizabeth calls "state-of-the-art cat care" while I was getting this book done.

Greg Zanfardino, media development business partner, for never losing sight of the movie possibilities.

Rodolfo Arredondo, cyber-artist extraordinaire of DarkMirror.com, for Web counsel.

To other friends and family who were supportive during the time of getting this book together:

Claudia Bielenberg Thorsrud, Marc Bielenberg, Billy Brady, Darryl Davis, Niko Endres, Ph.D., Andrea Fox, Chris Freeman, William Handley, Roberta Kenney, Don Kohrs, Pat Quillen, Steve Schemmel, Katherine and Chris Schwartzenbach, Nicholas Snow, Robert Taylor, Rick and Wynn Wagner, Daniel Vojir and Michael Ward, David Warren, Shirley and Cran Wisdom.

To someone in a category all her own:

Heather Chamberlain, for being on my horizon 30-plus years now.

Last but not least:

To Squeaky, for her unfailing presence. The Goddesses and Gods have assigned to domestic cats the big job of blessing a writer's manuscript by sitting on it whenever possible. This new title of mine bears her invisible furry seal of approval.

PATRICIA NELL WARREN NOVELS
SET IN THE AMERICAN WEST

One Is the Sun

"*This incredible book ought to be in the library of every woman and man who loves Mother Earth.*" – Michael Gorman, awardwinning author

Surviving a massacre in Yucatan, Mayan priestess Earth Thunder flees her temple and journeys into North America to teach those who wish to know Mother Earth and Her circles of life. While on her quest, Earth Thunder meets River Singing, a defiant slave girl who becomes her apprentice. Together they build a new circle of learning in the Deer Lodge Valley of Montana Territory. When enemies threaten, the Deer Lodge people will fight bravely and leave their mark in time.

Available from Wildcat Press in trade paperback. List price:$24.95
ISBN: 188913502X ISBN-13 9781889135021

Billy's Boy

"*Warren's ability to understand this character and tell his story in the lingo of 1990s youth is remarkable.*" – Library Journal

1997 Editors' Choice Lambda Literary Award

The second sequel in the Front Runner series, *Billy's Boy* is about a teenager's passionate search to know his deceased gay father.

Set in today's urban California, amidst issues around at-risk urban youth, in a region about to explode into the 1994 L.A. Riot. John William is just 14 years old and describes himself as "the science geek from hell." He loves astronomy and dreams of someday exploring the universe as a NASA astronaut. But lately his attention is focused on

his best friend Shawn, as well as his own awakening body.
Available from Wildcat in both hardcover and trade paperback
ISBN: 0964109948 ISBN-13: 9780964109940 $24.95
ISBN: 096410993X ISBN-13 9780964109933 $14.95

The Fancy Dancer

"*Warren has an uncanny ability in probing the male psyche, and her evocative descriptions of Big Sky Country are superb.*" – Bestsellers

Tom Meeker is a handsome rookie priest stranded in a struggling rural parish in Montana. Vidal Stump is a proud half-breed with a criminal record. Father Vance, his superior, is a cranky old-school cleric always looking to find fault. As Meeker dodges Vance's constant scrutiny, and that of the town busybodies, he is forced to choose between his sacred vows and his secret attraction to Vidal, that "fancy dancer" who lures him into a love forbidden by his Church.

Originally published three decades ago, this provocative novel was on the B. Dalton bestseller list for many weeks. It was the first bestseller to explore gay and lesbian lives in a small Western town.

Available from Wildcat Press in trade paperback List price: $14.95
ISBN: 0964109972 ISBN-13: 9780964109971

The Last Centennial

"*This impressive first novel...evokes the losing of the West... is almost Faulknerian in its depiction of the despoiling inheritors. Still, it ends with more optimism than the title suggests. Highly recommended.*" – Library Journal

Warren's first novel, published in 1971 by Dial Press under Warren's (then) pen name of Patricia Kilina. Soon to be back in print from Wildcat Press. Currently, copies of the first-edition hardcover can occasionally be found at Alibris.com or Bookfinders.com.

Place: the ranch-country town of Cottonwood, Montana. Time: the 1960s, and the town's upcoming centennial celebration, as seen through the eyes of three different people living there. An old rancher struggling to hold onto old ways. A teen girl who is disturbed about family and sexuality. And a champion Indian rodeo cowboy who was adopted by a white family as a child, now trying to find his way back to his ancient heritage. Optioned for feature-film development by Erik Lee Preminger.

For information on all Wildcat titles, and their distribution, go to:

www.wildcatpress.com

Or contact:

Wildcat Press
8306 Wilshire Blvd. Box 8306
Beverly Hills, CA 90211 - USA
Phone – 818/246-2766 Fax – 818/246-2767
Email – wildcatpress@aol.com